Diversity and Distrust

Diversity and Distrust

CIVIC EDUCATION IN A
MULTICULTURAL DEMOCRACY

STEPHEN MACEDO

HARVARD UNIVERSITY PRESS

Cambridge, Massachusetts, and London, England

Library of Congress Cataloging-in-Publication Data

Macedo, Stephen, 1957–
  Diversity and distrust: civic education in a multicultural democracy / Stephen Macedo.
    p. cm.
  Includes bibliographical references and index.
  ISBN 0-674-21311-4 (cloth)
  ISBN 0-674-01123-6 (paper)
  1. Public schools—United States. 2. Moral education—United States. 3. Citizenship—
Study and teaching—United States. 4. Liberalism—United States. 5. Multiculturalism—
United States. I. Title.
LA217.2.M33   2000
371.01/0973—dc21   99-41461

For David

Contents

Preface

At base, my concern in this book is with our attitude toward moral and religious diversity in a liberal democratic order. There are complex and difficult questions here that cut close to the core of the modern liberal democratic project. Putting deep moral and religious diversity in its place was, in a sense, the first item of business on the liberal agenda, and there it remains, a work in progress.

This book is also about the project of forming citizens in a modern liberal democracy, for it is the necessity of pursuing that project that makes diversity an issue. In American society, public schools have undertaken this project more directly and persistently than any other public institution. The controversial nature of the project is deeply etched in the history of this institution. Public schools are instruments for the most basic and controversial of civic ends. A glance at the table of contents and the structure and scope of the book should make it clear, however, that my interest is not limited to public schools, important as they are. The project of creating citizens is one that every liberal democratic state must somehow undertake. There are a variety of means at our disposal, many of them less direct than publicly controlled schools. American public schools do, however, embody our most visible and concerted effort to take political responsibility for shaping future citizens. American public schools have proceeded with this project, which Amy Gutmann calls "conscious social reproduction," even in the face of deep religious conflicts. Public schools are important instruments not only in their own right, but also because they reveal just what is at stake in this project of citizen formation.

Our civic project—which has a limited agenda and which is justified in terms of public values—nevertheless has broad and deep implications for our lives as a whole, including all of our deepest moral and religious commitments. This statement seems paradoxical, but its truth is inescapable. The success and health of a liberal democratic constitutional order depend upon the religious beliefs and other deep moral convictions that citizens form and act upon. The success of our civic project relies upon a transformative project that includes the remaking of moral and religious communities.

Can we justify this controversial enterprise? I believe that we can, and in doing so, I draw on the approach to political justification sketched by John Rawls in *Political Liberalism*. In formulating our shared civic ideals, we should leave aside many religious and philosophical controversies about which people have long disagreed, and focus instead on what Amy Gutmann and Dennis Thompson call "mutually acceptable reasons." Although this kind of liberal public justification may not rest on a particular conception of religious truth, it must assume that whatever is true as a religious matter is consistent with and supportive of liberalism.

What, then, of the value of deep diversity? Much of our thinking about such popular notions as "diversity" and "difference" is misguided. Indeed, it seems to me that we have not understood liberalism very well. Liberalism is about placing personal liberty and the defense of basic individual rights at the center of the political project. The freedom to choose, to pursue diverse religious and philosophical conceptions, is central to liberalism. But a liberal democratic society also counts on channeling the way that people use their freedom. Indeed, a liberal democracy counts on being nonneutral with respect to the patterns of moral and social life that arise and persist. Liberal democratic public institutions count on shaping wider social norms and expectations so that people are gently encouraged to behave in ways that are broadly supportive of our shared civic project.

If one looks at the political history of the latter half of the twentieth century in America and elsewhere, there can be little doubt that a preoccupation with individual rights and liberties at the expense of all other values can lead to an unbalanced conception of the free society—a conception that, in practice, pays too little attention to certain collective goods and social patterns that are integral to a free, self-governing *society*. The time is ripe for recovering a more balanced view. But we will not recover our balance by going outside of the liberal tradition; rather, we will do so by reappreciating the breadth of its insights and resources. We must not allow the foremost liberal principles to obscure other elements of liberal social theory that may also be crucial to the recovery of a more civic liberalism.

This book is, from beginning to end, about liberalism's transformative ambitions. The civic liberalism I defend rests on a circumscribed range of public principles and reasons, but its implications are broader and deeper than the proponents of "political liberalism" have typically allowed. On the basis of these circumscribed principles, we should seek to remake our social world.

Acknowledgments

I have benefited a great deal from associations with a number of important educational institutions over the last eight years, and a number of friends and colleagues have read drafts of parts of this book or made concrete suggestions that contributed to it. My accounting system for such debts is unreliable, and this list, therefore, is no doubt partial. Among those who have read parts of this work and commented helpfully are Sotirios Barber, Stephen Bates, Ronald Beiner, David Boaz, Shelley Burtt, Joe Coleman, Matthew Dickinson, Judy Failer, Robert Fullinwider, Tyl van Geel, Phillip Hogan, Jeffrey Isaac, James Johnson, Marci Kanstoroom, Chandran Kukathas, Meira Levinson, Sanford Levinson, Myron Lieberman, Jane J. Mansbridge, Frank Michelman, Judd Owen, Paul Rosenberg, Kim Scheppele, Nomi Stolzenberg, Ken Strike, Abigail Thernstrom, John Tomasi, and Melissa Williams. Eamonn Callan, Amy Gutmann, and Rogers M. Smith read the entire manuscript at a relatively late stage and provided very useful comments.

I had superb research assistance from Thomas Castleton, Kenn Cust, Jason Freier, Sourabh Gupta, Phillip Hogan, Lanethea Mathews, and Artemus Ward. I am deeply grateful.

I presented aspects of this work in a variety of forums, all of which were helpful to me. I am grateful to the organizers and participants: Harvey C. Mansfield and Delba Winthrop and their Program in

Constitutional Government lunchtime seminar at Harvard; Chandran Kukathas and his colleagues at the Political Science Department of the Australian Defense Force Academy; James Johnson, Jane J. Mansbridge, and their colleagues in political science at Northwestern University; Tom Anton and his colleagues at the Public Policy Center at Brown University; Shelley Burtt and the Yale University Political Science Department; James Johnson (again), Annabelle Lever, and their colleagues in political science at the University of Rochester; Will Kymlicka, Wayne Norman, and the Philosophy Department at the University of Ottawa; the Poynter Center for the Study of Ethics at Indiana University, with thanks to David Smith and his staff; and Judy Failer, Jeffrey Isaac, and their colleagues in political science at Indiana University.

In June 1996, I was fortunate to have the opportunity to exchange ideas at a day-long conference on the future of education research at Stanford University, sponsored by the Spencer Foundation. I am very grateful to the British Society for the Philosophy of Education for the chance to speak at a plenary session of their annual conference in Oxford in March 1996. My thanks to Nigel Blake for organizing this event.

I also presented aspects of Part Two in panels on "public reason" organized by George Kateb and the Political Theory Colloquium at Princeton, and at a meeting of the Conference for the Study of Political Thought, organized by Alan Ryan.

My thanks to the late Duane Smith for including me as faculty member at a National Endowment for the Humanities Summer Institute for High School Teachers in August 1997. Duane's premature death left William F. Harris IV to pick up where Duane left off. Will brought together a superb set of high school teachers, and I benefited enormously from several days of discussions.

Opportunities and funds for research leaves were provided by the Political Science Department of the Australian Defense Force Academy, where I learned a lot about moral and intellectual virtue from my old comrade Chandran Kukathas (and from his entire family). The Center for Social Philosophy and Policy at Bowling Green State University in Bowling Green, Ohio, provided a pleasant and productive semester to get started in earnest. My thanks to Fred M. Miller, Ellen Frankel Paul, Jeff Paul, Kory Swanson, and the wonderful staff, and to the other fellows that semester: Paul Greenberg, Chandran Kukathas, Myron Lieberman, and Ken Minogue.

Generous support was also provided by the Harry and Lynde Bradley Foundation, the Institute for Humane Studies, and the Earhart Foundation, which allowed me to take two semesters and two summers off from teaching to work on this book.

I owe a debt to my former colleagues and to the superb graduate students in the Harvard Government Department. What better place to think about liberalism than with liberal scholars as diverse as Judith N. Shklar, Harvey C. Mansfield, and Dennis Thompson, and with others as unsparing in their criticisms of liberalism as Michael Sandel and Seyla Benhabib. Most important to this book and to me were repeated conversations about liberalism and related issues—over more Thai food and beer than I care to recall—with Peter Berkowitz, Pratap Mehta, Glyn Morgan, and Leif Wenar.

My wonderful year at Princeton University's Center for Human Values was very important in moving this book along. I owe a very great debt indeed to center founder and former director Amy Gutmann. Her *Democratic Education* was an inspiration for this work in more ways than is probably apparent in the text. I also learned a great deal that year from the other center fellows and associated faculty: Daniel A. Bell, Chris Bobonich, Hillary Bok, Sam Fleischacker, Kent Greenawalt, Yael Tamir, and center associates George Kateb, Elizabeth Kiss, and Peter de Marneffe. As I returned to Princeton to join the faculty, Jameson Doig and Paul E. Sigmund provided several helpful suggestions. I appreciate deeply the support of Dean John Palmer and Senior Associate Dean Robert M. McClure at Syracuse University's Maxwell School of Citizenship and Public Affairs. I am also grateful to former constitutional law professor and university vice chancellor Michael O. Sawyer, who so inspired his students with his love of learning that they generously contributed to programs in his honor and the position that I was privileged to hold. My thanks also to colleagues Fred M. Frohock, Rogan Kersh, Elisabeth Lasch-Quinn, and Suzanne Mettler for their comments and conversations on aspects of this project. I owe a great deal as well to the excellent Syracuse graduate students who helped me think about these issues in the seminars "Liberalism and Its Critics" and "Constitutional Theory."

It has been a pleasure to work with an editor as patient and supportive as Michael Aronson. In addition, Julie Carlson made innumerable improvements in the text.

Finally, my greatest debt is to my partner, David Bernhardt, who exemplifies more of the virtues—civic, moral, and human—than I could ever describe. The family, as we know, is the foundation of all other virtues, and so I dedicate this book to him.

Some of the arguments in Chapter 1 were developed in "Transformative Constitutionalism and the Case of Religion: Defending the Moderate Hegemony of Liberalism," and "Reply to Flathman," *Political Theory* 26 (1998), 56–80, 85–89. Versions of portions of Part II appeared in "Liberal Civic Education and Religious Fundamentalism: The Case of God vs. John Rawls?" *Ethics* 105 (1995), 468–496; and in "Multiculturalism for the Religious Right? Defendidng Liberal Civic Education," *Journal of the Philosophy of Education* 29 (1995), 223–238. Permission to use this material is gratefully acknowledged.

Diversity and Distrust

Introduction:
The Place of Diversity

Diversity is the great issue of our time: nationalism, religious sectarianism; a heightened consciousness of gender, race, and ethnicity; a greater assertiveness with respect to sexual orientation; and a reassertion of the religious voice in the public square are but a few of the forms of particularity that stubbornly refuse to yield to individualism and cosmopolitanism. Economic divisions remain important, but in the never-ending contest over what defines us as a nation, the focus has shifted to the politics of identity.

These striking historical developments have been accompanied by a rising insistence among many political observers that greater weight be given to what distinguishes particular groups from others. Traditional liberalism—with its demand that political power should be guided by public reasons and standards of justice that can be shared by all—is increasingly regarded as unfairly homogenizing, "hegemonic," and exclusionary. Liberalism is held to be guilty of the cardinal sin of "denying difference" and is therefore condemned as outmoded and unfair.[1]

Many claims advanced under the banners of diversity, difference, and cultural pluralism are worth heeding, but we must heed them with an eye to liberal democratic principles and practices of liberty and equality that are more demanding than is often recognized. Talk of diversity and difference too often proceeds without taking adequate account of the degree of moral convergence it takes to sustain a constitutional order that is liberal, democratic, and characterized by widespread bonds of civic friendship and cooperation. Not every form of cultural and religious diversity is to be celebrated, and not all forms of what can be labeled "marginalization" and "exclusion" are to be regretted or apologized for. Profound forms of sameness and convergence should not only be prayed for but planned for without embarrassment.

This book is motivated by the conviction that much thinking surrounding the themes of diversity and difference is misconceived. Not all talk of diversity is misguided, to be sure. Often when people invoke the value of diversity, they mean to signal their opposition to unfair forms of exclusion, prejudice, and discrimination. At the broadest level, the typical invocation of diversity embodies an insistence that no one should be excluded from the American dream of equal justice based on arbitrary and irrelevant differences of skin color, gender, ethnicity, or sexual orientation. Given that our world is shaped by the enduring legacies of various forms of unjust exclusion, we may need to explicitly take into account forms of difference that have been the bases for discrimination.

Taking account of certain kinds of difference and diversity is sometimes a way of better pursuing basic principles of justice. The American dream of equal justice, properly conceived, need not be a blunt-edged insistence that the same rules apply to all, irrespective of differences of condition and circumstance. Whether or not one agrees that affirmative action policies, for example, do more good than harm, there is nothing wrong as a matter of fundamental justice with Supreme Court Justice Harry Blackmun's insistence that "to get beyond racism, we must first take account of race . . . in order to treat some persons equally, we must treat them differently." Blackmun's statement only sounds paradoxical: the principle of equality will *sometimes* require something more than formally equal treatment. Equality of concern and respect, for example, requires some sort of special access for the disabled. In many other instances as well, as Ronald Dworkin pointed out long ago, treating people as moral equals is often not the same thing as treating them all the same way.[2] Equal treatment—including a blindness to differences of color and other differences—may often be the best policy, but it is not required as a basic matter of justice. Even if our aim is the "expansion of individual opportunities and integrated inclusiveness within a common political culture" and not the "valorization of subgroup identities," as Rogers M. Smith insists, we should sometimes recognize and take account of "group disadvantages" when designing remedies. Indeed, while fairness and other basic moral principles are color-blind, Amy Gutmann rightly argues that when we apply those principles to an imperfect world in which individuals bear unequal burdens due to past and present discrimination, we should often take racial differences into account.[3]

Distinctive cultural practices may merit special accommodations and exemptions in the name of equality of concern and respect. Equal justice for all means being sensitive to many forms of difference. Categorical prohibitions should not be extended automatically or thoughtlessly. A prohibition on the wearing of hats in the military or elsewhere should not automatically extend to yarmulkes or Sikh turbans: the purposes and justifiability of the prohibition and the nature of the distinctive religious imperatives first need to be considered. At its best, talk of diversity, difference, and multiculturalism reminds us of the extent to which the promise of freedom and equality for all remains a work in progress: only partially realized, only partially understood.

Many forms of diversity have an important place in a liberal democratic society, but the core claim of this book is that diversity needs to be kept in its place: diversity is not always a value and it should not, any more than other ideals, be accepted uncritically. Diversity is sometimes invoked as a way of taking liberal democratic principles more seriously, but at other times the invocation of diversity and multicultural ideals undermines the very possibility of a public morality. The way I propose to put diversity in its place is by emphasizing the importance and legitimacy of a liberal educative project that shapes diversity for civic purposes.

I want to pick an intellectual bone not simply with certain critics of liberalism, but indeed with those liberals who focus single-mindedly on particular liberal commitments at the expense of a larger liberal democratic agenda. The freedom to choose among diverse ways of life and to help fashion new options is central to liberalism, but the commitment to freedom should lead us to plan for a political community characterized by tolerably peaceful, respectful, enlightened, and responsible freedom. Not only forms of diversity and difference, but the patterns of choices that individuals make need to be shaped or constituted for the sake of sustaining a liberal democratic political order that is civically healthy.

In part, what I want to do is make more explicit what is often already implicit when diversity is invoked. One often hears, for example, that America has become a much more diverse country. In many respects, however, we have become a much *less* diverse country over the past century and a half, and this is all to the good. We may talk about and celebrate many forms of diversity more than we once did, but we are no longer divided by profound regional differences, or by moral differences that threaten our nation's unity in the way that slavery did. The supremacy of the national government is virtually unchallenged. The ideal of basic freedom and equality for all is much more of a reality than was the case not long ago. National ideals of toleration and respect for individual rights are much more widely and deeply entrenched than they once were.[4] National media and communications link everyone to common sources of information. And although American religious communities may be more numerous and exotic than ever before, at a deeper level, one must be struck by the extent to which the major religions have embraced the basic commitments of liberal democratic life. Talk of a culture war is, as Alan Wolfe argues, exaggerated.[5]

The fact is that from the standpoint of the great moral alternatives that humans have faced throughout history, or even over the course of the American republic, today's celebrations of diversity and difference are often superficial, for they are often about celebrations of the broader extension of freedom and the fuller realization of equality. We would do well to be more conscious of the shared values that underlie much talk of diversity. We simply cannot say, in the abstract, whether "diversity" is to be lauded or not.

Aims and Plan of the Book

While social diversity is often a great asset, all political regimes, even pluralistic liberal ones such as our own, require a considerable measure of convergence on basic political values. Focusing too narrowly on today's political controversies is liable to obscure what should be the extent of our ambitions with respect to shaping diversity. Planning for the preservation of the liberal public order requires that we constrain and channel people's freedom, sometimes directly perhaps, but also in many indirect ways. We cannot avoid indirectly promoting some versions of the moral and religious life and discouraging others: indeed, we must do so in order to survive and prosper as a political community. Of course, we can avoid these troubling issues by making various unwarranted assumptions, as many commentators do. We can simply assume that people are good liberal democrats, or trust that they are led in the right direction by some sort of invisible hand, but then the edifice of our political thinking will rest on blind faith, sheer optimism, or some other variety of shallow thinking. In fact, I am all for making use of something like "invisible hand" mechanisms, but invisible hands need to be employed and directed by public policy, as Adam Smith recognized.[6] Political order should not be understood, at base, as the product of an invisible hand, but rather as a construction for discernible collective ends and purposes, including the preservation of a broad swath of liberty.

I want to argue here for what will to some sound like an oxymoron: a tough-minded version of liberalism. We need to circumscribe liberalism's aims appropriately, but then we need to take liberalism's educative ambitions seriously and face up to the fact that no version of liberalism will make everyone happy. Liberty should be the core principle of our regime, yet we must recognize that a single-minded preoccupation with liberty could undermine our ability to perpetuate free institutions. A prudent solicitude for the system of individual liberty does not counsel a stance of laissez-faire, but rather a willingness to intervene (gently and indirectly where possible) to promote shared liberal values and civic virtues.

I want here to defend a liberalism with spine. To preserve liberal toleration, we must do more than practice tolerance: we must recognize and respond to intolerance and other threats to liberal values. Of course, it is not always easy to say what constitutes a threat to justifiable civic values as opposed to a challenge to some reigning habit or opinion. In the face of this uncertainty, Americans have often veered in one direction or the other. We have sometimes been too ready to perceive as threats the behavior of immigrants, non-Protestants, or, more recently, all who fail to honor supposed "Judeo-Christian" values.[7] By some measures at least, the American public remains remarkably intolerant.[8] At other times, however, central aspects of our liberal public morality itself seem to encourage various camps—whether libertarians, cultural pluralists, or proponents of a "politics of difference"—to ignore or deride the project of constituting diversity for the sake of the liberal political community as a whole.

We have a history of nativism and of intense fear of diversity, as we shall see.[9] But increasingly many of us tend to concentrate single-mindedly on choice, freedom from political interference, and indiscriminate difference and otherness. Our fears of disorder may lead to unjustified incursions on freedom. Yet an uncritical embrace of diversity may obscure the need to promote citizenship and the elements of a healthy civic life. While we must try to respect the free exercise of religion, for example, and listen to those who feel oppressed by the rules, norms, and expectations of our public life, we must also see to it that the work that public schools are meant to do—of helping us negotiate our differences in the name of forging a public life—somehow is done, even if not by public schools as we know them. Of course, we should often seek to defuse or soften basic moral conflicts, and I will emphasize the importance of noncoercive, indirect means of civic education. Heavy-handed state interventions should often be put aside in favor of background statecraft that educates indirectly by shaping social norms and redefining the contours of the moral environment.

These large themes and problems will be explored here in contexts and episodes that are in some ways peculiarly American, though the larger lessons of this story are not limited to the United States. The central context to be examined is the institution of American public schooling, and the episodes are often conflicts between the asserted imperatives of civic education and the claims of families, churches, and other groups to be free to raise their own children in their own ways. On one side are the imperatives of civic education, on the other are a host of claims involving parental rights, the free exercise of religion, and the good of cultural and religious diversity. This book explores the question of how our deepest conflicts should be negotiated. Throughout, I insist that a steady eye be kept on the liberal civic ideals that are our best guarantee that diversity will remain a blessing rather than a curse.

Issues of diversity in modern liberal polities raise complex questions that call for a multifaceted inquiry. In Part One, I consider how our polity has confronted the challenge of normative diversity in the past and ask what we can learn from that experience. By looking to the past, we will not only see that many of today's deepest conflicts are variations on much older themes, but we can also reexamine episodes that shape today's attitudes and that are invoked on one side or other of today's controversies. I focus on several of the major clashes that swirled around public schools, the institution charged most directly with fostering a common civic life. This inquiry clarifies the vast and deeply controversial ambitions of a modern liberal democracy with respect to normative diversity. I argue that while racism, xenophobia, and anti-Catholic nativism were important elements in shaping nineteenth-century ideas about civic education, the common schools were deeply controversial not in spite of, but *because of* legitimate civic purposes. Indeed, Catholics were at the forefront of opposition to common schools not simply because some school materials and practices were anti-Catholic, but because some in the Catholic hierarchy rejected legitimate civic ends. The great rapprochement that has taken place between the Catholic Church and liberal democracy is indeed a great event of world historical significance, but it was made possible by profound changes within Catholicism, as we shall see.

Having explored the nature and magnitude of the problem of normative diversity in the historical inquiry, I turn in Part Two to questions of moral justification. How should a liberal public morality, properly understood, respond to the challenge of diversity? I defend a form of liberalism robust enough to do the political work that we should want done: not just the protection of basic individual liberties, but the generation of a healthy civic life capable of sustaining free self-government over the course of generations.

In Part Three, I return to the institution of public schooling—America's oldest and most extensive social welfare institution, and in many ways, the one that has generated the deepest and most persistent controversy. Today's debate over school reform is often carried on in a manner that is oblivious to our deepest educative ambitions, but that need not be so. There is, in fact, a powerful case for reform that takes our civic aims seriously.

The shape of our social lives is educative, and the shape of our social lives is influenced deeply by public policy. We can gain leverage over civic education indirectly by thinking about ways to influence and shape patterns of social life that, in effect, educate people of all ages. Doing so will not be a matter, once again, of simply unleashing group and associational diversity, but of imparting a very definite shape to associations, whether "public" or "private." That story, however, will be taken up elsewhere.[10]

Civic Liberalism

My employment of the label "liberal" here is bound to cause confusion among many outside the academy, and no doubt some within it. In our politics, "liberalism" has come to be associated with faith in federal government activism and a set of progressive public policies growing out of the New Deal, the Great Society, and the Warren Court. So far as many ordinary Americans are concerned, there is no doubt that Jonathan Rieder is correct when he observes that by the late 1970s, the term "liberalism" was associated with "profligacy, spinelessness, malevolence, masochism, elitism, fantasy, anarchy, idealism, softness, irresponsibility, and sanctimoniousness."[11] At the extreme, many academics and nonacademics from across the political spectrum portray liberalism as a kind of anemic nonjudgmentalism, a position that is morally uninspired and uninspiring, incapable of pressing even its own core values in the face of disagreement.[12] Needless to say, I want to disconnect the view I am defending from these unhappy associations.

In the face of such unflattering portrayals—not entirely unearned—it might seem prudent to simply surrender the label "liberal" to history. But that would be a profound mistake, for the great tradition of liberal political thinking deserves a better fate. It contains ample resources to respond to its critics, and I have no doubt that it deserves to weather the current academic and popular fashions.

I want to reject the view according to which "liberalism" is identified with an insistence that public policies be neutral with respect to conceptions of the good life. Liberalism properly understood is anything but neutral with respect to basic moral and political issues, and it does not stand for an ultimate commitment to fairness or impartiality. It is true enough that some contemporary versions of liberalism have tried to put these values at the center of our political morality, but this approach seems to me deeply mistaken.[13]

In a sense, the basic point of this book is to emphasize the vital importance of not allowing the foremost liberal values to obscure others on which the regime also depends. The liberal foreground is composed, first, of the basic liberties for all that are familiar from bills of rights: freedoms of religious practice, rights of association, and personal privacy, as well as freedom to express your opinion, to travel, and, as Benjamin Constant put it, "to be neither arrested, detained, put to death or maltreated in any way by the arbitrary will" of others.[14] Closely connected with these basic liberties are the familiar defensive mechanisms designed to check abuses of power and safeguard basic individual liberties against the encroachments of government: constitutional devices to check and regularize political power that include the separation of powers, legislative bicameralism, and the rule of law. The liberal foreground is composed of what might be thought of as *negative constitutionalism:* a sphere of individual inviolability (which Isaiah Berlin called "negative liberty") and the familiar constitutional mechanisms designed to ward off incursions on that sphere.[15]

Liberal political thought has often, and perhaps especially in recent decades, kept somewhat in the background the more civic dimensions of political life that are also vital to the liberal tradition. We have good reason to regard respect for certain basic liberties as politically paramount; having done so, we will do well to join Berlin in insisting that "participation in self-government is, like justice, a basic human requirement, an end in itself." The right to participate in the institutions of collective self-government is not only a safeguard of, but also a vital complement to, personal liberty.[16]

Constant famously defended modern "private" liberty against those who sought to revive a "collective freedom" that entailed the "complete subjection of the individual to the authority of the community." He recognized, nevertheless, the importance of tempering the potentially excessive privatism of modern liberty with a measure of civic spirit. The final lines of his famous speech are worth quoting:

> The work of the legislator is not complete when he has simply brought peace to the people. Even when the people are satisfied, there is much left to do. Institutions must achieve the moral education of the citizens. By respecting their individual rights, securing their independence, refraining from troubling their work, they must nevertheless consecrate their influence over public affairs, call them to contribute by their votes to the exercise of power, grant them a right of control and supervision by expressing their opinions; and, by forming them through practice for these elevated functions, give them both the desire and the right to discharge these.[17]

Modern liberalism counts on promoting certain kinds of civic character. All we know about modern politics suggests that under reasonably favorable conditions, opportunities for collective deliberation about public affairs help secure and complement personal freedoms of self-direction.[18]

Liberal political institutions and public policies should be concerned to promote not simply freedom, order, and prosperity, but the preconditions of active citizenship: the capacities and dispositions conducive to thoughtful participation in the activities of modern politics and civil society. A commitment to individual freedom as a paramount virtue is no warrant for neglecting the civic dimension of our lives: the character and capacities of free citizens are shaped by social and political institutions of various sorts. Liberal democrats need to think about the ways in which public policies and institutions of different kinds shape and educate in direct and indirect ways. The very fact that liberalism celebrates individual freedom above all creates a risk that other concerns will be allowed to slip out of the picture altogether. The success of the negative constitutional project of individual liberty depends on a more positive, transformative enterprise that aims to shape normative diversity in a basic way, to foster a civic life supportive of liberal citizenship.

Diversity and difference, like all good or potentially good ideas, can be taken to an extreme or grasped in the wrong way. A liberal democratic political order is complex rather than simple. Liberals are not wrong to place freedom and equality in the foreground of politics, and to relegate somewhat to the background concerns with virtue, character, citizen education, and the like. Making the promotion of citizen's virtue and personal excellence the overriding ends of our politics will overturn the liberties that we have good reason to prize.

Liberals cannot, however, leave aside altogether the project of moral education. A system of free self-government needs to encourage widespread convergence on certain shared attitudes and character traits, as well as the patterns of social life that support them. No liberal democracy can survive without citizens prepared to tolerate others, to act more or less responsibly, to take some part in public affairs, to stay informed, and to act for the good of the whole at least sometimes. For a liberal democracy to thrive and not only survive, many of its citizens should develop a shared commitment to a range of political values and virtues: tolerance, mutual respect, and active cooperation among fellow citizens of various races, creeds, and styles of life; a willingness to think critically about public affairs and participate actively in the democratic process and in civil society; and a willingness to affirm the supreme political authority of principles that we can publicly justify along with all our reasonable fellow citizens.[19]

The negative conception of liberalism is, on its own, deficient.[20] As Walter F. Murphy puts it,

> The goal of a constitutional text must . . . be not simply to structure a government, but to construct a political system, one that can guide the formation of a larger constitution, a "way of life" that is conducive to constitutional democracy. If constitutional democracy is to flourish, its ideals must reach beyond formal governmental arrangements and help configure, though not necessarily in the same way or to the same extent, most aspects of its people's lives.[21]

In what follows I want to bring the positive constitutional project and the civic ideals it supports closer to the liberal foreground. Doing so should further the project of responding to that legion of critics who argue that the public philosophy of liberalism is incapable of realizing, or even articulating, civic ideals.

Liberal self-government and the institutions, practices, and character traits that support it—which I want to call civic liberalism—make up a distinctive (though not comprehensive) moral ideal, and one that is worth planning for. Of course, we want to avoid trying to promote moral ideals in ways that infringe on fundamental liberties: an over-zealous concern to promote moral virtues may lead to infringements on individual freedom. But that is only an argument for guarding against excessive zeal. Civic liberalism, like all forms of moral life, needs not only options, but channels. Political institutions, social practices, and norms of all sorts encourage particular forms of behavior and discourage others: they help form the channels through which our lives flow. To respect freedom, we want to make sure that the channels are broad and not too deep, but there will always be channels, and we should try to make sure that they tend to promote our deepest shared values.

A final word about civic liberalism: I will refer frequently to liberal commitments, principles, and practices and the importance of designing policies and institutions to help promote them. This should not be taken to suggest that liberal principles are fully known and beyond contestation and criticism. Precisely the opposite is true: liberalism as I understand it is, at its core, committed to a self-critical process of giving and demanding reasons, a process in which all substantive commitments are provisional and none are beyond political challenge. Even the "constitutional basics" are properly subject to ongoing political debate, criticism, reinterpretation, and revision, as I have argued at length elsewhere. Liberal citizens at their best know that they have a share in helping to direct the fearsome powers of the modern state, and they know that this fact behooves them to seek mutually acceptable reasons for the ways they would direct this power.[22] To affirm this in no way undermines the importance of promoting the preconditions of political community: a liberal community of reason givers is a distinctive form of political community. The dispositions to question, criticize, and offer public reasons are among the distinctive virtues of liberal citizens.

We have no reason to take for granted either popular allegiance to liberal democratic principles or the skills and habits needed by good citizens. I will try to give both diversity and shared values their due by defending a reasonably confined but tough-minded liberalism: one determined to take reasonable measures to promote specifically political virtues but not ideals of life as a whole, one that would accept that doing so has unavoidable non-neutral consequences for the religious beliefs and ways of life that flourish in our regime.

My concern with issues of diversity lies not with this or that public policy, and I am not necessarily out to defend a larger federal government. Across the political spectrum, however, there is a tendency to take some of our deeper commitments for granted. Sometimes this tendency manifests itself in an unwillingness to look critically at claims advanced under the banners of diversity, but at other times the problem is a blind faith in market mechanisms. The common error, as I show in Chapter 1, is to focus on a part of the liberal political project at the expense of liberalism's deeper and broader ambitions.

I hope that this book is written in a spirit that recognizes the great good of a world in which many differences of religion and culture, race, ethnicity, gender, and sexual orientation can be sources of enrichment and celebration for all. My main purpose, however, is to suggest that diversity and difference are not always to be celebrated: political work needs to be done to shape a world in which forms of diversity can be considered valuable rather than sources of fear and violence.

CHAPTER 1

Diversity Ascendant

How can we, on the one hand, respect and protect the wide range of freedoms and the diverse patterns of religious and cultural life to which freedom naturally gives rise, while recognizing, on the other hand, that even a free society must act directly and indirectly to shape the ways that people use their freedom, in order to support and improve the civic life on which free self-government as a whole depends? Can we, in other words, imagine and devise an adequately *civic* liberalism: a political program that gives freedom its ample due while taking reasonable steps to promote good citizenship and thereby to preserve the social and political supports that freedom needs for future generations?

If our aim is to promote a political order that is characterized by a healthy measure of liberal democratic virtue, what are the implications for diversity? What is the relation between a liberal constitutional order, understood as a normative or moral structure, and the other normative structures that exist within a polity?

The main business of this book is to address these fundamental questions. First, however, I briefly consider some of the ways in which these questions have been derailed in recent discussions of diversity and education. In this chapter, I explore a series of retreats and evasions in the face of the need to shape and limit ultimate ideals and belief systems in order to support liberal democratic values. Liberalism's aims are deep and pervasive, but not everyone is prepared to recognize this fact.

This detour will help make it clear just how tempting it is to ignore what should be recognized as the unfinished business of our political order: the positive constitutional project of shaping diversity toward the demands of a shared public life. The temptation is nonpartisan, as we shall see by considering evasions from across the political spectrum. Indeed, the temptation often grows out of certain core liberal commitments: to freedom, to equality, to markets and choice, to limited government, and to a distinction between public and private. All of these are values central to liberalism, but all can also be grasped in the wrong way or pushed to an extreme, and then the liberal democratic whole is obscured.

Negative Legalism

Typical of the negative view of liberal constitutionalism is the "rule of law" ideal of politics. This simple picture of liberal legalism is familiar enough. It is the view that law, properly understood, is a framework of impartial rules within which individuals and groups may pursue their own divergent ends and independently defined conceptions of what constitutes the good life. The law furnishes a set of "baselines" for individual conduct, as Lon Fuller put it, but otherwise should be "noninstrumental" or "purposeless," in the sense that it does not seek to impose purposes or ends on free citizens.[1] Hobbes prefigured such a view, and so did Locke ("that ill deserves the Name of Confinement which hedges us in only from Bogs and Precipices").[2]

Government is necessary to enforce the law and regulate freedom. But it is also very important, according to this view, to ensure that political power is limited to the right sorts of purposes (to our "civil interests," as Locke put it), and is justified on the basis of reasons that we can share (as the social contract tradition hopes). So a vital task of constitutional law is to strike reasonable balances between private freedom and public power: to draw lines demarcating the proper spheres of conscience and religious association on the one side, and political authority on the other.

Liberal legalism helps sustain a set of familiar dichotomies: individual rights versus collective power, liberty versus coercion, private versus public. There are important debates about where to draw the lines, and I do not wish to deny the importance of the conflicts that these distinctions signify. At a certain level, these images are useful: law does help secure ordered liberty, and it does help individuals and groups know how they may go about pursuing their purposes under the law's protection. Thinking of the role of law in these terms alone, however, misses much of what is really interesting and important. It contributes to the erroneous idea that liberalism is based on a presocial conception of persons with interests that somehow preexist the constitutive effects of social practices and political institutions. Indeed, taking this view of law as the centerpiece of one's political philosophy—as many classical liberals and libertarians are apt to do—conceals some of the deepest ambitions of a liberal constitutional order. In much of what follows, I want to emphasize just how inadequate, even potentially misleading, is this simple picture of the social functions of law.

The rule of law and the distinction between public and private are, at one level, ways of directing and limiting political power. Yet at a deeper level, widespread acceptance of the rule of law and the distinction between public and private represent ways of constructing the world as a whole.

Liberal constitutional institutions have a more deeply constitutive role than the rule of law ideal signifies: they must shape or constitute all forms of diversity over the course of time, so that people are *satisfied* leading lives of bounded individual freedom. It is, after all, a profoundly important achievement for a society to converge on the notion that religious values and practices belong in a private sphere that is distinguishable from the sphere of political power. It is an accomplishment to come to a rough agreement that there are distinctively public reasons and purposes, in contrast to other reasons and purposes not properly pursued via political means. Successful constitutional institutions must do more than help order the freedom of individuals prefabricated for life in a liberal political order: they must shape the way that people use their freedom, and mold *people* in a manner that helps ensure that liberal freedom is what they want. If a democratic constitutional regime is to thrive, it must constitute citizens willing to observe its limits and able to pursue its aspirations.

The simple picture of law's purposes misses the transformative dimension of liberalism and the positive ambitions of constitutionalism. The rule of law ideal of politics captures the liberal desire to regularize and limit political power. But it misses the breadth and depth of liberalism's transformative aspirations. There is no reason to think that the dispositions that characterize good liberal citizens come about naturally: good citizens are not simply born that way, they must be educated by schools and a variety of other social and political institutions.

Libertarianism, Multiculturalism, and School Choice

The most ardent defenders of individual liberty and the most enthusiastic celebrators of free markets are often among those who neglect the positive, transformative ambitions of a liberal democratic political order. The common motivation often seems to be a profound distrust of politics. There is certainly good reason to doubt the success of many public policies, and greater use should often be made of market mechanisms. Nevertheless, it is hard to see how sentiments such as these entitle anyone to take civic education for granted. If society as it is constituted contains forces that shape citizen character and preserve civic habits, it behooves market advocates to spell these out, investigate their preconditions, and provide some assurance that we are doing what we must to preserve them. Instead, the problem of civic education is often simply ignored.

Increasingly, the celebration of markets and choice also seems to gain support from the language of multiculturalism or cultural pluralism. This trend is nowhere more striking than in debates over public educational policy. Here, perhaps more than anywhere else, greater reliance on market competition and choice speaks not only to the desire for greater efficiency and "improved performance," but also to the embrace of normative diversity. There is every reason to pursue our purposes, whether public or private, efficiently. What is striking in debates over public school reform is that the emphasis on markets, choice, and cultural diversity often seems accompanied by a profound loss of faith in civic purposes.

Suspicion of political control in education comes in two varieties. On the one hand, observers from left and right decry what they see as the ideological hegemony and intellectual homogenization promoted by politically controlled schools. On the other hand, advocates of market competition charge that the public education monopoly needs to end if educational achievement is to improve. Both classes of critics converge on a common prescription: get rid of publicly controlled education—allow schools to compete and parents to choose with few government regulations.

There are observers at both ends of the political spectrum who liken government control over schooling to the establishment of an official state religion, and who see no end to ideological and moral conflict until the institution of common schooling is eliminated.[3]

Consider Stephen Arons, who decries the intellectual homogenization that public schools, in his view, often attempt to impose on families and local communities that disagree about their religious and moral convictions. Arons describes harrowing incidents of censorship and community conflict provoked by struggles to control public school curricula, libraries, and ideology. He argues that because public schools are educational institutions that, by political fiat, must serve families with radically different values and ideals, they inevitably furnish many occasions for deep and irresolvable normative conflicts. We should get rid of these conflicts by redrawing the boundaries and eliminating public schools as we know them, claims Arons, and by replacing them with a much more diverse range of publicly supported educational institutions.[4]

Consider one of Arons's most striking examples. In 1977–1978, Warsaw, Indiana, passed through what Arons describes as a "massive seizure of anti-intellectualism." He writes, "By the time the crisis had passed, five books had been banned, three teachers had been fired, the student newspaper had been eliminated, nine literature courses had been cut from the curriculum, and local senior citizens had offered their 'vote of thanks' to the censors with a parking-lot bonfire fed by gasoline and high-school texts."[5]

The conflict erupted when an increasingly conservative local school board, influenced by Christian fundamentalism and anxieties about the erosion of "family values," decided to try and root out the progressive, cosmopolitan cultural influences that had become increasingly prominent in Warsaw's schools—as it had in many others—since the 1960s. Courses on black literature and science fiction were among those discontinued, books containing criticisms of "traditional roles for women" were among those banned, and forty copies of the textbook *Values Clarification* were burned.[6]

Such conflicts, for Arons, are the consequence of political control over schooling: public schools, which are meant to serve all children, implicate too many intellectual controversies over which there is no agreement. Cultural consensus cannot be forged by political control over schooling, any more than religious uniformity could be imposed by political fiat. Indeed, Arons argues, the wars over public school curricula—and over what will constitute cultural orthodoxy more broadly—*are* religious wars, and so he quotes a study by Dorothy Nelkin:

> The recurrence of textbook disputes suggests that the truce between science and religion, based on the assumption that they deal with separate domains, may be a convenient but unrealistic myth. Religion as well as science purports to be a picture of reality, a means through which people render their lives and the world around them intelligible . . . It is clear that for many people science, often unrelated to their experience, does not serve as a satisfactory explanation of reality on which to base their values.[7]

The conflict over public schooling "centers on which explanation of reality shall be certified by the government as valid for the next generation."[8] But the government has no business certifying a particular vision of ultimate reality: to do so, Arons asserts, is to resurrect theocracy.

Rockne McCarthy and his coauthors similarly charge that the role of public schooling is to shape the worldview of students, and that this task invades the sphere of religion because "all of life is religion." There is no such thing as a neutral or objective way of looking at the world: "We all wear perceptual glasses of some sort that shape our perspective of reality . . . The only question is, What kind of glasses shall we wear?" According to McCarthy and his coauthors, "That choice belongs freely to every community, for world-views always have a communal dimension . . . They are formed within the context of supporting communities of like-minded people, and are not individualistic or religiously neutral."[9] The essentially religious disputes that tear apart school districts cannot be settled, but only avoided, according to these critics. And avoiding them requires disestablishing educational orthodoxies by closing down the public schools.

Critics such as these insist that the First Amendment should be understood to protect not only the expression of beliefs and opinions but also their formation.[10] Arons would eliminate public control over schools (beyond banning racial discrimination) and provide public support to poorer families, so that all will be equally free to determine their own beliefs and pass these along to their children by choosing among competing schools. We could thus avoid passionate conflicts while protecting "the formation of individual belief and . . . individual political sovereignty."[11]

Michael McConnell similarly presses what he sees as the animating purpose of the First Amendment in order to argue against political control over schooling. The central problem for McConnell, as for Arons, McCarthy, and many others, is that the realms of religion and public morality overlap to a considerable degree. The Constitution's framers cared most about "liberty of conscience," according to McConnell, not civic virtue. Indeed, the fundamental radicalism of the Constitution was that by embracing an extended republic constituted by multiculturalism and religious diversity, the founders gave up on the idea of a nation united around a shared public morality.

McConnell insists that the "Religion Clauses of the First Amendment meant that we would *not* have a common civic culture at the most fundamental level. We would *not* have a common morality." The Constitution, he admits, "thus left a dangerous void" because the various sects, when left to their own devices, "might propagate all manner of pernicious doctrines," and the clergy might stir up antagonisms "making civic harmony virtually unattainable." Yet the founders "took the risk" and trusted to "private institutions for the propagation of moral culture." And so, according to McConnell, "[t]he principal purpose of the Religion Clauses is to ensure that decisions about religious practice, including education, are reserved to the private realm of individual conscience."[12]

McConnell's position seems to me astonishing, but he deserves credit for being clear-eyed and honest enough to state what so many others ignore: that the failure to take responsibility for creating a civic culture would open a "dangerous void" in our public life.

Multiculturalist critics of common schooling such as McConnell raise important questions. They rightly recognize that removing all religious exercises and teachings from the schools does not make the schools wholly nonpartisan with respect to religion: today's public school curricula may have the effect of undermining some forms of religious faith, especially those that espouse moral values in tension with liberal democracy.

I return to these controversies later, but let me here note one thing about these proponents of educational diversity: their cramped view of the proper educative ambitions of a liberal democracy. These critics are so opposed to the notion of government-imposed orthodoxy that they ignore all other causes of concern. Arons, for example, conflates parental control with individual freedom: "where the individual is too young to make an informed and voluntary choice, his parents ought to control it."[13] And yet shouldn't we worry about parental as well as governmental tyranny? Is it not also the case that religious communities may be deeply illiberal and anti-individualistic? Arons ignores the fact that all-encompassing private groups can be as oppressive as an overweening state. Simply curbing government control will not necessarily promote freedom—at least the freedom of the children involved—nor does it necessarily promote children's capacities for citizenship or a stable and orderly system of liberal self-government.

Arons ignores the potential conflicts between particular normative communities—families, religious communities, and other groups— and the liberal community as a whole: the great society of many communities. He expresses solicitude about the "search for community" among Protestant fundamentalists, and speaks of their desire to create a moral "cohesiveness or sense of shared belief" through Christian schooling.[14] But the children of fundamentalists are also future citizens, and our shared political institutions are proper instruments to plan for the cohesiveness of our *political* community. Whether we merely tolerate religious schooling or join Arons, McConnell, and others in seeking to subsidize it, some account needs to be provided of how future citizens acquire the character traits, habits, and virtues they must have if the liberal political project is to survive and thrive.

It does no good simply to assume that people will disagree peacefully if only public schools can be gotten rid of, if only the proper lines can be drawn between private freedom and public power. Arons and McConnell provide no account of where this good temper comes from. Like many others of a libertarian bent, they take for granted a mutually respectful desire to live in peace with those one believes to be damned. This desire is, however, a political achievement and not an assumption to be taken for granted. We need to avoid making the libertarian mistake of assuming that liberal citizens—self-restrained, moderate, and reasonable—spring full-blown from the soil of private freedom. As we will see later, Adam Smith did not make these blithe assumptions, and neither should we. Harry Eckstein gets closer to the mark by suggesting that "stable governments . . . are the product of 'accidental' (extremely improbable) conjunctions of conditions which do sometimes, but rarely, occur in actual societies."[15]

It may be that a greater reliance on educational choice and school competition makes sense from the point of view of educational policy. And it may be that we would do well to utilize the particular virtues and capacities of private groups and civil society institutions in the delivery of social services. The last thing we should do, however, is to simply ignore or assume away the civic ambitions that have been at the core of common schooling from the beginning.

It is one thing to disagree with particular means toward the end of creating a shared citizenship; it is quite another to altogether neglect the importance of that basic end. These critics may or may not be right to suggest the need for fundamental revision of public school policy, but no adequate judgment can be made on this score until we take account of the need to constitute citizens.

At their most radical, these critics seem to argue that the promotion of civic purposes in public schools is necessarily at odds with religious freedom. When the government mandates the teaching of science in schools, it certifies a particular "explanation of reality" as a whole and usurps the place of religious teachings. When government promotes a civic morality, it encroaches on the proper sphere of religious sects. The choice is a stark and simple one: either protect freedom or promote a common civic culture. The burden of much of this book is to argue that this choice is a false one. But to see that we will need to understand something of the history of the conflicts among civic purposes and religious communities in America, and we will need to reconsider how a public morality can be justified in the face of religious and philosophical diversity.

School Choice and Market Competition

First Amendment libertarians are at least attuned to the religious and political conflicts that surround school policy. Other proponents of parental choice and market-based school reform write as though the only thing that citizens should want out of schools is "academic achievement": good grades, low dropout rates, and high scores on standardized tests.[16]

Recent years have witnessed an increasing number of challenges to the public school system. While many of these challenges strike at the foundations of what has long been the central political instrument of moral and civic education, reformers often say surprisingly little, or nothing at all, about the civic dimensions of reform. At the extreme, critics of public schooling seem to believe that public control serves no purpose except bureaucratic self-interest.

John E. Chubb and Terry M. Moe blame the problems of public schools on the institutions of democratic control, which transfer authority from school principals and the recipients of school services to the politically powerful. The keys to effective organization, they find, are school autonomy, a clear sense of purpose, school competition, and choice for parents and students. Give schools and their principals autonomy, assert Chubb and Moe—leave them "free to govern themselves as they want, specify their own goals and programs and methods, design their own organizations, select their own student bodies, and make their own personnel decisions."[17] Better schools can be generated by the market mechanisms of product differentiation, competition, and consumer choice.

Who could be against "better" schools? That is, schools that do what public schools do—only better? And yet Chubb and Moe also recognize that "[t]aken seriously, choice is not a system-preserving reform. It is a revolutionary reform that introduces a new system of public education." Taking private authority over education seriously would *not*, then, give us a better version of what we have; it would give us something deeply new. Impressive as their study is, Chubb and Moe never describe this newness or discuss its merits. They claim to take institutions seriously, and in many ways they do, but they never address the civic dimension of public schools. Market incentives may be the key to reform, but we need to deploy categories of analysis rich enough to describe and assess the political and moral dimensions of those reforms.[18]

Discussions of education reform are too often transfixed by dropout rates, test scores, and other indices of academic achievement. In a way, the very fact that these indices of success are taken for granted is enormously revealing. That it could be taken for granted that the overriding educational goal of parents and local communities is worldly achievement might be, I suppose, a way of paying implicit homage to the success of civic education in the American regime. Neglect of the most basic civic *ends* might imply that these are, after all, really quite unproblematic, so all that we need to think about are the best *means*.

Still, one would like to know how this successful convergence on ends was brought about, and what must be done to preserve it. Did public schools as an institution have a role in bringing about Arons's peaceful religious coexistence, or the emphasis on "success" that Chubb and Moe assume? What is the plan for keeping America's families happily preoccupied with sober and regime-supporting (or at least regime-compatible) interests such as high math scores and fewer dropouts?

As Arons's account of intense intellectual conflict shows, any analysis of our political interests in the education of future generations that ignores passionate conflict is part fantasy. Parents do care about dropout rates, standardized test scores, and other indices of intellectual achievement, but those who think that Americans care *only* about academic achievement are far too sanguine. The work of constituting diversity is not complete; indeed, some worry that our shared political identity may be coming undone in important respects.[19]

Ironically, the narrow focus of the policy debate is not explained by any overwhelming evidence that reform would bring academic improvement. Academic achievement is very difficult to compare across schools, which differ enormously in terms of student preparation, family background, and other crucial determinants of academic success. Schools differ so widely in what goes into them that it is hard to isolate the effects of the schools on what comes out. So even were we to accept the narrow measure of success (for example, academic achievement, as measured in standardized test scores), the advantages of private schooling over public schooling appear to be modest, perhaps even trivial.[20] Were there reason to think that scrapping the current regime of public schooling would lead to truly remarkable advances in academic achievement, it might be more understandable to ignore other factors and conclude that "choice is a panacea."[21] As it is, crucial aspects of public educational policy are being ignored by many reformers in the name of perhaps only slight gains in academic achievement.

The Politics of Difference and the Distrust of Virtue

It is worth noting that while many seem to want to ignore issues of deep diversity, others seem to want to celebrate it uncritically. Invocations of diversity and difference are often used as critical levers against what some see as liberalism's unfair tendency to marginalize or homogenize social diversity. Many social practices need to opened up to greater criticism and contestation, and many public policies should be revised so as to be made much more respectful of those outside the cultural mainstream. As work by Michel Foucault and others demonstrates, deeply embedded structures of meaning may shape social and personal identities and limit freedom in subtle but profound ways.[22] Uncovering and articulating these deep structures, contesting settled meanings, is important work. It is surely not the case, however, that all social structures are oppressive or equally worthy of contestation, or that any deep social formations that limit diversity or marginalize particular social groups must be rejected.

Iris Marion Young insists that politics should more carefully attend to the voices of those groups that have been unfairly pushed to the margins of society. This is an honorable and important project. But some groups have been pushed to the margins of society for good reason, and the last thing we want is a politics of indiscriminate inclusion.

Young wants a politics that "attends to rather than represses difference," one in which no group "is stereotyped, silenced, or marginalized." She dismisses the ideal of impartiality and such notions as moral universality, human nature, essentialism, and various other "modernist" sins and vices, because all deny the basic significance of group-based differences: "Groups cannot be socially equal unless their specific experience, culture, and social contributions are publicly affirmed and recognized." Not surprisingly, Young rejects "melting pot ideals of assimilation and unity," arguing that the "desire for political unity will suppress difference, and tend to exclude some voices and perspectives from the public." She advocates "bilingual-bicultural maintenance programs" to preserve and affirm group-specific identities.[23]

A politics that does not, as Young puts it, "devalue or exclude any particular culture or way of life" is neither plausible nor attractive.[24] Young champions certain constituencies (blacks, native people, women, gays, the disabled) and simply leaves aside the complaints of

Nazis, fundamentalists, or even the Amish, all of whom could claim to be victims of oppression, at least as Young describes it.

The implicit selectiveness of Young's solicitude for groups allows her to ignore a more basic political problem: how to promote convergence on the fundamental but no means uncontroversial goods of tolerance, openness to social diversity, equality of concern and respect, and free self-expression. Young in fact advances a very definite, and by no means uncontroversial, ideal of life as a whole: the modern, culturally pluralist city life. Young calls her ideal of city life "a vision of social relations affirming group difference," and she characterizes the proper city-dweller attitude as "an openness to unassimilated otherness."[25] Like Young, I would much rather live in London, Sydney, or San Francisco than Russell, Kansas, or Hope, Arkansas. But the ideal of city life is far from equally hospitable to all ways of life. A healthy and vibrant city life requires more: a predominance of tolerance, mutual understanding and respect, cooperativeness and good will within groups and across group lines, a sense of ownership of public places, and a willingness to help the weak. Good citizenship in today's cosmopolitan cities entails distinctive virtues, which Young herself implicitly recognizes in her praise for "openness" to "otherness." The virtues that Young relies upon are not only distinctive but also controversial, for the peaceful patterns of urban interaction that they undergird will effectively "marginalize" and "silence" adherents of ways of life that do not thrive in cosmopolitan conditions—including orthodoxies that thrive only within narrowly circumscribed boundaries, closed societies, and tight social control. Of course, cities can tolerate (and perhaps in some ways benefit from) a certain measure of "deviance" from any and every norm. The point is not that every city dweller must live up to a strict code of conduct; it is rather that in lively and attractive cities, certain patterns of behavior and certain attitudes of civility prevail. The "otherness" that one encounters in a peaceful and tolerant, if unquiet, city square is *assimilated* to a common way of life.

Richard Flathman also sees the seeds of oppression in shared liberal ideals of justice and civic virtue; that is, in the hegemonic potential of liberal ideals themselves. Flathman criticizes those wrong-headed "virtue liberals" who are judgmental about some ways of life because these liberals are, as Flathman would have it, liable to permit "restriction and repression" of unhealthy and unreasonable ways of life.[26] The problem that Flathman shares with Young is that he relies on an account of citizen virtue without articulating it, defending it, and describing how it can and should be promoted. While spurning "virtue liberalism," Flathman allows—without making enough of the point— that his ideal of life depends upon a wider set of personal virtues, which include "[s]elf-control, moderation, magnanimity, respect for 'forms' and adverbial considerations, and conditions of life conducive to these"; all of these virtues and more are necessary or else "individuality disappears into herd behavior or deteriorates into self-indulgence and 'letting-go.'"[27]

Young, Flathman, and other proponents of "difference" and contestation have decided expectations about how people should behave: racists, nativists, sexists, homophobes, the corrupt, the violent, and no doubt many others will be marginalized in their favored regime. We must all hope that certain groups become and remain marginalized.

It is far from wrong to worry about the persistence of social prejudice and cultural expectations that constrain the free self-development of many people. Not all social norms are expressions of prejudice, however, and not all cultural expectations constrain freedom.

By all means, let us celebrate a mutually respectful liberal democratic diversity, let us approach settled social and political expectations in a critical spirit. But let us also recognize that the celebration of peaceful diversity behooves us to try and understand what must be done from a political standpoint to keep Sydney from becoming Sarajevo, or Boston from becoming Beirut. Our current notion of "difference" is far too thin and devoid of moral content to characterize what it takes to constitute the shared life of a reasonably stable, peaceful, and mutually respectful urban order. There are groups and ways of life that thrive on ignorance and the demonization of outsiders. Surely, a world in which such groups are marginalized is exactly what we want.

Diversity in Its Place

What is the common thread here? All of the foregoing celebrators of choice and diversity in fact presuppose orderings of moral values and accounts of political virtue without taking responsibility for articulating those civic values, defending them, and offering accounts of how these values should be promoted. Invocations of diversity and difference, market choice and freedom, cultural pluralism and multiculturalism are easy resorts: they represent the spirit of the age, and to invoke them against the forces of homogeneity is to play on some of the deepest chords of today's political thinking on both the left and the right. The problem is not that cultural pluralists, libertarians, free market advocates, and other critics of virtue liberalism are altogether misguided. Each grasps a part of what any sensible liberal citizen will care deeply about: freedom, productivity, equality, and critical individuality. But each of these camps picks up a part of the liberal project and seems to want to make it the whole. The result is that these narrow partisans ignore imperatives that must also be given their place in a social order that hopes to sustain over generations a decent and orderly system of free self-government. What all of these inadequate views represent are variations on the same theme: a neglect of the civic dimensions of our liberal democratic political project.

Let me not be misunderstood: these partial perspectives have their uses. The keen sensitivity with respect to diversity represents, in certain respects, an advance in our political tradition. It is only in the last forty years, after all, that the American polity has begun to set its mind to delivering the oft-postponed promise of full political equality for black Americans. We have a long history of prejudice with respect to Native Americans, African Americans, Catholics, Jews, women, Asian Americans, and many others, as Rogers M. Smith has ably chronicled. No one nowadays could plausibly deny that the American political tradition has, for long stretches, unfairly marginalized and excluded particular groups.[28] Gays, lesbians, and others continue to suffer unfair discrimination. Acknowledging the reality of unfair exclusion should not, however, lead us to make the opposite mistake of indiscriminate inclusion: the embrace of all differences, and a laissez-faire attitude to the civic dimensions of the project of liberal self-government.

Let me conclude this chapter, and this preliminary discussion, by going back to the beginning of the liberal tradition, when the transformative aims of liberalism stood out in sharper relief, perhaps because they were so far from being accomplished. This is one way of glimpsing what must be the positive agenda of liberal constitutionalism with respect to diversity.

It must be admitted, however, that once we glimpse the extent of the liberal transformative agenda it will become clearer why many commentators prefer to ignore it. In important respects, the scope of the liberal agenda seems to outrun the reach of liberal reasons. Whether this is so, and how we can best address the problem of justification, is something to which we will need to return.

Religious Toleration and the Transformative Agenda

I have so far mainly emphasized unpaid debts of liberalism's critics. It is time to consider the depth of liberalism's transformative ambitions and the magnitude of the problem we face: How adequate are the reasons that liberalism offers for what it seeks to accomplish? And do liberalism's transformative ambitions outrun these publicly stated reasons?

Our problems of diversity are, in certain respects at least, rooted in the founding documents of liberalism. The problem of normative diversity is the original problem of modern politics, and it is worth seeing just how difficult it is to address. To begin to think more adequately about what liberal ambitions mean with respect to diversity, we can consider a crucial founding document of the liberal tradition: Locke's *Letter Concerning Toleration*. As Stanley Fish has pointedly suggested, the surprisingly problematic nature of Locke's argument is a source of confusion to this very day.[29]

The aim of the *Letter* is nothing less than to settle the conflict between the concern with "men's souls," on the one hand, and "on the other side, a care of the commonwealth." Locke writes, "I esteem it above all things necessary to distinguish exactly the business of civil government from that of religion, and to settle the just bounds that lie between the one and the other. If this be not done, there can be no end put to the controversies."[30]

This, as Stanley Fish has pointed out, is an admirable expression of the "mission statement" of liberalism: to bring about a world in which conflicts over basic religious and philosophical commitments can be resolved in favor of mutual toleration and political freedom. Only thus, liberals have long believed, will there ever be an end to the religious controversies that have for so long plagued mankind.

What is Locke's argument for limiting politics in the ways he suggests? He offers a complex array of arguments that to modern eyes seem misleadingly self-evident. Let us consider Locke's argument and its limits.

Religious faith depends, Locke argues, on inward assent; religious belief is crucial and cannot be coerced: "I cannot be saved by a religion that I distrust, and by a worship that I abhor." Locke calls this "the *principal consideration* . . . which absolutely determines this controversy." It is simply irrational to engage in religious persecution: people cannot be saved against their will. This argument appears to land a "knock out" blow against intolerance, and it has been echoed by Jefferson, Madison, and many others.[31]

Still, Locke adds other arguments. "Every man," Locke insists, is for himself the "supreme and absolute Authority" in matters of religion because "no body else is concerned in it, nor can receive any prejudice from his conduct therein." It is, in other words, no harm to you if your neighbor goes to hell. Jefferson later emphasized the same point: "[I]t neither picks my pocket nor breaks my legs."[32]

In addition, Locke argues that religious truth does not need the help of politics. Truth will, he insists, win out in free public argument: "[T]he business of law is not to provide for the truth of opinions, but for the safety and security of the commonwealth, and of every particular mans goods and person. And so it should be. For truth certainly would do well enough if she were once left to shift for herself. She seldom has received, and I fear never will receive much assistance from the power of great men to whom she is but rarely known, and more rarely welcome."[33] As Mill would elaborate more fully later, the free clash of opinions is the best means to ensure the pursuit of truth.[34]

Locke adds still other arguments. Even if political persecution were efficacious, he writes, political leaders disagree about religion and have no special expertise in this realm, so they should not be trusted with the power to coerce uniformity. An expressed concern with saving men's souls can, in any case, serve as a cloak for the self-interested pursuit of power. Finally, Locke denies that public religious uniformity is a prerequisite for peace: social conflict is more likely to result from the demand for religious uniformity than from the freedom to profess one's beliefs.[35]

Locke's battery of arguments for toleration seems irresistible today. The upshot is that political authority and religious authority are entirely different. The church, says Locke, is "absolutely separate and distinct from the Commonwealth. The boundaries on both sides are fixed and immovable. He jumbles heaven and earth together, the things most remote and opposite, who mixes these two societies; which are in their original end, business, and every thing, perfectly distinct and infinitely different from each other."[36] Locke's rendering is conclusive: a complete and utter separation of the spheres of religion and politics. These arguments were accepted by few in Locke's day, and it took a century and a half for Locke's position to be accepted in Britain. The arguments were forceful, and in time they proved influential. A "wall of separation" has been erected between church and state, and it is believed to be erected on the solid foundations that Locke articulated.[37]

Locke's arguments, however, are not nearly as conclusive as they appear. Indeed, Locke's ambitions seem to outrun his political or civil reasons in important respects.

One thing that is immediately striking is the extent to which, in spite of Locke's insistence to the contrary, the boundaries between politics and religion are not "fixed and immovable." Politics cannot in fact leave religion to one side: it cannot leave the soul alone and care only for the body, for our deepest moral and spiritual commitments need to be shaped in accordance with political imperatives. This fact is clear from the start of the *Letter,* for the argument does not begin with an account of rights or an appeal to political values but rather with an account of our religious duties: of what is *right* as a religious matter.

The very first sentence of the *Letter* insists that toleration is "the chief characteristical mark of the true church." So toleration (the basic liberal virtue) is in the first instance defended *as a religious mandate.* And soon thereafter: "I appeal to the conscience of those that persecute . . ."[38] That Christ and the Gospels command toleration is, indeed, the principal theme of much of the *Letter.* All of this signals Locke's dependence on the prevalence of religious sensibilities that support toleration: toleration needs the support of private beliefs and practices; it depends on a certain ordering of the soul.

Perhaps most importantly, Locke's insistence that the spheres of politics and religion are "perfectly distinct and infinitely different" is belied by the fact that both spheres are concerned with a variety of forms of "moral actions." Locke seems to be thinking of laws against vices at odds with the public good, such as drunkenness and transgressions against prevailing sexual morality. These moral actions can be regulated by the state not to promote particular religious views, but for the sake of the public welfare.[39] Of course, religious authorities will also have an interest in the way these moral activities are regulated.

In addition, many public activities will directly impinge upon or indirectly affect religious life and religious practices, and vice versa. We cannot shield religious life from all these effects; indeed, Locke never guarantees that we can or should. So the impassable boundary between our civil and religious lives seems to be rather a broad and important swath of overlapping jurisdictions: actions that are relevant to religion can be regulated by the state for the sake of civil interests.

Locke's "impassable" wall turns out to be a remarkably narrow guarantee that *government will not act for the sake of religious reasons*. He never denies that public policies may burden religious practices as a collateral matter, or as a consequence of pursuing a legitimate public purpose. He never guarantees that government and public policy will be *neutral in their effects* on religion and other private ways of life. Ruling out religious reasons as a basis of lawmaking still means that the political and religious spheres will overlap—that is, there will be conflicts between political imperatives and individual consciences and religious communities.

Locke mentions examples of conflicts. Government cannot ban the sacrifice of calves (a religious ceremony), but it *can* ban the slaughtering of calves in the event of a famine. The government cannot require children to be baptized, but it can require them to be washed for health reasons. Just because public authorities act for only public purposes does not mean that there will be no conflict among those purposes, religious interests, and the conscientious scruples of citizens. Locke's hypotheticals can easily be multiplied, as demonstrated by real life cases:

- Quakers and other conscientious objectors seek exemptions from military service on the grounds that their religious beliefs forbid them from participating in combat.

- Christian Scientist parents withhold medical treatment from their children because they believe in the power of prayer to cure diseases, but public officials may regard this as an act of criminal negligence.

- The government prosecutes a "war on drugs," and Native Americans complain that they have a right to use peyote as part of their traditional religious ceremonies.

- The government decides a new highway is needed through a remote area, but it turns out that the ground is sacred to Native Americans.[40]

What happens when legitimate public purposes and private religious values conflict? Religious people might well think that public imperatives in any given case are trivial compared with the religious burdens that they suffer. Religious people might also suspect hidden motives: the government may ban the slaughtering of calves for health reasons or on account of a food shortage, but is this only a pretext? On the other side, public officials worry that making exceptions to generally applicable laws will unleash a torrent of conscientious objections.

What happens when clashes such as these occur? Locke's answer appears to be simple. Public authorities judge what the public good requires, and so long as the judgment is about a political matter and based on the public good, a citizen will have no *right* to be exempted based on reasons of conscience, which are private. "For the private judgment of any person concerning a law enacted in political matters, for the publick good, does not take away the obligation of that law, nor deserve a dispensation." At the same time, Locke also allows that if a private person sincerely judges that a law requires some act that is "unlawful" to his conscience, he should abstain from the action and take his punishment, "which it is not unlawful for him to bear." Indeed, Locke goes further and allows that "[t]he principal and chief care of every one ought to be of his own soul first, and in the next place of the publick peace." This implies the possibility of active resistance to the law, not only passive submission, when it is believed that the public good is being used as a pretext to cloak religious oppression.[41]

So if there is a conflict between perceived public and religious imperatives, basic religious duties will come first for many individuals, but political leaders will look first to the public good. Conflicts of interest are to be expected, especially when public officials and religious people have different experiences, worldviews, and values. And if political authorities and religious citizens disagree, Locke explains that there is no judge on earth between them: only God can judge, which is to say that they will fight it out on earth, and look to divine judgment in the next life. (We should not foreclose the question of "dispensations"—or religiously based exemptions and exceptions to generally applicable public policies—in the peremptory manner that Locke seems to embrace, but for now let us follow the deeper logic of Locke's position.)

The "clear and immovable" boundary between civil and religious spheres guarantees only that public authorities will not pursue a specifically religious agenda. This leaves us with an extensive overlap of public and religious concerns, which has important implications for political stability. The overlap suggests that absent a degree of compatibility and convergence among public and private purposes, public authority will be fragile, and conflict among public bodies and private communities will be frequent.

As liberal democrats, we want more than bare toleration and peace: we want citizens to be able to deliberate respectfully about shared concerns and to cooperate in formal institutions and less formal social settings. The subtext of the Lockean position—especially when transposed onto more explicitly democratic institutions—is that the civic health of liberal democracies depends not simply on a clear division of spheres, but on a deeper convergence of public and private values: a convergence of individual consciences and the public good powerful enough to ensure the political supremacy of public values and institutions against competing imperatives.

Perhaps the most dramatic evidence that the boundaries between politics and religion are not as sharp and "immovable" as Locke sometimes asserts is found where Locke describes the duties of Christian preachers:

> It is not enough that ecclesiastical men abstain from violence and rapine, and all manner of persecution. He that pretends to be a successor of the apostles, and takes upon him the office of teaching, is obliged also to admonish his hearers of the duties of peace, and good-will toward all men; as well as towards the erroneous as the orthodox; towards those that differ from them in faith and worship, as well as towards those that agree with them therein: and he ought industriously to exhort all men, whether private persons or magistrates, (if any such there be in his church) to charity, meekness, and toleration; and diligently endeavor to allay and temper all that heat, and unreasonable averseness of mind, which either any man's fiery zeal for his own sect, or the craft of others, has kindled against dissenters.[42]

Locke's political order counts on religious teachers and institutions to foster the virtues of civility and self-restraint on which the survival of the political order depends. Locke here acknowledges in effect that a good deal of moral education takes place in the norm-generating communities of the private sphere. The civil virtues of "charity, meekness, and toleration," among others, must gain the support of religious communities if a liberal social settlement is to survive and prosper. Indeed, Locke clearly hopes that the practice of religious toleration will drain the religious sphere of hostility and transform churches into schools of liberty. Accusations of church-based sedition would soon cease, he says, "if the law of toleration were once so settled, that all churches were obliged to lay down toleration as the foundation of their own liberty; and teach that liberty of conscience is every man's natural right, equally belonging to dissenters as to themselves." The peaceful coexistence of religious pluralism would, Locke hoped, itself be educative.[43]

Lockean politics cannot, any more than our own, leave private moral beliefs altogether to one side; it cannot leave the soul alone to care only for the body. It counts on a convergence of public and private, for a good deal of publicly relevant moral education is bound to be done by private communities. Civic education, in the broadest sense of that phrase, obviously becomes a central concern under these political conditions. Normative convergence must be fostered, but given the conviction that religious imperatives in certain respects transcend political concerns, this enterprise must be one fraught with controversy.

How might we ensure this convergence? How can we make certain that private consciences and religious communities do not deviate too far from what is supportive of the regime? How might we narrow the gaps between the shared political good and what various churches and individuals profess and promote? May the government do anything to bring about a convergence of public and private views, or would that be objectionable and dangerous: a trampling in the most private of spheres that could only offend religious sensibilities? It is hard to see what the explicit mechanisms of soulcraft are in the *Letter*, but it is worth noticing that what sometimes look like exercises in line drawing and boundary marking can also be seen as implicit attempts to reconstitute the private realm in a manner that will make it compatible with and supportive of the public.

First and most obviously, there are limits to the right to toleration in Locke, and those limits are marked out in accordance with the imperatives of the social compact itself. Members of sects that profess that "faith is not to be kept with heretics" forfeit a right to toleration, according to Locke, for this would mean that religious authorities could dissolve the political compact by excommunicating the sovereign. The limits of a right to toleration are reached, for Locke, when religious doctrines are advanced that deny the grounds and integrity of the social compact itself.[44] If the price of full citizenship and, more broadly, full public acceptance is that religious communities honor the integrity of the social compact, then citizens have important incentives to circumscribe their religious convictions to respect civic aims.

Locke asserts that it will be rare for churches to teach "doctrines of religion" at odds with "the foundations of society," because in doing so "their own interest, peace, reputation, every thing, would be thereby endangered."[45] This, from the point of view of Locke's day, seems like a bit of wishful thinking. He could, of course, *hope* for a future in which all churches would conceive of "their own interest" in terms of favoring, and being known to favor, freedom and peace. The important point is that what is in one's interests, and what makes for a good reputation, depend on the nature of the society in which one lives: its political institutions, its norms, and the beliefs of other citizens. Living in a political society that is based on tolerance and a social contract of shared civil interests would encourage religious communities to think about "interest, peace, and reputation" in terms supportive of the regime—at least as long as liberal norms succeed in determining the public grounds of respect.

Liberal politics itself may be educative in a variety of ways. In this regime, churches themselves must accept the political framework and mimic it to some degree, for they themselves must be voluntary associations with no coercive powers, in which individuals have a right of exit. As citizens, religious believers acknowledge a fundamental duty to persuade rather than coerce those believed to be in error over religion and other matters. So churches themselves must respect basic individual freedom and accommodate themselves to it.

The political role of citizenship should also be educative. As members of a political community, Locke's citizens would put their religious differences to one side for the sake of shared civil interests. They would be required to honor the equal political rights and equal political standing of fellow citizens of different faiths. According to this new political dispensation, religious differences (within limits) are not obstacles to political unity. In our political relations as fellow citizens, our religious differences are of secondary importance as compared with our shared concerns with peace, the security of rights, prosperity, democratic deliberation, and equal individual freedom.

This liberal democratic political order, which Locke only partially prefigures, counts on being more than just a set of limits on prepolitical interests and convictions. The success of this political order depends upon its ability to be educative at the deepest level.

The transformative ambitions of Locke's political order may help explain why Locke advances some political claims that seem dubious as a matter of principle: they are perhaps meant to push our thinking about religion in a certain direction, to help create a certain kind of religiosity and thereby a certain kind of society. Locke writes, for example, that "the care of each man's salvation belongs only to himself" because the "perdition" of one is no "prejudice to any other man's affairs" (once again anticipating Jefferson's comment that it "neither picks my pocket nor breaks my leg.")[46] But, as some of Locke's contemporaries immediately pointed out, are we not affected by those who live around us? Does not our ability to live an upright life depend upon a supportive social context? And what of our children's salvation? Locke's assertion that religious conviction cannot be coerced is also not quite as convincing as it at first appears, for persecution can concentrate the mind. Persecution might well reduce the availability of heretical ideas and the incidence of error. As Don Herzog has pointed out, however, the assertion of our religious independence may be questionable as a matter of fact, but fostering a belief in such independence may help bring about a society in which freedom and independence are respected.[47]

Finally, Locke notes that truth will triumph without the help of government, "for truth would do well enough, if she were once left to shift for herself." Well, we hope so, and we count on people believing this, but the way we pursue truth will influence the destinations at which we arrive. To embrace the notion that the truth is best pursued in conditions of freedom is to say something significant about the nature of truth. Free, individual truth seeking is itself a way of life: it defines a particular social framework within which beliefs will be formed. To say that truth does well enough in such a framework is, in part, to beg the question of what truth is. When Locke argued for the authority of individual judgment on religious matters, he argued against the authority of clerics, received traditions, and civil magistrates. Locke himself was a doctrinal minimalist who insisted on the positive and by no means uncontroversial claim that there could be no certainty on many disputed theological issues. Getting religious communities to accept a regime in which truth is allowed to fend for itself is a basic and substantive aim of liberalism.[48]

Conclusion

Today, Locke's arguments for toleration appear self-evidently true. That is misleading, for these arguments depend on premises that were contested by most believers for centuries, and that are rejected by some even now. Those premises importantly include the conviction that there is no religious duty to impose uniformity, and that the central religious duty is to look to your own conduct and salvation. The appearance of conclusiveness represents the extent to which religious and philosophical beliefs, at least in the United States and some other societies, now generally support liberal principles of toleration. This convergence is a very good thing from a liberal political point of view. But our shared political reasons can only partially justify this religious transformation, for we do not claim, as a polity, to have a public account of religious truth: we have only a shared account of basic civic values that impose limits on what can be true in the religious sphere.

It may seem hard for members of modern liberal democratic societies to see why people persecute others over religious matters. Yet the decline of religious intolerance is in no way foreordained. Intolerance of religious error may bespeak a seriousness with regard to religion and a concern with the well-being of others that is, according to some, missing in some modern liberal societies. Is part of the liberal settlement that people must not take religion too seriously? Is the watering down of religion and its relegation to the margins of life part of the liberal agenda? Many observers now charge that American public life has become a "naked public square," and that our public policies foster a "culture of disbelief." The religious voice is increasingly defensive and outspoken on this point. No less a figure than Pope John Paul II warned on his first trip back to Poland after the collapse of Communism: "We must take into account that, as time has passed, especially in the so-called modern age, Christ—as the creator of the soul of Europe, the creator of this freedom that has its roots in him—has been placed in parentheses and a new mentality has begun to form, a mentality which could be expressed by the following phrase: Let us think, let us act, as if God did not exist."[49]

It is, I believe, a profound mistake to identify religious seriousness with illiberal religiosity. We do not, however, have public arguments to show that a concern with eternity is best expressed in ways that accord with liberal democratic political institutions. There is something frightening in the reminder that on the religious side of the ledger are reflections such as those heard during the "Promise Keepers" rally in Washington, D.C.: "[W]e are only on earth temporarily, those who are born again will live together in heaven for ever."[50] Statements like these remind us that the reconciliation of religion and liberalism is still precarious and not to be taken for granted.

The basic problematic for modern society with respect to deep normative diversity is glimpsed in Locke's effort to divide the spheres of religion and politics. This division depends upon the support of religious reasons and religious communities—a support that can be encouraged by a liberal public philosophy but not altogether justified by it.

Liberalism is dependent on religion in two important ways. First, it depends on the reasons, norms, and moral convictions generated by religious communities. Jeremy Waldron has noticed the extent to which Locke's argument depends on supportive religious premises and implies that this is a weakness in Locke's argument: the last thing we want, Waldron suggests, is to have to come up with a new argument for toleration in response to every version of religious orthodoxy.[51] The problem, however, is that we cannot show that political aims and values override competing religious imperatives on the basis of political argument alone: the case for toleration and other civic values is, for religious people, bound to depend in part on how they construe their religious views. In justifying a liberal public philosophy, we cannot avoid setting certain boundaries as to what can be true as a religious matter, but we should avoid positing a particular view of religious truth. Indeed, as I argue in Part Two, today it is best to say even less about religious truth than Locke does. Even so, the convincingness and popular appeal of the public argument for toleration will depend upon the religious beliefs that people form and act upon. Liberal transformative ambitions outrun liberal public reasons.

Liberalism is dependent on religious and other nonpublic communities in a second, more positive way. To the extent that communities and associations of various sorts are important moral educators within a liberal democratic political order, then clearly the political order is dependent on the type of moral and political education promoted by religious and other normative communities. And indeed, Sidney Verba, Kay Lehman Schlozman, and Henry E. Brady provide evidence showing that religious communities are important civic educators.[52] Moreover, we live in an era, as I discuss elsewhere, in which increasing emphasis is placed on the importance of civil society to the civic health of the polity. Different people sometimes mean different things by "civil society," but in general it designates those associations and communities (other than economic enterprises) between the individual and the state. Active participation in associations and groups is seen as conducive to the habits and character of good citizenship. This renewed concern with civil society highlights the extent to which modern mass societies depend upon the quality of the moral and political education provided by the intermediate associations and communities, including churches.

Public and private institutions are mutually dependent. This interdependence sets much of the problem for what follows: How can we justify and realize liberal values consistent with the freedom of individuals and communities? That is, how can we constitute, in the positive, transformative sense, a liberal civic order?

As I explain next, anxiety about the popular capacity for responsible and reasoned self-government in the new American republic was intensely felt and at least partly understandable. This anxiety gave rise to a public institution designed to do what Locke, in the *Letter*, counts on private preachers doing. Horace Mann and others saw the common school as the fit instrument for pursuing the transformative purpose that must underlie any project of free self-government: a fit instrument because if the public ends are important, then adequate public means should be found.

American public schools have been, in many ways, where the tension between diversity and the felt need to promote shared values has played out most dramatically. This institution has, from its inception, been the principal direct public instrument for creating a shared political culture amid religious, racial, ethnic, and class diversity. Public schools are where what purports to be a liberal state has intervened between children and their parents and communities of birth to shape the deepest beliefs and commitments of "private" communities and future generations. The objections raised against the public schools allow us to examine critically some of the deepest divisions and most intractable conflicts that characterize the public lives of modern states.

PART I

Public Schooling and American Citizenship

Public schooling is not only America's oldest and most extensive social program, it is also one that intervenes in the most private of relations for the most sensitive of purposes. For its defenders, the American public school system epitomizes liberal democratic commitments to equal opportunity for all children, the promise of a common citizenship, and the freedom of all children to make their own way in the world even if doing so means rejecting the wishes of their parents and communities of birth. For its detractors and critics, the public school system represents nativist suspicion of foreigners, Protestant prejudice against Catholics, the desire of economic elites to standardize the children of working-class families, and a homogenizing zeal that belies the promise of freedom and equality.

Summarizing the standard historical view, Stephen V. Monsma insists that "anti-Catholicism and the common school ideal worked to reinforce each other." This is far from a matter of antiquarian interest, for as Monsma and others insist, "There is strong evidence that both the common school ideal and the suspicion of Catholic private education rooted in anti-Catholic prejudice are continuing factors shaping the mindset with which Supreme Court Justices and other policy elites approach the issue of public funds and K-12 schools." Or, as John E. Coons puts it: "The machinery of public monopoly was chosen specifically by brahmins like Horace Mann and James Blaine to coax the children of immigrants from the religious superstitions of their barbarian parents. Today that antique machinery continues its designated role."[1]

Public schools are, and have been from their inception, sites for some of the most interesting and intense conflicts in our polity. Here our concern will be with the conflict between the imperatives of civic education and the claims of diversity: the great and enduring struggle between those anxious about our ability to create a shared citizenship capable of sustaining our free constitutional order and those determined to preserve particular religious, moral, and ethnic ways of life. What may the state do to promote the attitudes and habits needed by liberal citizens? When should religious families and communities secure changes in or exemptions from aspects of the public school curriculum?

It is clear enough that in order to confront today's moral conflicts, we need to understand the historical struggles that shaped institutions such as common schooling. My aim here is not simply to follow the many others who have sought to uncover the pretenses and hypocrisy of claims to public school neutrality with respect to religion, and later, morality. The civic agenda of common schooling has often been pursued in a way that was exclusionary and unfair. Nevertheless, it is far too simple to say, as does Myron Leiberman, that "the *raison d'être*" for common schooling "was religious prejudice."[2] There have been and still are genuine conflicts between some religious groups and the civic life of a liberal democracy. Likewise, there is some truth to the claims of David Nasaw, Stanley K. Schultz, and others that the public school system has often been supported by business elites and shaped by the needs of a capitalist economy.[3] Nevertheless, these claims of elite dominance are easily exaggerated, for Paul E. Peterson has shown that public schools long enjoyed the support of labor unions and other working-class organizations.[4]

The American public school system, like other American political institutions, has been shaped by a history of prejudice and exclusion on grounds of race, gender, religion, nationality, and class. This history has been ably and amply documented by Rogers M. Smith, and I do not wish to minimize or discount it.[5] Yet I believe that we can also discern important and legitimate civic purposes in the history of the American public school system, purposes that are today in danger of being forgotten. We should credit the proponents of common schooling for recognizing what is too often overlooked today: that convergence on liberal democratic civic norms does not come about automatically, that in fact the health of our regime depends on its ability to turn people's deepest convictions—including their religious beliefs—in directions that are congruent with the ways of a liberal republic. The fact is that in the mid-nineteenth century as today, some opposed the legitimate civic aims of common schooling. Indeed, what I want to emphasize here is that to a greater degree than many historical sources allow, some of the most basic and widely discussed conflicts around public schools have been the consequence of religious opposition to basic civic ideals.

This part of the book depicts, in broad strokes, some of the primary civic aims pursued by the founders and shapers of public schools. My goal is not to treat this vast subject comprehensively. It is rather to uncover the civic ambitions of this institution and thereby to reveal something about the depth of the civic purposes that remain to be pursued. Many of today's controversies—especially over religious and cultural plurality—echo older debates that took place at the inception of the common school system. Tracing these roots and sketching these antecedents will help us better understand what is at stake in today's disputes over schooling, religious freedom, and multiculturalism. Our challenge, I believe, is to acknowledge the unfairness, small-mindedness, and prejudice that have often accompanied the project of promoting a shared civic identity, while insisting that the project is nevertheless inescapable, legitimate, and worthy of renewed attention.

CHAPTER 2

Civic Anxieties

The common, or later "public," school system is one of our most familiar—and most controversial—political institutions. By "public schools," I mean specifically those educational institutions that are publicly controlled and funded, and that are open as a matter of right to all children in a given geographical area. This is not an ancient institution, but one that began to take hold in America in the second quarter of the nineteenth century, for civic purposes that are worth exploring.

The United States is generally regarded as a leading exemplar of liberal individualism and small government. The American state is often said to have been slower to develop than its counterparts in Europe and never to have developed as full a range of social responsibilities. And yet with respect to public educational policy, Americans in the early nineteenth century seem to have been ahead of many of their European cousins in deciding that securing a universal education (at least for white males) was a public responsibility to be accomplished by a common, public institution. American public education policy was, and remains, strikingly decentralized. Yet the unity of purpose and broad zeal to secure for all children a common education in public institutions reflected a striking determination to promote a shared citizenship.

Anxiety and Early American Nationhood

American anxieties about the preservation of moral community are at least as old as the European settlements. European families arriving at the New World struggled not only to survive in the wilderness but also, as Bernard Bailyn emphasizes, to transplant their cultural inheritance and transmit it to future generations. Bailyn describes a people driven by cultural anxieties about the fragility of social norms, the "incipient savagery" of the young, and the difficulty of sustaining traditional moral standards and institutions in a wholly new environment.[1]

From the beginning, as Tocqueville reports, public provisions for education were among the means deployed to promote knowledge of scriptures, public morals, and good order. The Massachusetts Code of 1650 obliged every township to maintain schools and to enforce attendance.[2] A dramatic sign of concern with moral slackness is the profusion of seventeenth-century laws and admonitions requiring parental respect and punishing filial disobedience (which was elevated in Connecticut and Massachusetts to a *capital* offense). Throughout the colonial period, public authorities did not hesitate to insist that families fulfill their obligation to prepare children to be decent, orderly, and productive citizens. Some states had laws ordering that children found in "gross ignorance" should be removed from their families. The law stepped in to fortify the guardians of traditional morality—family, church, and local community—and, when necessary, to contrive supplements and substitutes for traditional sources of moral education.[3]

While local communities in the colonial era exercised wide powers over the education of children, the care of dependents, and the behavior of all adults, the mechanisms employed were, by our standards, remarkably localized and informal. Indeed, well into the nineteenth century the primary sources of protection and safety were the "wholesome restraint of public opinion," aided by the night watchman.[4]

The vast majority of Americans throughout the eighteenth century worked on family farms and lived in rural areas. In 1755, Philadelphia—by far America's largest city—had only 20,000 residents, while New York, Boston, Newport, and Charleston had fewer than 15,000 each. Even by 1790, out of approximately 4 million Americans, fewer than 125,000 lived in "cities" with more than 10,000 residents. Most goods were produced and consumed at home, and few Americans had contact with remote and impersonal economic institutions. Eighteenth-century Americans depended, and could depend, on voluntary efforts and cooperation for a host of civic purposes, including law enforcement, fire fighting, and the care of dependent and disabled neighbors. Early nineteenth-century observers found that even the largest American cities, such as Boston, retained the moral economy of villages, where the "character of every man" was "open to the observation of every other."[5]

Throughout the colonial period, therefore, and into the early nineteenth century, communities relied to a remarkable degree on local informal self-policing to control behavior. As David J. Rothman puts it, "[M]embers of the community were to supervise one another, to detect and correct the first signs of deviancy."[6] At the time of the American Revolution, as Barry Alan Shain has shown, and for many decades after, the assumption was that local communities would seek "to shape, in ethically intrusive ways, the 'souls' of their residents."[7]

The profound democratic currents that fed the American Revolution greatly increased the concern with popular enlightenment. Adam Smith's *Wealth of Nations* was first published in 1776, and it is worth recalling his insistence that the state has a responsibility to educate the common people, not only to keep them from sinking into torpor and stupidity, but also to prepare them for the office of self-government by rendering them capable of making judgments on public affairs. "A man, without the proper use of the intellectual faculties of man," is, argued Smith, "mutilated and deformed" in an "essential part of the character of human nature." The state should promote "the instruction of the inferior ranks of people," not only because education was important in its own right, but also because it would make them less liable to "the delusions of enthusiasm and superstition"—more capable of seeing through "the interested complaints of faction and sedition."[8]

After the American Revolution, many spoke of the need for an educated, disciplined, and patriotic citizenry. "In proportion as the structure of a government gives force to public opinion," Washington warned in his 1796 Farewell address, "it is essential that public opinion should be enlightened." Benjamin Rush likewise insisted that "[t]he business of education has acquired a new complexion by the independence of our country." And Noah Webster argued that education should be "the first care of a legislature"; all citizens, not only the wealthy, must be fitted "for places of trust." To fail publicly to support the education of all would mean that "[t]he constitutions are *republican* and the laws of education are *monarchical.*"[9]

Many leading Americans called for the founding of elaborate systems of public schooling, and even a national university. The grandiose schemes of national education came to nought. Among the leading state measures, Virginia's Bill for the More General Diffusion of Knowledge failed numerous times to win legislative support in the two decades after independence. Of Jefferson's comprehensive plan for state education—which included primary schools in every village or ward and a smaller number of regional academies for more advanced students—only the University of Virginia actually came to fruition in his lifetime.

Municipal and state subsidies to charity schools and academies increased in many places, but the construction of systems of public education as we know them today fell to a later generation. While public leaders agreed on the need for a dispersion of knowledge across the population, they disagreed about such basic matters as the constitutionality of national initiatives on education and the role of religion in public education.[10]

In the early decades of the nineteenth century, the pattern of informal surveillance and disorganized local education began to be regarded as inadequate. The eventual result was a host of rehabilitative institutions founded to act where it was believed that families were failing: almshouses, reformatories, penitentiaries, and asylums for orphans and the insane. These institutions supported, or if need be substituted for, the roles of families and local communities in building moral character and creating responsible citizens.

This striking upsurge of reformism in the early to mid-nineteenth century sprang from a variety of sources. The sheer growth of the American population, and especially its concentration in urban centers, was widely regarded with alarm. Small villages with relatively stable populations could count on informal mechanisms to monitor and control behavior, but during the early nineteenth century, northern cities received a huge influx of immigrants and grew at a spectacular rate. The population of New York City was 11 percent foreign born in 1825; thirty years later the figure was over 50 percent, and half of those were Irish Catholics. Cities began to experience crowding, poverty, and delinquency, all of which brought fears of disorder and mob violence.[11]

As populations swelled and became increasingly heterogeneous and mobile, city services that had long been provided on a volunteer basis—such as police, fire fighting, and street repair—gave way to paid municipal agencies. Moreover, early-nineteenth-century America experienced a general surge in state intervention: canals were dug, roads were built, and banks were chartered, all in the spirit of government-encouraged enterprise and improvement.[12]

With expanding commerce came expanding international competition. Horace Mann and other reformers were favorably impressed by what they saw as the forward-looking examples of increasingly active European states. Centralization, standardization, and systemization appealed to many social reformers of the early nineteenth century.[13]

Structural changes in the economy had important consequences for authority within the family. As manufacturing and commerce replaced agriculture as the primary economic activity, work and home became separated. Fathers left their homes for long periods to work, and this was thought to have adverse consequences for children's discipline. Public schools, it was believed, might help fill this void.[14]

People were also beginning to think in new ways about their shared civic lives. Republican government was, in the early nineteenth century, still a fragile experiment. Landholding had long been a crucial prop for citizen independence and virtue, but as wage labor became increasingly important and the population shifted toward the cities, many feared that commercial wealth and urban life would increase opportunities for vice of every sort. Property qualifications for voting fell away in the 1820s, and the proportion of adult white males actually voting soared. The widening franchise (among white males) provided a powerful and widely voiced argument for a universal right to education. "As property ceased to create citizens," Robert H. Wiebe has observed, "it also lost its power to shape their character." New measures were needed to promote citizen virtues such as good judgment, self-restraint, industry, and respect for the law. Educational reformers rushed into this breach. "That intelligence and virtue are the only support and stability of free institutions, was a truism a long time ago," argued Horace Mann; "If the multitude, who have the power, are not fitted to exercise it, society would be like a herding together of wolves. The only safety, then, is in the concomitance of qualifications and power." Free education was, as Judith N. Shklar puts it, "the one public activity that did not worry democrats."[15]

Amidst the many sources of anxiety and alarm, there emerged a sense that human intervention could ameliorate social ills. Ideas about the causes of social disadvantage were changing in the late eighteenth and early nineteenth centuries. Under the influence of the educational writings of John Locke and others, delinquency and poverty were increasingly attributed not to innate depravity but to environmental factors such as parental failure and poor upbringing, against which the community could and should act. "The mobs, the riots, the burnings, the lynchings, perpetrated by the *men* of the present day," argued Horace Mann, "are perpetrated, because of their vicious or defective education, when children." More and more people accepted Locke's teaching that the mind was like a tabula rasa, whose shape was determined not by inherited attributes but by experiences.[16] Childhood, many reformers believed, "made the man," and this belief gave communities powerful incentives to intervene to rectify the perceived shortcomings of many parents. "Children," argued teacher and education theorist Gideon F. Thayer in 1839, "are brought into life plastic, and for a time, passive beings; ready to receive . . . mouldings and impressions."[17]

Thus support for moral reform in general, and schooling in particular, was motivated not only by fear of the disordering consequences of social change, but also by confidence in the possibility of human progress. The spread of scientific sensibilities and the success of early efforts by people like Thomas Gallaudet to help the deaf, dumb, blind, and insane bred a confidence that, as Jonathan Messerli puts it, "problems long considered an inevitable part of human existence—poverty, disease, hunger, and ignorance—could now be eradicated."[18] Public support for general humanitarian assistance was increasing: before turning his attention to education, Horace Mann directed the establishment of the first state mental hospital in the United States. The schools played an increasingly important part in the effort to foster progress by improving moral character because they were seen as preventive rather than remedial. Mann's success in garnering widespread public support for asylums, schools, and other reforms shows that he was far from alone in believing that government's "great circle of duties" included "gratuitous education, universally diffused; laws repressing licentiousness"; and the furnishing of "all needful succor to those . . . [who] suffer without fault or offense of their own."[19]

Before common schools, there was public financial support for education in many places: many states mandated a certain period of education for all children. Charity schools and religious schools often enjoyed state and municipal subsidies, and public funds were sometimes allocated on a per-pupil basis, not unlike the voucher schemes that are much discussed today. Even the most advanced American cities such as Boston, however, had only a decentralized and miscellaneous collection of essentially village schools.[20]

During the first fifty years of the new nation's history, large increases occurred in school enrollments and in state and local government support. Unlike England, moreover, where some thought that schooling would breed disaffection among the lower classes, America saw virtually no opposition to popular schooling (at least for white males). Yet teachers were held in low esteem and were often poorly qualified, and even where some degree of school attendance was legally mandatory, as in Massachusetts, schools in the early decades of the republic were highly heterogeneous, locally controlled, and poorly funded.[21]

As in England, France, and elsewhere, various forms of education were widely available to Americans before the advent of public schooling. For poor children, apprenticeships remained common until the early nineteenth century and were the usual means to receive some education. There were also church charity schools, which mushroomed along with a host of voluntary associations and mutual aid societies. During the first fifty years or so after the American Revolution, "free" schools might also be operated by quasi-public societies such as the New York Free School Society. Charity schools were of poor quality, however, and were shunned by families that could afford to pay tuition. Pay schools served the middle ranks of society, including low-income workers who wished to avoid the stigma of charity schooling. The most affluent families hired tutors.[22]

During most of the 1820s, for every child in the New York Free School Society—the forerunner of the New York public school system—there were three in private schools and three in no school at all. A church or other group in New York City could start a school and simply apply to the state for funds allocated on a per-pupil basis. Quasi-public academies flourished in Massachusetts.[23]

In the early decades of the nineteenth century, public support flowed to many types of schools, Protestant as well as Catholic. The schools differed not only in their mode of funding and clientele, but also in their missions. Independent pay schools often served to complement and extend the educational role of the family. The same was true of the rural village school, in which the parents often took turns boarding the teacher. Urban charity schooling, however, was, as Carl Kaestle puts it, "an explicit attempt to intervene between the parents and children of a supposedly alien culture." Such institutions were thus often at odds with the child's family and peer influences.[24] The charity schools intervened between children and their parents, and so between children and their ethnic and religious communities of birth, to reduce delinquency, combat gross forms of ignorance, and pursue other civic purposes.

In the late 1830s and 1840s, state and local support for schooling was growing, but it was far from foreordained that aid would take the form of publicly run common schools with a monopoly on public funds. The older pattern of publicly supported educational diversity survived in many countries, where it continues to this day. It did not survive in America for a variety of reasons—including, importantly, that it was increasingly seen as inadequate for promoting shared civic purposes.[25]

By the late 1820s in New York, Philadelphia, and elsewhere, particular charity school organizations began to attain favored positions with city and state governments. In many cities, the dominant charity schools became the public common schools, and the era of government-subsidized diversity began to give way in the 1830s, 1840s, and 1850s to publicly run schools with a monopoly on taxpayer support. From a pattern of dispersed support for private schools, many city and state governments began concentrating their support on common schools: schools that would "comprehend the children of every class, and thus promote a harmonious intermingling of the youth of the community, as a social and public benefaction."[26]

Part of the rationale for this consolidation was that the dual system of charity and pay schools perpetuated class distinctions and offended democratic sensibilities. The "fundamental error of Europe," according to DeWitt Clinton, was to "confine the light of knowledge to the wealthy and the great." Lamentably, for Clinton and others, public education was synonymous with pauper education for many Americans. James G. Carter, chairman of the House Committee on Education in Massachusetts, warned in 1837 that if the propertied classes continued to establish private academies rather than free public schooling for all, the nation would be irreparably divided.[27] The stigma of charity schooling could be removed by transforming these institutions into free public schools open to children from all social, religious, and ethnic backgrounds. The superintendent of the St. Louis schools insisted that it was necessary to abolish tuition payments even for those who could afford to pay, for to maintain distinctions between paying families and charity cases would be to fan "invidious distinctions, bickerings, and heartburnings." The trustees of the New York City Public (formerly "Free") School Society urged in 1828 that common schools "should be supported from the public revenue, should be public property, and should be open to all, not as charity, but as a matter of common right." The trustees saw this as a hopeful and inclusive response to the "diversity, magnitude, and character of our population."[28]

The school reformers sought both bureaucratic consolidation (teacher examinations, textbook uniformity, and the more systematic gathering of information) and the elimination of private schooling. They soon managed to curtail public financial support for private education. Uniformity and system could, it was believed, improve the academic quality of the schooling available to all. It would, however, be wrong to think of the common system as a more effective way of pursuing all-purpose educational ends. The new system was meant to pursue a novel set of civic ends: consolidation under public aegises was essential to the institution's civic agenda.

What school reformers and most of the public increasingly wanted was a system of schooling that would meet public needs: schools that were, as Selwyn K. Troen has put it, "agents of the community and . . . dedicated to its service." Parochial schools addressed themselves to other ends: they served the interests of particular religious and ethnic communities. Hence, it was not surprising that, especially in the Midwest where large numbers of German and Slavic immigrants settled, the issues of separate language instruction and religious instruction were, from early on, closely connected.[29] Educational variety, it was believed, would thwart attempts to bring all children together under the auspices of a common republican culture. Arguing against his own fellow Congregationalists, the Reverend W. S. Dutton insisted in the pages of Horace Mann's *Common School Journal* that

> The children of this country, of whatever parentage, should, not wholly, but to a certain extent, be *educated together,*—be educated, not as Baptists, or Methodists, or Episcopalians, or Presbyterians; not as Roman Catholics or Protestants, still less as foreigners in language or spirit, but as Americans, as made of one blood and citizens of the same free country,—educated to be one harmonious people. This, the common school system, if wisely and liberally conducted, is well fitted, in part at least, to accomplish.[30]

A miscellaneous mix of educational institutions serving particular needs would not reliably forge a common moral and political culture in an increasingly diverse population. What was wanted was an institution that would be truly public.[31]

These old discussions stand in striking contrast with debates over educational reform today. Nineteenth-century reformers did believe that greater system, uniformity, and public support would pay dividends in the currency of academic effectiveness. At the center of school reform in the 1830s and 1840s, however, were civic imperatives. One great benefit of this new institution—the central benefit for many of the leading reformers—was its character as a shared civic space, one that embodied the aspiration to a common civic life.

Protestantism and American Democracy

We should avoid making the mistake of identifying nineteenth-century social progressivism with secular attitudes. Education and religion were typically seen as inseparable in the late eighteenth and early nineteenth centuries. The Northwest Ordinance of 1787 specified that because "religion, morality, and knowledge" were essential to good government, it was the legislature's duty to protect freedom of worship and "encourage schools and the means of instruction."

In the early nineteenth century and for many years later, popular confidence in human progress was fueled not only by scientific and economic advances, but by profound religious currents as well. Ernest Lee Tuveson has shown that Christian faith, rather than secular theory, provided the earliest grounds for popular confidence in human perfectibility. Evil was to be progressively conquered in history, according to the most popular American religious tracts of this period, and many Americans understood the United States to be God's chosen instrument for redeeming mankind. This millennial faith was an activist one: it prescribed not a watchful waiting but energetic efforts to hasten the consummation of God's work on earth. Of particular importance were reforms designed to alleviate social ills, combat vice, and spread knowledge. Reform initiatives such as temperance, Sabbath closing, and better schooling gained enormous impetus from these religious enthusiasms.[32]

Protestant religiosity was closely intertwined with and in many respects mutually supportive of democratic reform in the early republic. Nathan O. Hatch has written eloquently of the "democratization of American Christianity" in the half century after the Revolution. He describes a Protestantism revolutionized by the political ideals of the Declaration of Independence. American Protestant denominations, especially the Methodists, denied the "age-old distinction that set the clergy apart" and "refused to defer to learned theologians and traditional orthodoxies"; they "instinctively associated virtue with ordinary people rather than elites, [and] exalted the vernacular in word and song."[33] The democratic enthusiasts of religious revival emphasized the personal and the charismatic, rather than the learned, the traditional, and the institutional. The primary impulse, as Richard Hofstadter emphasizes, was "the feeling of direct personal access to God." The enthusiastic sects thus tended to espouse popular choice and lay control; they also spawned sectarian "division and subdivision" and vigorous competition for converts. They elevated popular spiritual enthusiasm over concern with doctrinal orthodoxies, and helped "make Christianity itself a liberating force; people were given the right to think and act for themselves rather than depending on the mediations of an educated elite."[34]

The complementarity between the religious and political spheres was striking. Just as democracy broke up aristocratic centers of political power and distributed that power to each individual (meaning for some time of course, to each white, male individual), so too did the increasing fractiousness of American Protestant denominations help to fragment religious authority, and to distribute it to each believer and his private judgment. This convergence of attitudes toward structures of authority was hardly accidental: the popular embrace of the Declaration's political ideals helped transform American Protestantism. Denominational enthusiasm, in turn, poured forth on behalf of democratic ideals: sermons, hymns, camp meetings, and other expressions of religious enthusiasm and revival all were brought to bear as instruments for inculcating and spreading democratic ideals among the common people. American camp meetings were "festivals of democracy," according to one foreign observer.[35]

The Protestant enthusiasts' faith in human progress helped fire a broad and interdenominational zeal for a wide range of political and social reforms, prominent among which were education and common schooling. Common school crusaders, as David B. Tyack and Elizabeth Hansot put it, translated "the quest for enlightenment, economic opportunity, moral improvement, and a new kind of citizenship, into support for a particular institution, the common school. Not separatism, but a consensus based on schooling as a common and public good became an enduring legacy of . . . [the] millenial faith."[36]

Needless to say, this confluence of republican and religious enthusiasms was not unproblematic in a nation characterized by increasing religious pluralism. By the middle of the nineteenth century, not only in eastern cities but in frontier communities as well, "leading citizens assumed that Americanism and Protestantism were synonyms and that education and Protestantism were allies."[37] Public schools, as Lawrence Cremin emphasizes, may have helped take the place of established churches as guardians of public morality: they were less sectarian than the religious establishments that had fallen away, far more capable of securing the support of a broad consensus of support, and so more efficacious in crafting a shared identity among new generations of Americans.[38]

Many Americans viewed Protestantism as a crucial part of the matrix of ideas advanced by the public schools, not only because it was the dominant religion, nor simply because religious uniformity was sought for its own sake. Indeed, Protestantism was seen by many as the intellectual and moral font of republicanism. Horace Mann, the intellectual leader and one of the most progressive and liberal of the early school reformers, rejoiced in America's "Protestant liberty," which sustained both free institutions and common schooling: "It may, indeed, be said, that it was freedom of thought, constituting as it did, the main element of Protestantism, which has given superiority to the communities where common schools have flourished. But if Protestantism, from which systems of public instruction emanated, has always tended toward free institutions, yet could Protestantism itself have survived without the alliance of a system of public instruction?"[39]

These sentiments were far from idiosyncratic. Nearly everyone found a purely secular public education simply inconceivable. In 1858, when it was proposed that Bible reading be eliminated from Wisconsin classrooms, the superintendent replied that "Christianity is everywhere incorporated in the law of the land." To remove the Bible from schools would endanger "all we now hold dear and sacred: our homes, our country, Christianity and the Bible."[40]

Many people viewed Protestantism as inseparable from the American republican idea.[41] The religion of the early common schools was intended to be broadly acceptable: the core religious exercise was Bible reading without commentary. "Sectarian" intrusions—attempts to advance particular theological and doctrinal claims—were otherwise forbidden. A remarkably broad consensus supported the new common schools, which could only succeed in a religiously pluralistic environment if they were viewed by the vast majority of people as religious but nonsectarian; that is, as capable of inculcating basic moral precepts rooted in religion while avoiding sectarian impulses.[42]

It is worth emphasizing that the interdenominational spirit that infused the schools was not simply a matter of compromise, but represented a shared commitment to fostering a common civic identity, one grounded in what was widely regarded as the only firm foundation for morality: a "pure, unsectarian, Christian culture."[43] As time went on, and especially when the problem of religion in the schools was debated at length, the argument that was increasingly relied upon was not that Protestantism per se was crucial to American republicanism, but that public morality required *some* religious basis: if the common schools were to be capable of providing a common moral instruction as well as intellectual instruction, then some religious element would be necessary. A common moral education was described, therefore, not as Protestant rather than Catholic or Jewish, but as "religious" rather than either "sectarian" or "infidel." A public moral education was possible, argued Daniel Webster, because all Americans believe in "certain great religious truths": "All believe in the existence of God. All believe in the immortality of the soul. All believe in the responsibility in another world for our conduct in this . . . And cannot all these great truths be taught to children without their minds being perplexed with clashing doctrines and sectarian controversies? Most certainly they can."[44] In the middle decades of the nineteenth century, when Americans made the case for including some—any—religious element in the common schools, the argument was increasingly advanced in terms of purely civil interests.

The pressure to broaden the religious element in common schooling was not simply a matter of trying to make the schools acceptable to a broad range of Protestants, as historical accounts often suggest. There was an element of basic principle: a recognition of the fact that civil purposes might be invoked to justify a religious element for the sake of teaching children to be moral, but that no such civil purpose could justify the teaching of more particular sectarian doctrines. The common schools were to be "purely of a civil character . . . for civil purposes," as defenders of common schooling in New York City put it in 1840, and "[t]he injustice of taxing the whole community for the support of sectarian schools is so manifest, and it is so glaringly incompatible with the genius of our political institutions, that the naked proposition would seem to carry with it its own refutation." As a proponent of Bible reading in the public schools was to put it in Cincinnati three decades later, "Religion . . . not theology, not dogmas, not creeds—is to be taught in the schools; and it is to be taught to the end that the pupils may become intelligent and virtuous citizens."[45]

Without denying the existence of anti-Catholic prejudice and nativism, it should also be recognized that common schooling succeeded in the early republic in part because American Protestants were readier than citizens of other nations—such as England—to put aside their sectarian differences for the sake of nonsectarian common schooling. This is one reason for the popularity in America of the "Lancastrian" method of monitorial instruction, named after Englishman Joseph Lancaster. True enough, this approach was economical and made it easier for public agencies to take responsibility for educating the children of the poor. It was also a keystone of Lancaster's system, however, that children of all faiths should be educated together in a nonsectarian common school. Lancaster insisted that the problem of educating poor children was a "national concern," and that the chief obstacle to effective common action was the "pharisaical sect-making spirit" of the denominations. Common schools could, Lancaster insisted, inculcate the necessary basics of morality—"duties to parents, relations, and society . . . civility without flattery, and a peaceable demeanor"—without violating "private religious opinions." Lancaster promoted a nonsectarian but still religious education and was, like Horace Mann and many other public school supporters after him, criticized for reducing the Gospel "to a mere system of ethics." (In England, for example, opposition to Lancaster focused on religious issues.) The American embrace of Lancaster shows how much further than in England the interdenominational consensus on behalf of common schooling had progressed. The cross-sectarian cooperation that was unacceptable in Britain was achieved in the more fragmented denominational climate of America. By the time Lancaster had visited America in 1818, his system was already flourishing here.[46]

What seemed nonsectarian to some appeared sectarian to others. With ever larger numbers of Irish Catholic immigrants arriving in the United States, the religious dimension of public school morality soon became a locus of intense controversy. In the face of this hot debate, the Protestant majority insisted with increasing vehemence that public support for education should be concentrated in what they regarded as "nonsectarian" schools.

New Diversity: The Catholic Problem

There was no great influx of immigrants during the years immediately after the Revolution, and attitudes toward newcomers were fairly relaxed (250,000 people arrived during the quarter century after the Constitution's ratification). A liberal and confident naturalization law was passed in 1790, which required only a two-year wait for immigrants to become naturalized citizens. This period was extended to five years in 1795, due mainly to anxiety about the loyalties of those fleeing the French Revolution. Immigrants were also now required to take oaths renouncing foreign titles and allegiances. Federalists temporarily increased the naturalization period to fourteen years in 1798, and passed the infamous Alien and Sedition Acts, but the Republicans turned it back to five in 1802, and there it remained for over a century.[47]

Federalists were not alone in their worries about immigration. Jefferson also worried that immigrants "will bring with them the principles of the governments they leave, imbibed in their early youth; or, if able to throw them off, it will be in exchange for an unbounded licentiousness, passing, as is usual, from one extreme to another. It would be a miracle were they to stop precisely at the point of temperate liberty." Jefferson warned that immigrants trained in the habits and principles of other political cultures would transmit these habits to their children and "in proportion to their numbers" to legislation, rendering the polity a "heterogeneous, incoherent, distracted mass."[48]

After the War of 1812, immigration to America increased and then skyrocketed. One million immigrants arrived between 1830 and 1845, and during the next decade the new arrivals totaled nearly 3 million. Among the arrivals were vast numbers of Irish Catholics. In 1790, the 35,000 American Catholics accounted for barely 1 percent of the nation's population of 3.2 million. By 1850, there were more than 1.5 million Catholics in America, and by 1860, over 3 million.[49]

The Catholic problem, as it was conceived, had several dimensions. There was no doubt a great deal of inherited prejudice to be dealt with. The English colonists, and especially the Puritans, brought with them to America a profound disdain for "popery," and many Americans long believed that the basic loyalties of Catholics would always be to Rome. Catholics suffered some form of discrimination in every colony but Rhode Island. At the time of the nation's founding, Catholics enjoyed the privilege of equal citizenship in only five of the original thirteen states.[50]

The vehemence of the native prejudice against Catholics was no doubt fed by the swelling sense of national destiny. The notion that Americans were God's chosen people was a powerful one in the nineteenth century. America's territorial expansion and growing power were believed to manifest the nation's Anglo-Saxon superiority and its messianic mission to redeem the world for Christian principles. America represented not only the perfection of Protestant principles, but also an especially uncorrupted and vigorous segment of the Anglo-Saxon race: "Surely, to be a Christian and an Anglo-Saxon and an American in this generation is to stand on the very mountain-top of privilege."[51]

Many popular works in nineteenth-century America were devoted to showing that Anglo-Saxon or Teutonic people had a special role in realizing God's plan, in part because of preordained mental and moral characteristics manifested in historic achievements. These characteristics included an "intense and persistent energy," an "indomitable perseverance," an "instinct or genius for colonizing," and a "love of civil liberty."[52] "Gauls," on the other hand, were naturally "a priest-ridden race," and the Celts were subjects ripe for subservience and superstition. Only by "disintegrating" the Celtic race, according to John L. Motley, "grinding it small and mixing it liberally with other elements," could it be saved from itself.[53]

Behind the new racialism were burgeoning "sciences" such as phrenology and comparative ethnic studies, as well as a Romantic preoccupation with the distinctiveness of particular peoples. "It was," Reginald Horsman argues, "unusual by the late 1840's to profess a belief in innate human equality and to challenge the idea that a superior race was about to shape the fates of other races for the future good of the world."[54]

Without minimizing the racialist element in nineteenth-century Americanism, we should also not let it obscure other factors that were at work, including the clear opposition between the American political creed and the doctrines of the nineteenth-century Roman Catholic Church. Many Americans, including many Catholic Americans, feared institutional Catholicism's hostility to free self-government, and not without reason. They could see that the still young republic's core principles of individual freedom and democratic equality were at odds with the church's authoritarian institutional structure, its longstanding association with feudal or monarchical governments, its insistence on close ties between church and state, its endorsement of censorship, and its rejection of individual rights to freedom of conscience and worship (which Pius IX in 1864 called the "liberty of perdition").[55] In case republicans were apt to discount these worries, Rome issued brisk reminders in the form of papal encyclicals in 1832, 1834, and 1864, which contained fulsome denunciations of the basic principles of American democracy. As Pope Gregory XVI asserted, "We greatly deplore the fact that, where the ravings of human reason extend, there is somebody who studies new things and strives to know more than is necessary, against the advice of the apostle. There you will find someone who is overconfident in seeking the truth outside the Catholic Church, in which it can be found without even a light tarnish of error."[56] No doubt, American attitudes to Catholicism were shaped by long-held prejudices and an intense anticlericalism. The fact is, however, that Rome furnished ample grounds for many to wonder whether it was possible to be a good Catholic and a good republican.

Of course, many ordinary American Catholics rejected Rome's reactionary pronouncements. Just as it is unreasonable today to equate the beliefs of American Catholics with the dictates of Rome, so it was in the nineteenth century. Even the upper echelons of the American clergy had their doubts. As one American archbishop sardonically observed to another on the occasion of Pius IX's infamous Syllabus of Errors, "It is consoling to think that our Holy Father has in all his official acts a light of guidance from on High—for according to all the rules of mere human prudence and wisdom . . . [the Syllabus] would be considered ill timed."[57]

From early on, many American Catholics—especially lay persons— plied a distinctly pro-American and pro-republican line. John Carroll, who later became the first bishop in the United States, was an enthusiastic supporter of the Revolutionary cause. Early American Catholics welcomed religious freedom, the separation of church and state, and the live-and-let-live ecumenism that generally prevailed for a time after the Revolution. When Bishop John England of Charleston addressed Congress in 1826, he endorsed the separation of the religious sphere from that of politics, and granted that "our civil rights, our civil concerns" fall within the purview of the state: "You have no power to interfere with my religious rights; the tribunal of the church has no power to interfere with my civil rights."[58]

Some American Catholics went so far as to argue that the American Catholic Church should be reformed to comport with republican principles: that congregations rather than bishops should, for example, control church property and have a greater hand in hiring parish priests. American Catholic lay trustees did, in some instances, assume extensive control over parochial administration, but a line was crossed in the early 1850s when several Catholic congregations claimed the right to dismiss their pastors. Rome dispatched a papal nuncio to America to put down the "trusteeship" movement.[59]

Racism was not, therefore, the only factor behind the fear of Catholicism. Nor is it obvious that the most avid opponents of Catholicism wished to use the public schools to establish Protestantism as such. It is worth noting that the anti-Catholic Know Nothings of the 1850s did not condemn Judaism. No doubt one reason for this, as Tyler Anbinder points out, was the tiny number of American Jews. These quintessential American nativists nevertheless argued that, unlike Catholics, Jews never allowed "their religious feelings to interfere with their political views." Jews could make fine American citizens, said the Know Nothings, because "however repugnant their religion may be, their religion is Republican . . . Indeed, the Jews were the first Republican people in the World." Because of the republican propensities deemed evident in the democratic administration of Jewish congregations, at least some nativists held that Jewish immigrants would never pose a threat comparable to that posed by Catholicism.[60]

This discussion is not an apology for nineteenth-century American nativism, anti-Catholic prejudice, or racism. But it would be wrong to attribute the civic anxieties of this period to racism alone, or to a simple desire to use public institutions to promote Protestantism for its own sake. It was not unreasonable for Americans to worry about the fragility of their experiment in self-government. There were also civic, secular reasons for fearing that an education in orthodox Catholicism could be hostile to republican attitudes and aspirations. Racism and anti-Catholic prejudice were not the all-consuming motives of the era. When it came to immigrants, moreover, racist antipathy was, for the vast majority of Americans, subordinated to the hopeful conviction that with a proper education, immigrant and native-born Americans could share a common citizenship.

The Birth of Common Schooling

It was out of this complex mix of motives—a variety of prejudices, not unreasonable anxiety, and a genuine hopefulness about the potential for a common civic life—that the impetus for common schooling emerged and spread. The ethnic and religious diversity that increasingly characterized American cities in the second quarter of the nineteenth century contributed powerfully to calls for an institution that could inculcate a common culture, the English language, and republican sensibilities by educating the children of different faiths and classes in one institution dedicated to forging a shared citizenship. In spite of the mix of racialism and prejudice that greeted many of the new arrivals, it was also held that if Protestant and Catholic children interacted in the same schools, they "would form similar associations, cultivate kindred political and social feelings, and in their manners and customs become peculiarly American."[61] The old system of publicly subsidized educational variety would leave educational institutions to reflect rather than transform "the great diversity of religious sects into which the people are divided." The new institution of common schooling was a very direct way of exercising greater political leverage over the intellectual development and moral character of future citizens: to educate children together in a common institution would help fit them for citizenship.[62]

One great example of the consolidation of many different schools into a public school system occurred in New York City. Established in 1805 by a group of Quakers, the New York Free School Society gradually consolidated many of the city's charity schools under its aegis. Early on, the Presbyterian and Episcopal churches discontinued their charity schools and turned over their shares of government funds to the Free School Society. In 1825, the Society convinced the city's common council that no funds should be distributed to denominational schools, which included those expanding competitors associated with the Bethel Baptist Church and with Roman Catholic churches. The state legislature sided with the Free School Society and its claim that no public money should go to "sectarian" schools. Having gained control of most of the public education money, the Society changed its name to the Public School Society in 1826 and invited all children to attend its schools. Tuition was at first charged to those who could afford it, but instruction was made free to all students in 1832 after the passage of property taxes for school support.[63]

The public school system enjoyed overwhelming though not unanimous Protestant support: most Americans wanted a common educational institution from which "sectarianism," as they understood it, was excluded. Most Protestants were prepared to put aside their differences in favor of a common educational institution.[64]

The common school was to serve as an instrument of public moral community, to forge an identity capable of unifying a diverse polity. Common school advocates sought to accomplish their task by bypassing "sectarian" quarrels, and most citizens were prepared to lend their support, despite any desire they might have to use schooling to advance their own religious view. Horace Mann and many other school reformers advocated staying to the middle and avoiding sectarianism. The problem was that what Mann and his many allies saw as an effort to enlighten and elevate democracy, and to stick to a civic agenda "neutral" with respect to competing sectarian views, others saw as public partisanship on behalf of Protestantism.[65]

The vast majority of Americans believed that without a grounding in a broadly conceived biblical religiosity, moral education was inconceivable. Children might learn to know what is right, but they would not be motivated to do it. So the public welfare argued for a measure of religious instruction. "It is a political maxim that the welfare of a republic is dependent upon the virtue and intelligence of its citizens," argued a Cincinnati attorney. "It is upon this ground that the State assumes the right to educate its youth." The argument that only civic purposes could justify taxing people for the support of educational institutions, and indeed, that only civic purposes of the first order could justify the state institution embroiling itself in such bitter controversies as those over religion in the schools, had its effects over the course of time: the charges of sectarianism were taken seriously and the common schools were made fairer and less sectarian.[66]

Few seriously proposed excluding religion altogether from the public schools; doing so would have been unacceptable to the vast majority of nineteenth-century Americans who regarded religion, and especially the Bible, as the font of morality. The common schools were defended as nonsectarian but religious. The aim was to avoid "the particular tenets or creed of some denomination" and to teach "religion," by which was usually meant a standard set of everyday virtues— "the duty of man to man, the obligation to truth and personal purity, charity, virtue, intelligence, cleanliness, honor"—buttressed by a belief in God and an afterlife.[67]

Was the reason for including Bible reading in the school at base religious, rather than civic? Was the point of public school religious exercises to favor a particular view of religious truth? Or was the strategy that was chosen, on the whole if not in every detail, a way of building support for a common educational institution at a time when very few people believed that a moral education could be severed from religious moorings? These questions are difficult if not impossible to answer. From a Catholic point of view, there were good reasons to perceive the schools as favoring Protestantism: schoolbooks, for example, contained anti-Catholic passages. Protestant sectarians, on the other side, were willing, for the sake of a common institution, to surrender in part their ability to teach their children their own particular creed: they supported common schools in spite of the oft-stated charge that the schools were agents of Mann's Unitarianism, as they may well have seemed from a Baptist or Presbyterian point of view. Some Catholics, especially laypersons, agreed with the view that was dominant among Protestants: one of New York City's two Catholic newspapers *(The Truth Teller)* maintained that religious training belonged in the home and the church, and it openly favored public schools that embraced all classes and religions. It was the Catholic hierarchy, and New York's other Catholic newspaper *(The Catholic Register)*, that insisted on seeing the conflict as one between "Protestant Public Schools" and equally public, to their way of thinking, Catholic schools.[68]

Indeed some Catholics tried to play on Protestant sectarian suspicions, arguing that everyone should fear that public schoolteachers might make improper comments on biblical passages, for "the teachers in our public schools, by whom and under whose direction the Bible is read, are not abstract, non-denominational Christians; they are or may be, some or all of them, Lutherans, Presbyterians, Methodists, Baptists, Trinitarians, Unitarians, etc. Each one has his religious bias."[69] If Protestants regarded the public schools from their denominated standpoint, they too could view those schools as sectarian.

Because the public schools allowed only Bible reading without commentary and excluded specifically "sectarian" religious teachings, they were charged with favoring Protestantism, Unitarianism, or infidelity, depending on who was the accuser. "The Public School Society failed to recognize that its version of nonsectarianism was sectless Protestantism," as Diane Ravitch puts it.[70] The matter was not quite so simple because the religious elements advanced by the common schools were in important respects tailored for specifically *civic* ends, and that is how they were being defended, by some in the 1840s, and by increasing numbers of people thereafter.

A central tenet of the common school religion was that charity toward others should take precedence over different and more particular claims to religious truth. Horace Mann captured the essence of the public school creed in an anonymous article in his *Common School Journal* entitled, "What Shall Be My Sabbath Reading?":

> Is there not a danger of my becoming proud even of my religious opinions? . . . I must, therefore, not read anything that diminishes my charity for my fellow-creatures,—for their character, their purposes, or their opinions. Whatever is written in an uncharitable spirit, no matter what name it has, I will endeavor to avoid . . . [no less if it is] under the cloak of a sermon or a religious tract . . . Whatever renders me uncharitable must be wanting in that Christian spirit.[71]

The common school creed was ecumenical and antisectarian. It held that concern with particular truths—truths that divide rather than unite different religions—is positively un-Christian and un-American.[72] Insofar as the common schools reflected Horace Mann's ecumenical spirit, the religion of the common schools was specifically tailored for civic ends: to enable citizens of different (and often warring) faiths to converge on a civic identity. Some Catholic objections to common schools had much to do with this civic mission.

Of course, concentrating public funds in schools with this "nonsectarian" religious content did not appeal to many Catholic citizens, though some of these undoubtedly preferred that *some* religion be taught (even if not their own) as opposed to *no* religion. But the common school religious settlement, as noted, was not equally attractive to Protestants either. The common school agenda was bound to be more congenial to tolerant and ecumenical Christian sects than to less ecumenical sects.

From early on, a variety of groups opposed the unified common school system. Many Germans and Italians wanted dual-language schools. Some Lutherans and Mennonites dissented and resisted the public schools. A few opposed centralization of authority in large districts because they wanted the schools to teach the local orthodoxy rather than what they saw as the watered-down Protestantism promoted by Horace Mann and other school reformers. Localists could also fly the banner of parental control.[73] The point of contention was not whether children would be educated, but who would teach them and what they would be taught.

Catholics were the most numerous and important opponents of the new public school regime. In New York and elsewhere, intense conflicts over the religious character of the common schools erupted from the start. Catholics at first sought concessions from public school establishments to make those schools acceptable. In 1834, New York Catholic bishop John Dubois asked that a school near St. Patrick's Cathedral hire a Catholic teacher of his choosing, use only textbooks that he had approved, be opened to Catholics for Sunday school instruction and religious instruction in the evenings, and allow him to visit the school and from time to time make recommendations to the Public School Society. The Society rejected these requests as special privileges incompatible with common schooling. The Society did offer, however, to join with Catholics in identifying and erasing anti-Catholic or other sectarian passages from public schoolbooks, and the Society declared its willingness for classrooms to be used after hours by any religious society. Catholics rebuffed these offers of cooperation and insisted on their right to a share of the school fund. An opportunity for compromise was lost, and soon the nonconfrontational Bishop Dubois was replaced by a much more fiery bishop, John Hughes, who was determined that Catholic children would have a Catholic education.[74]

In 1840, Catholic parents in New York petitioned the city's common council to restore public funds for their schools. Governor William H. Seward was sympathetic to complaints about the anti-Catholic tone of some textbooks and the unfairness of reading the King James version of the Bible. He proposed that, rather than letting Catholic children go uneducated because their community was unwilling to patronize schools biased toward Protestantism, the state should aid in the establishment of parochial schools for the Catholics. Much of the public was outraged by this act, which it took to be evidence of Catholic clannishness and separatism.[75]

It was not without reason that many saw the Catholic petition as a threat to the very idea of common schooling, for within days of the Catholic petition for a portion of the school funds, similar petitions arrived from the Scotch Presbyterian Church and the Jewish community. Both groups said that they had not previously intended to seek a pro rata share of public education monies, but that they would do so if the common council acceded to Catholic requests. Many of the city's other churches—Methodist, Episcopalian, Baptist, and Dutch Reformed—quickly followed suit, arguing that while they were prepared to accept the state's policy whereby only public schools would receive public monies, if the city were to accept the Catholic request for a "perversion of the Public School Fund," then they would "ask and claim . . . an equitable proportion." The Catholic petition was unsuccessful, but it provoked days of widely reported public debates, at which the Catholic position was stated with great eloquence by Bishop Hughes, who was answered by a wide variety of advocates for the Public School Society.[76]

Conflicts similar to those in New York played themselves out elsewhere. In Philadelphia, compromise was attempted on the issue of Bible reading in the public school classroom. Catholics had sought to have Catholic children read their own Douay Bible, rather than the Protestant King James version. Local school officials had refused, but had allowed Catholic children to be released from the classroom during Bible readings. The supposed disruption caused by the new policy caused complaints and disputes, which escalated into riotous clashes between nativist and Catholic mobs. More than a dozen lives were lost in the Philadelphia Bible riots of 1844.[77]

The proponents of public schooling, especially early on, sometimes seemed to simply fail to recognize or admit their own partisanships. In one of his annual reports on Massachusetts's schools, Mann praised the Massachusetts public school system as the "one place in the land where the children of all the different denominations are brought together for instruction, where the Bible is allowed to speak for itself."[78] For Mann and many others at midcentury, this was the preferred vision of common school nonsectarianism: reading the King James version without commentary, stressing the importance of biblical morality, and otherwise avoiding sectarian controversy.

Bible reading without commentary conveys a substantive message about who has the authority to interpret scripture. Mann's message is anathema to Catholics, as Dr. John Power, a vicar general in the New York diocese, observed in 1840: "The Catholic church tells her children that they must be taught their religion by AUTHORITY—the Sects say, read the bible, judge for yourselves. The bible is read in the public schools, the children are allowed to judge for themselves. The Protestant principle is therefore acted upon, slyly inculcated, and the schools are Sectarian."[79] For nineteenth-century Catholics, as for many religious people since, a truly nonsectarian public school system is an impossibility.

There were, and are, two obvious ways in which a kind of school neutrality toward religion could be maintained. One option was to exclude religion altogether from the public schools and to seek neutrality through exclusion. Some favored this option.[80] But to many Catholics, this was also unacceptable because, as Bishop Hughes put it in the 1840 New York City debates: "To make an infidel, what is it necessary to do? Cage him up in a room, give him a secular education from the age of five years to twenty-one, and I ask you what will he come out, if not an infidel? . . . They say that their instruction is not sectarianism; but it is; and of what kind? The sectarianism of infidelity in its every feature."[81] If we read "sect of infidelity" as "secular humanist," Bishop Hughes could be speaking to today's controversies over the exclusion of school prayer, Bible reading, and creationism from the public schools. Then, as now, many believers charged that a purportedly "neutral" school policy that excludes religion from the schools is actually a way of inculcating atheistic secular humanism or the "sect of anti-religion."[82]

A second possible route to neutrality was through inclusion: to present the various versions of religious truth present in the polity to children in an evenhanded way. Many Catholics and others objected to this option, for they believed this would imply that religion is a mere choice, like styles of dress.[83] A variation on this option was proposed in some places: since Bible reading was the core religious exercise, it was proposed that children should be allowed to read any version of the Bible at the beginning of the school day, including the Catholic Douay version. This was rejected as an option by at least some Catholics, who argued that "the reading of the Bible, even in the Douay version, without note or comment, involves the right of private judgment, a right which, in the sense in which it is asserted by the Protestant, the Catholic denies . . . [T]he Catholic apprehends danger from the uncommented and indiscriminate reading of the Bible."[84] Nineteenth-century Catholics denied the right of private judgment in matters of religion. The response by advocates of common schooling was that biblical excerpts were to be read as moral, not sectarian religious, teachings. The Catholic hierarchy's unwillingness to view matters in this light caused many to doubt that the Bishops wanted Catholic citizens to think for themselves about morality and politics.

Many Protestants, not only nativists and zealots, felt exasperated with Catholics for refusing to check their religious beliefs at the schoolhouse door. Bishop John Hughes expressed his version of the Catholic position at some length in the New York City school debates of 1840, and his position was complex and equivocal. His objections, at base, were not so much a matter of a certain aspect of common schooling, but to the enterprise as such. His conditions for an acceptable regime of common schooling were, by his own admission, impossible. For one thing, he seemed to require that an acceptable school policy should have only neutral effects on the religious beliefs of children. Only if the public schools could be "constituted on a principle which would have secured a perfect NEUTRALITY of influence on the subject of religion, then we [Catholics] would have no reason to complain. But this has not been done, and we respectfully submit that it is impossible."[85] He was surely right about the impossibility of an educative regime that would be required to have neutral effects on the varied religious beliefs of citizens, for surely any form of civic education would have non-neutral effects on those religious beliefs that conflict with the civic morality.

Hughes's position also appeared self-contradictory. He admitted that common schools that left religion aside altogether would not as an "*active* process" promote infidelity, but would suit the "infidel" and as an indirect matter promote such leanings. At the same time, he conceded that it would be wrong to tax people to support educational institutions with a direct and purposeful religious mission, and therefore admitted that if Catholic schools received public monies they could not teach religion but must confine themselves to the "neutral ground on which our children may learn to read and cipher." But that neutral ground appeared to be the very neutrality through exclusion—the "cold indifference" to religion—that Hughes had elsewhere rejected as promoting infidelity.[86]

In response to Hughes, the most reasonable advocates for the Public School Society, such as Theodore Sedgwick, conceded that Catholics may have had grounds to complain of biases in public schoolbooks and instructional materials. "If there is any thing in our system which, rightly considered, prevents their enjoyment of its advantages, the system is in that respect wrong . . . is radically wrong." If, he insisted, "the books used in the schools are hostile to Catholics, and promote the Protestant interest . . . they ought to be expurgated; and if they cannot be satisfactorily expurgated, the books themselves ought to be abandoned, and their places supplied by others."[87] Sedgwick and others responded to Hughes by insisting on their commitment to make the common schools truly common: "The State intends to give a 'secular' and moral, but not religious education," steering "entirely clear of all doctrinal or sectarian principles."[88] Sedgwick also renewed earlier pleas to Catholics to join in compiling a set of biblical abstracts that would be acceptable to both sides for use in the schools. Catholic leaders repeatedly refused to cooperate.[89]

Catholics agreed that morality could not be taught without a religious foundation, but they would not agree to Bible reading without comment. The Catholic insistence on using the Douay Bible, with its authoritative marginal notes and comments, raised a basic problem for Sedgwick: "This objection is a fundamental one in principle. The Catholic Bible is filled with marginal notes which inculcate dogmas proving, or seeking to prove, doctrinal points—transubstantiation, for instance, or the necessity of the fasts and penance . . . [T]he truth of these doctrines is not of the slightest importance. I do not care whether the Protestant or Catholic be right." The problem, rather, was the propriety of introducing any doctrinal disputes into the schools, for the whole point of the institution was to carve out a common space to one side of these disputed theological matters:

> Mankind has never disagreed as to the propriety of robbing, or cheating, or bearing false witness; but about these dogmas, these doctrines, the race has been cutting each other's throats for the last ten centuries. For the last four centuries these doctrines have dyed Europe with blood. It is these recollections, these reminiscences, which have dictated our legislation on this subject. It is these prodigious evils that American statesmen have striven to avoid.[90]

In these common school debates in New York City in 1840, Bishop Hughes and his allies showed themselves uninterested in common schooling in principle and opposed to it on any terms. The advocates for common schooling, at their best at least, emphasized the importance of a civic institution in which sectarian differences would be put aside, and through which civic identities would be forged across doctrinal lines. Hughes, on the other hand, continually stressed an interpretation of American ideals according to which private conscience "is supreme": America, he insisted, is "a country which makes no law for religion, but places the right of conscience above all other authority."[91] Given Hughes's uncompromising insistence on the rights of private religious conscience, a common educational institution was, in principle, impossible. As Diane Ravitch puts it: "Bishop Hughes abhorred common schools. He was no assimilationist. The arguments used in favor of common school education—its contribution to social equality and social harmony—were irrelevant to Hughes." Hughes's mission was to keep Catholic children on the Catholic path, a goal best achieved by Catholic educational separatism. He had no intention of cooperating with public authorities in making the common schools more acceptable to Catholics.[92]

Public school reformers in the nineteenth century faced an obvious problem, and their response was shaped by prudence as well as principle. A broad political coalition needed to be built around the idea of a unitary school system, and such a coalition required forging a fairly inclusive intellectual agenda, including a broadly acceptable civil religion. Inclusiveness required compromise. Religious differences would have to be downplayed if the public schools were to be acceptable to most families in conditions of religious pluralism. Where there were large German-, Slavic-, or French-speaking populations, for example, accommodations might be made with respect to bilingual education. Oregon went so far as to permit monolingual German schools. By 1900, over 200,000 elementary schoolchildren in cities like Milwaukee, Cincinnati, Baltimore, and St. Louis studied German, including the majority of children in the upper elementary and high school grades in Chicago.[93]

Building a broad consensus for public schooling required avoiding some controversies and compromising on others. The common schools did *not* take a stand, as is sometimes charged, for Unitarianism over Trinitarianism. This theological controversy was avoided, as were many others. Sidestepping sectarian controversy was understood to be the whole point, and the common schools would otherwise have failed. Of course, too much avoidance could squeeze the moral substance out of the schools altogether. Reaching out too far, embracing the truly lowest common denominator, would forfeit the support of the core constituency—the vast majority of whom could not conceive of republican citizenship without a moral base, and could not imagine moral education without a religious element. As it was, Frederick Packard, a vocal critic of Horace Mann, worried: "What doctrines of revealed religion will remain, to be connected with a system of public instruction, after subtracting those about which there are conflicting creeds among men?"[94]

The profession of nonsectarianism was widely if not unanimously supported, and it allowed the public schools to claim a monopoly on public funds. The common school regime, at least as defended by relative liberals like Mann and Theodore Sedgwick, may have been as nonsectarian as a common educational institution could have been in nineteenth-century America. Persistent Catholic complaints, and the fact of religious pluralism more broadly, helped minimize the religious content of public education.[95] The controversies over sectarianism in the common schools, and the civic justifications offered in response, likely contributed to reducing the religious content of public schooling. In Cincinnati, for example, the school board decided in 1829 that Bible reading should begin the school day. In 1842, the rule was amended to allow parents to object and have their children exempted. In 1852, the policy was again modified so that children could read any version of scripture they wished. Finally, in 1869, public authorities tried to persuade Catholics to accept a consolidation plan by banning all religious instruction, including Bible reading, during the school day. Catholics rejected the plan.[96]

But it was not simply the need to forge a broad political coalition that led public school proponents to minimize the religious elements of public education. There was also the principled matter of what could be justified in civil terms as advancing legitimate civil interests. Common schools were defended as nonsectarian institutions, and through the middle decades of the nineteenth century, religious instruction was increasingly rationalized in purely political terms. Certain fundamental religious truths must be taught, Josiah Strong put it later, "not because the child should know them in preparation for a future existence,—the State is not concerned with the eternal welfare of its citizens,—but because immorality is perilous to the State, and popular morality cannot be secured without the sanctions of religion." Strong conceded that "the advocacy of religion on the ground that it serves as moral police is not very exalted; but," he continued, "if our ground is to be broad enough for upwards of 60,000,000 people to stand on, it must needs be low. The top of the pyramid is too narrow." Only on grounds of self-preservation, Strong was to argue in 1886, could the state justify teaching the existence of God, the immortality of the soul, and man's ultimate accountability. According to Strong, no more than this, and no peculiarly Protestant doctrines, should be taught.[97]

Against the proponents of parental choice and educational diversity, Horace Mann's vision largely prevailed. Then as now, unanimous support for a common educational institution was impossible. Evenhandedness of treatment was attainable under the older regime of government supported diversity, but that option required abandoning what was perceived to be a powerful and necessary instrument for building a shared public culture.[98]

Compromise and accommodation were by no means a complete success. By midcentury, most Catholics were uninterested in common schooling in principle: they wanted a share of school funds in order to educate their own children in their own schools. Having failed to secure a share of public funding or other concessions, the First Plenary Council of American Catholic Bishops, meeting in Baltimore in 1852, condemned American public schools as irreligious and decreed that Catholics should maintain their own schools and educate their own children. Increasingly, and especially after the Civil War, Catholics followed the lead of Bishop Hughes and shifted from seeking accommodations from the public school establishment to opposing common schooling altogether.[99] Poor Catholic immigrant communities needed public assistance for education, and they continued to seek it. But they were repeatedly denied a share of public funds because to grant them public money would have defeated the dominant public purpose: to cast the public's weight behind a publicly controlled institution that could be trusted to bring together children of many faiths and to inculcate a common political, moral, and religious perspective.

There were powerful elements of xenophobia, racism, ancient religious prejudice, and class conflict bound up in the response to Catholic immigration. The common schools could have and should have been more inclusive and more flexible, especially with respect to Bishop Dubois's requests in 1834. Nevertheless, the "perfect neutrality of influence" that Bishop Hughes required was impossible, and by 1840 prominent American Catholics such as Bishop Hughes had rejected common schooling on any grounds. This response was no doubt due partly to the incompatibility of Catholicism and a common republic education, but it also surely had something to do with the beleaguered and defensive nature of American Catholicism: as a poor immigrant church, it was subject to significant hostility and discrimination.

Nativists increasingly interpreted Catholic attempts to secure a share of public funds as efforts to overthrow the common school system. Nativist anger in the 1850s helped promote the "Know Nothing" party—whose central tenet was the opposition between Catholicism and American republicanism, and which was dedicated to extending the naturalization requirement to twenty-one years and to excluding Catholics and other foreigners from public office.[100] In Massachusetts public schools, Roman Catholic children lawfully could be, and were, beaten for refusing to read aloud from the King James Bible.[101] The Boston School Committee argued for the need to bring Catholics into the common schools in language that paraphrased St. Augustine on the need to persecute heretics: "We must open the doors of our school houses and invite and compel them to come in. There is no other hope for them or for us."[102]

Irish Catholics served with distinction in the Civil War. This helped put an end to the Know Nothing party and for a time quieted nativist anxieties. Economic expansion after the war promoted what John Higham calls "an age of confidence" that helped make immigrants seem more of a blessing once again.[103] Catholic complaints received a more respectful hearing, and nativism dissipated. Nevertheless, Catholic schools were established in large numbers after the war, and Catholics began to compose a sizeable and increasingly assertive political bloc in a number of northern cities. The common school controversies have never entirely disappeared.

Constitutionalizing the Common Schools

Renewed Catholic efforts to secure a share of state aid for their schools led, in the 1870s, to a new push to deny all forms of public support to the Catholic and other "sectarian" schools. This time, the opponents of public aid to "sectarian" schools sought to enshrine in the Constitution the common school and its claim to a monopoly of public funds for education. The debate over the Blaine Amendment is often regarded as simply another episode of anti-Catholic prejudice and nativism. No doubt these factors were at work. Yet it is once again striking to note how far the proponents of common schooling went to try to accommodate religious diversity, and to justify the institution of common schooling strictly in terms of shared civic values.

Political partisanships played an important role. President Ulysses S. Grant's administration was plagued by scandal, and he badly needed a cause to rally the voters for the upcoming elections. Grant found his rallying cry when he warned in 1875, "If we are to have another contest in the near future of our national existence, I predict that the dividing-line will not be Mason and Dixon's, but between patriotism and intelligence on the one side, and superstition, ambition, and ignorance on the other." To secure the republic's foundations against internal divisions, Grant urged his countrymen to "[e]ncourage free schools, and resolve that not one dollar of money appropriated to their support, no matter how raised, shall be appropriated to the support of any sectarian school." "Keep the church and state forever separate," he insisted, by which he did not mean to argue against Bible reading in public schools or other public institutions such as reformatories, prisons, or hospitals. As before the war, the Bible was still widely regarded as a "religious and not a sectarian book," and as a crucial prop for public morality and civic education.[104]

A few months after Grant's speech, Republican Congressman James G. Blaine introduced a constitutional amendment that would have written the aims of the common school movement into the Constitution. The "Blaine Amendment," as it became known, banned the use of state funds for sectarian schools.

The point of the Blaine Amendment, as Gary D. Glenn argues, was to extend the First Amendment's disestablishment of religion clause to the states, and to incorporate the aims of the common school movement into the Constitution. As introduced by Blaine, the amendment read:

> No state shall make any law respecting an establishment of religion or prohibiting the free exercise thereof; and no money raised by taxation in any State for the support of public schools or derived from any public fund therefore, or any public lands devoted thereto, shall ever be under the control of any religious sect or denomination, nor shall any money so raised or lands so devoted be divided between religious sects or denominations.[105]

The Blaine Amendment, like the common school movement, did not aim to drive all religion out of the public schools: the Senate version of the Amendment explicitly stated, "This article shall not be construed to prohibit the reading of the Bible in any school or institution." The point, rather, as Glenn argues, was to deny public monies to schools "under the control of any religious sect," or, in the broader Senate version, to *any* institution controlled by "any religious or antireligious sect or denomination."[106] According to its defenders, the amendment aimed to constitutionalize the judgment that "[i]nstitutions supported by the money of all persuasions . . . are not to be made schools for teaching presbyterianism or catholicism, unitarianism, or methodism, or infidelity, or atheism."[107] They were to be instruments, rather, of public purposes bolstered by a broadly inclusive biblical religiosity.

Indeed, in a statement of ecumenism that was remarkable given the energy that had been spent in some places defending the exclusive rights of the King James Bible, Senator Frelinghuysen of New Jersey defended the Senate version of the amendment on the ground that it prevented the exclusion of any version of the Bible from the public schools, whether "the [Catholic] Douay or the King James version. I am for the broadest toleration, but I would never agree to a constitutional amendment that would exclude from the schools the Bible. The

Constitution should neither say that it should or should not be read in the schools." Not only Protestants and Catholics, said Frelinghuysen, but also the "Israelites" join in denying that the Bible should be excluded from the schools. The amendment stood for the broadest toleration compatible with the accommodation of an exercise deemed to be a crucial prop for public morality: Bible reading without comment. The only religious teachings permitted in public schools would be

> That pure and undefiled religion which appertains to the relationship and responsibility of man to God, and is readily distinguishable from the creeds of sects; that religion which permeates all our laws, which is recognized on every sentence against crime and immorality, which is invoked in every oath . . . that religion . . . which sustains the pillars of our liberty, is a very, very different thing from the particular creeds or tenets of either religionists or infidels.[108]

Speaker after speaker in the Senate agreed that particular religious sects and denominations should not be supported out of general funds. All argued in favor of a principle of fairness among different "sects and denominations." The disagreement, once again, was over what was required for fairness and evenhandedness.[109]

Senator Kernan, a Democrat who opposed the Senate version (which disallowed the flow of public funds to denominational hospitals, asylums, reformatories, and other charitable institutions), argued that public schools should be places of strictly "secular learning"— like schools to teach "mechanics." Any religious element was a cause of legitimate offense to Catholics and "Hebrews or others." Those who "cannot adapt themselves" to such purely secular schooling, he admonished, should resort to private school.[110]

Against Kernan it was insisted that some religious element—not Protestantism in particular—was crucial to popular morality and free government. Senator Edmunds was categorical: "[W]e must conserve the public interest by instructing the youth of this country in those things essential to the preservation of the Government itself." "Liberty of conscience," he insisted, cannot "stand in the way of these great and necessary acts" in which the "security of the Republic is bound up."[111] Even Senator Randolph, who helped defeat the Senate version, argued, "There is a general belief that good government requires by some sufficient means religious as well as secular education. Protestants and leading American Catholics agree in this."[112] More than one senator, including Frelinghuysen, quoted Washington's Farewell Address to the effect that "[o]f all the dispositions and habits which lead to prosperity, religion and morality are indispensable supports." "National morality" cannot prevail, Washington had argued, "in exclusion of religious principle."[113]

The Blaine Amendment was approved by a vote of 180 to 7 in the House of Representatives. A revised and broadened version was debated vigorously in the Senate, but it fell just short of the required two-thirds majority, passing by twenty-eight to sixteen. Different versions of the amendment were introduced twenty-seven times in subsequent years, most recently in 1938, and Blaine-type amendments have in fact been added to several state constitutions.[114]

The Blaine Amendment and its heirs failed for a variety of reasons. Many doubted that there was any great danger of sectarian control over substantial sums of public money. Others did not want to extend federal authority over state and local affairs. The revised Senate version overreached: it would have barred state and local aid not only to schools under denominational control, but to all other institutions as well—including religious orphanages, insane asylums, reformatories, and hospitals.

At the moment when the country came closest to explicitly writing the common school movement's aims into the Constitution, these debates show the extent to which a number of senators felt it was necessary to pare down and broaden the religious elements of the public schools, and confine those religious elements to what could plausibly be defended in terms of civic purposes.

Ten years later, the Reverend Josiah Strong's widely read assimilationist tract, *Our Country: Its Possible Future and Its Present Crisis*, argued once again that public schools should contain only the minimum religious instruction necessary to preserve the moral foundations of the republic: children were to be taught about the existence of God, the soul's immortality, and man's ultimate accountability. "But," Strong asked, "does not the teaching of religious doctrine which is undenominational violate the rights of agnostics as much as inculcating the dogmas of one sect wrongs the adherents of others?" "By no means," he insisted, because "the teaching of the three great fundamental doctrines which are common to all monotheistic religions is essential to the perpetuity of free institutions, while the inculcation of sectarian dogmas is not."[115]

Indeed, Strong insisted that "the public schools are not Protestant, because *distinctively* Protestant doctrines are not taught in them." He argued, indeed, that proponents of public schooling must resist the tendency "to Protestantize the public schools," for "in the eyes of the average voter it would make valid the Catholic argument for a division of the school fund," which would spell the end of common schooling.[116] "Sectarian dogmas," Strong insisted, "are not essential to popular morality. The State, therefore, has no right to teach them, and to do so would be radically wrong in principle, and oppressive to many citizens." The danger to common schooling, Strong observed, came not simply from many Catholics, but also from Protestant immigrants, especially the Lutherans, most of whom "have been trained in denominational schools." The division was not, therefore, between Catholic and Protestant, but between advocates of common schooling and civic purposes, on the one hand, and sectarians of all stripes on the other.[117]

Granting the widely held notion that morality and religion are inseparable, the supporters of the Blaine Amendment, and later defenders of common schooling such as Josiah Strong, went very far indeed in allowing only those religious elements deemed necessary to basic public purposes. Against the prevailing view, a small minority held that public monies could only be fairly appropriated for entirely nonreligious institutions. But there were also those who argued that the thin religiosity of the common schools was hardly distinguishable from a purely secular education. Indeed, in the latter half of the nineteenth century, and especially after the Civil War, Catholics generally stopped seeking concessions from public school administrators that would allow Catholics to attend the common schools, and instead sought to establish their own separate system.[118]

Unstable Alliances?

In the latter half of the nineteenth century, the public school system was consolidated and extended, largely fulfilling the aims of the common school proponents. Catholics established a separate system of parochial education, but their schools were long regarded as second-rate institutions that tended to educate mainly poor immigrants. Catholics never gave up on their efforts to secure a share of public funds.

In 1881, Isaac T. Hecker prefigured an alliance of the future by trying a new tack on behalf of Catholic school funding. In an article entitled "Catholics and Protestants Agreeing on the School Question," Hecker argued that the religious content of public schooling had become so watered down as to be virtually nonexistent. Protestants who took their religion seriously had been duped, he argued, and were gradually discovering "that what had been prepared by designing men to decatholicize the children of Catholics has loosened the hold of the Protestant religion" on Protestant children. Thanks to the common schools, the country was being peopled by "a generation of doubters, sceptics, and infidels, if not atheists." Protestants themselves were coming to recognize what had long been obvious to Catholics, Hecker argued—namely that "a more religious education is absolutely needed" if religion and morality were to be maintained.[119]

Hecker believed that in the 1880s the signs of religious indifference were growing, and that the time was right for a great realignment on the school question. Protestants who were serious about their religion should now join with Catholics and agree on the need to combat the common enemy: the infidel promoters of secular education. In Hecker's view, both great religions needed to recognize that the current educational regime "strikes at the very foundations of Christianity, at morals, at the family, and at the state." These historic antagonists should now unite on the need for a more sectarian education: that is, for schools that are "directly religious and positively Christian."

Hecker proposed that the evil of infidelity could be combated only by establishing a fair and truly American system of school funding: a return to something more like the era of educational diversity. He proposed that a "quota" should be paid by the state to every school for that portion of instruction to children which the state deems necessary for making them "intelligent voters and good citizens." By providing a voucher (in effect) to all schools for the civically useful and publicly valued component of education, parental rights and religious freedom could be respected, and the republic could also secure a more robust religious base for public morals.[120]

Politically, Hecker's effort to form a grand coalition against the common school system was unsuccessful, but his account of the religious trajectory of the common schools was prescient. The ever-increasing pluralism of the American religious scene meant ever more conflicts over the content of the public school religion, and greater conflict helped make it ever harder to justify "nonsectarian" religious exercises in shared civil terms. Hecker's argument also helps show, however, that it is too simple to regard the nineteenth-century school controversy as one strictly between Protestants and Catholics. In significant respects the conflict could be reframed as one between religious particularisms of various sorts, on the one hand, and a common institution pursuing common civic aims, on the other.

In the 1940s, the Supreme Court belatedly implemented some aims of the Blaine Amendment by prohibiting many forms of state aid to religious schools.[121] The Court also applied the First Amendment to public schools in ways that proponents of the Blaine Amendment would have disowned. The Court ruled that "nonsectarian" school prayer and Bible reading in public schools were impermissible state establishments of religion.

Today's public schools must avoid directly advancing any religious views at all. But given the unpopularity of the Supreme Courts decisions on school prayer, it seems unlikely that state legislators and local school boards would ever have completely eliminated religious exercises from the public school curriculum. Public dissatisfaction with the current regime no doubt has helped erode support for public schooling as such. One consequence of the Court's interventions was that more Americans believe that public schools promote what was once called the "sect of infidelity," or what is now more often described as "secular humanism."

Were it not for the Supreme Court, many of our public schools would have a greater religious component than they do, but there would also likely be more public monies flowing to private religious schools than is now the case. As we will see, there are those who feel that such an arrangement would not only be fairer, but also superior from the standpoint of civic education. Among the most vocal defenders of today's school reform are Catholics and Protestants, who believe that religion is a crucial component of education and that parents should have greater freedom to choose the religious affiliation of their children's school. The Catholic-Protestant coalition that now supports publicly funded vouchers and parental choice is reminiscent of Hecker's call for a realignment on the school question.

Conclusion

These old conflicts over the ends of common schooling remain uncomfortably vivid, in part because their memory plays a role in today's debates about school reform. Common schooling always was a myth, according to many commentators, and it still is.[122] By no means do I wish to justify everything that was done in the name of common schooling. There were no doubt many who were out to "Protestantize" America, and racist beliefs were rife. Catholic Irish Americans faced religiously based bigotry and racism. Nevertheless, we need to be careful not to discount the legitimate civic purposes behind the common school movement or dismiss the real efforts that were made to make the common schools fairer to Catholics and others.

Part of the reason that Protestants were more accepting of the common schools is that they were, compared with important Catholic leaders like Archbishop Hughes, more willing to live with religious diversity and more ready to embrace the rights of individuals to judge for themselves in matters of religion. Consider one of the passages that Hughes found particularly annoying among the "infidel" books used in public schools. It concerns a father taking his son, Edwin, to see all of the different churches to which various people were going on a Sunday morning:

> A Roman Catholic congregation was turning into their chapel; every one crossing himself, with a finger dipped in holy water, as he went in.
>
> The opposite side of the street was filled with Quakers . . . A spacious building was filled with an overflowing crowd of Methodists . . .
>
> Presently the services began. Some of the churches resounded with the solemn organ, and the murmuring of voices following the minister in prayer; in others a single voice was heard; and in the quiet assembly of the Quakers not a sound was uttered . . .
>
> Edwin . . . observed them all with great attention, but did not so much as whisper lest he should interrupt any one. When he was alone with his father, "Why," said Edwin, "do not all people agree to go to the same place and to worship God in the same way?"
>
> "And why should they agree?" replied his father. "Do you not see that people differ in a hundred other things? Do they all dress alike, and eat and drink alike, and keep the same hours, and use the same diversion?"
>
> "In those things they have a right to do as they please," said Edwin.
>
> "They have a right, too," answered his father, "to worship God as they please. It is their own business, and concerns no one but themselves."
>
> "But has not God ordered particular ways of worshipping him?"

At this point, as Vincent Lannie puts it, "Hughes wryly commented that Edwin had more sense than his father." In the story, Edwin's father replies to his son: "He has directed the mind and spirit with which he is to be worshipped, but not the manner. That is left for every one to choose. All these people like their own way best."[123]

Bishop Hughes paraphrased this story in the 1840 public school debates and concluded with a rhetorical question: "I ask you if there is no infidelity in that? I ask if it is a proper lesson to teach children, that, as they have a right to form their own tastes for dress and food, they have a right to judge for themselves in matters of religion . . . children are too young to have such principles instilled into them."[124]

Edwin's question is a difficult one for a public schoolbook to address. His father offers a familiar argument for religious diversity: these variations in worship are indifferent as far as God is concerned. The problem is that Edwin's father is advancing an essentially religious defense of religious diversity: from an ecumenical standpoint, one can say that these religious differences are unimportant, but such a statement will not be acceptable to those who believe that theirs is the "one true church." It would have been better for the public schoolbook to have confined itself to the civic dimension of the issue: Edwin's father should have spoken only to the civic rather than the religious aspects of the question of religious diversity, saying something such as "They are all good citizens, and none of these differences matter to us as members of a common political society." The question remains, however, of whether Hughes would have been satisfied with this solution.

My aim here has not been to justify everything done by the supporters of common schooling. On the one hand, there are still many Americans who believe—perhaps with less fervor than the first generation of common school founders—that public institutions for all are uniquely appropriate means of pursuing civic educational ends. In an immigrant society, it is hard to wholly discount the value of an inclusive institution that represents our civic ambition to forge a respectful community of fellow citizens. Yet such an institution is bound to stand in tension with the goals of more particular normative communities, especially those that do not altogether accept core civic values.

It would be wrong to deny the reality of many forms of prejudice and exclusion. Much of the popular understanding of Catholicism was based on centuries-old prejudice, suspicion of foreigners, racism, and other forms of narrow-mindedness. Had there been a livelier appreciation of the extent to which many ordinary American Catholics were seeking to be good citizens of a free republic, ways might have been found to accommodate Catholics within the public system.

Greater fairness and flexibility would not, however, have quieted these controversies. The proponents of many orthodoxies, especially perhaps integral and totalistic belief systems, will not be happy with educational institutions that include all of the children within a pluralistic community. We cannot pursue shared civic ends without making it harder for the proponents of some moral and religious doctrines to perpetuate their views.

Even when specifically religious issues are set aside, and the proper limits of civic education (as best we can discern them) are observed, many people will object to the liberal civic project itself. To see why, let us return for a moment to Mann's original project and consider to what extent his articulation of the common school ideal can still be seen to have merit. Recall the admonition, published in Mann's *Common School Journal*, about the dangers of "becoming proud" even of one's "religious opinions," and his consequent determination not to read anything on the Sabbath "that diminishes my charity for my fellow-creatures." The common schools held that a prideful commitment to particular truths—truths that divide rather than unite different religions—is un-Christian, and they advocated this, at least in part, to generate adequate support for the shared political project, and to encourage mutual respect among fellow citizens.

The public schools were thought to be an appropriate public instrument for promoting the reasonableness and cooperation among citizens that a healthy liberal political order depends upon. Concentrating public funds in schools with an ecumenical, nonsectarian religious content was bound to have the result of favoring tolerant and ecumenical beliefs and practices, and thereby of reforming religion to suit the political project of liberal democracy. Even if the religious content of the public school curriculum was low—and even if it had been *nonexistent*—its mission with respect to religion and other "private" normative domains was crucial: to promote tolerant and "charitable" forms of religious and ethical belief.

All of this will seem to many like the height of illiberality. If liberalism stands for anything, after all, it is the separation of church and state: the conviction that politics should respect religious freedom. But basic political values of equal freedom for all apply within the religious sphere and all other spheres (including the family, as we see later). The fact is that many "private" communities in mid-nineteenth-century America—including some religious ones—*did* need to be transformed in order to generate greater support for liberal democratic principles.

To what extent did Mann and the common school idea go beyond the proper aims of a liberal constitutional order? Recall that for Locke it was a duty of Christian preachers "industriously to exhort all men, whether private persons or magistrates . . . to charity, meekness, and toleration; and diligently endeavor to allay and temper all that heat, and unreasonable averseness of mind, which either any man's fiery zeal for his own sect, or the craft of others, has kindled against dissenters."[125] Locke's account of religious duties are virtually identical to the creed that Mann prescribes for the common schools. Liberal political institutions count on private normative communities embracing, or at least accepting, a rule of toleration and charity toward nonbelievers. Whereas Locke exhorts private preachers to teach the Christianity of "charity, meekness, and toleration," Mann sees the common school as the fit instrument for this purpose: fit, presumably, because if the public ends are important, then adequate public means should be found.

For a liberal public morality to be widely shared, let alone shared by all, a good deal of political work needs to be done. And this work is far from complete, for this morality—even if conceived and presented, as indeed it should be, in more strictly political terms than was the case in seventeenth-century England or nineteenth-century America—is far from equally appealing to all religious communities. It was, is, and will be regarded as unacceptable by those who reject Locke's tolerant Christianity, and all who resist the rule of equal freedom.

Today one can see, however, that it would have been far better, as a matter of principle, to have focused more resolutely on specifically civic issues, while leaving aside the religious dimension of these matters. It may be easier to embrace a common citizenship with those with whom one disagrees in religious matters if one is not excessively proud of one's particular sectarian view, as Mann suggests. Nevertheless, public institutions have no business addressing the specifically religious dimensions of civic questions: public institutions should simply allow that there are a variety of ways of reconciling oneself, as a religious matter, to a civil society such as liberalism.

A greater public adherence to a specifically public agenda would likely not have much altered the course of this controversy. When we reframe the aims of civic education in more purely civil terms, Hughes would still have had reasons—perhaps even greater ones—for objecting to a "cold indifference" toward religion. Hughes did not want a "fairer," more truly public, system—rather, he wanted Catholic children to have a Catholic rather than a public education. Common schools simply will not appeal to parents or moral communities that place great weight on passing along to member children particular viewpoints that are not part and parcel of the liberal democratic viewpoint. Today the public schools are more consistently civic in their orientation; that is, they do a better job of simply leaving religious issues to one side. Even now, complaints such as those that Hughes advanced are still heard, though the complainants are more likely to be fundamentalist Protestants than Catholics. This is partly because Catholics were successful in establishing their own school system, but it is also because the doctrines of the Catholic Church have been decisively transformed, at least partly on account of the Catholic encounter with America.

CHAPTER 3

Civic Excess and Reaction

It is too simple to say that the early common schools were in the business of "Protestantizing" Catholic immigrants or imposing dominant class values on lower classes. To a significant degree, the common schools represented a shared civic vision. Convergence on that vision could not, according to those who shaped these institutions, be taken for granted.

Our common civic project, however formulated, has profound implications for people's deepest normative commitments, including their religious commitments. If Catholics were most vigorous in their resistance to the common school regime, it was not only because anti-Catholic and anti-immigrant prejudice marked public school materials and teachings (which they did); it was also partly because of the genuine tension that existed between American republicanism and the nineteenth-century Catholic hierarchy. In our post–Vatican II era, those tensions have largely abated, but that is because of significant changes within the Catholic Church, changes that may be regarded as concessions to liberal democracy.

In this chapter, I carry the historical story forward into the present. I consider the resurgent assimilationist sentiments of the 1890s and subsequent decades and take stock of two famous Supreme Court cases from the 1920s—*Pierce v. Society of Sisters* and *Meyer v. Nebraska*—that were decided near the culmination of that resurgence. Here, the Supreme Court insisted on the rights of parents and religious communities and ruled against state attempts to prohibit private schooling and foreign language instruction in the schools.

As with the other historical episodes we have examined, these cases are frequently invoked in today's debates over parental rights, multiculturalism, educational choice, and religious diversity. They are regarded as lodestars of what Michael McConnell calls our "multicultural constitutional ideals" and stand in opposition to the "civic republican ideal of the common school movement." *Meyer* and *Pierce* are cases in which, as Kenneth B. O'Brien Jr. puts it, "the idea of the priority of the rights of the parent to supervise the education of his children was emphatically reaffirmed."[1] How broadly should we interpret these cases' principles of parental control and educational diversity?

Today's public school debates are shaped by another set of related normative and institutional conflicts that also came to a head in the early decades of this century: namely, the tension between the cosmopolitan ideals of the Great Society and the virtues of small communities. Why was control over school administration centralized? What are the tradeoffs between local control and more centralized and professional administration? How should we feel about the charge that individualism and bureaucratization have driven community and shared values out of the common schools?

The New Immigration and Americanism

From the founders to Crèvecoeur to the late nineteenth century, an enlightened minority of Americans supported a fairly cosmopolitan and hopeful view of our national identity, one comporting with the abstract ideology of the Declaration of Independence. The liberal immigration law enacted by Jeffersonians in 1802—with its five-year requirement for citizenship—remained in place for over 120 years. Nevertheless, as Rogers Smith has ably documented, blacks, Indians, Asian laborers, and women were excluded in whole or part from citizenship. Other immigrants encountered pressure to assimilate, much of which emanated from the common schools.

In its most generous incarnation, assimilation was understood as a process of mutual engagement and common adjustment. In St. Louis, for example, Germans were numerous, prosperous, capable of supporting a rich array of cultural institutions and associations, and able to marshal political power. They were also bearers of an esteemed culture, and of a racial stock understood to have close affinities with the dominant Anglo-Saxon race. William Torrey Harris, the influential superintendent of St. Louis schools from 1868 to 1880, never questioned that the common language of instruction would be English, but he did not insist that it be the exclusive language of instruction. In his view, the schools should allow and even encourage students of German ancestry to maintain ties with their cultural traditions, at least as a stepping-stone to a "new homogeneous nationality." Assimilation would be a gradual and mutual process that would alter the "peculiar idiosyncrasy" of the "Anglo-American." Each group would benefit from the peculiar virtues of the other. In the 1870s, where ethnic groups enjoyed substantial political power, foreign language instruction was not uncommon. At the other end of the spectrum, those groups that lacked political power—blacks in the south and Asians in California—were either educated in separate and grossly inferior facilities or denied public education altogether.[2]

During the last two decades of the nineteenth century, a vast new surge of immigration occurred. In 1882 alone, the same year that the first federal legislation was passed barring the entry of convicts, "idiots," paupers, and Chinese, 800,000 immigrants entered the country. Most of the new immigrants were from Southern and Eastern Europe (indeed, of the 13 million immigrants arriving between 1897 and 1914, fully 10 million were from these areas), and many Americans viewed the new arrivals as racially inferior. The industrial downturn of 1883–1886 also persuaded many wage earners that the stream of new arrivals threatened their livelihood. Urban and industrial unrest, especially the Haymarket riots of 1886, gave rise to a dread of imported anarchy that swept the country. In the years after 1884, Catholics increased their efforts to multiply dioceses and to build parochial schools, which, along with renewed efforts to secure state aid, provoked new anti-Catholic sentiment.[3]

The national consensus on immigration was changing at the end of the nineteenth century, and the conviction spread that more intense efforts at Americanization were needed lest the nation become, in Theodore Roosevelt's words, a "contemptible knot of struggling nationalities."[4] "It is urgently necessary to check and regulate our immigration," Roosevelt argued in an 1894 essay entitled "True Americanism," "by much more drastic laws than now exist . . . to keep out laborers who tend to depress the labor market, and to keep out races who do not assimilate readily with our own."[5] Now as before, anxieties about assimilation were tempered by a hopefulness about the ability to build a common polity through institutions such as the common school.

For Josiah Strong, America's spread westward and its growing prosperity and power were the consequence of the superiority of America's dominant Anglo-Saxon or Teutonic stock, as well as manifest signs of God's favor. It was not necessary to exclude those of inferior stock, but only to control their entry, for the most advanced scientific views held that some "commingling of the races" would strengthen the dominant strain. Care needed to be taken to control immigration, argued Strong, for America was preeminently the place where the "Anglo-Saxon race is being schooled" for "the final competition of the races." "We stretch our hand into the future," Strong prophesied, "with power to mold the destinies of unborn millions."[6]

These racialist convictions—absurd as they now appear—were held by many early progressive reformers.[7] John R. Commons, professor of political economy at the University of Wisconsin, began his study *Races and Immigrants in America* by qualifying the Declaration of Independence's assertion that "All men are created equal." The reality, he insisted, is that "[r]ace differences are established in the very blood and physical constitution."[8]

Ellwood Cubberley, the first dean of the Stanford School of Education and a widely influential advocate of many progressive education reforms, warned in 1909:

These southern and eastern Europeans are of a very different type from the north Europeans who preceded them. Illiterate, docile, lacking in self-reliance and initiative, and not possessing the Anglo-Teutonic conceptions of law, order, and government, their coming has served to dilute tremendously our national stock, and to corrupt our civic life . . . Everywhere these people tend to settle in groups or settlements, and to set up here their national manners, customs, and observances. Our task is to break up these groups or settlements, to assimilate and amalgamate these people as a part of our American race, and to implant in their children, so far as can be done, the Anglo-Saxon conception of righteousness, law and order, and popular government, and to awaken in them a reverence for our democratic institutions and for those things in our national life which we as a people hold to be of abiding worth.[9]

Cubberley's prejudices—his belief in the inherent superiority of white, male, native-born, Anglo-Saxon Americans—were widely shared by his fellow educators.[10]

The early progressives were not all racialists—and it should be stressed that progressive racialists typically believed in the efficacy of education and other reforms to elevate immigrants into good citizens—but all shared a desire to promote a more nationalized vision of citizenship. As before, reformers viewed both social problems and their potential solutions as importantly moral. Some causes of concern were similar to those expressed in the early nineteenth century: immigration, industrialism, urban crowding, poverty, and crime. In addition, there was a growing revulsion at political corruption and machine politics, labor unrest, and a rising fear of political radicalism spread by foreigners. The school system was, once again, seen as a key public institution to be deployed for republican uplift and assimilation.[11]

Cubberley worried about a "general weakening of the old social customs and traditions," which had contributed to the moral education of the young. Churches were declining, and fewer and fewer people lived in "small and homogeneous" communities in which "every one's actions were every one's business," and where a "code of conduct" supplied by the "older members" was enforced. Home life was loosening its grip on children, apprenticeships were no longer available, and factory work made it "undesirable that children should labor." The "little homogeneous community with its limited outlook and clannish spirit" was fast being displaced by urban conditions, a "cosmopolitan population, and a much freer and an easier life." It was believed, and not for the last time, that substitutes for the old sources of moral education and discipline needed to be found.[12]

The progressive response was, as Cubberley put it, "very paternalistic, perhaps even socialistic, in the matter of education." Progressives believed that the public school regime should be extended, and that control over it should be centralized and professionalized. Centralizing management, Cubberley explained, would increase efficiency, as well as promote greater equality and uniformity among school districts. Attitudes toward the control of children needed to change fundamentally. In Cubberley's words, "Each year the child is coming to belong more and more to the state, and less and less to the parent . . . when neglect, abuse, and the deprivation of the child of any natural right takes place, the child belongs to the state . . . The plea in defense that 'the child is my child' will be not be accepted much longer by society. Our welfare is too thoroughly in the keeping of the child to permit such a policy." Democracy, Cubberley insisted, requires a well-educated and morally upright citizenry. If state governments are weak, inefficient, and corrupt, then "fundamental moral and economic principles must be taught to the masses, so that they may realize the importance of civic righteousness."[13]

Cubberley's intense commitment to moral reform and his confidence in science and centralized control were widely shared by other progressive reformers and helped lead to the establishment of national bureaus of education and naturalization. Private voluntary activity also thrived at this time: settlement houses were founded, evening schools were instituted to teach English and civics, and the crusade for temperance (or prohibition) continued. But the progressives, along with activists such as Jane Addams, did not believe that private action was adequate: the problems of urban poverty and overcrowding were viewed as too vast to be adequately addressed by private charitable action.[14]

Theodore Roosevelt called for an Americanism that was available to all who gained admittance, but that required a wholehearted embrace: "We do not wish, in politics, in literature, or in art, to develop that unwholesome parochial spirit, that overexaltation of the little community at the expense of the great nation, which produces what has been described as the patriotism of the village." A crucial means toward Americanization was continued support for the public school system: "We stand unalterably in favor of the public school system in its entirety." English alone should be the language of instruction, and there should be no state aid to parochial schools.

The great benefit of common schools, for Roosevelt as for earlier proponents, was that when "Catholics, Protestants, Americans of every origin and faith" are "brought up in them," they "inevitably in after-life have kindlier feelings toward their old school-fellows of different creeds, and look at them with a wiser and manlier charity, than could possibly be the case had they never had a chance to mingle together in their youth . . . But this kindly feeling can never exist if one side has legitimate cause for the belief that it is being discriminated against by the other."[15]

Roosevelt insisted that the schools and other public institutions should be rigorously nonsectarian and nondiscriminatory: religion should not be a point of contention or discrimination in national life.[16] Roosevelt meant it when he said "we don't wish any hyphenated Americans," but his Americanism was available to all: "Americanism is a question of spirit, conviction, and purpose, not of creed or birthplace." Roosevelt insisted that nativism and Know Nothingism are "repugnant to true Americanism": no one who was willing to make the effort to assimilate should be excluded from the American project. He denounced those who believed that Catholics or members of certain ethnic groups could not be good Americans. Americanism meant giving "men of all races equal and exact justice." It was an un-American outrage to take people's religious or ethnic affiliations into account when voting or in any exercise of political power: for Roosevelt, Americanism meant putting all such considerations aside and judging fellow Americans on the grounds of merit and character alone.

Unhyphenated Americanism was available to all, but as an imperative, not merely an option. Immigrants should be given two years to learn English, Roosevelt argued, or be sent back home.[17] The "ideal attitude" was expressed for Roosevelt by a German immigrant to Wisconsin: "We are Americans from the moment we touch the American shore until we are laid in American graves. We will fight for America whenever necessary. America, first, last, and all the time."[18] By the second decade of the twentieth century, many Americans had embraced Roosevelt's call for "100% Americanism."

World War I brought renewed anxieties about loyalty, and the Bolshevik Revolution in Russia encouraged fears of working-class anarchism and subversion. In 1917 a federal espionage act was passed, and the next year a sedition act.[19]

Meyer and Pierce

Evidence of the more insistent nationalism of the 1920s can be found in the political initiatives that gave rise to two notable Supreme Court decisions of the decade: *Meyer v. Nebraska* and *Pierce v. Society of Sisters*. In *Meyer* the Supreme Court struck down a state law requiring all young children to be taught only in English.[20] In *Pierce*, the Court overturned a state law requiring that all children between the ages of eight and sixteen attend *public* schools.[21]

Sanford Levinson points out that many constitutional interpreters regard these cases, especially *Pierce,* as keys to the real meaning of religious liberty in America. If, as Levinson observes, *Pierce* is read as standing for a "constitutional principle which should be supported and perhaps even venerated," then perhaps we are obliged not only to grant parents the right to withdraw their children from public schools, but also to subsidize that right for religious parents who cannot afford to exercise it. For why should the exercise of a right so closely connected with a family's ability to express its basic religious values depend on the ability to pay?[22]

In the words of Ronald Dworkin, important constitutional cases have "gravitational force": they exert an influence far beyond their immediate legal effects. But the gravitational force of important cases depends upon how we understand them.[23] If the principles for which *Meyer* and *Pierce* stand are singularly clear and unyielding, then the gravitational force of these cases will be great. If, on the other hand, *Meyer* and *Pierce* are themselves fraught with competing principles and conflicting values, then the gravitational force is less.

Were the judgments in each case fair? On balance, these cases seem to me to have been correctly decided, but the motivations for the state laws at issue, and the Court's reasons for overturning those laws, are both a good deal more ambiguous than the usual accounts allow. The ambiguities of *Meyer* and *Pierce* need to be appreciated, for by oversimplifying the meaning of these cases, we are liable to displace competing considerations and elevate the cases as keystones of a constitutionalism of parental rights, educational choice, and multiculturalism at odds with the liberal democratic civic agenda. We would do better to read these cases in their contexts, with their ambiguities intact and their principles suitably circumscribed.[24]

The conservative Court of this era is generally decried for ushering in a great dark age of constitutional law, in which the doctrines of "substantive due process" and "liberty of contract" were invoked to overturn progressive legislation emanating from states and national attempts to regulate the economy. Minimum-wage laws and maximum-hours legislation were overturned in cases such as *Lochner v. New York,* which lent its name to the Court of this era. Eventually, the *Lochner* Court overturned many provisions of the New Deal. Although the constitutional vision of this era is widely decried, *Meyer* and *Pierce* stand out as forerunners of a more enlightened jurisprudence of privacy and personal liberty, which the Court was to embrace decades later.[25]

Meyer v. Nebraska

The first of the two cases, *Meyer v. Nebraska* (1923), concerned the constitutionality of a state law that prohibited the teaching in any private or public school of any modern languages other than English, to any child who had not passed the eighth grade. There is no doubt that bigotry and xenophobia played important roles in passing language laws, but the motivations were not quite so simple.

The language laws are usually portrayed simply as the consequence of anti-German sentiment in the wake of World War I. The conflict behind the laws was, however, not simply between immigrants and native-born Americans, but also between different generations within immigrant communities. English language education laws were not only widespread in the early 1920s, but also had a long history. The law at issue in *Meyer* was passed by the Nebraska state legislature in 1919. Sixteen states enacted similar laws in that year, and by 1923, thirty-one states had laws mandating English as the sole language of instruction, either in public or in all schools. A number of states and localities had laws mandating English language instruction in all schools as far back as the middle of the nineteenth century.[26]

These laws were motivated by genuine and not altogether unreasonable worries that immigrant groups in the Midwest and the Great Plains were forming isolated enclaves, with their own schools, churches, banks, stores, and insurance companies. Ethnic separatism was not only a provocation to nativists, as Barbara Woodhouse has usefully emphasized, but also worried progressives, who feared that ethnic isolation would deny the promise of equal opportunity to immigrant children.[27]

For progressives, the public schools represented common republican ideals, opportunities open to all, and the hope that all the children of a community would meet and learn from each other. Popular accounts such as that in the magazine *Literary Digest* (which was prepared with the help of the Education Department and intended as a teaching aid for high schools) argued that "Americanism" includes not only understanding and appreciating each other's culture, but also learning a common political language and ethos.[28] As Woodhouse explains, many progressives were concerned that equal opportunity and full participation in American life could not be achieved for immigrant children if their parents shaped their education to reaffirm the traditions of the Old World. Fluency in English had long been seen as a sine qua non of full citizenship, and with good reason: English was the language of political deliberation, and the absence of a common tongue would stymie such core political values as mutual understanding and cooperative relations, the capacity to comprehend and negotiate differences, and reasoned public deliberation.

Historians disagree about whether there really was a substantial problem of immigrant children not learning English, but in some locations, there may well have been grounds for concern. Studies of schools in Nebraska, Chicago, St. Louis, and elsewhere found many children being taught in a foreign language much of the time, and some children being instructed wholly in a foreign language. In St. Louis in the 1870s, when bilingual education was being debated, Selwyn Troen points out that German was the native tongue of nearly half of the adult males.[29] In a Nebraska study in 1918, seven counties reported having schools whose instruction was altogether in German.[30] When laws were passed in Wisconsin and Illinois in 1889 and 1890, respectively, mandating that all elementary school instruction, whether public or private, be conducted in English, the very same bills also contained prohibitions on child labor and strengthened the compulsory schooling laws. The Illinois law was repealed after Republicans lost control of the legislature, and twelve years later, according to one study, over half of Chicago's Catholic schoolchildren were in ethnic parish schools in which much of the child's schooling was conducted in foreign languages.[31]

The Supreme Court in *Meyer,* speaking through Justice James C. McReynolds, admitted the legitimacy of the state's interest in fostering a "homogeneous people with American ideals prepared readily to understand current discussions of civic matters." And it conceded the "power of the State to compel attendance at some school and to make reasonable regulations for all schools, including a requirement that they shall give instructions in English." Nevertheless, the Court determined that it was going too far to prohibit foreign language instruction, so it struck down the law as an unreasonable interference with the liberty of parents and children. On balance that seems right.

On the one hand, "homogeneity" is too broad a public end. The state has a legitimate and indeed basic interest in promoting fluency in the shared language of our civic life, but it does not have a valid interest in stamping out the knowledge of other languages or the cultural attachments that are perfectly compatible with our shared civic culture. Though nativism and prejudice were not the only grounds for the Nebraska law, they provided a significant impetus absent which this draconian measure cannot be rationalized. Indeed, Manley's study of Nebraska emphasizes what Woodhouse does not: that the language law in Nebraska was part of a campaign to remove every vestige of "der Vaterland" from the state, a campaign in which the German language was decried as the "language of betrayal"—a permanent link between the immigrant and the Old World.[32] We have every reason to applaud judicial interventions when there is evidence of widespread prejudice. The intense prejudices of this era are an important part of the justification for the *Meyer* decision, but even here we should not allow the fact of prejudice to blind us to all other factors, including the legitimacy of the state interest in counterbalancing the educative influences of particularistic communities. We should not read *Meyer* as standing for the proposition that parental rights to direct children's education routinely trump the public interest in providing for all children the prerequisites of a common civic life and the equal opportunity to lead an independent existence.

Pierce v. Society of Sisters

Pierce v. Society of Sisters (1925) concerned Oregon's Compulsory Education Act of 1922 (passed by popular initiative, a device favored by progressives), which required all children between the ages of eight and sixteen to attend *public* schools. Noncompliant parents faced heavy fines and jail terms. This law, now seen as an extraordinary exercise of state power, is usually explained simply as an upsurge of some of the least attractive strains of Protestant nativism.

The act, according to Clement Vose and other scholars, was inspired by the Ku Klux Klan and actively promoted by the Freemasons and various patriotic organizations. Public documents offered in support of the legislation placed great emphasis on assimilating and educating foreign-born citizens: "Mix the children of the foreign born with the native born, and the rich with the poor. Mix those with prejudices in the public school melting pot for a few years while their minds are plastic, and finally bring out the finished product—a true American. The permanency of this nation rests in the education of its youth in the public schools . . . where all shall stand upon one common level."[33]

The Freemasons proclaimed their belief in compulsory tax-supported public education in which children would be educated "in the English language only without regard to race or creed as the only sure foundation for the perpetuation and preservation of our free institutions."[34] Opponents of the act, especially Catholics, argued that democracy needed private educational institutions in order to prevent the public schools from becoming "autocratic and arbitrary."[35] The law was approved, however, by 53 percent of those voting.

A challenge to the constitutionality of the act was initiated by the Hill Military Academy and joined by the Society of Sisters, which operated parochial schools in Oregon. A federal court restrained the state from enforcing the act, and Governor Walter M. Pierce appealed to the Supreme Court. A brief filed on behalf of the state by the Freemasons argued:

> If the Oregon school law is held to be unconstitutional it is not only a possibility but almost a certainty that within a few years the great centers of population in our country will be dotted with elementary schools which instead of being red on the outside will be red on the inside. Can it be contended that there is no way in which a state can prevent the entire education of a considerable portion of its future citizens being controlled and conducted by bolshevists, syndicalists and communists?[36]

In June 1925, a unanimous Supreme Court found the act to be an unconstitutional infringement on the property rights of those conducting private educational institutions, as well as an unreasonable interference with the liberty of parents to "direct the upbringing and education of children under their control": "The fundamental theory of liberty upon which all governments in this Union repose excludes any general power of the state to standardize its children by forcing them to accept instruction from public teachers only. The child is not the mere creature of the state; those who nurture him and direct his destiny have the right, coupled with the high duty, to recognize and prepare him for additional obligations."[37] On balance, I believe that here again the Court did the right thing. We should, however, also take account of legitimate considerations advanced on behalf of the Oregon law, for it was not simply motivated by anti-Catholic prejudice.[38]

The Oregon mandatory public school attendance law that was struck down in *Pierce* had come close to passing in Nebraska and Michigan and had gained substantial support in other states.[39] It was supported by populists, who were led in Oregon by Governor Pierce.

Along with the antiforeign, anti-Catholic prejudice, supporters of the law also emphasized the importance of a common educational institution that could not only promote cultural assimilation, but also overcome class barriers and promote equal opportunity. The argument printed on the official ballot included the assimilationist sentiments quoted earlier, but also this: "Our children must not under any pretext, be based upon money, creed, or social status, be divided into antagonistic groups, there to absorb the narrow views of life, as they are taught. If they are so divided, we will find our citizenship composed and made up of cliques, cults and factions, each striving, not for the good of the whole, but for the supremacy of themselves."[40]

One central point of the legislation, as Woodhouse emphasizes, was "to bring children of all races and creeds together." Among the motives behind these laws were KKK-backed prejudices, no doubt, but also populist egalitarianism and democratic reformism. Governor Pierce had been an elector for William Jennings Bryan in 1900, who later supported a wide array of progressivist legislation (a state income tax and a tax on timber interests), opposed criminal syndicalism legislation, and backed FDR and the New Deal.[41]

On the other side, there was, as Woodhouse emphasizes, a close connection between opposition to compulsory schooling and opposition to child labor laws. Woodhouse argues that many of the Catholics and business leaders who were against both mandatory schooling and child labor laws were influenced by attachments to old ideals of patriarchal family rule. Many of those who opposed both measures in the early twentieth century did so on the broad ground that children belonged to their parents.[42]

It is worth recalling that the same Justice McReynolds who wrote the Court's opinions in *Meyer* and *Pierce* was the Court's staunchest advocate of property rights and part of the Court majority that invalidated the federal anti–child labor statute.[43] The chief spokesman for the Catholic community in the *Meyer* and *Pierce* cases—the man who argued that the state laws at issue in these cases stood for the "communistic" child-rearing practices of Plato's *Republic* and represented a radical subversion of parental control—was none other than William Dameron Gutherie, a principal architect of the doctrine of "substantive due process" (the doctrine that furnished the main constitutional rationale for protecting private property against state interference).[44] William Jennings Bryan, who was arguing the Scopes case when the

Pierce decision was handed down, joined other fundamentalist Protestants in insisting that "the Oregon case affirms the right of parents to guard the religious welfare of the child and this, I think, is decisive in our case."[45]

As someone who has argued that the most vehemently criticized decisions of the old *Lochner* Court were not all bad, I find some measure of perverse satisfaction in arguing that its most revered decisions were not all good.[46] I do not, however, want to go so far as to argue that *Meyer* and *Pierce* were wrongly decided; I only want to suggest that we should pause before making the principles of these cases into templates of a new jurisprudence of multiculturalism, choice, and parental rights. Woodhouse, for example, seems to me to play down the degree of prejudice at work in Nebraska and elsewhere. The usual textbook accounts of *Meyer* and *Pierce* are not all wrong, they are just too simple, and thus claim an unwarranted force and sweep for the principles of these cases.

We need to allow for complex motives when assessing these and other episodes, and to hold in mind the reasons that can be mustered on both sides. We must remember, in particular, that not only the state but also parents can obstruct the freedom and equality of children. The 1920s were without question a time of resurgent nativism and mounting anxiety over immigration, but these anxieties allied themselves with confidence in the efficacy of common schooling and a belief that the promise of American life should be available to all. We need to be alert to the multiple sources of possible oppression. In our zeal to guard against state-backed efforts to monopolize education and to homogenize all children, we should also remember that the parental freedom to control the education of children can itself be a form of tyranny—especially if such control extends to a view of the child as the parents' property.

So it is worth regarding *Meyer* and *Pierce* in a critical light and heeding the revisionist objections of critics such as Woodhouse, who argues that *Meyer* announced "a dangerous form of liberty: the right to control another human being. Stamped on the reverse side of this coinage of family privacy and parental rights," she continues, "are the child's voicelessness, objectification, and isolation from the community."[47] We can and should accept what the Court did in these cases, I believe, so long as we place at the core of the Court's holdings

McReynold's insistence that the state retains important and extensive powers to promote "American ideals" and to regulate all schools, including compelling all to teach English. It seems hard to believe that states could not have encouraged the vast majority of immigrants to learn English through means less severe than those embodied in these laws. The Court plays a legitimate role in reminding the populace that it should not pursue legitimate aims with excessive zeal, or in such a way that unreasonably discounts freedom.

Ham-fisted public incursions into the lives of families and religious communities are often a poor strategy for promoting inclusion. It may often be more effective to lure the children of families from minority religious cultures into common institutions by making those institutions more attractive to them. In this regard it is worth recalling William Torrey Harris's openness to bilingual education for German students during his tenure as St. Louis school superintendent from 1868 to 1880. In 1860, one-third of the city's 15,000 pupils—80 percent of the German-American students—attended private schools in which the official language of instruction was German. To lure these children to the public schools, St. Louis school authorities rescinded their English-only policy and introduced German into the public school curriculum. Within twenty years, 80 percent of the German-American children were attending public schools. Unfortunately, in St. Louis and in other cities, this milder strategy ran into political opposition, and the accommodations failed to garner adequate support at the polls.[48]

Harris did not advocate permanent pluralism, but rather favored an eventual homogenization and amalgamation of ethnic groups. Nevertheless, at least during a transitional period, Harris accepted that it would be harmful to children if, by learning only English, they lost the thread of continuity with older generations: "[C]onsciousness of one's ancestry and the influence derived from communication with the oldest members of the family is very potent in giving tone to the individuality of youth and ripening age, and indeed to a community or people as a whole." A break between younger and older generations caused by a sudden breach in easy communication would, Harris allowed, be a "calamity" to both generations. The goal, for Harris, was to lessen the shock of immigration by respecting cultural traditions while working to avoid a permanent tribalization of society. His goal, as Troen puts it [quoting Harris], was "a transitional ground on which each group would neither confine itself to the 'narrow limits of its inherited nationality' nor 'fall suddenly into cosmopolitan indifference' and thereby lose 'the vital springs of energy and aspiration.'"[49] This strategy seems sensible: there are severe costs to both sudden assimilation and "intransigent isolation." One wonders how many of those who sought to ban foreign language instruction gave due weight to the interests of immigrant families?

If the nativism of this era quieted after 1924, it was on a note of triumph. In that year the first immigration quota was established, limiting total immigration to 150,000 per year and banning most immigration from Asian countries altogether. Racialism played an important role in establishing the National Origins Quota system, which was meant to reflect and reinforce the composition of the polity in 1890. The quota system remained in place until 1965, but in the 1940s racialism was powerfully undermined by the specter of Nazism in Europe and the greater seriousness with which racial equality was taken during World War II.[50]

Horace Kallen and the Pluralist Reaction

The prejudices and excesses of this era are undeniable. Anxieties about immigration certainly encouraged people to recognize that a shared civic sphere—and the attitudes and behaviors that sustain it—is a political artifact worthy of attention, not a fact of nature to be taken as given. Nevertheless, governments pursued civic ends in ways that were overly broad, zealous, and often mean-spirited. The early decades of this century helped give assimilation and "Americanism" bad names from which they have never recovered. It is hardly surprising that the excesses of assimilationism called forth simplistic alternatives that made the opposite mistake of taking a shared civic life for granted.

In response to the excesses of Americanizers, proponents of "cultural pluralism" have often neglected supporting institutions and practices designed to encourage groups to converge on patterns of peaceful interaction and mutual respect. The phrase "cultural pluralism" was first introduced by Horace Kallen in a widely read *Nation* article in 1915. Kallen attempted to use American ideals against nativists and assimilationists: he insisted that the lofty goals of the Declaration of Independence, properly understood, support respect for strong and distinctive group identities, which lie beyond the scope of choice: "[T]he political autonomy of the individual has presaged and is beginning to realize in these United States the spiritual autonomy of his group." Anticipating some of today's most prominent communitarians, Kallen asserted, "Men may change their clothes, their politics, their wives, their religions, their philosophies, to a greater or lesser extent: they cannot change their grandfathers."[51] Recasting the ideas of the racialists in a positive light, Kallen insisted that the melting pot was an impossibility because ethnic differences were inherited and deeply imbedded in human nature. It would be better to think of America as a mosaic, a "multiplicity in a unity, an orchestration of mankind," and to adopt a new political ideal appropriate to the fact of "inalienable" national identities.[52]

Kallen attempted to use American ideals against assimilationists by reinterpreting the nation's history as a march toward cultural federation. The ideal of liberty motivating the Revolution and the decades thereafter, he argued, was local and collective: it was a liberty that protected the "distributive sovereignty of each state" without touching deeply the "internal organization" of the states.[53] This ideal of liberty existed in tension with the ideal of union written into the Constitution, and that tension was resolved in favor of union only by the Civil War. The triumph of the Union overturned the older liberty of local groups protected by states and put in its place a new liberty of individuals protected by the national government. These national ideals reached a climax in the progressivism of Roosevelt and Wilson, Kallen argued, in which state sovereignty was practically abolished.[54]

Kallen claimed that America's political integrity was assured. An individual American's citizenship in the commercial order is voluntary—a matter of contract, not status, that can be given up when citizens "find it incompatible with their other ideals." Government "is a tool, not a goal," instituted only for the sake of individual happiness. Politics in this order is not itself constitutive of happiness.[55]

The problem is that the New Nationalism—built on individualism and centralized power, especially in an active executive—breeds "government by indifference" and an "indefiniteness of outlook." It "throws men back on themselves," desocializes them, and makes them "mere units." All of this results from the decline of "civil conscience," which was once enforced by "fellowship in the smaller state-group."[56] Throughout, Kallen echoed Tocqueville's warning that excessive centralization leads to narrow self-concern and mutual disinterest.

The new immigration, however, once more transformed the union: it made manifest that the individual is "as a link in an endless historical chain which is heredity," and that "it is what we are by heredity and early family influence that comes nearest to being inalienable and unalterable." Immigration, industrialism, and the triumph of nationalism had set the stage for a new ideal of democracy, Kallen argued: one founded on "the perfection and conservation of differences," that is, a new federalism based on permanent, natural differences of national character. Instead of the melting pot, Kallen saw an ever more pronounced ethnic separatism: ethnically based neighborhoods, churches, parochial schools, libraries, associations, newspapers, books, and more. Instead of assimilation, he saw "a process of dissimilation" in which "the arts, life and ideals of the nationality become central and paramount." Rejecting the contention advanced by several studies in the 1920s (and since vindicated) that ethnic intermarriage would promote assimilation, Kallen argued that "intermarriage or no intermarriage, racial quality persists, and is identifiable."[57]

Kallen argued that it was time to embrace a new ideal of Americanism and democracy, one in which "each might attain the cultural perfection that is *proper to its kind*," with the "kind" being inherited national character. The new democratic model was to be federal: not the old federalism of arbitrary local units, but one rooted in the real, national differences. Kallen also defended hyphenated Americanism: a hyphenation not of states and union, but of nationality and union. The new ideal would be variety in union involving "a give and take between radically different types, and a mutual respect and mutual cooperation based on mutual understanding."[58]

The great obstacles, Kallen argued, are the powers of reaction: those who anxiously insist that the immigrants give up their language, their clothes, their folklore and music and assimilate to Anglo-Saxon culture. Members of the dominant national culture, anxious about their status and more fearful of "difference" than of challenges to their economic supremacy, seek to maintain their hegemony in the name of guarding "the fundamentals of the nation." Luckily, Kallen argued, most Anglo-Americans are committed not only to cultural dominance but also to the more abstract and inclusive ideals of the Declaration of Independence. Force would be required to maintain cultural dominance—especially the complete nationalization of public schooling, the elimination of private schooling, and a ban on the teaching of foreign languages. Cultural unity could only be the product of a forced forgetting incompatible with America's basic liberties.[59]

Kallen offered a stark choice: either the country would be handed over to the most reactionary proponents of "100% Americanism," or it would have to embrace his ideal of cultural pluralism and federation. The choice was between "Kultur Klux Klan or Cultural Pluralism": the infantile defense of cultural uniformity versus radical and permanent cultural diversity.[60]

When Kallen wrote of America as a federation of cultural groups, he appeared to mean primarily a cultural rather than a political federation: cosmopolitan political and economic relations would overarch group-based cultural and religious differences. But Kallen said little about political institutions, or about how this divorce between the cultural and the political was to be sustained. His vision of cultural pluralism was of group-based diversity without prejudice, ethnocentrism, or serious tensions among groups.[61] It is as though he wanted people to live in the ghetto but not harbor any of the prejudices and narrowness that so often are a feature of life in homogenous enclaves.[62] The great weakness of Kallen's posture was that he said little about political institutions, or about how this wedding of cultural particularism and political cosmopolitanism would be sustained.

"Surely," Kallen argued, "the more cohesive and flexible, the more adjustable and self-sustaining are these communities," the more they will contribute to the happiness of all. But how does one promote national groups that are, as Kallen wanted, radically different yet harmonious and even cooperative? How does one promote groups that are autonomous, cohesive, and self-sustaining, but also flexible and "adjustable"? Kallen appeared to regard Jews as a model: in his view, they are the most group-conscious of people, and yet the most "flexible and accommodating" in adjusting to their social environment.[63] Assuming that this generalization is true, there is no particular reason why it should apply beyond groups, such as Jews, with a long history of pariah status—that is, these groups may have had the greatest incentive to fit in. While Kallen appeared to see the need for balance between groups and the common political identity, his tendency is to rhapsodize about ideals rather than develop a political science of group life.[64]

What do we make of Kallen's call for cultural pluralism? Important components of Kallen's vision, most notably his racialism, are startlingly unacceptable. In addition, his insistence on the permanence of national differences and the irrelevance of intermarriage have been given the lie by ever increasing proportions of mixed marriages.[65]

Federalism, moreover, is simply too radical a model for American cultural pluralism. Kallen gave too little weight to our shared political identities. He failed to recognize that political institutions grounded in the ideals of the Declaration are not merely "tools" (as opposed to "goals"): those ideals embody shared moral aspirations of a high order.

Kallen's account of what we share as citizens was, for the most part, far too limited: he seemed to view our politics as a modus vivendi among cultural groups federated for certain limited purposes. And yet at other times, he spoke of citizenship as a "Great Vocation." Indeed, he criticized vocational education on the ground that while it feeds "the insatiable greed of the industrial machine . . . , the Great Vocation is forgotten, This vocation is citizenship. In a democracy it is fundamental, for a democracy dares to endow each citizen with the task that Plato, who was so wise in his own democratic generation, left to a hardily trained and expert few."[66]

Kallen seemed, politically speaking, to want it both ways. He seemed to want not only the deep diversity of a minimalist cultural federation, but also the shared civic commitments of a robust democratic project—one that makes citizens both guardians of the state and "world citizens" who sympathetically recognize and understand the differences of others. In the real world, tradeoffs between particularity and cosmopolitanism seem inevitable, but not in Kallen's ideal: "The cultivated Man, whether he be an Englishman or a German, is essentially a citizen of the world because from his firm seat in his own home, he understands and cooperates with spiritual expressions having a different base, a different background, and a different import from his own."[67] Kallen seems to have wanted citizens who are both firmly situated in permanent national groupings as well as cosmopolitan and open to outsiders. A happy result, but a sustainable one? And how do we get there?

Kallen's political vision was not entirely coherent. He was, however, far from wrong to echo Tocqueville's warnings about the dangers of excessive centralization within a mass commercial order. In part at least, Kallen appears to propose nationality-based local communities as correctives to the atomizing and homogenizing tendencies of the Great Society. Kallen rightly argues that we should not attempt to concentrate all allegiances at the political center—that decentralization plays an important role in maintaining social diversity and, thereby, individual freedom and creativity. He rightly predicts that in America, ethnic differences (while they may not have the permanence and rigidity he claimed) combat a deadening homogeneity and check the tendency toward regimentation: ethnic communities are, he notes, among "the reservoirs of individuality, the springs of difference."[68]

Kallen rightly points to the need to preserve group life: those associations and identifications intermediate between the family and the nation as a whole. At times, he even gestures in the direction of what is really needed: a political science of group life that shows how local differences can coexist peacefully and, indeed, promote shared ideals of citizen virtue. Kallen comes closest to the right sort of political science when he writes of the inevitability in an immigrant society like America of multifaceted identities: of complexly divided allegiances and multiple memberships, among which nationality is only one (though always, he insisted, the most important). The problem is that in Kallen's framework these bits and pieces are all undeveloped, and we are left with only the unsupported hope that radically divided cultural groups will harmoniously cooperate in an "orchestration of mankind."[69]

If we wish to allow, with Kallen, that cultural diversity and group-based difference are important components of a healthy liberal democracy, the task still remains of showing how group difference can be reconciled to the overarching demands of liberal democratic values. In Parts Two and Three, I attempt to show how diverse local communities can not only peacefully coexist, but also promote some of the virtues needed by liberal democracy. The best political science for liberal democratic citizenship draws on resources provided by local community life, but it must also shape those resources in distinctive ways to render them supportive of liberal democratic civic ideals.

Horace Kallen was alive to the dangers of investing the national project with the whole of our moral energies, and he was right to remind us of the enduring importance of communities and allegiances intermediate between individuals and families, on one side, and the state on the other. By viewing heredity as destiny, however, Kallen offered a cramped version of individual freedom. By embracing a model of cultural federation, he shortchanged the important role of our national ideals in guaranteeing the freedom and equality of all individuals. And in neglecting to explore the importance of institutions and practices that might shape diversity to guarantee peaceful coexistence and democratic respect, he failed to grapple with the hard questions posed by the tensions between deep diversity and our shared civic ideals in modern societies.

Kallen's reaction against the excesses of assimilation was in many ways understandable, but it was excessive in its own right. It took for granted the need for an overarching civic framework and gave too much weight to cultural particularity. It furnished a model for the future that was attractive but inadequate to civic purposes. It did not say enough about the political work that needed to be done to ensure that group particularism and localism would help serve our largest civic purposes.

CHAPTER 4

The Decline of the Common School Idea

As Horace Kallen vividly reminds us, one way in which the tension between diversity and our most inclusive civic ideals manifests itself is in the conflict between characteristically national ideals of individual freedom and equality and the more local allegiances and norms of smaller communities. The scope and structure of governance matters, as the Antifederalist proponents of small community and decentralized control had argued in opposition to the Constitution. Madison and others among the founders also knew that to embrace many interests in a single representative district or other institution would, over time, amplify some voices and mute others, altering the nature of those interests.[1] To close this episodic historical overview, it is worth noting the extent to which debates over the values of expertise and efficiency, aided by centralization of control, deeply mark the twentieth-century common school system and help structure debates about school reform today.

By today's standards, nineteenth-century school governance was remarkably decentralized. Major cities had, for example, both central and ward-based school boards. Until 1911, each of the thirty-nine subdistrict boards in Pittsburgh raised its own taxes, hired its own teachers, and built and maintained its own schools. Rural school districts elected their own superintendents, and the one-room schoolhouse was common.[2]

During the twentieth century, there has been a vast growth of public schools, and also, thanks in part to progressive reforms, structural changes in the way schools are organized. School reform in the first half of this century was marked by a shift from control by laymen to professionals. An increase in administrative centralization further bolstered the autonomy of professionals and led to a turning away from localism.

The New York City public schools that helped assimilate the millions of immigrants who settled in the metropolis between 1890 and 1920 were neighborhood based and often remarkably homogeneous. A 1905 survey found that one school district of 64,000 pupils was 94.5 percent Jewish and ten of the district's thirty-eight schools were 99 percent Jewish. Immigrant families often jealously guarded their neighborhood schools: in 1904, Jewish parents angrily refused to allow 500 of their children to be shifted to less crowded schools outside their neighborhood. Some reformers despaired that this "flocking together" only reinforced the immigrants' resistance to Americanization.[3]

Urban political machines helped connect city neighborhoods to city hall, and they helped mediate conflicts between immigrant communities and public officials. They also contributed to the patronage, construction, and textbook-purchasing scandals that enraged progressive era reformers.[4] Many reformers distrusted localism and ward politics, for they seemed to promote scandal and corruption, whereas good government was increasingly understood in terms of professionalism and a disinterested expertise above mere politics. Muckraking journalists from the 1880s on tied local political machines to administrative corruption in the schools. A St. Louis newspaper portrayed boss-dominated school politics this way:

> A number of noisy, possibly half-drunken men form the "cell-germ" of our political system, the primary ward meeting. In the midst of this howling mob we see two or three men, who are struggling to bring their followers to the enthusiastic endorsement of a "slate" which they have arranged in the calm seclusion of their own dram shops. This is the Democratic primary. The Republican meeting is the twin-brother to it, possibly controlled in the secret councils of the bosses by precisely the same men.[5]

The enemy of reform, according to muckraker Adele Shaw, was "the old village prejudice and the tenacity of association that prefers to see in office a bad neighbor rather than a good man from a remoter street." According to the Public Education Association, "all merely local and artificial divisions should be abolished both in the management of the schools and in the appointment of members of the Board of Public Education, so that the interest of the whole community may always be kept in view." The schools must be taken "out of politics," a key St. Louis reformer argued, and control must be shifted toward "men of standing and position in the community."[6] "The community cannot afford to purchase local interest in the schools at the price now paid for it," argued a New York reformer.[7] Elwood Cubberly was more sarcastic: "José Cardoza, Francesco Bertolini, and Petar Petarovich are elected as school directors," he lamented. "The process is of course educative to these newcomers, though a little hard on local government."[8]

The reforms shifted the emphasis of the public system away from neighborhoods and lay control, away from localistic pluralism, away from what Teddy Roosevelt called the "patriotism of the village," and toward that of the great community, represented by autonomous professionals and impartial experts.[9]

The opponents of these reforms were not simply corrupt city bosses and the beneficiaries of patronage, as they were contemptuously portrayed by reformers. The prereform New York City school trustees of 1896 were, according to Diane Ravitch, "solid, if unrenowned, middle-class citizens." The city school board "recognized the right of representation of all sects and nationalities," and the local school boards "reflected their districts."[10] Opponents of centralization often regarded the reformers as self-righteous Yankee Protestant snobs, "old maids in the Civic Club."[11] They made a political case for the virtues of a pluralism, localism, and decentralization. The proponents of local, ward-based control of the schools warned that an "aristocracy" was seeking to usurp the people's power. Popular trust in the schools would be maintained, they argued, only so long as the schools were kept in close touch with the people. As the president of the New York Board of Education put it: "If you do away with the trustee system you do away with the people's schools. The trustees are in touch with the schools, and none others are or can be but those who live in the locality of the schools. We have a peculiar population, made up of all nationalities . . . There is a fear on the part of these people that we are going to interfere with their religion. If we have ward trustees representing all classes, confidence will be maintained." According to the weekly newspaper *School*, "The larger number of persons who can be kept in touch with and interested in the public school system, the better it will be for the schools."[12]

The stereotype about progressive reformers was also not true: they were not all blue-blooded snobs or business elites, and their involvement was helpful to public schools. School reform went hand in hand with the expansion of public education, and both enjoyed widespread popular support.[13] Likewise, in spite of the sort of sarcasm evident in Cubberley's remark, the increased voting strength of ethnic groups in urban areas makes it hard to believe that elites could impose reforms on working-class immigrants. Between 1880 and 1910, as Paul E. Peterson shows, German, Irish, and other immigrant groups garnered a more equal share of educational resources and political power: immigrant children do not seem to have been educated in larger classes, and the Irish in particular secured increasing numbers of positions as teachers and principals. So long as immigrants had the vote (from which blacks and many Asians were excluded), they had an increasing say in school governance.[14] The reforms generated changes in the structure of democratic governance—they shifted control from localities to city and state-wide electorates, and to elected rather than appointed superintendents—but these shifts were themselves democratically supported. Indeed, once divisive social antagonisms, charges of corruption, and intense partisanships were in some measure transcended, popular interest in and support for education seems to have increased. As Selwyn Troen argues in his study of St. Louis, "Between 1916 and 1947 the public never failed to endorse appeals for more revenues. Only since World War II, and particularly in the 1960's as the emergence of a large black population aroused the kind of communal discord that had obtained in the nineteenth century, have successive boards been increasingly frustrated by a lack of support."[15]

The progressive reformers enjoyed some real successes. In rural areas, districts were unified and control shifted from district officers to county or state educational authorities. The number of one-room schoolhouses in America declined from approximately 200,000 in 1910 to 20,000 in 1960. Larger regional high schools likewise replaced local high schools.[16]

A leading plank of urban school reformers such as Nicholas Murray Butler was that the nineteenth-century system of ward-based school control needed to be overturned in favor of more centralized and professional control. There were obvious means at hand to pry urban public schooling away from what were perceived (not without reason) to be the corruptions and inefficiencies, nepotism and favoritism, and backwardness of local control: the size of school boards was greatly reduced, and board members were henceforth elected in at-large rather than district contests. Indeed, the average number of central board members in big-city schools across the country was reduced by about two-thirds between 1893 and 1923. In 1917, the New York City School Board was reduced from forty-six to seven members. The ward school boards all but disappeared. And in many cities, school board independence was increased and the influence of mayors over school administration reduced. The point of these moves was to shift control from local communities toward more remote administrative centers, and to increase the autonomy of professional administrators and teachers.[17]

School district consolidation continued after World War II: in 1945–1946 there were over 100,000 school districts in the country; by 1983–1984, fewer than 16,000 districts served a much larger population. Public school authority was extended outward as uniform standards and the equal distribution of resources were imposed across districts of expanding size: it became harder, as a consequence, for parents, local communities, and neighborhood leaders to exercise influence over the schools. School support shifted from local taxes to state aid (in 1930, 17 percent of school revenues came from state aid, compared to 40 percent in 1950).[18]

In addition, the reach of the public system was extended to older children in the decades before World War II as high school education expanded and older children were kept in school longer. Here too the public schools achieved remarkable success: in 1890 nearly a third of all high schoolers were enrolled in private schools, whereas by 1940 the figure was only 6.5 percent.[19] Vocational schools were also founded in great numbers.

The rise of vocational schools at midcentury is often linked to a decline in the ideal of a universal liberal education. Likewise, the proportion of academic subjects in the curriculum declined precipitously in the middle decades of this century in favor of more directly "useful" subjects that would prepare children to be "home makers, workers, and citizens."[20] This decline in intellectual content is often decried as a sign of a lowering of intellectual standards and expectations, and that indeed may be part of what occurred. Richard Hofstadter emphasizes, however, that one important reason for the change was simply the newly widespread conviction that high schools should be available to all instead of being a luxury for the few. If schools were going to catch dropouts, it was believed that they would need to focus to a much greater degree on "real life problems" rather than intellectual training.[21] The "dumbing down" of the curriculum at midcentury was thus, in part at least, a consequence of high schools becoming mass, rather than merely elite, institutions. In addition, drugs, crime, broken families, and a host of other problems present the schools with difficulties unimagined in previous generations.

In any case, thanks in part to the successful efforts of reformers, by the end of World War II, the public schools enjoyed a near complete monopoly on elementary and secondary education.

The Changing Substance of Public School Morality

Changes in the structure of school governance—school districts of vastly greater size and authority increasingly removed from the neighborhood level—were accompanied by parallel changes in the moral ethos of schools. Since World War II, a more individualistic and inclusive public school ethos has emerged. At the constitutional level, meanwhile, a greater emphasis has been placed on respect for the individual rights guaranteed to all as a matter of national citizenship.[22] Most dramatic, perhaps, was the relatively quick shift in the Supreme Court's attitude to the loyalty-building exercise of mandatory flag salutes in the public schools. In 1935, some children of the Jehovah's Witnesses faith refused, on religious grounds, to participate in the morning flag salute ceremony, which was a long-standing custom in the public schools of Minersville, Pennsylvania. The local school superintendent became adamant, and—with the consent of the state attorney general—got the school board to pass a resolution making the ceremony mandatory. In 1940 (as Nazis marched across Europe) the Supreme Court rejected the challenge on the grounds that, as Justice Frankfurter put it, local authorities have the right to promote "the binding tie of cohesive sentiment" on which all of our liberties depend.[23] The ceremony did not directly interfere with freedom of religious belief and assembly, Frankfurter said, and so it did not conflict with the First Amendment.

The Court reversed itself in 1943, and held that First Amendment guarantees of freedom of speech mean that government officials cannot compel professions of political allegiance. As Justice Jackson put it in his opinion for the Court,

> Struggles to coerce uniformity of sentiment in support of some end thought essential to their time and country have been waged by many good as well as by evil men. Nationalism is a relatively recent phenomenon but at other times and places the ends have been racial or territorial security, support of a dynasty or regime, and particular plans for saving souls . . . Probably no deeper division of our people could proceed from any provocation than from finding it necessary to choose what doctrine and whose program public educational officials shall compel youth to unite in embracing . . . freedom to differ is not limited to things that do not matter much.

The state may not promote loyalty by coercing professions of belief, even professions of belief in liberal democratic values. Justice Jackson, however, underestimated the controversy of educating for freedom when he expressed the hope that "[f]ree public education, if faithful to the ideal of secular instruction and political neutrality, will not be partisan or enemy of any class, creed, party, or faction."[24]

A generation later, in the midst of another war, the Court insisted that public school students "are entitled to freedom of expression of their views." In the same institutions in which Catholic students had a century earlier been whipped for refusing to read the King James version of the Bible, the Supreme Court now held that students (in high school and junior high) who wore black armbands to school to express their opposition to the war in Vietnam were protected by the First Amendment. School officials could not take disciplinary actions against this silent expression of antiwar sentiment unless they could show that such conduct would "materially and substantially" interfere with school discipline.[25] The Court has also required that high school and junior high school authorities do not have unfettered discretion to remove books from school libraries because of opposition to the ideas expressed in them. While substantial control of the curriculum would allow school officials to inculcate community values, the school library was to be understood as a place for "voluntary inquiry."[26]

Court decisions and policy changes in schools in the 1960s extended important aspects of freedom of expression and due process to students. At the same time, the Court has also consistently reaffirmed the role of public schools in "inculcating fundamental values necessary to the maintenance of a democratic political system."[27] As we saw above, the Court in *Meyer* allowed that states might require that all students learn English, and in *Pierce*, while insisting that the option of private schooling cannot be foreclosed, it also allowed that states may require private schools to teach "certain studies essential to good citizenship."[28]

More recently, the Court has allowed school officials to draw lines limiting forms of student expression in order to enforce standards of civility. Consider *Bethel School District v. Fraser*, a case in the 1980s involving disciplinary action against a high school student who made lewd references in a speech at a student assembly, provoking hooting and sexual gestures from the audience. At first, a lower court vehemently rejected the idea that school officials can inculcate standards of civility and "decency": "We fear that if school officials had the unbridled discretion to apply a standard as subjective and elusive as 'indecency' in controlling the speech of high school students, it would increase the risk of cementing white, middle-class standards for determining what is acceptable and proper speech and behavior in our public schools."[29]

The Supreme Court rejected this view, however, and reaffirmed the schools' role in preparing pupils "for citizenship in the Republic," which included respect for the proprieties of reasoned discourse: "The process of educating our youth for citizenship in public schools is not confined to books, the curriculum and the civics class; schools must teach by example the shared values of a civilized social order."[30] The Court has also ruled that the permissive standard of *Tinker* does not apply to the content of high school student newspapers produced as a part of the official curriculum. School officials may exercise editorial control in order to "set high standards for the student speech that is disseminated under its auspices."[31]

Important changes in public school governance have been brought about by the Supreme Court's more vigorous interpretation of the Constitution's prohibition of establishments of religion. The 1947 case of *Everson v. Board of Education* was most famous for Justice Hugo Black's invocation of Jefferson's famous "wall of separation" metaphor for the proper isolation of church from state: "The 'establishment of religion' clause of the First Amendment means at least this: Neither a state nor the Federal Government can set up a church. Neither can pass laws which aid one religion, aid all religions, or prefer one religion over another . . . No tax in any amount, large or small, can be levied to support any religious activities or institutions."[32]

In spite of these broad sentiments—which some have interpreted as signaling a stance of hostility toward religion—the Court in *Everson* permitted the state to pay for transportation to not-for-profit private schools, including religious schools. The public provision of "general government services," such as "police and fire protection, connections for sewage disposal, public highways and sidewalks," may all be permissibly extended to religious institutions, for "State power is no more to be used so as to handicap religions than it is to favor them."[33] The Court has also allowed states to loan secular textbooks chosen from a list approved by the state to all schoolchildren in the state, including children in religious schools. And it has permitted state income tax exemptions for expenses incurred in providing for the education of children in parochial schools, so long as the exemptions are broad-based enough to include expenses incurred by parents of public school children as well as children in a variety of private schools, including secular schools.[34]

In other cases that would be more pleasing to supporters of the Blaine Amendment, the Supreme Court has disallowed state attempts to subsidize the salaries of teachers of secular subjects in nonpublic schools. The monitoring necessary to ensure that the subsidy is not used for religious instruction would, the Court insisted, foster an excessive entanglement with religion.[35] And the Court has repeatedly expressed the fear that large public subsidies to religious institutions could risk injecting religious disagreements into politics: "The recurrent nature of the appropriation process provides successive opportunities for political fragmentation and division along religious lines, one of the principal evils against which the Establishment Clause was intended to protect."[36] State "neutrality" toward religion is no easier to define now than in 1840.

In important respects, the modern Supreme Court has bolstered the nineteenth-century common school settlement with respect to religion, but it has also moved to rid the public schools of those "nonsectarian" religious exercises once deemed essential to moral education. The Court has prohibited "nonsectarian" school prayers, including nonsectarian prayers at high school graduation ceremonies, and it has disallowed Bible reading and the posting of the Ten Commandments in public schools.[37]

While at least some of the cases mentioned above—those allowing public provision of transportation and textbooks to parochial school students—can be viewed as victories for religious parents, Michael McConnell complains that these cases represent "a serious setback for pluralism," for what they represent is the principle that public subsidies must be confined to public purposes, and this itself is "a powerful inducement to homogeneity." As McConnell notes, only those forms of assistance that "could not be imbued with a religious element (such as diagnostic tests, school lunches, or the grading of standardized tests) would be permitted." The problem, for McConnell, is that "religious schools could receive public money, but only at the cost of adopting the secular curriculum of the public schools." But what exactly is the alternative? Are we to tax people to support the specifically religious aspects of religious institutions? It seems to me better to say about the current state of the law that the Supreme Court's establishment clause jurisprudence is generally intended to ensure that public monies are spent appropriately for civic purposes such as promoting literacy and other branches of learning. It is hardly objectionable that the Court prohibits public monies from being used to subsidize programs whose primary justification is religions. Indeed, McConnell himself admits that, in some respects, the unavailability of many forms of state aid reduces the incentives for religious schools to tailor their convictions in order to qualify for public aid.

McConnell, however, opposes the overall contours of these judicial decisions because he opposes the common school tradition as a whole, root and branch. In his view, it is better to replace public schools devoted to public values with a voucher system committed to multiculturalism and parental choice. In reviving the Catholic argument of the 1830s and 1840s, McConnell admits that the "genuine" multiculturalism he would put in the place of a public system poses "great risks" of balkanization and group division—but he urges that we take those risks in the name of free choice and diversity. I believe, however, that we have no good reasons of basic principle to take these risks. If we permit greater parental choice, it should not be in order to realize "multicultural" ideals at odds with our shared civic project, but in order to improve the quality of common education.[38]

Does the combination of expressive rights for students, and the prohibition of religious images and exercises in the schools, signal a positive hostility to religious values? Critics such as Michael McConnell and Stephen Carter echo Justice Stewart's dissenting opinion in the Bible reading case, and argue that the current public school regime puts religion at an "artificial and state-created disadvantage":

> For a compulsory state educational system so structures a child's life that if religious exercises are held to be an impermissible activity in schools, religion is placed at an artificial and state-created disadvantage. Viewed in this light, permission of such exercises for those who want them is necessary if the schools are to be truly neutral in the matter of religion. And a refusal to permit religious exercises thus is seen, not as the realization of state neutrality, but rather as the establishment of a religion of secularism, or at the least, as government support of the beliefs of those who think that religious exercises should be conducted only in private.[39]

There are several problems with Stewart's argument. First, the holy grail of government neutrality "in the matter of religion" will never be found. Neutrality is a mirage. So-called nonsectarian state prayers (such as the prayer composed by the New York State Regents) that were struck down by the Court in 1962 will appear to many to be the state establishment of a wishy-washy form of religious beliefs.[40] The Bible reading without commentary that Stewart here defends will not be acceptable to those who want their children to be instructed in religion by particular religious authorities, as we have seen, so Stewart's own position fails his test of neutrality.

Another problem with Stewart's position, which I develop further in Part Two, is that it is wrong to say that those who would exclude religious professions from the official curriculum of the public school must either be proponents of "the establishment of a religion of secularism" or people who believe that "religious exercises should be conducted only in private." There are many religious people who do not want the public school to meddle in religion, take sides on religious controversies, or compose prayers. Likewise, to exclude officially sponsored religious exercises from public schools does not mean that religious expression is confined to private places. Anyone who doubts that there are many public fora available for the public expression of religiosity has either not spent much time in America, or has not been paying much attention. Of course not all religious people are equally happy with a public educational system that excludes religion from the curriculum. But there is a perfectly good civic case for confining political institutions to civic purposes and materials. Most important, there is no educational regime—just as there is no government policy—that is perfectly neutral in its effects, and we should stop looking for it.

I return to complaints such as these in Part Two, but before leaving this matter it should be noted that the courts have allowed religious institutions, along with other charitable and non-profit institutions, to enjoy tax-exempt status. And more recently, the Court has insisted that if after-hours access to school facilities is made available to student groups generally, schools may not refuse access specifically to student groups that are religious in nature. To do so violates the students' rights to freedom of expression. Indeed, the Court has gone so far as to say that if a portion of student activity fees at a state university is allocated to fund independent student groups—such as publication costs for organization mailings—a state university may not deny student religious organizations equal access to the student fee.[41] It is arguable that the Court here went too far, for the student fee could be recategorized as a public fund allocated to a religious organization for the pursuit of religious purposes. Yet the allocation of student fees in this case is part of "a generally applicable University program to encourage the free exchange of ideas by its students," as Justice O'Connor put it in her concurring opinion. To pick out religiously oriented student organizations—even after the state has explicitly declared that the independent student groups are not the university's agents—would truly place religious messages at a state-created disadvantage.

The basic contours of the Court's jurisprudence seem to me defensible. If those contours have jagged edges, it is because the Court is weighing competing values that are not easily gauged. Here, even more than in other areas of constitutional law, hard cases and difficult matters of judgment abound. Sweeping rules and the embrace of one horn or the other of the dilemma would make for a tidier but less defensible arrangement. While schools lacking a specific religious purpose may indirectly favor certain religious perspectives, they are fairer in a pluralistic society than public schools that directly teach liberal Protestantism. The current system has a justification that does not depend upon the truth of a particular religious view.

Leaving religious questions to one side is the best that our educational establishment can do with respect to religion. Indeed, maintaining an educational establishment that teaches children that important public issues can be deliberated upon without considering religious questions is itself part of the education for liberal democratic citizenship properly understood.

Now, as in the past, many parents object to the fact that their children's schools do not reinforce their particular religious beliefs. Now, as in the past, many such parents abandon the public system. In recent years, fundamentalist parents have founded over 10,000 private schools enrolling over 1 million students. There are now over a million children more being home schooled.[42] Yet part of the reason why some parents reject the common school settlement is because they discount or reject the legitimate civic purposes of common schooling.

An Education without Values?

Do expressive rights for students, and the prohibition of religious images and exercises in the schools, reveal a school system that has no positive moral agenda? The public schools have, some critics say, simply abandoned efforts to teach basic values.

Some polls show that while the vast majority of parents want "moral values" taught in public schools, most teachers resist the idea. At least some teachers worry about "lifting the moral standards of students above those of their parents."[43] Some teachers worry, moreover, that explicit efforts at moral education will always antagonize some parents, and they are probably right. Nevertheless, teachers' loss of a sense of moral purpose is a striking phenomenon because the core purpose of public schooling is to promote civic ideals. The public schools' origins and history may be fraught with moral purposes—sometimes for good, sometimes for ill—but has the normative sap run out of the institution?[44]

The notion that public schools do not teach any moral values is wrong. Today's public schools give less preferential treatment to traditionally privileged cultural groups, and there is more of a desire to treat individuals fairly in spite of differences of religion, race, gender, and ethnicity.[45] We take liberal democratic strictures more seriously than we used to—for example, by excluding a wider range of sectarian exercises from the public schools. No doubt such exclusion upsets many of those who—in the name of "moral values"—would like to see the return of public school prayer, Bible reading, and the Ten Commandments. But although the morality that informs the public schools may be "thinner" and more latitudinarian than it once was, the same could be said of the American family and our society more broadly. Public schools have changed in part because we are exercising our shared political power in a way that is more consistent with mutual respect, religious diversity, and individual liberty. It would be rash to conclude that public schooling is now morally empty. At their best, public schools exemplify a spirit of mutual respect, reciprocity, and mutual curiosity about cultural differences.

Yet although public schools are not morally vacuous, many schools and teachers have retreated to a position of moral subjectivism in the face of moral conflict and disagreement. According to some observers, public schools foster nonjudgmental attitudes and a moral subjectivism according to which each person's values are held to be equally defensible. Consider, for example, the approach to moral education known as "values clarification," which according to a 1975 poll of public school teachers was the most widely approved approach to moral education.[46]

Values clarification may epitomize the nearly substanceless proceduralism for which "liberalism" is so often pilloried.[47] According to its leading textbook, this approach is to be distinguished from "moralizing," which is the notion that adults have superior wisdom due to greater experience, and that they should seek to inculcate that wisdom in youngsters. Moralizing does not work well because children are bombarded with many different messages from adults, and mere moralizing does not help them decide among conflicting values (this is also the problem with moral education based on looking up to role models). Moralizing, moreover, promotes hypocrisy, as it teaches children only to mouth values that they do not really believe in.[48]

Values clarification cuts through the problem of selecting among conflicting values and role models by focusing on the process instead of the content of valuing. The purported aim is not to instill any particular set of values, but to help students clarify and form their own beliefs, weigh the pros and cons of different options, and decide which of their beliefs they are willing to stand up for. Rather than imposing beliefs on students, values clarification encourages them to ask questions like, "Am I really getting what I want out of life?" It can be taught through classroom exercises with names such as "Dialogue with Self," "All about Me," and "Who Are You?"[49]

Values clarification portrays itself as a value-neutral means of moral education, a nonjudgmental matter of process rather than substance.

The best that can be said about it is that it is not as nonjudgmental as it claims to be. Critical thinking about one's own convictions is an important part of moral education. A leading text in the field also emphasizes the importance of nonconformism, pride in one's convictions and a willingness to stand up publicly for them (whatever they may be), sensitivity to others, and foresight.[50] Implicit in this program are important virtues: clarity of purpose, consistency, introspection, sociability, fortitude, and foresight.

But values clarification is also insipid. It encourages children to see their own nascent dispositions as the source of all moral insight. It seems to encourage children not so much to examine critically inherited beliefs and traditions, but to ignore them altogether. It suggests, as Gerald Grant points out, that adults have no greater role in moral education than to help children and young adults clarify their convictions. It treats "every moral conviction as equally worthy," as Amy Gutmann observes, and "encourages children in the false subjectivism that 'I have my opinion and you have yours and who's to say who's right?'"[51] While it is true that children will often get conflicting advice from adults—and indeed from traditions and great figures who serve as role models—receiving this advice calls for reflection and critical judgment, not for the narcissism of thinking that all moral insight comes from looking within and being true to one's own convictions.

Some will no doubt regard the pseudo-nonjudgmental proceduralism of values clarification as the very epitome of a "liberal" approach to moral education. Michael J. Sandel, for example, argues that the crux of liberalism as a public philosophy in the late twentieth century is its insistence on remaining "neutral" in the face of moral and religious controversy: according to this view of liberalism, if people disagree about their moral convictions, the only appropriate course is to bracket our disagreements.[52] Here, as elsewhere, neutrality is a ruse, for particular procedures always embody or advance particular values. It must be allowed, however, that what Sandel and other critics of liberalism such as Stanley Fish mean to criticize is precisely the embarrassment in the face of moral judgment: the failure to identify and take responsibility for the substantive values that inform a liberal public philosophy, and the resort to procedures in the vain hope that doing so provides a way to avoid direct judgments about what constitutes a good life—which some people will not accept.

In his nifty skewering of this nonjudgmental stance, Stanley Fish points to oft-cited lines from a 1967 Supreme Court case: "The classroom is peculiarly the 'marketplace of ideas.' The Nation's future depends upon leaders trained through wide exposure to that robust exchange of ideas which discovers truth 'out of a multitude of tongues, [rather] than through any kind of authoritative selection."[53] I join Sandel, Fish, and others in disparaging the notion that our core moral commitment should be to remain neutral in the face of moral conflicts, to avoid taking sides. No one, in fact, lives this way, and liberals, in particular, have every reason to take a stand when basic liberal values are at stake. We cannot live "without authoritative selection," at least in the sense that we have, provisionally at least and in a self-critical spirit, committed ourselves to certain institutions and certain ways of conducting our public affairs: preeminently through appeals to sovereign public reason.

Where I part company from Sandel and Fish is in rejecting their apparent conviction that liberalism and weak-kneed neutralism are one and the same. I do not believe that liberalism properly understood issues in the sort of nonjudgmentalism that Sandel decries, as I show in Parts Two and Three. Sandel and Fish are right, however, that certain varieties of liberalism give aid and comfort to the sort of moral squeamishness represented by values clarification.[54] And yet any public philosophy can be misunderstood and perverted. Fairminded criticism should try and seek out the best version of what is being attacked.

Reconsidering the Common Schools

Schools that are somewhat detached from the particular values and prejudices of families and neighborhoods, and that seek to include the diversity of society in a setting that insists on mutual respect and seeks to cultivate mutual understanding, may be especially good at teaching a range of liberal virtues: not only tolerance and mutual respect, but also openness to change, self-criticism, moderation, and respect for the norms of public reasonableness.[55] It may be, therefore, that what some parents object to in today's public schools is not the absence of moral values, but the substance of the moral values that are indeed present. Some parents object to a liberal civic education, as we shall see in the next chapter. Now as before, some complain because public schools do what they are supposed to do: intervene between parents and children to teach children civic virtues, to prepare children in various ways to be good citizens of our regime and not only followers of parental beliefs. Public schools continue to educate for character, and many parents (though not always the same ones) continue to object.

It should not be forgotten that a controversial centerpiece of the more inclusive public school system has been racial desegregation. For many decades after the infamous Supreme Court decision of *Plessy v. Ferguson* in 1896, the Court allowed that the guarantee of equal protection would be satisfied if states maintained "separate but equal" public facilities for blacks and whites. The reality was that spending on schools was vastly unequal for the two races.[56]

School desegregation was a priority of the NAACP because it was seen as a key to the entry of blacks into the American mainstream: equal educational opportunities were a crucial part of making black Americans equal members of society. Opponents of school integration, especially in the South, responded to the Supreme Court's landmark desegregation order in *Brown v. Board of Education*, (1954), by reasserting the long tradition of local control of schools. In 1957, President Eisenhower ordered federal troops to Little Rock, Arkansas, to force the integration of all-white Central High. That was the beginning, rather than the end, of a long struggle over racial integration, in which racism and local control of schools were often allies.[57]

Federal antipoverty initiatives also targeted schools for aid. The Elementary and Secondary Education Act of 1965 provided federal monies to help schools that served substantial numbers of the poorest children, who had heretofore barely been reached by the institution of common schooling. The Head Start program was another federal initiative designed to help three- and four-year-olds from deprived backgrounds get ready for school, "so poverty's children will not forever be poverty's captives," as President Johnson put it.[58]

During the 1960s and 1970s, great strides were made toward racial inclusion. Paul Peterson argues that the very effectiveness of the public school monopoly allowed the schools to try to satisfy the new demands, taking their middle-class constituency for granted. Egalitarianism and inclusiveness were always part of the rhetoric of the public schools, but these values came to the fore in the 1960s and 1970s. Of course, in many instances the schools did not embrace inclusiveness but had it thrust upon them. The courts played an important role in forcing desegregation of the schools, as well as providing more equal access for handicapped students.[59]

There are, of course, a number of oft-heard grounds for complaint with respect to public schooling, including bloated bureaucracies, high costs, and declining academic achievement. The fact is that substantial amounts of extra money are being spent on public schools because they have been asked to pursue a number of social goals beyond academic achievement narrowly conceived (including education of the handicapped, nutrition programs, and school busing for racial integration). I return to these complaints in Part Three. One complaint is that public schools no longer provide the kind of moral training that many parents want: the public schools educate for pluralism—that is, they inculcate respect for diversity—but, the charge often goes, little else is taught.[60]

In the face of school integration and the arrival of new generations of immigrants, many middle-class whites fled to the suburbs or to Catholic schools, leaving inner-city schools to poor whites and minorities. New York City, for example, lost 800,000 white residents in the 1950s and gained 750,000 black and Puerto Rican residents. Population shifts such as these often simply overwhelmed public efforts at integration.[61] Urban public schools have lost important parts of their core constituency, and more people seem open to the idea of fundamentally revising the system of common schooling.

I do not mean to suggest that we should resist all school reform measures that entail a fundamental revision of the structure of common schooling. It may be that we have good reasons on balance to introduce school competition and parental choice into the public system. In some places, giving parents the means to choose private schools might help us pursue public purposes. But although we should be open to new and more effective ways of pursuing our aims, we must not abandon or ignore civic purposes that remain vital.

Much of the dissatisfaction is focused on today's large and impersonal urban high schools. Early public schools, as we have seen, were extensions of local communities, and because America was far more homogeneous then, most families and local communities tended to unite in support of these institutions.[62] Today's public high schools, in contrast, embody the variety and choice of the Great Society: they are

designed to provide children with perspectives that transcend particularistic communal norms, but it may be that the scale of these institutions prevents them from themselves becoming communities. Some
liken today's big public high schools to shopping malls: they are environments

> where a do-your-own-thing attitude prevails. High schools take few
> stands on what is educationally or morally important. Yet one thing they
> cannot be neutral about is diversity itself. Pluralism is celebrated as a
> supreme institutional virtue, and tolerating diversity is the moral glue
> that holds schools together. But tolerance further precludes schools' cele-
> brating more focused notions of education or of character. "Commu-
> nity" has come to mean differences peacefully coexisting rather than
> people working together toward some serious end.[63]

These schools represent respect for diversity and individuality, but as
Powell, Farrar, and Cohen describe them, they are too large to cultivate an internal sense of community and shared purpose, and in this
they stand in sharp contrast with religious schools.[64] Part of education should be holding people responsible for their actions and
choices, but a large anonymous educational institution may make
such a goal difficult or impossible. Consider this report of a high
school principal's remarks:

> Adolescence, he suggested, is a time of normal disorganization; it is
> therefore psychologically counterproductive to impose restrictions on
> teenagers. "Freedom is a major learning experience . . . We don't believe
> in restraining kids. We want to give them choices with support, and let
> them make mistakes." . . . It is healthy for teenagers to be exposed to the
> admittedly unhealthy things that sometimes happen in school, such as
> vandalism and snowball fights. 'The school represents these paradoxes
> rather than attempts to control them,' the principal said. During Dr.
> Nelson's celebration of freedom he was informed that his son's locker
> had just been blown up.[65]

Powell, Farrar, and Cohen find that inclusive, pluralistic, choice-
oriented public high schools shun even the idea that academic excellence or effort are important: a premium is placed on getting everyone
through and bolstering the self-esteem of all. No particular notion of
excellence is to be imposed on students. The public schools seem to
stand for the sort of nonjudgmental pluralism represented by the "values clarification" model of moral education.

Gerald Grant tells a similar story in his account of the paradigmatic American high school, which he dubs "Hamilton High." It is, he allows, "a racially, ethnically, and economically integrated public school that also serves a sizable number of disabled youngsters." But it is also a largely demoralized environment: "more democratic" than the pre-1960s high school, "but also more bureaucratic, more adversarial, and officially value neutral."[66] Due process and student freedom have been allowed to replace moral leadership by adults. The ACLU, as Grant reports, composed a manifesto for this environment when it advised, in 1968, that freedom implies the right to make mistakes and that therefore students must sometimes "be permitted to act in ways which are predictably unwise so long as the consequences of their acts are not dangerous to life and property, and do not seriously disrupt the academic process." "Students and their schools should," the ACLU warned, "have the right to live under the principle of 'rule by law' as opposed to 'rule by personality.'"[67] The consequence, according to Grant, is that the moral authority of adults within schools was greatly undermined. Our response should not be to overturn wholesale guarantees against arbitrary treatment forged in the 1960s and thereafter, but Grant rightly insists that unless adults set moral standards and expect students to live up to them, schools cannot be effective educational environments, from either an academic or moral standpoint.

Conclusion

How should we assess today's loss of faith in public schools? Will a reformed school system that places greater emphasis on parental choice and the moral authority of particular communities prove an obstacle to liberal democratic political education? Is the current push for reform a sensible reaction to bureaucratic lethargy and poor performance? Or does it proceed in ignorance of civic educational ends that we have no reason to take for granted?

No doubt, there are reasonable grounds for criticizing important aspects of the system of public schooling as it has evolved. It is hard to believe that most big-city schoolchildren will thrive in educational institutions that are as large and anonymous as many of today's urban public schools. The growth of school bureaucracies may have made it harder to hold principals accountable for educational outcomes. Centralized control and rigid unions dampen innovation and the esprit of schools and teachers. At the same time, it is clear that public schools often get blamed for failing to solve problems that other social institutions—such as the family—thrust upon them.

There is every reason to welcome vigorous discussion of public school reform, especially in the nation's cities. Particular policy controversies should not be allowed to obscure the fundamental civic purposes of the common school. We need to disentangle debates over *means* from debates over basic civic *ends*. How, one wants to know, should we feel about the larger project of common schooling, which after all predates many of the institutional features—the centralization of school districts, the rise of the large urban high school—that are the subjects of so much complaint? By all means let us debate and seek to improve our policy instruments, but let us not abandon the political project of shaping diversity for civic ends. Reform should not be an occasion for ignoring basic civic purposes; it should rather be an opportunity to devise ways of pursuing our civic purposes more effectively.

Reasonable measures to promote civic virtues are to be distinguished from the extremism of those who tried to force Catholic children to read the Protestant Bible, the nativist proponents of "100 percent Americanism," and the Klan. Prejudice against Catholics is also to be distinguished from perhaps reasonable fears that those educated in relatively authoritarian religious doctrines may be more prone than others to reject liberal democratic political norms and institutions. While the animus against Irish Catholics was indeed based partly on race prejudice, there were more substantial and honorable grounds for worrying that the teachings of the Roman Catholic Church before Vatican II were inconsistent with liberalism. Let us close this part of the book by returning to the Catholic question.

CHAPTER 5

Civic Ends: The Dangers of Civic Totalism

American Catholics have been central antagonists in this account of liberalism and the public schools, an account that will have undoubtedly struck many as representing an unremitting sequence of prejudice and oppression. I do not by any means wish to endorse all that was done in the name of Americanism. Our nation has witnessed appalling episodes of anti-Catholic hysteria and violence, powered partly by racialist theories that we can now see rest on crude and absurd stereotypes.

In addition, as we shall see in the concluding sections of this chapter—when we turn to a monumental figure so far ignored here, John Dewey—even the most enlightened and human proponents of public education have not altogether respected the proper limits of civic education. This is a difficult area of public policy in which to strike a proper balance. I want to emphasize the importance of liberalism's transformative project, but begin to develop an account of its limits.

No doubt many American Protestants sought to favor Protestantism in the common schools because they believed it to be the true religion. I certainly do not mean to endorse the nineteenth-century common school program in its entirety. Yet it seems to me well worth recalling what older generations of liberals never forgot—namely, that free self-government is not compatible with every normative orientation, let alone unlimited diversity and difference. Part of the reason for the Catholic rejection of early common schooling was the incompatibility of Catholicism and the republican civic aims of the schools.

Any tolerably complete account of our disposition toward diversity needs to take account of the dependence of our political order on the habits, values, and interests formed in "private" communities, including religious communities. The degree of support that these communities provide for our shared political project is a vital public concern, indeed, there is ample reason to think that a modern mass liberal democracy cannot survive—or at least thrive—without the support of certain patterns and kinds of groups and associations. Modern liberal democracy needs the right sort of civic culture, and many (not all) religious communities are an important part of this culture.[1]

American Catholicism and the Triumph of Transformative Liberalism

The American Catholic Church made important contributions to the Americanization of masses of Catholic immigrants. It provided an intermediate refuge for immigrants and an important source of social assistance.[2] In addition, the church has always been relatively flexible and open to the values of the larger liberal democratic society. The nineteenth-century "trusteeship" movement among American Catholics included calls for congregational authority over parish property and the selection of priests. It reflected the sense of many ordinary American Catholics that something was amiss with the structure of authority within the Catholic Church, a sense that was surely related to their embrace of republican citizenship. The American Catholic Church also accommodated the rise of labor unions more freely than did its European counterparts, which according to John Tracy Ellis probably helped moderate the American labor movement.[3] We should not forget, however, that Rome characterized this Catholic embrace of liberal democratic values as the "heresy of Americanism" because this tendency was especially characteristic of the American Catholic Church.

The fears and suspicions of "Americanizers" were only in part the product of religious prejudice, xenophobia, racism, and an exaggerated sense of political and moral fragility. Recent research supports the notion that institutionalized Catholicism in its traditional form, with its "vertical" patterns of authority, discourages the formation of an associative civic culture supportive of liberal democracy. Robert Putnam, for example, provides evidence showing that in those areas of contemporary Italy in which traditional Catholicism is strong (especially the south), patterns of civic community and political engagement are weak. In northern Italy, the church itself is characterized by a greater degree of the sort of trusteeship that manifested itself in nineteenth-century America—with active lay control and relatively "horizontal" patterns of authority. Only where the Catholic Church itself adopts the sort of leveling of authority that is associated with Protestantism does it appear to promote a social order supportive of active citizenship and healthy liberal democracy.[4]

Consider an even more striking finding. Students of democratization movements around the world have argued that until the mid-1960s (pre–Vatican II), "the greater the proportion of the population that is Protestant, the higher the level of democracy."[5] Having surveyed much of the evidence, Samuel P. Huntington concludes that "[t]he social scientists of the 1950s were right: Catholicism then was an obstacle to democracy. After 1970, however, Catholicism was a force for democracy because of changes within the Catholic Church."[6] A historic transformation was apparently brought about in the 1960s.

After centuries of often quite effective opposition to liberal democracy, the Catholic Church reversed its position and became a positive force for democracy around the world. Those changes within Catholicism were, in important respects, concessions to liberal democratic political values, and were also in part the consequence of the Catholic experience in America. Of the factors that made the Catholic Church more supportive of democratic reform around the world, the influence of the United States and the American bishops was "particularly important," according to George Weigel. Their influence culminated in Vatican II and its Declaration on Religious Freedom, which was "a child of the American experience and experiment," and especially of the American theologian John Courtney Murray. The consequence was nothing less than what Weigel rightly calls the "Catholic human rights revolution, in which the Catholic Church finally insisted on the fundamental right of all human beings to freedom in matters of religious worship and inquiry."[7]

The importance of this story can hardly be overestimated. The suggestion is that the Catholic encounter with America contributed to the eventual liberalization of the Catholic Church itself, making that institution a positive and in many places decisive force for liberalization around the world. In this way the indirect, educative effects of American liberal democracy may have helped alter not only the beliefs of American Catholics, but also the official doctrine of the Roman Catholic Church itself, and thereby the beliefs of Catholics worldwide. After centuries of often quite effective opposition to the basic tenets of liberal democracy, the Catholic Church became a powerful and indeed revolutionary vehicle for the spread of liberalism around the world. The transformation within the Catholic Church was also the product of longstanding internal debates and no doubt a host of other factors.[8] Nevertheless, in some measure this story represents a dramatic triumph of the transformative potential of civic liberalism.

The range of significant normative diversity in America and in the world has been reduced by this transformation in the Catholic Church. For that matter, a world without the Inquisition is a world with less diversity; it is in a sense a less interesting world (in the sense of the old Chinese curse "May you live in interesting times"). Who needs this kind of interest? What we want are healthy forms of diversity, and from a political standpoint that means forms of diversity supportive of basic principles of justice and a liberal democratic civic life.

A liberal democratic polity does not rest on diversity, but on shared political commitments weighty enough to override competing values. The mere celebration of diversity and difference is no substitute for a shared public morality: the abstract ideals of liberal justice lay claims of mutual respect on every group in society, whereas the claims of particularity advanced by pluralists create no necessary claim for tolerance or respect.[9] Assimilation is not to be despised; it is rather to be embraced—if we assimilate in nonoppressive ways and toward justifiable values.

Although racism and narrowmindedness have often characterized anxieties about "Americanization," we should not ignore the partisanship of our regime and the fact that it depends upon the existence of character traits that cannot be taken for granted. Those traits are the consequence of deliberate educational efforts, as well as of authority patterns of civil society that exist in communities and groups below the level of the state. While tolerance and respect for individual rights must be watchwords in a regime that claims to live according to the ideals of the Declaration of Independence, nothing about those ideals bars us from taking reasonable measures to promote citizen virtues, both directly through formal educative measures and indirectly by seeking to shape patterns of associational life in the "private" sphere.

Admittedly, it may be hard to attribute to the American public school system what seems to me to be the salutary influence of liberalism on Roman Catholicism, for many American Catholics formed their own schools and educated their own children. And yet American Catholics have long been relatively liberal by Catholic standards, and certainly have proved themselves to be loyal and patriotic citizens well before Vatican II. Nevertheless, this transformation of American Catholicism did not occur accidentally; public policy played a vital role.

One significant instrument of religious liberalization—a crucial if indirect liberal transformative device—may be precisely the separation of religious and political spheres. Decades ago, Will Herberg went so far as to argue that the "segmentation" of religious and political spheres lies at the very root of the American civil religion. The price of assimilation into the American way of life, he argued, is that religious people must be prepared to regard their religious views as politically irrelevant. All three of the great American religions share this view, Herberg argued (in 1960, a bit prematurely perhaps): all three have cooperated in establishing their own political irrelevance and have thereby promoted the moral supremacy of the belief system of "Americanism," on which the three great religions have become mere variations.[10]

We might almost say that American Catholics (though perhaps not fundamentalists as of yet) have come to accept the American rather than the Catholic position on the separation of church and state. To be American is to have a religion (we have very few village atheists these days), but any religion will do. As President Eisenhower put it: "Our government makes no sense unless it is founded in a deeply felt religious faith—and I don't care what it is."[11] This is an odd view of religion, when one thinks about it.

Consider the *Ladies Home Journal* poll conducted in 1948. In it, Americans were asked to "look within [themselves] and state honestly whether [they] thought [they] really obeyed the law of love under certain special conditions." As Herberg reports,

90 percent said yes and 5 percent said no when the one to be "loved" was a person belonging to a different religion; 80 percent said yes and 12

percent no when it was the case of a member of a different race; 78 percent said yes and 10 percent no when it concerned a business competitor—but only 27 percent said yes and 57 percent no in the case of "a member of a political party that you think is dangerous," while 25 percent said yes and 63 percent said no when it concerned an enemy of the nation.[12]

These findings are incredible for several reasons. First, as Herberg says, "no people on earth ever loved their neighbors as themselves as much as the American people say they do."[13] More to present purposes, Americans apparently feel that

> they *ought* to love their fellow men despite differences of race or creed or business interest; that is what the American Way of Life emphatically prescribes. But the American Way of Life almost explicitly sanctions hating a member of a "dangerous" political party . . . or an enemy of one's country . . . while the Jewish-Christian law of love is formally acknowledged, the truly operative factor is the value system embodied in the American Way of Life.[14]

It has been remarked that, contrary to appearances, the Supreme Court follows the election returns. According to Herberg, the three great religions of America have also followed, if not the election returns, at least the basic imperatives of political liberalism in America. And most importantly, it may be the very segmentation of religion and politics that has helped indirectly to establish the practical supremacy of shared liberal democratic values.[15]

Consider as well the ritual that Catholic judges and candidates for president have had to pass through in their quest for high office. As Sanford Levinson observes, Catholics have effectively "been forced to proclaim the practical meaninglessness" of their religious convictions as a condition of being allowed to serve.[16] Jewish judges such as Frankfurter have often not had to make similar public professions, Levinson argues, but only because their secularism seemed indisputable.

Such rituals are bound to be educative, and they reflect a deeper mindset played out in innumerable public institutions, practices, and less formal expectations and norms. They express our commitment to ensuring that political power will be exercised on the basis of reasons that we can share, for purposes that we can hold and justify in common, notwithstanding our religious differences. One consequence of these public rituals may be to reconfigure many people's religious convictions—especially religious convictions that exist in some tension with liberal democratic values. Here, then, is the "hidden" or "silent" curriculum writ large: an educative agenda inscribed in the value patterns of liberal democratic institutions and practices as a whole.

None of this necessarily calls for regret, apologies, or adjustment, it seems to me. Why should we find this surprising or objectionable? We share a great confidence in our basic constitutional values and practices. We should hardly be surprised, or find cause for regret, in the fact that those communities—religious or otherwise—that set themselves against such valuable and successful institutions will lose adherents. It is to be hoped that in a healthy liberal democracy beliefs in tension with fundamental liberal democratic commitments will gradually be diminished in importance. Transformative liberalism makes use, I would suggest, of many mechanisms, practices, and expectations that shape our commitments and habits very deeply.

If all of this seems deeply illiberal, one thing should be kept in mind. The point of the transformative mechanisms (as they are endorsed from a liberal civic point of view) is *political.* They are deployed in liberal politics, and their effects are welcomed insofar as they secure a system of political liberty and other basic political goods. The political aim is to secure our civil interests, not to promote Protestantism over Catholicism, and even less to promote atheism. From a strictly political standpoint (the perspective of a judge, for example, justifying constitutional arrangements in official terms), the religious dimensions of these changes are generally irrelevant: it is enough to emphasize that there are adequate public reasons for what we seek. The operation of these institutional tendencies and biases is also *gentle* rather than oppressive, influencing people's deeply held beliefs without coercion or force. A range of religious ways continue to thrive within liberal political arrangements, and people remain free to practice whatever religion they choose within the bounds of legality. That the system as a whole tilts in a certain self-supporting direction, and that extrapolitical communities of all sorts tend to adjust to the tilt in their distinctive ways, is perfectly legitimate and politically helpful. No one has a right to a level playing field.

Not everyone agrees that the transformation of extrapolitical normative systems is to be applauded. My worry is that those who argue for greater "fairness" toward religious people in our public life might cripple the subtle and indirect means of turning religious and other systems of private belief in directions that support the regime.[17]

My point here is only to emphasize the importance of transformative ends; I consider later the question of means. The transformative ambitions that underlay the common school movement should not, it seems to me, be regarded as alien to liberalism properly understood. Whether the means of public schooling as we have traditionally known it was ever, or is today, a fair and prudent means for pursuing these ends, is a different and perhaps more difficult question, to which I return later.

We face competing concerns in thinking about public education. The task of building a common political culture is work that must be done, if not by public schools as we know them, then somehow. We should insist that all children are provided with the basic intellectual tools needed to perform the duties of citizenship and to fashion responsible, productive lives for themselves. We have ample reason to go beyond these basic requirements and to promote a wider set of civic virtues, such as cooperativeness and mutual respect. And yet we must honor the limits of liberal political authority. Those limits have not always been adequately noted.

We should also allow that Catholicism has contributed to the health of the American project in important ways. The belief in natural law, for example, is a useful check on the democratic tendency to see the popular will as the final arbiter on all moral questions. The Catholic principle of "subsidiarity" lends support to the traditional American emphasis on the importance of small communities to the moral economy of the Great Society. In these ways and others, the Catholic Church has helped remind Americans that the political good is not the whole of the human good. As an Ohio court put it in 1820: "Government is an organization for particular purposes. It is not almighty, and we are not to look to it for everything."[18] The transcendence of religious aspirations, including Catholic ones, helps prevent people from investing politics with the entirety of their moral energies, and this seems to me quite useful. In these ways and others, Catholicism has contributed to a moralized but morally limited public realm in America. It is precisely this sense of the moral limits of politics that some of liberal democracy's warmest proponents have neglected.

Dewey and the Problem of Civic Totalism

John Dewey's influence over American education was no doubt very great and very diffuse, as excellent recent discussions by Robert Westbrook, Alan Ryan, David Steiner, and David Fott make plain.[19] I will focus on one aspect of his thought: his attitudes toward normative diversity, and especially religious diversity—attitudes that stand in counterpoint to those of Kallen. Dewey seems to me to flirt with a civic totalism that leaves too little to the extrapolitical dimensions of the human experience. Liberalism itself should be devised in such a way as to accommodate some religious and philosophical pluralism. It is not only religion that needs to be reshaped in order to help generate support for our shared civic project.

Dewey was not a fanatic: he opposed the Oregon law that the Court overturned in *Pierce,* saying that it struck "at the root of American toleration."[20] He was, however, a thoroughgoing democrat, and he rightly observed that in a vibrant liberal democratic society, the habits of critical reflection that are fostered in politics will spill over into other areas of life. Contrary to what some argue, this is not necessarily objectionable view.

The problem is that Dewey seems to argue that our public morality should make comprehensive claims to truth, and in this we shall want to decline Dewey's lead.

Dewey set himself firmly against traditional religions—not some religions, but religion as such: any fixed ideas about dogma, God, creed, or organization; any beliefs that "ascribe peculiar religious force to certain literary documents and certain historic personages." Dewey did support what he called a belief in the "religious" in experience, by which he meant "a better, deeper and enduring adjustment in life," a "harmonizing of the various elements of our being" that improve our sense of well-being. The religious is experienced "through allegiance to inclusive ideal ends, which imagination presents to us and to which the human will responds as worthy of controlling our desires and choices."[21]

Dewey saw a deep and irreconcilable opposition between religions and the religious in experience. The religious "can be emancipated only through surrender of the whole notion of special truths" and the admission that there is "but one method for ascertaining fact and truth—that conveyed by the word 'scientific' in its most general and generous sense."[22] There is, he said, "but one sure road of access to truth—the road of patient, cooperative inquiry operating by means of observation, experiment, record and controlled reflection." The gulf between traditional religions and Dewey's religious experience is not a matter of this or that belief, but "centers in the question of the method by which *any and every* item of intellectual belief is to be arrived at and justified."[23] For all dogma and doctrine, we must substitute "supreme loyalty to the method by which truth is attained."[24]

Dewey flatly rejected the notion of any common ground between his philosophy and religion: "The opposition between religious values as I conceive them and religions is not to be bridged. Just because the release of these values is so important, their identification with creeds and cults of religions must be dissolved." He rejected agnosticism as "a shadow cast by the eclipse of the supernatural" and a mere "halfway elimination" of error. He scorned liberal Protestantism, and noted wryly that at least the fundamentalists realize what is at stake.[25] Religion, in Dewey's view, breeds fatalistic passivity; it draws off precisely the moral energies needed for social reform and must be altogether eliminated to make room for the "comprehensive community of beings" dedicated to science and art, intercourse and communication.[26]

Dewey's progressive democratic enthusiasms have a comprehensiveness that puts him at odds with liberalism properly understood. He wanted to dissolve traditional religions in order to transfer religious energies to the common political project of progressive reform and the advancement of science and culture: "Surely to fuse into one the social and the religious motive, to break down the barriers of Pharisaism and self-assertion which isolate religious thought and conduct from the common life of man, to realize the state as one Commonwealth of truth—surely this is a cause worth battling for."[27]

Dewey's aspirations for reform had a comprehensiveness equal to those of the religionists he scorned. Like the millennialists, he too sought to hasten the Kingdom of God on Earth, which for him was industrial democracy:

Democracy thus appears as the means by which the revelation of truth is carried on. It is in democracy, the community of ideas and interest through community of action, that the incarnation of God in man (man, that is to say, as organ of universal truth) becomes a living, present thing, having its ordinary and natural sense. This truth is . . . made a common truth enacted in all departments of action, not in one isolated sphere called religious.[28]

Dewey's Kingdom of God had its prophets: early in his career, he proclaimed that "the next religious prophet who will have a permanent and real influence on men's lives will be the man who succeeds in pointing out the religious meaning of democracy." And it would be hastened by prayer: "prayer is the 'seek and ye shall find,' the inquiry of science."[29]

The high church of this civil religion for Dewey, as for earlier reformers such as Horace Mann, was the public school. In 1908, Dewey called for a moratorium on the teaching of religion in public schools, but only as a temporary measure. There were, he said, "types of religious feeling and thought which are consistent with modern democracy and modern science." The schools "shall keep hands off and shall do as little as possible" with regard to religion, but only until "the non-supernatural view is more completely elaborated in all its implications and is more completely in possession of the machinery of education."[30] There could be no doubt that eventually the schools would preach a comprehensive democratic creed:

[I]t is the part of men to labor persistently and patiently for the clarification and development of the positive creed of life implicit in democracy and in science, and to work for the transformation of all practical instrumentalities of education till they are in harmony with these ideas. Till these ends are further along than we can honestly claim them to be at present, it is better that our schools should do nothing than that they should do wrong things.[31]

The partisans of secularism could count on ultimate victory, Dewey claimed, because the system was already rigged in their favor in important respects. Even if public schools do not preach the secular humanist gospel as such, the very fact that they bring together children of "different nationalities, languages, traditions, and creeds," and assimilate them to what is common and public, constitutes "infinitely significant religious work. They are promoting the social unity out of which in the end genuine religious unity must grow."[32] The crucial thing is to preserve such institutions, to maintain the "integrity of the state as against all divisive ecclesiastical divisions." The "full logic" of such a situation, Dewey strikingly asserted, is "the subordination of churches to the state (falsely termed the *separation* of church and state)" in which "state consciousness" would take the place of religion.[33]

Dewey's great aim, therefore, was to promote a society unified around a progressive democratic religion. For Dewey, unceasing criticism and social adjustment would replace all dogmas, the school would supplant the church, and this-worldly happiness would take the place of any belief in otherworldly rewards. As Robert Westbrook points out, it is hardly surprising that Dewey today appears as a star witness for fundamentalist parents, who claim that the public schools advance a religion of secularism.[34]

It should be emphasized that while dogmatic religions bore the brunt of Dewey's critical ire, his ideal society implied a general critique of associations and groups. Industrialism and modern mass commercial society had destroyed traditional local community life, Dewey asserted, and a new basis needed to be found to make the Great Society a Great Community. The imperative was to get people to understand their new interdependence and to rise above the narrow group-consciousness and parochialism that, in Dewey's view, left the public confused, apathetic, and effectively absent from politics. The popularity of dogmatic religious communities was emblematic of a larger deficiency of public criticism and open communication of information about social problems and potential solutions. Dogmatic religious communities—closed to outsiders and organized around a "private inspiration and outlook" fixed in advance of critical reflection[35]—were only the most dramatic obstacles to the ideal of a society dedicated above all to critical, scientifically based social improvement.

Good citizens would belong to local communities and particular groups, Dewey allowed, but these should interact "flexibly and fully" with others and remain conscious of their dependencies. Groups should be constantly open to new information, communication with others, critical assessments of the group's aims, and so to consequent "reconstruction" or "adjustment."[36] Dewey's ideal groups are not constituted by inward-looking group loyalties, but are merely convenient loci for the better pursuit of cosmopolitan aims. All groups should exhibit a constant and pervasive concern with scientific inquiry and progress because only continuous, connected inquiry yields true public opinion. At his most utopian, Dewey suggested that the daily press should concern itself with explaining the latest social scientific findings—people would take a genuine interest, he believed, if the material were only properly presented.[37]

Such is Dewey's version of the progressive ideal of a national community: a comprehensively unified group in which subgroups participate fully and without reservation in democracy's great pursuits.

There is certainly much that is humane and admirable in Dewey, but his vision of a democracy united by a common faith in the "one sure road to truth" is disturbingly totalistic. This unsettling quality is also apparent in Steven C. Rockefeller's sympathetic account of Dewey: "He understood as few others have that, if men and women in contemporary civilization are to find the wholeness, meaning, and inner peace that are the fruit of a healthy religious life, and if the violent conflict and suffering of twentieth-century history are to be overcome in the social sphere, then religious life and social life must not only be reconstructed, they must also be fully integrated."[38]

One would have thought that the lesson of the twentieth century was precisely the opposite of what Rockefeller suggests: that we should beware the insistent quest for "wholeness," especially when it involves concentrating all of our loyalties in a "fully integrated" vision of religious, social, and political life. The breadth of Dewey's vision and his impatience with those who dissented from his progressive faith, while rarely stated so baldly today, are not altogether absent from contemporary defenses of liberal democracy.

It seems right to insist that scientific findings often have a kind of public, political authority that special claims to authority—including some religious claims—lack. We think it unfair to exercise coercive political power except on the basis of public reasons and evidence that can, in principle, be shared with all who will be subject to political authority. But can we claim as a public matter that science has an exclusive claim to authority in our lives as a whole? Can we justify advancing a comprehensive program such as Dewey's in public schools, even though some of our fellow citizens—who are prepared to accept the authority of public reasons in political institutions—continue to believe in the authority of traditional organized religion? How should we regard those whose faith does not, like Dewey's, find ultimate significance in a this-worldly democratic project?

Dewey was not wrong to insist that liberal democracy has broad ambitions with respect to the transformation of religious communities and other associations. For reasons we have already seen, and others that will be elaborated on—we have good reason to believe that the health of a liberal democratic political order depends on encouraging widespread convergence on patterns of authority, group life, and moral character that are congruent with liberal democratic political norms. And yet we cannot regard religion as simply an adjunct to our political lives.

We need not and should not go as far as Dewey. We do better, I think, to adopt a political stance that is robustly ethical and does not shirk from attending the need to construct and maintain a shared civic space, but that does not lay comprehensive claim to the whole truth of the human condition. We need a liberalism less comprehensive than Dewey's, though one that is robustly civic.

Dewey realized that liberal democratic respect for diversity—as epitomized by the "separation of Church and state"—could not be taken at face value, for he saw quite clearly that democratic practices and convictions would need to find support in the extrapolitical institutions in which so much of education takes place. He was right to see the benefits of congruence among public and private sources of intellectual and moral authority. Nevertheless, we should resist the insistent totalism of Dewey's democratic ideal. We do want to ensure that our civic values find adequate support in religious and other normative communities, but we should also be prepared to live with a certain fragmentation of authority and purpose. National ideals of liberty and equality indeed should be supreme, and the civic ideals that inform the Constitution are certainly very great values: we should not only hope that they will regulate and inform all of our lives; we should plan to make it likely that they will do so. But it goes too far to think that the civic lives of modern states, important as they may be, should seek to encompass the moral life as a whole. What we should want is a civic liberalism that is robust but less than fully comprehensive from a moral standpoint, one that can accept the fact that citizens will invest our shared political project with something less than their entire moral energies.

Indeed, as I have already suggested, it may be one of the great advantages of the religious life as it exists in America that it encourages a salutary division of loyalties. Ronald F. Theimann has put it nicely: "Recognizing the penultimate character of the public realm, believers will not seek their final resting place in this sphere of power and persuasion."[39] The impetus to merge religion and politics can come either from political or religious convictions. So, George Weigel notes, the "politicization of the Gospel" has recently been most clearly represented by liberation theology. This "resacralization of politics" represents a total "politicization of existence" at odds with the transcendence of ultimate religious aims.[40]

Many religious communities help remind us that no democratic procedures are guaranteed to yield just outcomes. Religious communities help keep vivid the notion that there are standards of right and wrong that transcend the outcomes of democratic process. In this respect, the teaching of Catholic natural law supports liberal justice: we must subject democratic outcomes to the higher tests of principles of right and wrong.[41] The Catholic Church and other religious communities have been among the principal forces resisting communist totalitarianism in the decades since World War II. Many religious communities are vital components of liberal democratic civil society.

Diversity Is Not Enough

Public schools intervene in the most private of relationships, for the most sensitive of purposes. They deny parents complete authority over the upbringing of their children, and they may well interfere with the ability of parents and religious communities to teach their particular beliefs to their children. Some condemn the entire enterprise of common schooling and its assumption that the public ought to take a direct hand in childrearing to promote civic virtue. Such complaints should be taken seriously, but we should not embrace the complacency about national unity and civic virtue on which this variety of libertarianism often rests. Too often, libertarians and cultural pluralists simply fail to think seriously about what Amy Gutmann has called "*conscious* social reproduction."[42]

It is easy for us, from the standpoint of the late twentieth century, with liberal constitutionalism triumphant, to condemn as small-minded and prejudicial the anxieties about immigration and diversity that have been discussed here. True enough, prejudice has played an important role, and Americans have often betrayed the abstract and inclusive ideals of the Declaration of Independence. And yet we should not altogether condemn nineteenth-century Americans for dwelling anxiously upon the fragility of free government: they were, after all, custodians of a unique political experiment and had every reason to believe that free government was fragile. They were, as well, not wrong to think that free self-government depends on the existence of character traits that cannot be taken for granted.

A liberal polity does not rest on diversity, but on shared political commitments weighty enough to override competing values. Promoting liberal attitudes and values is not the same as imposing "Anglo-conformism" or WASP hegemony. As Philip Gleason usefully reminds us, the Protestant Americans of British descent who played a leading role in founding this country wrote abstract and universalistic principles into our basic law—principles that, properly understood, do not warrant the political imposition of cultural uniformity beyond what is relevant to our shared civic project. The mere celebration of pluralism (or a "politics of difference") is no substitute for a shared public morality: the abstract ideals of liberal justice lay claims of mutual respect on every group in society, whereas the claims of particularity advanced by pluralists create no necessary claim for tolerance or respect.[43] Assimilation is not to be despised; it is rather to be embraced, if we assimilate in nonoppressive ways and toward justifiable values.

Liberalism properly understood is complex and contains built-in tensions. Our Constitution guarantees not only that our government will refrain from establishing a religion, but also that it will respect the free exercise of religious beliefs. If we do everything we might to promote liberal attitudes and values, there could be very little room left for families and private communities to exercise religious and other freedoms. A government too insistent on promoting the character traits and the shared way of life of a liberal democratic regime—such as the states that passed the laws at issue in *Meyer* and *Pierce*—could undermine liberty itself. What is needed is a capacity for prudent judgment in the face of competing values. Were the survival of free institutions really to depend upon it, and were it efficacious to do so, a law making *public* school attendance mandatory would not be incon-sistent with basic liberal values. But in conditions as we have known them, including in the 1920s, such laws went beyond the bounds of a reasonable solicitude for our shared civic project.

On the other hand, we cannot give carte blanche to everything that claims the cover of religious freedom. Some religious beliefs are at odds with liberalism itself. We should tolerate the intolerant, as long as they do not genuinely threaten the survival of free institutions, but we need not bend over backward to make life easy for them.

Toward a Civic Liberalism

In the chapters that follow, we will for the most part leave histori-cal matters behind. Noble civic energies and narrow-minded anxieties have informed the institution of public schooling. The task of bringing together children from different backgrounds and communities of be-lief, of helping them negotiate their differences and develop friend-ships across these bounds, even if very often badly undertaken, is important political work. If the institution of public schooling requires fundamental reform, as indeed it may, the aim of civic education must be attended to.

In Part Two we consider objections to public schooling from Dewey's most radical opponents, Protestant fundamentalists. Funda-mentalists take Dewey at his word: they too regard public schools as engines of a totalistic worldview that they bitterly oppose. The chal-lenge of Part Two is to articulate and defend a civic version of liberal-ism capable of reaching beyond Deweyite "true believers." I offer there a foundation from which we might both defend the authority of the public school to teach core liberal values and circumscribe the school mission so as to more adequately respect those who dissent from the religious dimensions of Dewey's faith.

PART II

Liberal Civic Education and Religious Fundamentalism

This part carries forward our inquiry into the extent and nature of civic purposes and the value of diversity in a liberal democratic constitutional order such as the United States. My fundamental concern here is not with constitutional law in the narrow sense of the term, but with the broadest questions of political morality and statecraft: What can we do to promote civic ideals in the face of religious complaint? Nevertheless, cases and ongoing controversies in American constitutional law furnish interesting and important contexts in which to explore principled conflicts. Indeed, the two great religion clauses of the American Constitution—the "non establishment" and "free exercise" clauses of the First Amendment (which read, "Congress shall make no law, respecting an establishment of religion, or prohibiting the free exercise thereof")—express two of the principled commitments that liberal regimes should embrace with respect to religion. Each clause also poses important questions about how liberal commitments should be interpreted and applied.

What constitutes an "establishment" of religion? The Supreme Court has held that the sorts of supposedly "nonsectarian" religious exercises that have long been a staple of the common school curriculum—Bible reading and "nonsectarian" prayer—are, in fact, impermissible state establishments. But what about a curriculum that has expunged these and other religious exercises and has no explicit religious content? Might one object that when the public school curriculum lacks any religious content a message is sent that religion is unimportant? Recall Bishop Hughes's question: what else does it take to produce an "infidel," or non-believer, but to require him or her to endure an exclusively secular education? Or as Justice Stewart put it more recently, does not the state, in imposing on large parts of a child's life a curriculum emptied of religious exercises, effectively put religion at an artificial and state-created disadvantage? Should not a state that wishes to be religiously neutral provide for the expression of religious sentiments during the school day?

And what does free exercise require? Having disestablished religion, having taken the government out of the business of promoting or fostering religious sentiments or exercises as such—even ecumenical religious sentiments—the "free exercise" clause suggests that there is additional work to be done to make sure that religion can be practiced freely. Some have suggested that the addition of the free exercise clause requires public officials to go well beyond merely refraining from establishing religion, that they must positively accommodate those whose free exercise is burdened by general laws or policies.[1] The clause seems to suggest that after we have tried to make sure that laws have legitimate public justifications, we should go further to accommodate those whose particular religious practices and beliefs mean that they will suffer some special burden by complying. But how much further should we go? When public efforts to inculcate basic liberal values interfere with the free exercise of religious beliefs, which values should give way? What does this clash tell us about the justifiability and partisanship of our liberal regime?

These questions become especially pointed when we note that powerful religious communities can usually ensure that laws are designed in a way that accommodates their needs. Those groups that resort to the courts to plea for accommodations and exemptions will often be outside of the cultural and religious mainstream. While we must not forget the very real possibility that the interests of religious minorities will be unfairly neglected, we must also remember that such religious communities may often raise objections that go to the core of legitimate civic aims. *Some communities are outside the mainstream because of their resistance to basic civic values.*

As we grapple with the demands of religious nonestablishment and free exercise, we should remember an implicit constitutional principle that is even more basic, and that is sometimes left too far in the back-

ground of these controversies—namely, what we might call the constitutional "self-establishment" provision. We need, that is, to try and
guarantee religious freedom, and to avoid impermissibly establishing
any religion, in a way that keeps in focus the basic political project of
sustaining a shared political order, including the directly and indirectly
educative institutions needed to foster civic virtues. There is no more
basic constitutional task than the project of taking reasonable measures to secure the survival and health of our liberal civic order. In no
small measure, we must maintain political institutions and practices
that work to transform the whole of the moral world in the image of
our most basic political values.

The questions I have raised, and that I address at greater length later,
are not mere academic puzzles, but are causes of bitter and perhaps
increasing controversy. Liberalism emerged under the banner of religious toleration, but one might be forgiven for wondering whether
the liberal settlement will turn out to have been a long but temporary truce. In recent years, resistance to state regulations of Christian
schools has landed parents and ministers in jail, churches have been
padlocked, and states have threatened to terminate parental rights.[2]
Some leading scholars charge liberals with obliviousness in the face of
weighty religious objections to public institutions such as the schools.[3]
One leading scholar professes a "sense of crisis about the current state
of religious liberty" in America.[4] Another calls for a wholesale reex-
amination of the meaning of religious liberty in the name of multiculturalism.[5]

In this part and the next I sketch what seems to me the best way of
carrying forward the liberal political project. I argue that civic liberalism offers the hope of deliverance from both politics as holy war and
politics as the embrace of nonjudgmental, unqualified pluralism. Our
task might be easier, at least as a matter of basic principle, were we to
affirm one of the sweeping approaches to religious diversity examined
earlier: Dewey's comprehensive version of democratic truth, or Kallen's embrace of a deep cultural pluralism. Instead, I try to respect
reasonable forms of religious diversity while caring for a robust but
less than fully comprehensive civic life.

Public school controversies, today as a century and a half ago, help
reveal the principal fault lines between religious communities and the
secular state: the conflicts that occur here go to the heart of the liberal

public settlement. Public schools inevitably (if indirectly) favor certain patterns of religious life (although liberalism does not stand for a particular version of religious truth). Still, one can be more or less fair, and one can allow more or less freedom. The balance between a prudent preservation of order and a magnanimous accommodation of minorities seeking relief can be struck in different ways. My aim here is to explore how this balance should be struck by looking at particular cases. The hard fact is that we cannot make everyone happy. Trying to do so can sell short liberal ideals and practices that are and will remain partisan and controversial.

CHAPTER 6

Multiculturalism and the Religious Right

One of the great constitutional questions of our time is whether and when public officials should accommodate or exempt religious believers who argue that some general public rule or widely applicable policy imposes special burdens on them. The high water mark of judicial accommodationism was the famous Amish education case, *Wisconsin v. Yoder*, in which Amish families sought an exemption for their high-school-aged children from a Wisconsin law requiring school attendance for children up to age sixteen. The Amish did not object to having their children attend public grammar school to learn basic skills such as reading and arithmetic, but they did object to the two years of mandatory high school attendance on the ground that "secondary schooling, by exposing Amish children to worldly influences in terms of attitudes, goals, and values contrary to beliefs, and by substantially interfering with the religious development of the Amish child and his integration into the way of life of the Amish faith community at the crucial adolescent stage of development, contravenes the basic religious tenets and practice of the Amish faith, both as to the parent and the child."[1] Formal high school attendance was objectionable not only because of the specific values of high schools, but also because any formal schooling at this stage outside the Amish community would take children "away from their community, physically and emotionally, during the crucial and formative adolescent period of life."[2]

The state of Wisconsin had refused to grant the Amish request for an exemption from the mandatory education laws, but the Supreme Court held that in doing so the state violated Amish religious rights of the parents and children. Chief Justice Burger, writing for the Court, emphasized that the Amish provided their children with an education that was fully adequate for life in the Amish community. Indeed, he suggested that the Amish were unusually successful at educating their children, as evidenced by their very low crime rates and refusal of welfare benefits. Burger's defense of the Amish drew on conservative values ("It cannot be overemphasized that we are not dealing with a way of life and mode of education by a group claiming to have recently discovered some 'progressive' or more enlightened process for rearing children for modern life") and multicultural ideals: "[T]he Amish communities singularly parallel and reflect many of the virtues of Jefferson's ideal of the 'sturdy yeoman' who would form the basis of what he considered as the ideal of a democratic society. Even their idiosyncratic separateness exemplifies the diversity we profess to admire and encourage." Not surprisingly, Burger also reached back to the Court's landmark decision in *Pierce* for support; "However read, the Court's holding in *Pierce* stands as a charter of the rights of parents to direct the religious upbringing of their children."[3]

The great question raised by *Yoder*, as by *Pierce* half a century before, was whether these cases' central principles—of parental rights and religious diversity—would prove to be the basis for a constitutional and moral revolution. Would the Supreme Court, or the political community more broadly, embrace a new regime in which normative diversity would trump civic purposes? In the quarter century after *Yoder*, the Supreme Court has never again gone so far in insisting that particular religious communities have a basic right to exemptions from generally applicable laws. Indeed, if *Wisconsin v. Yoder* was the high water mark for accommodationism, the low water mark came twenty years later in *Employment Division of Oregon v. Smith*.

The *Smith* case concerned two men who were dismissed from their jobs with a private drug rehabilitation program because they ingested peyote as part of a Native American religious sacrament. They were subsequently deemed ineligible for unemployment compensation on the ground that they had been discharged for work-related "misconduct." The case raised the question, therefore, of whether Oregon had violated the free exercise clause by including "religiously inspired peyote use within the reach of its general criminal prohibition on use of that drug."[4]

A sharply divided Supreme Court denied that the state was required to make an exception to the drug laws for the sacramental use of peyote. The Court went further. In a sweeping opinion by Justice Antonin Scalia, the Court insisted, "We have never held that an individual's religious beliefs excuse him from compliance with an otherwise valid law prohibiting conduct that the State is free to regulate."[5] So long as criminal laws have public justifications and apply to citizens generally—so long, that is, that laws are backed by legitimate public purposes and are not *designed* to impose some special burden on a particular religious group—the Court will *never* require exceptions or accommodations to be made.

The *Smith* decision caused a torrent of academic and political outrage. Scalia did not simply say that in this case the state had available to it very important reasons for not making exceptions to the drug laws (drug laws, he might have said, are extremely important laws, partly designed to send a message to young people that drug use is bad, and the force of these laws would be undermined if exceptions were made for the use of drugs in religious ceremonies). Rather, Scalia sweepingly rejected the general notion that states should have to offer a "compelling interest" before denying the right to an exemption from a generally applicable law on free exercise grounds: "What principle of law or logic can be brought to bear to contradict a believer's assertion that a particular act is 'central' to his personal faith?" Courts, Scalia insisted, should never engage in the project of making exceptions to general laws on the ground that the laws place special, albeit incidental, burdens on particular religious groups without adequate justification. Hearkening back to a long-repudiated opinion by Justice Frankfurter (in *Minersville School District v. Gobitis*, which upheld state laws making public school flag salute exercises mandatory in spite of religious objections by Jehovah's Witnesses), Scalia argued that the task of exception making should be left to the political process.[6]

Politicians as well as academics from both ends of the political spectrum denounced the *Smith* decision. In the House of Representatives, liberal Congressman Stephen J. Solarz found himself in the company of arch conservatives such as William Dannemeyer: "You know, Mr. Chairman, it took Deng Xiaoping, through the massacre in Tiananmen Square, to bring Mr. Dannemeyer and myself together on a China policy. I see it has now taken Mr. Justice Scalia, in his opinion in *Oregon Employment Division v. Smith*, to bring us together on the question of religious freedom."[7]

Officials from the ACLU called *Smith* "the *Dred Scott* of First Amendment law" (thereby likening it to the most infamous Supreme Court decision of all times, *Dred Scott v. Sanford*, in which the Court had ruled that slavery was protected as a matter of constitutional principle).[8]

Congress promptly answered the Court by enacting the Religious Freedom Restoration Act (RFRA), which President Clinton signed into law in November 1993. The bill explicitly sought to reestablish the "compelling state interest" standard for cases involving government actions that have "a substantial external impact on the practice of religion."[9] Any government action burdening religious liberty could be challenged in court as a violation of the free exercise of religious belief, at which point the government would have to show that the action furthers a "compelling state interest" and is the "least restrictive means" available to further that government interest. This is the most stringent test that the Court applies to violations of fundamental liberties.

In signing the bill into law, President Clinton echoed Justice Burger's *Yoder* opinion by invoking both traditional values and multicultural concerns: "Religion helps to give our people the character without which a democracy cannot survive . . . [R]eligion and religious institutions have brought forth faith and discipline, community and responsibility over two centuries." In addition, the president asserted, we are "the most truly multiethnic society on the face of the Earth," and RFRA would help preserve that diversity.[10]

In 1997, the Supreme Court replied to Congress and the president by striking down RFRA as unconstitutional. The Court held that Congress cannot expand constitutional rights like the free exercise of religion without encroaching on the powers of the states, and that Congress has no business telling the Supreme Court how to interpret the Constitution. Once again, the decision was greeted by vigorous dissents from many quarters, and there is every reason to think that the Court's latest pronouncement will not be the last word in this ongoing conflict.

Striking down RFRA was the right thing to do. But neither the

Court nor the Congress seems to me to have responded adequately to this controversy, which raises questions at the very heart of our civic life about the appropriate stance toward normative diversity. On the one hand, the Court majority went too far in suggesting that it should never make accommodations and exceptions to generally applicable laws that impose substantial but indirect burdens on religious believers. On the other hand, RFRA goes too far in insisting that the law must, short of the most exacting forms of justification, accommodate pleas for these religious exemptions and accommodations. The Court and Justice Scalia made the mistake of insisting on an excessive and unnecessary form of judicial inflexibility, thereby provoking an extreme reaction. But Congress and the president, in passing RFRA, introduced too much flexibility into our system—flexibility that would encourage religious objections to generally applicable laws of all sorts, encourage people to constantly regard the law from the point of view of their religious beliefs, and impair the Constitution's transformative function.

The usual analyses of religious accommodation and exception making are plagued by a broader and deeper weakness: the mistake of thinking about these conflicts within the narrow confines of judge-made constitutional law. Neither the courts nor Congress seem disposed to put these and other cases in the larger context we have been examining: the fundamental political project of shaping diversity for civic purposes. That fundamental constitutive project—a basic task of positive constitutionalism—has not been given the attention it deserves. When we give the liberal transformative project due weight, I believe the entire project of accommodations looks different.

Mozert v. Hawkins: The Intolerance of Educating for Tolerance?

Mozert v. Hawkins involved a complaint lodged in 1983 by fundamentalist Christian families against the local school board in Hawkins County, Tennessee. The complaint began when some parents and their children objected to the Holt, Rinehart, and Winston basic reading series (the Holt series) used in the children's public schools in the first to the eighth grades. The parents had a variety of complaints about the readers, not all of which are worthy of being taken seriously. It was alleged that the texts taught, among other things, value relativism, disrespect toward parents, the theory of evolution, humanistic values, and the notion that any belief in the supernatural is adequate to attain salvation.[11] These families also charged that the readers denigrated their religious views, both by their lack of religious "balance" and by the uncommitted, evenhanded nature of the presentations. If their children were to be taught about the religious views of others, the parents insisted, they should learn that the other religious views are false while theirs are true.[12] Vicki Frost, the parent who gave the most extensive testimony explained that "the word of God as found in the Christian Bible 'is the totality of my beliefs,'" and she and other parents insisted that it would be sinful to allow their children to use the readers.[13]

The parents seemed, in part at least, to object not that any particular religious claim was directly advanced by the readings, but that the program taken as a whole exposed the children to a variety of points of view. This very exposure to diversity, they claimed, interfered with the free exercise of their religious beliefs by in effect denigrating the truth of their particular religious views. I want here to focus on this complaint, which was central to the way the courts handled the case. In fact, this complaint is surprisingly revealing and indeed pivotal with respect to our deepest civic purposes.

The *Mozert* complaint recalls Bishop Hughes's objection in 1840, discussed at the end of Chapter 3, to having Catholic children exposed to reading selections describing the peaceful coexistence of New York City's religious communities in respectful terms that, he feared, might make religion seem like a matter of choice. To a remarkable degree, today's fundamentalist complaints resemble the Catholic dissent voiced at the beginning of the common school regime, including Bishop Hughes's insistence that only an impossible "perfect neutrality" would make the common schools acceptable.

The *Mozert* families asked school officials to allow their children to opt out of the reading program, and that program only, while remaining in the public schools. They agreed to cover the missed reading classes at home and have their children take the same statewide reading tests as other students. Some schools at first allowed these students to participate in an alternative reading series. Within a few weeks, however, the county school board had resolved to make the Holt series mandatory for all students, and to suspend children who refused to participate in the reading program.[14] A number of children were indeed suspended, after which some withdrew and went to Christian schools, others resorted to home schooling, some transferred out of the county schools, and a few, too poor or unmotivated to do otherwise, returned to their public schools.[15]

The families were not satisfied with the school board's decision, so they went to federal court, charging that the mandatory nature of the reading program interfered with the free exercise of their religion as protected by the First Amendment. The parents and supporting witnesses testified that permitting their children to read the Holt series violated their duty to protect their children from "all influences of evil that might lead them away from the way of God." These parents claimed that to allow their children to read the Holt series would violate their understanding of biblical commands and cause them to risk eternal damnation.[16] Along the way, the parents gained legal support from various national Christian organizations such as the Concerned Women of America. The school district, on the other hand, received assistance from Norman Lear's People for the American Way.[17]

The litigation was complex and protracted, and we need not follow all of its twists and turns. A lower federal court at first dismissed the case without a trial on the grounds that "mere exposure" to a "broad spectrum of ideas and values"—even ones that children or their parents find offensive—could not amount to a constitutional violation. There simply was no showing, according to the lower court, that any religious belief was presented by the readers or the schools as *true* rather than as a "cultural phenomenon" to be studied.[18]

This initial "summary" judgment was reversed.[19] After eight days of testimony, the federal district court decided that there had been a violation of free exercise: the court determined that the state had presented the parents with the choice of either exposing their children to certain ideas that they find religiously offensive, or giving up the right to a free public education.[20] The state, moreover, had not shown that the uniform use of this reading series was essential to the pursuit of its important interest in promoting literacy and good citizenship. Other reading texts were approved by the state, and some of those were apparently acceptable to the parents.[21] The judge granted the Mozert family their claimed right to opt out of the reading program and to retire to the library or study hall during reading sessions.[22]

This decision was, however, finally reversed by a federal appeals court, which upheld the school board and left the *Mozert* families without their claimed right.[23]

Mozert raises fundamental questions in an apparently moderate posture. The families did not seek to impose their ideas on anyone else through the public school curriculum and did not (apparently) challenge the general legitimacy of secular public schooling. They wanted only to opt out of a particular program while remaining in public schools—how much harm could there be in that? And yet, the *Mozert* objections went to the heart of civic education in a liberal polity: how can tolerance be taught, how can children from different religious and cultural backgrounds come to understand each other and recognize their shared civic identity, without exposing them to the religious diversity that constitutes the nation's history?[24]

The relatively restrained posture of the *Mozert* families—seeking only an exemption from a generally applicable policy—is unlike the "balanced treatment" act that was passed in Louisiana, which required evenhanded treatment of the theories of evolution and creationism in public school curricula. The Supreme Court struck down the Louisiana statute as a thinly veiled attempt to introduce religious views of man's origin into public schooling. That seems right. The logic of opting out, as in *Mozert,* is quite different: public monies and authority are not placed behind the views of religious families, but those children are merely allowed to remain in public schools while being exempted from exposure to ideas that they and their parents find religiously offensive.[25]

Mozert is reminiscent of the Amish education case discussed already, *Wisconsin v. Yoder.* As in *Mozert,* the Amish did not challenge the state's authority to promote basic skills such as reading and math and at least some civic virtues, such as law-abidingness. One thing that made *Yoder* politically easier was the fact that the Amish, unlike fundamentalist and evangelical Protestants, are not an especially large or powerful group. Sects such as the Amish pose no threat to the health of the wider liberal society, not only because of their small numbers, but also because of their lack of involvement in the wider political community.[26] Protestant fundamentalists are different. They are far more numerous and powerful, and they are actively engaged in political activity and are part of both our social and political orders. These elements make *Mozert,* in some respects, a harder and potentially more important case. From the point of view of the children's interests, the cases may not be so different.

Mozert raises two very basic issues. Can respectful exposure to diversity interfere with the free exercise of religious beliefs? And if so, do state officials—operating on the basis of their democratic mandate—have the authority to condition a benefit such as free public schooling on the willingness of parents to have their children exposed to diversity, or does doing so violate fundamental rights or run afoul of some other principled limit on public authority? Should the school board and local officials have accommodated the Mozert parents' complaints? And if public officials had refused, should a Court have stepped in and required an accommodation as a matter of basic constitutional right?

Judge Lively, writing for the appeals court, reasserted the trial court's initial view—namely, that mere exposure to ideas could not constitute a violation of the free exercise of religion. The matter would have been quite different were the state directly to inculcate particular religious ideas, insist that children perform particular acts forbidden by the student's religious convictions, or require affirmations or professions of belief (such as the mandatory flag salute struck down by the Supreme Court in *West Virginia State Board of Education v. Barnette*).[27] Mere exposure to diversity, however, could not constitute a constitutional infringement. Judge Lively approvingly quoted the school superintendent's claim that the reading program was, in effect, neutral with respect to religion: "[P]laintiffs misunderstand the fact that exposure to something does not constitute teaching, indoctrination, opposition or promotion of the things exposed . . . neither the textbooks nor the teachers teach, indoctrinate, oppose or promote any particular value or religion."[28]

Other judges conceded that the reading program interfered with the parents' ability to pass along their religious values. Judge Danny J. Boggs argued that the reading program could be likened to requiring Catholic students to read items on the Catholic Church's official index of prohibited books. Requiring students to study these books is not "mere exposure," he said, but is state-imposed "conduct" at odds with plaintiff's religious beliefs.[29] The *Mozert* families can take advantage of the important benefit of public schooling only if they do things that they view as at odds with salvation—that is, if they read these books or allow their children to read them.[30] Of course, the children are free to go to Christian schools or resort to home schooling, but even the modest tuition charged by the Christian schools to which some plaintiffs had resorted, Boggs noted, was equivalent "to about a doubling of the state and local tax burden of the average resident."[31]

The disposition of this case, Boggs argued, seemed to imply that local school boards had only to avoid directly teaching the truth or falsehood of particular religious views; beyond that they could require any curriculum, no matter how one-sided and objectionable on religious grounds:

> [P]upils may indeed be expelled if they will not read from the King James Bible, so long as it is only used as literature, and not taught as religious truth . . . Jewish students may not assert a burden on their religion if their reading materials overwhelmingly provide a negative view of Jews or factual or historical issues important to Jews, so long as such materials do not assert any propositions as religious truth.[32]

In spite of all these forcefully expressed concessions to the fundamentalist complaints, Boggs nevertheless joined the decision of his fellow judges on the basis of his convictions about judicial restraint.

I believe that we should begin by joining Boggs in conceding that the mandatory reading program interferes with the *Mozert* parents' ability to teach their children their particular religious views. The effects of a reading program that evenhandedly exposes children to religious and moral diversity may not be apparent from the perspective of those whose religious views have adjusted to the fundamental principles of our political order, but they are abundantly clear to people who hold certain religious views. Whether there is a violation of *moral or constitutional rights* here is another question. To address it, we will need to look more closely at just what sort of interference with freedom of religion might be involved here, and what is at stake from a civic standpoint. Let us begin by considering how some commentators have embraced the fundamentalist cause in the name of a "fairminded" extension of multicultural concern to the political right.

Mozert and the Multiculturalist Temptation

In Chapter 1 we examined the illusion that notions as abstract and morally contentless as diversity and difference are adequate for describing a civic life characterized by mutual understanding, peaceful cooperation, and a capacity for common deliberation. The temptation of at least certain versions of multiculturalism is similar: it leads otherwise thoughtful commentators to suppose that it is always right to adopt a posture of accommodation in the face of the claim that some public policy or social practice is biased against a particular culture and imposes special burdens upon it.[33]

Nomi Stolzenberg, writing in the *Harvard Law Review*, has defended the *Mozert* families' charge that teaching "diverse viewpoints in a tolerant and objective mode threatens," as she puts it, "the survival of their culture." Teaching the children of fundamentalist communities about the religious diversity that constitutes so vital a part of this nation's history is thus portrayed by Stolzenberg as a liberal means of assimilation, "that insidious cousin of totalitarianism."[34]

The *Mozert* parents insist that exposure to religious diversity interferes with their ability to teach their particular convictions to their children. They have a point. And yet the most basic forms of liberal civic education would be swept aside on the basis of the uncritical embrace of multicultural respect. The *Mozert* parents' claims seem based on certain liberal sensibilities. Freedom and equality are, after all, central commitments for liberals. People should be free to revise and shape their own deepest convictions and overall patterns of life, and all people merit what Ronald Dworkin has referred to as "equal concern and respect."[35] This freedom and equality is often allied with the notion that people almost always pursue their favored conceptions in groups of like-minded others. On these grounds, an imperative of multicultural concern seems to flow directly from liberalism.[36]

Stephen Bates, who has written an important account of the *Mozert* conflict, approvingly quotes a remark of two British educators: "What makes a particular culture identifiably that culture might include essentially sexist or racist practices and principles . . . Sexism can be, in theory, rooted in beliefs which are among the most strongly held and which are crucial to cultural identity. That is, they can be the very sort of belief which those of us who value a multicultural society think that minorities have the right to preserve."[37] Bates defends the accommodation of the *Mozert* parents because "tolerating everything except intolerance is circular. As Tom Lehrer once put it, 'I know there are people in this world who do not love their fellow men. And I hate people like that.'"[38]

Bates insists that those who refuse to accommodate dissenting families and communities misunderstand the American Constitution and its liberal guarantees: "The First Amendment requires the *state* to treat all faiths as equally valid. But *citizens* aren't obliged to follow suit. On the contrary: The separation of church and state is intended to safeguard each citizen's liberty to believe that his faith is valid and, if he chooses, that all others are heretical."[39] But Bates makes a mistake of his own by taking a narrow view of what it means to sustain a liberal democratic constitutional order. Such a political order makes demands not only on the state but on citizens as well.

While it is true enough that our liberal Constitution protects the freedom to proclaim that the religious doctrines of others are heretical, a more complex dynamic is at work here. A liberal democratic polity cannot endure without citizens willing to support its fundamental institutions and principles and to take part in defining those principles. We are citizens of a liberal democratic society, after all, not subjects of a state. Political power is our shared property and not something that is wielded over us. Liberal citizenship carries with it not only privileges but also obligations, including the obligation to respect the equal rights of fellow citizens, whatever their faiths. These obligations are part of the civic side of liberalism.

Citizens remain free to practice their religion and to condemn alternative belief systems. The lives of liberal citizens are in a sense properly divided: we have a public and a private side, and the public (or political) side is guided by imperatives designed to make our shared life together civilized and respectful. This division of spheres is only part of the story of the relation between liberalism and various systems of normative diversity, including religion. Liberalism does not simply divide our lives, and from certain angles at least, it really only divides our lives in a superficial sense. In a deeper sense, as we have begun to see, liberal institutions and practices shape all of our deepest moral commitments in such a way as to make them supportive of liberalism. That work is both legitimate and at odds with the notion that our basic commitment is to difference, diversity, or versions of multiculturalism designed without keeping civic aims in view.

Stolzenberg, Bates, and others neglect the civic side of liberal democratic politics and leap too quickly for accommodation. Our constitutional order must shape citizens, and not only establish political institutions. Citizens, not courts or legislatures, are the ultimate custodians of our public morality. We have every reason to take seriously the political project of educating future citizens with an eye to their responsibilities as critical interpreters of our shared political traditions—that is, as participants in a democratic project of reason giving and reason demanding.

But how should we go about justifying our common civic project? Can a moral education for citizenship avoid being a religious education? Is a truly public justification for our basic political commitments possible?

CHAPTER 7

Diversity and the Problem
of Justification

How can we justify basic political principles in a society in which people disagree about their religious convictions and philosophical ideals? *Mozert* provides an interesting test case for the problem of moral justification in conditions of deep diversity.

One straightforward approach to this problem is to begin by defining an objective human good, such as that offered by Plato in *The Republic*. Social justice consists of discerning the character and aptitudes of each individual, and assigning them to social roles based on their innate potential to realize particular aspects of the human good. The just city takes its bearings from an authoritative account of the human good as a whole. Plato was far from alone in wanting to justify political morality based on a "comprehensive" account of the truth as a whole (to use John Rawls's terminology).[1] John Dewey argued that the scientific method is the "one sure path" to truth and, as we have seen, Vicki Frost claimed that the whole truth could be found in the Bible.[2]

The most straightforward way of justifying the Holt reading program debated in *Mozert* would be on the basis of a broad and individualistic ideal of life, one centered on the value of individual moral autonomy and the importance of critically reflecting on all of one's inherited beliefs—political, religious, and otherwise.

The problem with comprehensive approaches to political morality is that people disagree about their views of truth as a whole: about man's highest good, for example, or about the nature of religious truth. The modern world is characterized by a diversity of religious and philosophical views; a diversity deep enough to convince many that people of different faiths cannot live together in the same political society.[3]

Resorting to a comprehensive philosophical ideal such as moral autonomy also seems to claim too much: Do we really want to premise political authority on the view that critical thinking is the way to attain religious truth? Should we base political morality on so broad a claim, given that the question of how best to pursue religious truth is, as Rawls emphasizes, a matter about which even reasonable people have long disagreed? The last thing we should want to do is to turn the conflict over the reading program in *Mozert* into a broad and implacable clash of comprehensive worldviews.

We do not have public, mutually accessible standards for adjudicating claims about the truth as a whole. As Theodore Sedgwick said in defending the purely *civil* character of the common school curriculum, injecting disputes over theological dogma into politics has been the source of centuries of bloody conflict. Comprehensive moral ideals— including apparently liberal ones such as critical moral autonomy— claim more than we should want to claim on behalf of our political order.

It may be that political orders are never really supported by reasons or adequate public justifications. Our only real alternative may be the one suggested by Thomas Hobbes. Irresolvable moral and religious disagreement is a fact of life, a Hobbesian would say. Political decisions are made, hopefully according to procedures that people have agreed to, but having been resolved one way or the other we simply cannot say that the resolution was just or unjust based on some reasoned standard. The Hobbesian judge might even concede, with Judge Boggs, that the burden being imposed on the *Mozert* families is similar to that of Catholic children being required to read books on the Catholic Church's index of prohibited books. A Hobbesian judge, however, would concur with Judge Boggs that there is no remedy, apart from an appeal to the sovereign people.[4] The law is the only public morality that we have.

The Hobbesian dispensation may be the best that we can do. If we follow Hobbes, however, we give up a lot. Hobbes's skepticism eliminates the possibility of shared moral limits on political authority. It is simply absurd, according to Hobbes, to say that the law is unjust. Convictions such as these are radically incompatible with the Declaration of Independence and with much of what is noblest in the American political tradition.

The Hobbesian dispensation cannot be easily dismissed, and it remains influential: it underlies Justice Scalia's opinion in the *Smith* case, as we shall see. Yet despite Hobbes's enduring appeal, most Americans believe that we can share a public morality that includes the principles of liberty and equality. The challenge is to try to do better than Hobbes while admitting the problem of religious and philosophical diversity.

There is a third possibility for responding to the problem of public justification amidst diversity. It owes something to the social contract view of John Locke and it resonates in the opinion by Judge Lively, who suggests the possibility of a public morality focused on shared civil interests.[5]

This alternative would put aside the many religious and philosophical questions about which people have long differed and instead attempt to justify the most basic matters of justice on grounds widely acceptable to reasonable people—and not only to those who share our particular view of the whole truth. Judge Lively took this alternative route. He defended the authority of public schools to teach values "essential to a democratic society," including toleration; they may "acquaint students with a multitude of ideas and concepts" so long as they avoid direct "religious or anti-religious messages." Lively also drew an important distinction. Public schools, he said, may teach "civil tolerance," which is the notion that "in a pluralistic society we must 'live and let live.'"[6] But schools may not teach "religious toleration," which claims that "all religions are merely different roads to God."[7] "No instrument of government" could legitimately "require such a belief or affirmation." Public schools may, in effect, teach that all religions are the same in the eyes of the state, but not that they are all the same in the eyes of God.[8]

If the schools stick to legitimate civil concerns and avoid advancing specifically *religious* teachings—even those that support our civic project—there is no principled requirement for them to go further and fashion a curriculum equally acceptable to every sect. By construing the public doctrine of toleration as strictly civil, Lively was able to accept *Mozert* parent Vicki Frost's insistence that "We cannot . . . accept other religious views on an equal basis with ours."[9]

Public Reasonableness and Liberal Citizenship

There is a striking similarity here with an approach to the problem of justifying liberal principles called "public reason." John Rawls is the greatest exponent of this approach, which he calls, when combined with substantive liberal principles, "political liberalism." Amy Gutmann and Dennis Thompson have developed a not dissimilar view, which they advance as central to democratic deliberation.[10] I do not here want to defend the details of Rawls's version, though I will draw on it freely. I will try to display the promise of a liberalism that has a central place for the aspiration to public reasonableness. The view I want to defend is, I believe, consistent with what Rawls advocates, but it goes beyond his concern with basic constitutional principles. I will use the label "civic liberalism" as a way of emphasizing the importance of the wider civic life of liberal democracy in practice, as well as liberalism's educative ambitions. Civic liberalism includes an account of the political institutions and social structures that help promote a publicly reasonable liberal community.

The idea of public reasonableness is an attempt to surmount the hurdles I have mentioned: disagreement about attempts to capture the entire religious or philosophical truth, the related difficulty of discerning publicly justifiable philosophical or religious foundations for shared political ideas, and resistance to accepting the Hobbesian invitation to abandon our public moral aspirations in favor of skepticism, will, and power. Rawls has discerned more clearly than anyone else that we have available to us public ideals and principles that have emerged in and around liberal democratic institutions, and which—when suitably elaborated are themselves adequate to justify a public morality without any further philosophical grounding. A public morality—substantive principles and processes of public justification—can be understood as self-supporting.[11]

Rawls's political liberalism starts with the conviction that reasonable people disagree deeply and permanently about their religious beliefs and philosophical ideals of life. The liberalism of public reason bids us to acknowledge that, given the difficult matters of judgment involved, people may reasonably disagree about the justifiability of even purportedly liberal ideals of life as a whole, such as Kantian autonomy or Millian individuality. That the good life is characterized by a pervasive commitment to autonomy is properly regarded as one more sectarian view among others, one no more worthy of commanding public authority than other philosophical and religious ideals that reasonable people might reject. Political liberalism extends the principle of toleration, as Rawls puts it, from religion to contestable philosophical ideals of life.[12]

Liberalism understood in this way focuses our attention on shared political values without requiring or expecting agreement on ultimate ends or a comprehensive set of philosophical values. The basic motive behind this liberalism is the desire to respect reasonable people. In a free society, many of our fellow citizens hold fundamental moral and religious beliefs that we believe to be false, but that we can also allow are within the bounds of the reasonable for political purposes.[13] A publicly reasonable liberalism asks us not to renounce what we believe to be true, but to acknowledge the difficulty of publicly establishing any single account of truth for the whole of life.[14] When it comes to laying the basis for common political institutions, political liberalism invites us to search for grounds accessible to our reasonable fellow citizens: appealing to reasons and arguments arising out of common experience and "to generally shared ways of reasoning and plain facts accessible to all." There are upper bounds on how complex arguments can be, and we should avoid the appeal to special metaphysical, philosophical, or religious doctrines. As Rawls put it in *A Theory of Justice*, the "principles of evidence are adopted for the aims of justice; they are not intended to apply to all questions of meaning and truth. How far they are valid in philosophy and science is a separate matter."[15] To philosophy and science, we could add religious inquiry. Liberal public reason invites us, therefore, to join with others who reject some of our (possibly true) beliefs for the sake of laying the groundwork for common political institutions. In accepting this invitation, we are not moved by the power of those with whom we join, but by respect for their reasonableness. We do not seek to respect pluralism or diversity as such, but reasonable pluralism.[16] Citizens who disagree about their highest ideals and their conceptions of the whole truth (including their visions of "ultimate reality," discussed in Part One) can nevertheless agree on public aims such as securing the equal enjoyment of a broad array of freedoms, establishing democratic institutions, and providing a basic social safety net.

Convictions such as these are far from peculiar to Rawls. Ronald Dworkin has argued that liberals should seek principles that we and our successors "will find easy to understand and publicize and observe; principles otherwise appealing are to be rejected or adjusted because they are too complex or are otherwise impractical in this sense."[17] Citizens, assert Gutmann and Thompson, must reason "beyond their narrow self-interest" and consider "what can be justified to people who reasonably disagree with them."[18]

The commitment to public reasonableness is characterized by a commitment to two basic virtues. First, good citizens should seek to discern and abide by *fair terms of cooperation*. Reasonable people are, explains Rawls, "ready to propose principles and standards as fair terms of cooperation and to abide by them willingly, given the assurance that others will likewise do so." At the core of this aspect of public reasonableness is, as Gutmann and Thompson stress, the virtue of reciprocity.[19]

The second cardinal virtue of public reasonableness is what Rawls calls a willingness to acknowledge the fact of reasonable pluralism: a willingness to allow that reasonable people who are worthy of respect will nevertheless differ profoundly over their highest conceptions of the human good and their views of religious truth (or, in Rawls's rather stylized way, that reasonable people "recognize the burdens of judgment"). His idea is simply that with respect to many longstanding questions of human existence, and many though not all basic philosophical and religious matters, there is room for reasonable disagreement. By "burdens of judgment," Rawls means to indicate that there are commonsense explanations for why reasonable people sometimes disagree: the evidence bearing on some problems is often "conflicting and complex, and thus hard to assess and evaluate." Even where we agree that certain considerations are relevant, we may weigh them differently. Concepts and principles are often vague and difficult to apply. The way we assess evidence and weigh moral and political values is to some degree shaped by "our total experience, our whole course of life up to now." Finally, we often have to make intrinsically hard decisions, where we are forced to choose among "cherished values" that cannot all be fully realized.[20] While "burdens of judgment" sounds somewhat exotic, it is hard to dispute Rawls's observations about why reasonable people disagree about many things.

Gutmann and Thompson's account is similar in spirit to the Rawlsian view and fully compatible with liberal public reason as I defend it. When we rely on empirical evidence, explain Gutmann and

Thompson, we should honor "relatively reliable methods of inquiry" and eschew implausible assertions. We should do this so that public discussions can, insofar as possible, be carried on in terms that are mutually accessible. In addition, it is illegitimate to appeal to "*any* authority whose conclusions are impervious, in principle as well as practice, to the standards of logical consistency or to reliable methods of inquiry that themselves should be mutually acceptable." The point is not to exclude appeals to religious authority per se, but to exclude appeals to *any* authority impervious to critical assessment from a variety of reasonable points of view. For public power is held in common by us all, and we should exercise it together based on reasons and arguments that we can share in spite of our differences. The authority that remains is the authority of reasons that we can share in public as fellow citizens.[21]

Some religious people may reply that their religious reasons are readily accessible to anyone who leads a good life. Vicki Frost might say that anyone who leads a good life and reads the Bible with a pure heart will understand the moral and religious truth as a whole. But Gutmann and Thompson rightly insist that this is not a reasonable demand to make, for "any claim fails to respect reciprocity if it imposes a requirement on other citizens to adopt one's sectarian way of life as a condition of gaining access to the moral understanding that is essential to judging the validity of one's moral claims." The point of public reasonableness is, after all, to accept the fact of reasonable pluralism, which means trying to discern principles that can be assessed and accepted by individuals who are committed to a wide range of different ways of life.[22] In this way, citizens honor a duty of civility to one another.

The liberalism of public reason does not, it should be emphasized, "silence" religious people or limit First Amendment rights to free speech. There may be a variety of ways, indeed, in which religious speech can *support* political liberalism by clarifying the depth of one's commitment to liberal principles and the political authority of public reasons.[23] The crux of the matter is not speech at all, but the legitimate grounds of coercion. When deciding how we are going to direct coercive political powers on matters over which citizens have serious moral disagreements, we should seek and articulate adequate public reasons that we can share with our reasonable fellow citizens. If we recognize additional religious reasons and offer these to coreligionists, that is surely permissible. Acknowledging the authority of public reasons is one mark of a virtuous citizen. People are, however, within their rights not to be virtuous, here as elsewhere.

The fact is that Americans do enjoy widespread (though not perfect) consensus on the sorts of basic guarantees that constitute the core of a political morality. These civil interests and political principles include a shared belief in the legitimacy of democracy constrained by respect for basic liberties, due process and the rule of law, and at least a basic safety net. Here, then, is the response to Hobbes: at the foundational level of philosophical argumentation, and when it comes to defining the highest human good, citizens may indeed disagree radically. There is nevertheless a reasonable consensus on certain shared matters of urgent political concern, a consensus that is freestanding in the sense that we do not need to agree on any one comprehensive religious or philosophical grounding. We also disagree about many matters of moral principle, such as abortion. We are saved from Hobbesianism, however, by an important range of substantive agreement, as well as by the fact that we are prepared to honor certain deliberative procedures and principles where we disagree.

The emphasis on public reasonableness and the centrality of public justification to the liberalism I want to defend helps make sense of why and how we can continue to see the idea of a "social contract" as central to liberalism. The idea is not that political legitimacy is based on an actual social contract, in the sense that people are obliged to obey a particular set of laws and institutions because they have actually consented—whether explicitly or tacitly—to be bound by that system of law. As Rawls acutely observes,

> The government's authority cannot. . . be freely accepted in the sense that the bonds of society and culture, of history and social place of origin, begin so early to shape our life and are normally so strong that the right of emigration (suitably qualified) does not suffice to make accepting its authority free, politically speaking, in the way that liberty of conscience suffices to make accepting ecclesiastical authority free, politically speaking. Nevertheless, we may over the course of life come freely to accept, as the outcome of reflective thought and reasoned judgment,

the ideals, principles, and standards that specify our basic rights and liberties, and effectively guide and moderate the political power to which we are subject. This is the outer limit of our freedom.[24]

The point of a contractualist approach to public justification is not to provide opportunities for actual consent, which, in any case, would be a rather hollow option for the reasons Rawls indicates ("America— consent to it or leave it!"). The point rather is to suggest that political legitimacy—and our own peace of mind, morally speaking—depends on our ability to discern basic principles of political morality that we believe on reflection could be justified to all reasonable people. The aim is a public moral order: a constitution informed by moral principles and a rationale that all reasonable people should be able to accept and affirm publicly before one another. Bringing about such a political order is a basic aim of liberalism as I understand it, even though the profile of this aim is often lower than the defense of basic liberties. The pursuit of public reasonableness is an end in itself, a way of thinking about the kind of political community that we should try for. This pursuit will itself shape the sorts of institutions and policies that we can accept and affirm in politics.

As citizens of a democratic polity, we are each partly responsible for the way that political power gets used. And when push comes to shove, political power involves all of the coercion and force that modern states can muster. The basic practical question that every citizen faces is what, if anything, ultimately justifies the use of political power? What guiding principles and limits might suffice to make a system of political power morally acceptable, or even worthy of our support?

Back to *Mozert*

Where does all this get us with respect to *Mozert?* Judge Lively's notion of civil toleration bids us, in effect, to extend political liberalism to the defense of public schooling. We focus on shared public principles and leave the religious dimensions of the question aside. The public school curriculum and teachers would in this way avoid directly confronting or denying the *Mozert* families' contention that the Bible's authority should be accepted uncritically. "When asked to comment on a reading assignment" Lively said, "a student would be free to give the Biblical interpretation of the material or to interpret it from a different value base." There should be no "compulsion to affirm or deny a religious belief" or, presumably, any other comprehensive moral view.[25] By simply leaving aside the religious question as such, Lively rightly leaves the school door open to reasonable fundamentalists—that is, to those willing to acknowledge *for civic purposes* the authority of public reasonableness.

Civic liberals must walk a tightrope, emphasizing the great weight of shared political aims but, so far as possible, avoiding taking sides on the wider religious dimensions of political matters and allowing that reasonable citizens may disagree about their religious and some of their basic philosophical views. Children should not be chastized for saying in class that God created man, though they might also be asked to describe scientific theories and evidence on the issue of human origins. Political liberals might well applaud the concurring opinion of Judge Chambliss, in the Scopes "Monkey Trial," who tried to save the Tennessee law at issue by construing it not as a ban on the teaching of evolution, but as a ban on the teaching of any theory that positively denies a role for God in the creation of the universe.[26] This Solomonic move could be seen as a political liberal attempt to keep public authority from directly endorsing or disparaging any particular religious view: it defends the place in public schools of widely accepted scientific evidence while not taking a position on the question of how—or whether—God fits into the whole business.[27] Chambliss would have allowed the teaching of theories of evolution on this condition.

It is tempting to say that the only real difference between civic and comprehensive liberalisms is that proponents of the latter are simply more candid in admitting that liberal institutions are based on an ideal of life as a whole, and that "civil" toleration inevitably promotes "religious" toleration. Candor is not, however, the crux of the matter: political liberalism stands for a measure of restraint that would be unnatural for one committed to a vision of the good life as a whole informed by autonomy or individuality. Acknowledging the authority and limits of public reasonableness provides principled reasons for avoiding taking a stand, as a political matter, on the question of religious truth. Civic liberals will reject in principle a public program that teaches a *religious* doctrine of toleration or one that advances John Dewey's claim that science is the "one sure road of access to truth."[28] We should focus on shared civic virtues and values, and keep the liberal door open to those who reject the wider philosophical ideals of Kant, Mill, or Dewey.

Public schools once preached a gospel of liberal Protestantism, but civic liberalism supports the current constitutional prohibitions on such exercises because they can only be justified as attempts to promote particular religious beliefs. Civic liberals will insist that public schools refrain from promoting a religion of "liberal" Protestantism, secular humanism, or atheism. Public schools should avoid denying that faith and revelation may be keys to understanding the ultimate significance of human life, and this should count for something with fundamentalists and others. Nevertheless, civic liberalism does not guarantee that the effects and broad consequences of the educational regime it supports will be equally amenable to all, for that would be inconsistent with the very aspiration to bring about a political community dedicated to equal freedom and public reasonableness.

In practice these distinctions can be difficult to apply. It may well be that a public school program that teaches civil tolerance will have the effect of indirectly promoting religious tolerance. Whether particular curricular materials teach religious or civil doctrines of tolerance will often be a matter of judgment and of the spirit in which they are used. One reading selection to which the *Mozert* parents objected was similar to the story that offended Bishop Hughes in the 1840 New York City debates. The modern selection is the well-known poem "The Blind Men and the Elephant," in which six blind men each feel a portion of an elephant and, on the basis of their limited experience, arrive at laughably various judgments about what the whole must be like. The poem concludes:

> And so these men of Indostan
> Disputed loud and long,
> Each in his own opinion
> Exceeding stiff and strong,
> Though each was partly in the right
> And all were in the wrong!
>
> Moral
>
> So oft in theologic wars,
> The disputants, I ween,
> Rail on in utter ignorance
> Of what each other mean,

And prate about an Elephant
Not one of them has seen![29]

This poem could be taught as an allegory about the burdens of judgment and the difficulty of arriving at publicly justifiable religious truths. The problem is that, like the story to which Bishop Hughes objected, it could be understood to assert as a religious matter that anyone who thinks they have religious truth is really in ignorance. The message would then be a religiously based lesson in skepticism, which is in principle out of bounds. The reader was saved, according to the district court judge in *Mozert*, by the fact that the poem is simply presented "for what it is worth": it is not advanced as a true account of religious controversies.[30] Still, one can understand how even those fundamentalist parents disposed to accept a political liberal settlement might well look with suspicion on the poem and the readers as a whole. One wonders how many depictions of fundamentalism the readers presented "for whatever they are worth."

The *Mozert* families did not simply object, in any case, to any particular readings so much as to what they understood to be the overall message of the readers as a whole. But the court decided that where explicitly religious ideas were expressed, as in the poem, the effect was only to present a possible point of view, not to teach that view as religious truth. Where a positive view on toleration was taught in the readers, it was one of civil rather than religious toleration.[31] This kind of inquiry is obviously an inexact science, and the court here seems to have performed its task reasonably well. It is, however, important to keep legitimate religious sensitivities in mind. A public school regime committed to liberal principles should regard religious questions as beyond the bounds of its authority. All we have to say about religious truth, as a public matter, is that it is possible for many (hopefully all) religious traditions to accommodate and support our liberal democratic civic life in their own way.

Public Reason and Civic Liberalism

Public reasonableness is an account of legitimate reasons or justifications: it tells us that it is illegitimate to fashion basic principles of justice on the basis of religious reasons—or reasons whose force requires that one accept a particular religious or philosophical framework—for these are matters about which reasonable people disagree. These guidelines will help us to address some complaints about schools and other public institutions.

It is worth observing that, as we saw in Part One, some people will believe that there are *civil reasons* for supporting religious exercises, such as Bible reading, in public institutions. Many nineteenth-century school reformers, including some of the most "liberal," seemed sincerely to believe that Bible reading was a crucial prop for popular morality and thereby for good government. One who believes that popular civic morality depends upon the perpetuation of Bible reading or prayer sponsored by public schools obviously has a civic reason for religious exercises in schools.

The commitment to public reasonableness may help resolve some controversies and shape how many others are approached, but by itself it will not get us very far.[32] Some thinkers have advanced civil purposes and public reasons for deeply illiberal practices. The concern with peace led Hobbes to insist on a public rule of religious uniformity.[33] Locke argued that atheists could not be trusted to keep their oaths. Rousseau denied toleration to religions that taught that those outside the true church would be damned, for he saw such religious narrow-mindedness as inconsistent with the shared bonds of citizenship. He also advocated the inculcation of a civil religion: "a purely civil profession of faith . . . not exactly . . . dogmas of religion, but . . . sentiments of sociability, without which it is impossible to be a good citizen or a faithful subject." Rousseau's aims are purely civil, and so if the sovereign banishes anyone for rejecting the civil religion, it will be "not for being impious but for being unsociable."[34] Emphasizing the authority of public reasons does not necessarily yield a *liberal* political theory.

At a more basic level, however, the whole thrust of a political belief in the need for religious uniformity cuts against the core aspiration of political or civic liberalism. That aspiration is, after all, for a political community of principle in which citizens share not only a common effective authority, but also public moral principles and a mutually acceptable and convincing rationale for those principles. Civic liberalism stands at base for the idea that such a community of political principles is compatible with religious and philosophical diversity. If it turns out that popular political morality needs the support of state-sponsored religion, then civic liberalism's aspirations will have to be radically rethought. If the public, mutually acceptable arguments for liberal democratic principles are really not very weighty for most people when compared with the deeper but nonpublic religious and philosophical reasons that they also have, then the society in question does not really share a public morality.

In a sense, civic liberal aspirations can be fully realized only when people no longer believe that public morals depend upon politically sponsored religious expressions. Political liberals can and should eschew the support of public school prayers and Bible reading.

Is Liberalism the Indirect Establishment of Religion?

As an account of how to think about justifying our basic political principles, liberal public reasonableness shows us how to avoid certain vexing religious and philosophical disputes about which reasonable people have long differed. Nothing in my defense of liberalism should be taken to suggest, however, that it is uncontroversial or equally accommodating of all religious beliefs. The goods promoted by liberalism's civic agenda (tolerance for reasonable forms of diversity and respect for a wide array of freedoms) will not be valued equally by people of different faiths. More to the point at hand, promoting (in public schools and elsewhere) core liberal virtues—such as the importance of a critical attitude toward contending political claims—will probably have the effect of encouraging critical thinking in general. Liberal civic virtues and attitudes will spill over into other spheres of life. Liberal institutions, policies, attitudes, and virtues are far from neutral with respect to the forms of life that are likely to prosper and gain adherents in a liberal society, as Rawls puts it. Even a suitably circumscribed liberalism will still have the effect of promoting certain broad patterns of life.[35]

Liberalism properly understood is neutral with respect to ideals of life as a whole only in the very limited sense of not relying on the justifiability of any particular comprehensive ideal or view of the whole truth.[36] Political liberal principles are neutral only in being justified *independently* of religious and other comprehensive claims. As a public matter, it is hoped, people need not invoke their religious or deeper philosophical ideals, because there are adequate reasons available that can be shared by reasonable people who disagree about their ultimate ideals.

There are much more demanding forms of neutrality or fairness than that offered by political liberalism. One might argue that public policies should have *neutral effects* on all the religions of society. At the very outset of the common school movement, Bishop Hughes insisted that only a regime of "perfect neutrality of influence" would be acceptable to Catholics. He was also entirely correct to describe such a regime as impossible.[37]

Whether or not such a regime would be possible to realize, establishing neutrality of effects as a public standard, and then trying to realize this standard, would greatly encourage social division. Citizens would, under such a scheme, continually invoke their deepest moral and religious commitments in the public realm as a yardstick for measuring the acceptability of basic public principles. Encouraging people to invoke their ultimate commitments—religious, philosophical, and so forth—in politics might reflect a desire to reaffirm, respect, and preserve their group-based identities and convictions, or the commitments that "constitute" people's identities at a basic level and that some communitarians are so solicitous of.[38] In some places—quite apart from what theorists might like—people will simply refuse to put aside religious and ethnic group-based sensitivities.

The Indian Constitution contains a guarantee of state "equidistance" from all religions, which seems to stand for a guarantee of neutrality of effect. Such a guarantee might be based on the presupposition that people cannot or should not put aside their religious commitments for the sake of public reflection on shared secular aims and interests. The requirement of equidistance seems to reflect the desire to respect and preserve group-based identities and convictions—or perhaps it simply acknowledges that, in India, to ignore religious and ethnic group-based sensitivities is to court violent conflict.[39]

Political liberalism asks people to proceed differently: it advances an ideal of citizenship according to which we formulate and defend basic principles of justice by relying on public reasons that we can share while disagreeing about our ultimate commitments. It aspires to a polity in which we can share a morally principled citizenship while disagreeing at a deep level about our ultimate religious and philosophical beliefs.

Of course, the very aspiration to think about politics from a perspective that is independent of religious views and other controversial comprehensive conceptions is not-neutral: its appeal will vary greatly among people of different faiths. Totalistic faiths (such as Vicki Frost's belief in the Christian Bible as the "whole truth," or the corresponding belief that the Catholic Church possesses the entire and "unvarnished" truth) will be especially resistant to thinking about politics (or anything else) from a public point of view not dependent upon their particular religious views.

It does no good to deny that some will find the strictures of liberal public reason burdensome. To refrain from relying solely upon religious beliefs when exercising public power will come naturally to many who have grown up within a pluralistic liberal order, but that should not be allowed to obscure the significance of this form of self-restraint. Niklas Luhmann, for example, seems to want to downplay liberalism's significance by arguing that a liberal society stands for nothing as a whole. Indeed, he suggests, seeking a meaning or point of the modern social order as a whole is fundamentally anachronistic, for ours is a "differentiated society," a fragmented social order divided into distinct spheres of life: economic, political, religious, educational, and so on. In his view, principles apply in particular spheres, but not across the entire society.[40]

The problem with this view is that a differentiated society does stand for something as a whole—several things, in fact. Luhmann himself allows that the division of society into many spheres allows individuals facing unwanted constraints in one sphere to flee to another.[41] A differentiated society thus serves the cause of freedom, and promotes moral laxity as well as a certain kind of individualism. All this is exactly what fundamentalists object to. In such an environment, parents will have a hard time teaching their children that the "totality" of truth is found in the Christian Bible. Many forms of discipline will be hard to sustain in the differentiated society, which indirectly fosters distinctive forms of personality, culture, and even religious beliefs, and which is, then, a particular type. We should avoid the common tendency to underdescribe the pattern of life that is promoted by even a circumscribed political liberalism.

If candor compels us not to minimize what liberalism stands for, we should also avoid the increasingly popular tendency to exaggerate the constraints on freedom and diversity in a liberal regime. Nomi Stolzenberg commits the latter error, I believe, when she argues that when liberals ask people to bracket their religious beliefs for the sake of public reflection on political principles, they take sides in a debate within Protestantism.[42] If Stolzenberg is right, liberalism—even political liberalism—is so close an ally of progressive, modernist, "liberal Protestants" that it and Protestant fundamentalism are directly at odds.[43]

Stolzenberg's view gains some plausibility when we consider how fundamentalism emerged at the turn of this century. One important source of controversy within nineteenth-century American Protestantism was the issue of how far to go in making peace with progressive cultural forces such as science. "Protestant modernists" went very far indeed in adapting their religious teachings to modern society. These successors of Unitarianism argued that God is immanent in human culture: modern progress is progress toward the Kingdom of God.[44]

As Protestant modernism advanced, a central point of contention was the proper relation of religion and science. The shifting stance of Horace Bushnell, a leading religious figure of his time, illustrates the path of many modernists. He began his career insisting that Christianity must define the place of science in our understanding of the universe, only to retreat to the position that alleged scientific laws must "pass both houses" of scientific proof and religious scrutiny. Bushnell eventually abandoned this epistemic bicameralism and allowed that the teachings of religion must conform to science or else dispense with the claim to truth.[45]

In line with the modernist Protestants' willingness to adapt their beliefs to changing scientific understandings, many also embraced the "Higher Criticism" emanating from Europe, which argued that religion itself should be studied "scientifically." Higher Criticism sought to place received religious teachings in their historical context based on the contention that those utterances cannot be understood apart from that context.[46]

Fundamentalism was a response to what many saw as the equivocation and empty comprehensiveness of "liberal" Protestantism.[47] Fundamentalists complained that liberals and modernists abandoned historically transcendent and revealed truths and preached nothing but social progress.[48] Instead of regarding the Gospels as the revealed word of God, Higher Criticism bracketed the truth question in order to place the Gospels in a historical context and study them "objectively." These disagreements were not unrelated to issues of class, for as Nathan Hatch points out, and as its name implies, Higher Criticism was elitist: it suggested that historical learning was needed to interpret scriptures properly. The literalist hermeneutic of the fundamentalists was far more accessible to common people.[49]

Against the Protestant modernists, the fundamentalists insisted on the need to preserve timeless revealed truths and not hold them hostage to the latest findings of science. Fundamentalists resist bracketing the truth of religious claims, Stolzenberg insists, for they believe that such a stance lacks religious seriousness. The "essential point" for fundamentalists is that "the objective study of religion, and objective approaches to knowledge in general, are quintessentially secular humanist activities."[50] According to Stolzenberg, the liberal demand that we forbear from invoking religious truths in politics—out of respect for the reasonableness that we might come to share—gives the *religious* opponents of fundamentalism all that they seek. Fundamentalists have every reason, therefore, to make holy war against liberalism.

This conclusion is far too hasty because Stolzenberg's analysis, provocative as it is, does not capture the aims of the liberalism that I have defended. Liberal public reason avoids saying anything about how religion is to be studied: that is left to churches and other private groups. The political liberal can live with the notion that fundamentalism may be the truth in the religious sphere—so long as it does not claim political authority.[51] Political liberals will, moreover, make common cause with moderate fundamentalists to deny political power to any—including Deweyite secular humanists—who would use public institutions to promote their view of the whole truth.[52] Space is cleared, in this way, for a broad range of religious orientations to converge on a shared political view. Finally, political liberalism asks of fundamentalists only what it asks of others, including proponents of secular ideals such as Dewey's humanism: to put reasonably contestable comprehensive ideals to one side in the political realm, and to focus on values such as mutual tolerance and freedom that can be shared by reasonable people.[53]

There is, then, a crucial difference between political liberalism's insistence on the political authority of public reasons and the theological controversies between fundamentalists and their opponents. Proponents of Higher Criticism advocate bracketing the truth question (or putting aside your belief in inherited truths) for the sake of religious study, whereas liberals want us to recognize that one party's religious truth cannot provide a public basis for basic principles that will guide the coercive power we hold together as a political community. We should not sell this concession short, and it is not obvious that fundamentalists (at least reasonable fundamentalists) will do so. Political liberalism is not, therefore, as partisan as Stolzenberg suggests.

Stolzenberg is not alone in her premature leap for the proposition that fundamentalism and liberalism are at war. Stephen Carter, whose book was invoked by President Clinton in support of his decision to sign RFRA, proposes

> that in its stated zeal to cherish religious belief under the protective mantle of "neutrality," liberalism is really derogating religious belief in favor of other, more "rational" methods of understanding the world. The great risk lying a bit further down this path is that religion, far from being cherished, will be diminished, and that religious belief will ultimately become a kind of hobby: something so private that it is as irrelevant to public life as the building of model airplanes.[54]

Another worry might be that religious people will increasingly understand the liberal settlement in Carter's terms and so make holy war against it.

Carter believes that liberalism rests on the authority of a model of reason that is secular, scientific, and at odds with fundamentalist religious communities and biblical hermeneutics. For Carter, liberalism chooses science over religion, and in the name of neutrality tells religion to get lost. As a way of ensuring fairness, Carter would broaden political justification to include the religious voice, and would invite people to operate in politics as proponents of this or that religious view.

Liberalism is not grounded in a comprehensive commitment to scientific as opposed to religious reasoning: reasonable people may believe that in some areas science pulls up short, and liberal public reason does not settle the matter of just where or when. The point is not to put science in the place of religion—or to settle their proper relation—but only to insist that public institutions should operate based on mutually accessible reasons. We should avoid upping the ante with Carter, and for good reason. Consider what happens when Stanley Fish embraces Carter's characterization of our public life. Liberalism claims, he says, to be ultimately tolerant, fair, and dependent only on reason—a court of appeal above the ideological and sectarian fray. But, Fish charges, there is no "reason" above the fray, no ultimate fairness or neutral standpoint. Liberalism places its faith in scientific reason, which has no privileged claim to transcendence, only pretensions thereto. Because liberalism defines itself by its nonpartisanship, writes Fish, "one can only conclude, and conclude nonparadoxically, that liberalism doesn't exist."[55]

Civic liberalism attempts to defuse this war of absolutes. It seeks ground shared by reasonable people and leaves it to individual citizens to connect shared political values with their non-public beliefs about the truth as a whole. We will not share a common account of liberalism's ultimate philosophical or religious foundations, because we do not share a common conception of the whole truth. That does not mean that liberalism is grounded in skepticism, or that it is ungrounded in a transcendent view: if one of the comprehensive views that supports liberalism is true, then liberalism is grounded in the true transcendent view. (And in that case, as Rawls says, those liberals who espouse false comprehensive views at least have true political views.)[56]

But liberalism's justification is neither uncontroversial nor nonpartisan. *Every* political theory is both controversial and partisan—noticing that is no great victory for Fish. Because political liberalism, properly understood, does not claim to be nonpartisan, Fish would be rash to conclude that it does not exist.

Civic or political liberalism is not the only possible response to Carter's dilemma. Comprehensive liberals could shout "Charge!" and rush to defend science, autonomy, individuality, and John Deweyism as the paths to the whole truth about the human good. Liberals could sound a strategic retreat and settle for a modus vivendi or peace treaty among fundamentally opposed groups who lack shared grounds for principled agreement. These strategies have their eloquent defenders. Civic liberalism attempts, instead, to head off the clash of ultimates and to avoid both liberalism as holy war and liberalism as uneasy peace.

The distinction between religious and civil toleration helps mark off the space on which to construct a principled but politic liberalism: a liberalism not grounded in the authority of science per se, but in shared standards of reason. Civic liberalism is not neutral in its effects, but it at least disallows the use of political power to directly promote anyone's contestable comprehensive ideals. It aims to promote a reasonable consensus and trust among those who might otherwise be as deeply opposed as Carter suggests, and that is at least worth trying for.

Liberalism is not as directly partisan as Stolzenberg, Carter, and Fish imply. It does not require that people "bracket" the truth question when studying religion (the *Mozert* contest is over a reading program, not a religion class); it does not endorse secular humanism or the scientific study of religion. A liberal citizen can hold that in religious matters one should defer to sacred books or higher authorities. Of course, accepting the political authority of a public point of view may be harder for many fundamentalists than it is for most of today's Roman Catholics and members of "mainline" Protestant denominations. But to ask less of people is to renounce the notion that good liberal citizens should justify basic political principles in terms they can share not only with members of their own sects, but with their reasonable fellow citizens.

Some fundamentalists may reply that it is the essence of their religious view that truth in every sphere of life is to be sought only in the Bible. To disencumber oneself of one's religious beliefs—even in the sense of offering public justifications for political principles that leave the religious foundations of those beliefs in the background—is to disparage the seriousness of beliefs that are supposed to govern the whole of life. At this point there may be nothing more to say to such people, except to point out that their religious beliefs are, unfortunately, inconsistent with the demands of good citizenship in a religiously pluralistic society.

Unfortunately, many people now misunderstand the nature of liberal public reasons, and such misunderstandings have political as well as philosophical consequences. When President Clinton signed RFRA, he said that he joined Carter in bemoaning "a climate in this country in which some people . . . are embarrassed to say that they advocate a course of action simply because they believe it is the right thing; because they believe it is dictated by their faith, by what they discern to be, with their best efforts, the will of God." "[L]et us never believe," Clinton said, "that the freedom of religion imposes on any of us some responsibility to run from our convictions."[57]

Civic liberalism does not require people to run from their religious faith. It is, indeed, prepared to affirm that many religious communities make a vital contribution to liberal civil society. Civic liberalism does argue, however, that when we seek to shape the political power that is our common property as citizens—when, that is, we act as *citizens* as opposed to private people—we owe our fellow citizens reasons that they can share with us. This is not antireligious; it is simply a basic requirement of mutual respect. It is also a duty of political civility that is in danger of being compromised by a misguided notion of fairness and toleration.

CHAPTER 8

The Mirage of Perfect Fairness

Liberal public reasonableness offers a promising way of bypassing some divisive religious and philosophical conflicts. It should help us recognize that our shared political beliefs and institutions have important but not unlimited aims: preserving a free, peaceful, and stable political framework within which individuals, churches, and voluntary groups can pursue their own visions of what is of ultimate value in life while cooperating together for shared political aims.

But any policy or program, though well justified in shared public aims and values, will impose disparate burdens on adherents of different comprehensive religious and moral views. There will likely always be groups with comprehensive moral or religious conceptions in decided tension with liberalism—conscientious dissenters to the liberal political order.[1] Clearly enough, even publicly justifiable principles and programs will have nonneutral effects and impose disparate burdens on adherents of different comprehensive religious and moral views. How should we comport ourselves with respect to conscientious dissenters? Should civic liberals insist resolutely on the evenhanded application of reasonably justified public rules? Or can we, consistent with the authority of public reasons, bend generally applicable public rules and proceed to a second stage of exceptions and exemptions? If exceptions are to be made, on what grounds should they occur?

Fairness might seem to suggest that at some point we should examine the disparate effects of publicly justified policies, especially on groups outside of the political and cultural mainstream. These will often be groups whose comprehensive conceptions exist in decided tension with the shared values of the political order. One way to do this is to provide public justification with a second stage: a stage where, having constructed a reasonable public view, we consider pleas from marginal groups for accommodations and exemptions. Fundamentalists are not powerless, but they are certainly outside of the cultural and intellectual mainstream, especially with respect to the educational establishment; so they would seem to deserve a sensitive hearing. Should public justification have such a second stage of principled exception making, and if so, should its aim be the kind of maximum feasible accommodation that some advocate?[2] And, more to the case at hand, should the fundamentalist families in *Mozert* be allowed to opt out of the reading program because of its disproportionate impact on their faith community?

Honoring the authority of public reasons means that we should avoid relying on "private" grounds when fashioning the principles that underlie the basic political institutions of society. It also means that we should count as private grounds not only such things as faith and personal inspiration that cannot be subjected to public scrutiny, but also philosophical ideals of life too disputable to gain the consent of a wide range of reasonable people. A second stage might be a way to grapple with the charge that liberalism deploys merely formal principles of neutrality and fairness. Public reason puts conflicting comprehensive views aside: it does not seek a compromise or balance among those wider views, and it does not furnish any sort of guide for weighing and assessing the disproportionate effects of various public laws and policies. Those wider effects can be discerned only if we take up the comprehensive normative perspectives of those who dissent from the liberal order.

Understanding the special burden that public rules sometimes impose on religious or cultural minorities requires adopting the minority perspective; that is, it requires dropping the resolute focus on public aims and shared secular interests. To fully understand the liberal settlement, we need to look at it from the perspective of those whose largest conceptions of meaning and value stand in some tension with liberalism.

The full import of life in this regime can be seen only if we leave its formal strictures behind and take up the normative perspectives of those who object deeply to what it requires and stands for. A more substantial ideal of neutrality or fairness would take up these comprehensive perspectives and assess the burdens that liberal policies place on particular groups or persons when viewed from *their* comprehensive perspectives, balance these burdens against public aims, and grant exemptions and accommodations in the name of securing "real" neutrality and fairness.[3] Solicitude for group-based diversity might well argue for more substantial notions of fairness and neutrality. A second stage would, moreover, help give independent meaning to the Constitution's free exercise clause, which it would seem to lack if all that is required is the assurance that laws have reasonable shared grounds (which is a way of cashing out the establishment clause).[4] Is this something that public officials should be prepared to do? Is it something that a commitment to public reasonableness allows them to do?

In considering these questions, we must not mistake the character of what public reason leaves aside. Comprehensive religious and moral conceptions are regarded as inappropriate grounds for determining the shape of basic political institutions (because these conceptions are sources of reasonable disagreement). But that does not mean that what has been put aside is valueless or irrelevant to individual citizens. Quite the contrary, much of value is outside of the shared grounds of a liberal public morality. Indeed, since our shared political perspective is only possible because it leaves aside the religious and ultimate philosophical foundations on which reasonable people disagree, that shared perspective is too limited to offer any guidance about the weight of these extrapolitical values and concerns. Political liberalism's guarantee of a formalistic neutrality seems implicitly to narrow our view and to imply a measure of real arbitrariness: some valuable ways of life (such as that of the Amish, perhaps) will suffer severe disproportionate burdens in this regime, and there might seem little that we can say, as a public matter, to justify this apparent inequity.[5]

Hobbesian Warnings

Taking up the clashing comprehensive grounds that liberal public reason purposefully puts aside seems fearsome: a second stage of justification would thrust comprehensive religious and philosophical ideals into the political arena and might threaten the overlapping consensus itself. If political liberalism is right about our inability to bring order to conflicting comprehensive views, moreover, then exceptions made on such grounds would seem bound to have an ad hoc and unprincipled character. In a second stage, the political sphere would surrender its independence from comprehensive views, the independence that alone secures its status as a shared perspective.

Warnings against exception making are far from frivolous. Judge Kennedy, as we saw, worried that giving the *Mozert* families their claimed right would open a floodgate of complaints and requests for exemptions within public schooling. Public officials would be faced with the need to weigh the costs and threats of accommodation in each particular case: "You Amish are law-abiding and, in any case, nonthreatening, so you can be exempted. You Fundamentalists are too scary and politically powerful, so you must stay in the schools."[6] Such decisions expose the rawest and deepest divisions within the polity, divisions for which we have no principled basis of resolution. Should we, then, regard all such exception making as a matter of sovereign legislative grace, not to be reviewed by the Courts or regarded as a matter of basic constitutional and public principle?

The intransigent position is ably defended by Walter Berns, who argues that the only way to have a common rule of law is resolutely to refuse to allow judge-made exceptions on grounds that, from a public standpoint, must be regarded as private. He would not, as a matter of constitutional principle, have exempted the Amish children in *Yoder* from the requirement of attending public high school.[7] To grant draft exemptions for conscientious objectors must similarly be regarded as a matter of legislative grace that may be extended only to traditional God-centered religions and not to philosophical pacifists, if that is what the legislature chooses.[8]

Berns worries that the courts increasingly allow individuals to substitute their private judgments for the public will of the sovereign (which in a democracy is the private will of the majority made law), making every citizen a law unto herself: "According to liberalism, one renders unto Caesar whatever Caesar demands and to God whatever Caesar permits." The price of civil peace is the resolute public insistence on keeping religion subordinate to law, on denying any political authority to private judgment. All this means that religious beliefs must be regarded in public as irrelevant, as mere opinions.[9]

Berns's position is simple: just as religious commitments must be put completely aside in lawmaking, so they must not be admitted through the back door as a principled ground for exceptions to generally applicable laws. His position is fully consistent with the requirement of offering reasons for generally applicable laws, but it is also fully compatible with very serious real inequalities of impact and burden. We do not really treat Orthodox Jews and Christians equally when we require heads to be uncovered in the military, knowing full well that this interferes with the religious practices of one group and not the other.[10] If we leave the task of exception making altogether to legislative grace, moreover, we abandon minority religious communities and other complainants to the power of democratic politics.

The intransigent position was adopted by the Supreme Court in the peyote case, *Employment Division of Oregon v. Smith*.[11] The *Smith* Court held that a state may, consistent with the Constitution's free exercise clause, prohibit sacramental peyote use in Native American religious rites and deny unemployment compensation for work-related misconduct based on use of the drug. Justice Scalia insisted for the Court that the state's interest in controlling drug use is a legitimate secular basis for banning the use of peyote, along with other drugs. The ban is neutral in the required sense: there is a good secular basis, and no particular religion is intentionally targeted. Even though the free exercise of Native American religion is indeed interfered with, the state need not meet the heavy burden of showing a "compelling interest" and of demonstrating that the means selected are the least restrictive available for achieving its purpose. All the state need have to justify such laws (with a few exceptions) is a "rational basis"—which is a very easy standard to meet.

Scalia's rationale was straight Berns: to require the state to show a compelling interest whenever it imposes burdens on religious practices

would be courting anarchy, but that danger increases in direct proportion to the society's diversity of religious beliefs, and its determination to coerce or suppress none of them. Precisely because "we are a cosmopolitan nation made up of people of almost every conceivable religious preference" . . . and precisely because we value and protect that religious divergence, we cannot afford the luxury of deeming *presumptively invalid*, as applied to the religious objector, every regulation of conduct that does not protect an interest of the highest order . . . [That] would open the prospect of constitutionally required religious exemptions from civic obligations of almost every conceivable kind—ranging from compulsory military service . . . to the payment of taxes . . . to health and safety regulation . . . to animal cruelty laws.[12]

To begin to make exceptions to publicly justified and generally applicable laws is to open a Pandora's box of religious complaints that cannot, as a public matter, be sorted, ranked, and weighed. To start down this path in pursuit of perfect justice for religious dissenters in each particular case would ruin the imperfect but sustainable fabric of a generally applicable rule of law, which stands for an admittedly rough but easily visible standard of equal treatment.[13]

The Berns-Scalia position, in its insistence on excluding private judgment from politics, resurrects Justice Frankfurter's long-repudiated opinion in the *Gobitis* case, in which the Court denied a challenge by Jehovah's Witnesses to public school regulations requiring students to salute the flag.[14] This jurisprudence is essentially Hobbesian in its conviction that public authority is a construction that must not be measured against natural or transcendent standards of justice; in its intransigent denial of the authority of private judgment; and in its acknowledgment that, at the end of the day, not everyone can be accommodated within a particular public order—not everyone is sufficiently moved by our sociable and pacific this-worldly ideals, and so some must, like irregular stones that "hindereth the building," be cast away.[15]

Do we, then, do enough when we insist that policies have legitimate public grounds? Or should we go beyond Berns, Scalia, and Hobbes and try to weigh the real burdens imposed (even if indirectly) by publicly justified policies? Can we afford to do more than insist on the evenhanded application of general rules with reasonable public grounds?

Worries about divisiveness could, of course, cut both ways. If it is divisive to accommodate dissenting religious groups, surely it could be divisive not to do so. One consequence of the school board's refusal to accommodate the parents in *Mozert* was that many of these children left the public school system altogether and enrolled in Christian schools, as have thousands of other children in recent years. (In the nineteenth century, as we saw in Part One, Catholics set up a parallel school system only after failing to secure accommodations within the public system.) If public schools do a better job of promoting tolerance and other civic virtues, then the children who were pushed out of those schools could be future sources of political divisiveness in other political arenas. It is certainly not clear that political divisiveness overall is being minimized by pushing fundamentalist children out of public schools: doing so eases the problem only for school administrators, not for the polity.[16] The whole point of the common school is to be a primary arena where children from the different normative perspectives that compose our polity encounter one another in a respectful setting, learn about one another, and discover that their differences do not preclude cooperation and mutual respect as participants in a shared political order. This is crucial work in any polity that is characterized by deep diversity. Yet if we widen our view and consider all of the religious complaints that might be advanced against not only public schools but every other government policy and institution, then the prospect of entertaining and thereby encouraging such complaints could seem terribly daunting and perhaps simply impossible.

The intransigent position is a powerful one. In spite of its association with a conservative desire to preserve public order, it should not be identified with a mere hardheaded or hardhearted refusal to acknowledge the genuine complaints of religious minorities. The intransigence of Berns, Scalia, and Hobbes is in some ways an insistent reminder of the considerations that undergird the resort to public reason: the fact of deep and unreconcilable disagreement with respect to religious values and ultimate ideals of life, and the need, as a consequence, to find other grounds to serve as a basis of our shared public order. Intransigent liberalism adds to the fact of disagreement the not unreasonable suspicion that to begin to make exceptions to public rules on religious grounds attempts the impossible and courts chaos: we cannot on the basis of public principles distinguish the weights of different religious complaints.

If exception making is to be allowed at all, Berns, Scalia, and other Hobbesians maintain, it must be entrusted to the repositories of sovereign legislative discretion, rather than to the guardians of basic principle: to legislators, executives, and administrators, that is, rather than to the courts.[17] There is no shared reasonable ground for weighing these claims, so if they are to be weighed and sorted out, it must be on whatever basis that the sovereign people and their representatives wish. To curtail judicial scrutiny of these cases dramatizes the fact that such judgments have no grounding in shared principles but must depend upon sovereign grace, hopefully informed by prudence. This cannot be a happy conclusion for liberals committed to trying to justify power on the basis of public reasons, but perhaps we cannot do otherwise.

If we embrace the notion that political authority should be grounded in a publicly reasoned consensus, then how can we allow exceptions or exemptions to public rules to be made on the basis of the very grounds—comprehensive moralities, transcendent religious beliefs, and so forth—that we have labored so hard to exclude from politics? The intransigent insistence on the supremacy and evenhanded application of publicly justified rules may be the best way of fulfilling the demands of political liberalism and public reason. Rawls may entail Scalia.

Prudential Accommodationism and Civic Aims

But not so fast. The Hobbesian position appears intellectually powerful, but in fact its skepticism is overdrawn. We do not in fact abide by the rule advocated by the intransigents: judges have sometimes made exceptions to accommodate religious complaints to schooling and elsewhere.[18] While the courts may not have done a very good job of articulating clear standards for determining when free exercise claims will be honored, we are not on a quick slide into the abyss.[19] In universities and other large organizations, moreover, we do our best to accommodate a widening array of student religious observances and restrictions. Even in the absence of clear public standards (which we lack in many areas of public policy), it may still be that peace and justice are best served when we accommodate religious minorities on those occasions when it seems, on balance, that we can do so at reasonable cost to civic aims and values, and without provoking an avalanche of indistiguishably plausible claims for exemptions and exceptions.[20]

The skeptical heirs of Hobbes may be right that we are unlikely to be able to articulate general rules or a complete set of principles to fully guide the process of exception making, but that does not mean that if we sometimes make exceptions we are flirting with chaos. It is, after all, a convenient and familiar bureaucratic retort that "I simply cannot make an exception in your case, because then I'd have to do it for everyone." To say that is to say that we cannot distinguish exceptional cases in a nonarbitrary way. But such an assertion may be itself arbitrary: in many settings, and given an overall willingness to go along with the law, exceptional cases can often be distinguished. Our standards for allowing students to miss an exam, say, will often be somewhat open-ended (a death in the family, a serious illness, or something on a similar magnitude) but not completely arbitrary or unworkable in practice.

It does not seem to me, in the end, that we are barred from considering exceptions and accommodations on religious grounds, though we must proceed cautiously and be careful not to exaggerate what can be achieved. We can advance to a stage of exception making so long as we banish unreasonable expectations of achieving "perfect fairness" and keep in view the need to preserve widely applicable institutional arrangements that serve civic aims.

Indiscriminate aspirations to fairness or neutrality would require that we weigh *all* public programs and policies against private religiously based complaints. If more substantive conceptions of neutrality and fairness are offered as alternatives to political liberalism, their attractions are more apparent than real. Pursuing the mirage of perfect fairness would, first of all, be utterly debilitating: How could we possibly ensure that public policies have neutral effects on the innumerable faiths and worldviews in our regime? Announcing an ideal of perfect fairness or neutrality of effect would, moreover, heighten group consciousness, group-based grievances, and political divisions.[21] "Perfect fairness" is also unappealing: it means being fair to reasonable and unreasonable views, to those who recognize the political authority of public reasons that can be shared by people who disagree and those who do not. If liberalism is not about indiscriminate toleration, neither is it about indiscriminate fairness or political neutrality.

We need, for one thing, to consider from a civic standpoint the nature and grounds of the complaints that are being advanced. In the *Mozert* case, the religious beliefs that were forwarded as a basis for the claimed right to an accommodation were especially troubling, in that the families asserted a totalistic belief system that led them to refuse to acknowledge the political authority of reasons that could be shared with their fellow citizens. This in turn led them to confuse political arguments for religious tolerance with religiously based arguments for skepticism or indifference toward religion. Certainly not all the consequences of life in a liberal society are positive, but why should we apologize if disparate burdens fall on proponents of totalistic religious or moral views who refuse to concede the political authority of public reason? It is hard to see why we should bend over backwards to accommodate such people, or cry crocodile tears over forms of non-neutrality that make life hard on the intolerant, or on those who refuse to acknowledge, for political purposes, the force of reasons that can be shared by fellow citizens of different faiths and comprehensive convictions. We need to remember how such people would behave if they had political power. Becoming transfixed by the mirage of perfect "fairness" could make us forget to be fair to ourselves, and to the important values that support the liberal practices and institutions that compose a liberal civic sphere.

It is hardly a criticism of liberalism, likewise, to say that it denies the existence of a public standard or scale that would allow us to weigh religious claims against public goals in a way that will satisfy everyone. Who has such a scale? Such a standard is provided only by a comprehensive moral or religious view, but these views are the subject of deep and reasonable disagreement and so are totally implausible candidates for providing fair grounds for political cooperation. The disabilities of liberal public reason are no more than the disabilities of our shared reason.

There is a danger, finally, of being overwhelmed by a kind of postmodern angst about our inability to establish publicly a comprehensive scheme of human values. Liberalism accepts the fact of reasonable disagreement about comprehensive moral and religious ideals. That acceptance should do nothing to corrode our confidence in those midlevel principles and aims that pass the test of public reason. Political liberalism does not assert a particular view of the whole truth, but that does not mean that there is no truth about these larger matters, or that political liberalism is untrue. It simply means that there are many reasonable accounts of "the whole truth," and we want to respect all of those reasonable views in politics. If any of the reasonable, comprehensive views that support the liberal public morality is true, then liberalism is true.[22] Nothing about reasonable pluralism should shake our confidence in the overriding weight of shared public principles: indeed, it seems to me that the fact that it can be converged upon by people representing different religious and philosophical backgrounds strengthens the case for a liberal public morality.

It is not right, then, to say that liberalism makes do with mere "formal" neutrality and "formal" fairness when more substantive and publicly reasonable accounts of these ideas are available. There is as much substance in liberalism's conceptions of neutrality and fairness as our shared standards of reasonableness—and respect for reasonable disagreement—allow.

We should not pursue a mirage of perfect fairness, but that does not mean that we should never consider pleas for accommodations and exemptions. Where public imperatives are marginal and the burdens on particular groups are substantial, accommodations will sometimes be justified. We should, however, enter into the process of exception making critically, and without aiming at anything quite so broad as the "maximum feasible space" for difference that William A. Galston advocates in the name of his ideal "Diversity State."[23]

The *Smith* Court fell prey to unreasonable inflexibility because of its overly abstract worries about the impossibility of weighing the conflicts between particular religious viewpoints and public purposes. The fact is that we engage in this weighing all the time, without rulelike guidelines, but without, in most cases, courting disaster.

There is also, however, an opposite danger from that of the intransigents on the *Smith* Court, and that is establishing too strong a presumption in favor of the rights of religious exemptions and accommodations. It was no doubt the fear of this opposite extreme view that in important part motivated the *Smith* Court, and we should not altogether dismiss this fear. Congress and the president committed this opposite error, I believe, in enacting the Religious Freedom Restoration Act, which attempted to instruct the federal courts that they should always apply their most exacting standards of scrutiny to pleas for exemptions or exceptions based on religious grounds. The standard of judicial scrutiny that RFRA insists on has, in other contexts, been called "heightened in theory, fatal in practice," because the standard represents a strong presumption that the government is acting unreasonably. RFRA required that Courts should always grant religiously based requests for exemptions or exceptions to general laws unless public officials met a heavy burden of proof. That standard of proof, as specified by Congress, would have required public officials to show that granting an exception or exemption would impair the public's ability to pursue some extremely important or "compelling" state interest, and that that interest could not be achieved in any alternative manner that would be less burdensome with respect to the religious liberty interest being asserted.

Theoretically, this was the standard that was in place before the *Smith* case, but in fact the courts found ways to hold that alleged infringements on religious liberty were not really infringements on religious liberty. The appeals court did precisely this in the *Mozert* case, arguing, in effect, that it knew better than Vicki Frost and the other parents what constituted a burden on their religious beliefs. With a "nudge and a wink," the Supreme Court could have swallowed RFRA. Indeed, as I mentioned above, it could have refused to make an exception to the nation's drug laws in *Smith* without being so dramatic about it, and without seeming to revise constitutional practice more radically than it did.

To take RFRA at its word, and really apply the same level of constitutional suspicion to free exercise complaints that is applied to laws that discriminate on racial grounds, would have been a disaster. The problem is that if we take laws and policies individually, and apply the standard that RFRA announces literally, it will very rarely be the case that a given law or policy can be said with confidence to represent the least burdensome way of advancing a compelling need. How often will we be able to say that there is no alternative way of, for example, promoting an understanding of different religious ways of life, as in the reading program at issue in *Mozert?* How often will it be true with respect to a particular set of complainants who come to court representing a minority religious community that exempting this particular group will cause a serious political disruption that could be addressed in no alternative way? James Q. Wilson has warned with respect to judicial interventions on behalf of complaining individuals or small groups that "the effects on a community of many individuals taking advantage of the rights granted to an individual . . . are often qualitatively different from the effects of a single person."[24]

The danger of RFRA is that it seems to represent too strong a presumption in favor of accommodation, too flexible a policy of accommodationism. It would have stoked the fires of the sort of new multiculturalism advocated by Michael McConnell. Congress and the president were right to be dissatisfied with the Court's *Smith* decision, but we should try to do better than responding to one extreme with another.

It has to be allowed that RFRA supporters were perhaps encouraged to take the route they did by the rigid rules that the Court has developed to decide what "level of scrutiny" it will apply in constitutional cases. As Justices Marshall and Stevens, among others, have long argued, the Supreme Court has too often responded to the complexity of the conflicts it must adjudicate by setting up rigid categories.[25] A hallmark of the "categorical approach" is that the Court applies either an extremely high or an extremely low level of scrutiny depending on whether a law runs afoul of a "preferred freedoms" or whether it classifies people on a basis that is "suspect" (such as race). If a law falls into the category of "strict scrutiny," the Court will assume that it is unconstitutional. If a law falls outside of the categories of strict scrutiny, the presumption is supposed to be equally strong that the law is constitutional. These ham-fisted judicial rules have encouraged the standoff between two unsatisfactory alternatives: the excessive inflexibility of *Smith* and the excessive permissiveness of RFRA.

Smith's Hobbesian stance clearly makes it much harder for religious minorities to show in Court that their interests have been discounted for no good reason. The vice of RFRA may be a bit more subtle. An overall political order that is too flexible in the face of pleas for accommodations and exemptions will not do the work that I described at the end of Part One: that of transforming various forms of diversity in liberal democratic directions. Of course we should weigh requests for accommodation. But especially when core civic aims are at stake, we also want to make sure that democratic deliberative institutions have some flexibility in pursuing public aims. What is needed is a more intermediate standard of scrutiny in this area: one capable of acknowledging that religiously based claims—and indeed conscientious claims in general—often have a special weightiness not shared by mere interests and preferences. But because religious and conscientious claims are so various and not easily subject to public scrutiny and assessment, and because the public needs a generally applicable system of law in which exceptions are not the rule, we should approach religiously and conscientiously based claims for exceptions without a strong presumption that they will be granted, but with a determination that they will be listened to and seriously considered. To do more or less would be unfair either to the religious complainant or to the civic order itself. As Mary Ann Glendon and Raul Yanes have argued, the most sensible thing in this sphere would be to adopt what some Justices have long championed in the face of the rigid system of two-tiered review: a more flexible intermediate standard that would ask whether the law being challenged advances important governmental objectives in a reasonable manner.[26]

Back to the *Mozert* Complaints

It must be said that the particular claims of the fundamentalist families in *Mozert* are weak. The reading program at stake there may indirectly impose disproportionate burdens on parents attempting to inculcate fundamentalist religion, and shield their children from knowledge of other religions. But we must remember that the source of the apparent "unfairness," the cause of the "disparate impact" here, is a reasonable attempt to inculcate core liberal values. The state is within the limits of its rightful authority in requiring public school children to learn about the religious differences that peacefully coexist among their fellow citizens. It is hard to see how schools could fulfill the core liberal civic mission of inculcating toleration and other basic civic virtues without running afoul of complaints about "exposure to diversity." Because such exposure is a necessary and well-selected means for teaching a basic civic virtue, objections to it cannot support a fundamental moral or constitutional right to be exempted from an otherwise reasonable educational regime.

There are, of course, uncertainties as to the real effectiveness of this reading program, and of all other efforts to instill moral virtues.[27] It would be extremely hard to show that any particular school program is crucial for realizing the core liberal value of toleration (another reason why the traditional "strict scrutiny" standard is inapplicable here). The Hawkins County school board presented no evidence of the program's effect on student's attitudes. Perhaps the presumption should shift to accommodating the *Mozert* families' desire to opt out of the reading program, at least until its efficacy is shown?

Empirical questions in this area are intrinsically hard to settle, however, and judgments about fundamental rights should turn on other grounds.[28] The program stands as a reasonable effort to familiarize students with diversity and teach toleration. The basic question of principle is: Do people have a moral or constitutional right to opt out of reasonable measures designed to educate children toward very basic liberal virtues, because those measures make it harder for parents to pass along their religious beliefs? Surely not. To acknowledge the legitimacy of the fundamentalist complaint as a matter of basic principle would overthrow reasonable efforts to inculcate core liberal values. It would provide religious fundamentalists with a right to shield their children from the fact of reasonable pluralism. Liberal civic education is bound to have the effect of favoring some ways of life or religious convictions over others. So be it.

As a matter of basic principle at least, we have good reason to refuse the *Mozert* families' request to opt out. If intransigence here appears to be at odds with religious freedom, it must be remembered that rightful liberty is civil liberty, or liberty that can be guaranteed equally to all. All of us must accept limits on our liberty designed to sustain a system of equal freedom for all. Each of us can reasonably be asked to surrender some control over our own children for the sake of reasonable common efforts to ensure that all future citizens learn the minimal prerequisites of citizenship. There is no right to be exempted from measures necessary to secure the freedom of all.

Further, we are dealing with children who are not mere extensions of their parents. The parents' religious liberty does not extend with full force to their children. Adult Christian Scientists might be allowed to refuse medical treatment, but not for their children. Insulating children from diversity is less serious than keeping them from needed medicine, but awareness of alternative ways of life is a prerequisite not only of citizenship, as we have seen, but also of being able to make the most basic life choices.[29] This ground alone might well be adequate to deny the claimed right to opt out.

Some will object to my intransigence here, pointing out that we allow people to exclude themselves from public schooling and go to private schools, parochial and fundamentalist schools, and even school at home.[30] How, then, can we justify intransigence in *Mozert?* I have conceded the right to opt out of public schooling (which the Supreme Court affirmed in *Pierce*), but that right should be understood to be conditioned by a public authority to regulate private schools to ensure that civic values are satisfied and the child's right to freedom is preserved.[31] True enough, in most states private schools and home schooling are only minimally regulated, especially with respect to civic education.[32] That states do not fully exercise their rightful authority, however, does not mean they do not have it. So while there is a (moral and constitutional) right to opt out of public schooling, there is no moral right to opt selectively out of those basic civic exercises that the state may reasonably require for all children. Concomitantly, private schools have no right to resist reasonable measures to ensure that all children learn about the many ways of life that coexist in our polity.[33]

If the intransigence I have argued for in *Mozert* seems harsh, we must remember that political basics are at stake here: toleration and knowledge of our society's diversity. This is not to say that we should never accommodate religious dissenters. Only the most basic public purposes will routinely trump religious complaints and warrant intransigent support. When heavy religious burdens are imposed on people for the sake of trivial public purposes, we should of course take the project of accommodation seriously. For example, the fundamentalists in *Mozert* might have objected to aspects of the curriculum far more incidentally or marginally related to the pursuit of basic civic aims: to art or gym classes, for example; then we would approach their complaints differently.[34]

One can easily imagine more reasonable religious complaints that should have gained a favorable hearing. The fundamentalists might have conceded the legitimacy of the core civic mission of the readers, while mounting an objection based on public values themselves. They might have objected, say, that the purported "diversity" of views in the readers lacks respectful depictions of religious ways of life. They might have charged the readers with combining glowing portrayals of secularist, this-worldly ideals of life and disparaging portraits of more conservative forms of religious belief.[35] While it would be unreasonable to insist on perfect "balance" in school readers or other parts of the curriculum, political liberals can sympathize with objections to a reading program so heavily biased against a particular comprehensive view that it appears designed to denigrate that view and promote alternatives. The proper response in a case such as this would not be to allow fundamentalist children to opportunity out, but to change the books so that all children learn proper respect for one another.

We can do more, therefore, than insist intransigently on core liberal values: we should also insist on political respect for fundamentalists who acknowledge the political authority of liberal public principles. Such fundamentalists are reasonable fellow citizens whose religious convictions should not be gratuitously disparaged in readers that profess to expose children to diversity and teach toleration. The political liberal will hold, after all, that children from religious families are not the only ones who may need lessons in tolerance. The children of evangelical atheists and of those who espouse totalistic versions of liberalism may also need to learn political respect for fellow citizens who hold other reasonable views.

We may, then, sometimes consider claims for accommodations, exceptions, or even adjustments in public policies based on comprehensive grounds. Liberals need not deny that it is sometimes legitimate to invoke comprehensive moral and religious views in politics as grounds for possible accommodations or exceptions.[36] There will sometimes be good grounds for wondering whether the public reasons of others are mere fronts for their comprehensive moral or religious agenda. (Are Sunday closing laws publicly justified on civil grounds as a common day of rest, for example, or are they actually just ways of favoring the dominant Christian community?)

Religious Accommodations and Transformative Liberalism

But what of the conservative charge that in taking up conscientious requests for exceptions and exemptions we are opening the back door to the very comprehensive sources of irresolvable conflict that political liberalism works so hard to push out the front?[37] In a sense, we are doing just that, but the context is all-important. Basic political issues have been settled in accord with the strictures of public reason. Most people affirm liberal principles and accept the vast bulk of public policy without deep conscientious reservations. When we take up the question of accommodations and exceptions, moreover, it will not be with the expectation that the political order as a whole will be reexamined for its "substantive" neutrality or fairness. There is absolutely no possibility of reexamining every public measure to ensure that people are equally happy about them when viewed from the perspective of their comprehensive conceptions of meaning and value. We expect only that some extraordinary burdens on particular groups may be lessened without great damage to the basic integrity of the public order.

If these moments were the stuff of politics as a whole, political liberalism would be impossible. If all of politics were a matter of particularistic requests for exceptions, if there were constant demands that every public policy be "fair" when judged from the perspective of each group's or person's conception of the good as a whole, then governance in even a moderately heterogeneous society would be impossible, and there would be no such thing as the rule of law.[38] But so long as most people accept political liberal values and strictures with regard to most basic matters of principle, and so long as most people are prepared to concede that general lawmaking is a blunt instrument, then we can safely proceed to consider comprehensively based pleas for exceptions and accommodations, as indeed we do. It is neither necessary nor possible to completely banish comprehensive considerations from politics. Indeed, as I have argued, listening to complaints may sometimes allow us to improve the law. The conservatives, then, are not entirely wrong to worry about the consequences of taking up religiously based pleas for exceptions, but they exaggerate the dangers.

Conservatives may also ignore the extent to which exception making and accommodation can help promote support for a just regime. I have argued that the *Mozert* families have no right to be accommodated, at least on the basis of principled grounds. But besides principled reasons for exception making and accommodation, political liberalism also suggests certain strategic and prudential reasons.

Liberalism is misconceived if it is thought of as simply an attempt to draw boundaries around people with prepolitical conceptions of the good life and beliefs about religious truth. Rather, another aim of a liberal civic order should be to promote patterns of belief and action that are supportive of liberalism, to transform people's deepest commitments in ways that are supportive of liberal politics. The transformative ambitions of civic liberalism themselves suggest certain principles of accommodation, for these ambitions represent an aspiration toward a kind of civil society in which people share a public moral order and respect one another as common participants in that order. Because a liberal public morality is always (more or less) in a state of coming-into-being, we should accommodate dissenters when doing so helps draw them into the public moral order; that is, when it helps transform a modus vivendi into a deeper set of shared commitments. To the extent that we can make mainstream public institutions more accessible to cultural and religious outsiders, we may help integrate them into our shared institutions.[39] In the case of the *Mozert* families, this points to the relevance of the consideration mentioned earlier: will the refusal to accommodate drive these families out of public schools altogether and into Christian schools? Can we accommodate the families while only minimally compromising our principled concern with teaching toleration?

From this prudential standpoint, it might well have been better for the school board to have softened its intransigent line, which led many of these children to withdraw altogether from the public school system. While one can appreciate the school board members' worries about a future filled with many such requests for accommodation, flexibility might help stem the flood of children into Christian schooling.[40] Still, the school board's judgment was not completely unreasonable: if a deluge of "conscientious" complaints to various aspects of public schooling were to materialize, the result would be a "buffet style" curriculum in which every child partakes only of those courses that accord with his or her family's personal views. This kind of curriculum would mean the end of common schooling.

Although the *Mozert* families had, therefore, no fundamental moral right to be accommodated (and no judicially enforceable constitutional right so far as I can see), school administrators who anticipated the withdrawal of these families should have tried to accommodate them in order to keep the children within the public system. The Hawkins County school board could have been more flexible, but some parents made bizarre demands, and administrators became annoyed. Bates suggests that members of the board wanted to get the *Mozert* parents out of their hair: intransigence was backed by the hope that the parents and their children would leave the public schools. If a court applying the more flexible constitutional standard I have recommended could have helped preserve informal accommodations to keep the *Mozert* children in the public school system—without imposing unreasonable burdens on the school system and without creating misguided constitutional principles—that would have been all to the good.[41]

In addition, it is not good enough to simply assert an abstract, blanket concern that every time we grant a request for an exemption or exception to a general rule we are opening a Pandora's box. A court may rightly require some evidence that there are many others in the wings who are prepared to make requests indistinguishable from the original. The specter of the proverbial "Pandora's boxes" should not be allowed to work as an unexamined talisman for refusing to listen to religious complaints or other objections to laws. A rigid insistence on the sanctity of exceptionless rules may reflect nothing more than bureaucratic convenience. To unfairly marginalize even unreasonable people is to fan their alienation and resentment, to encourage their disaffection with our political system.[42]

To say that the practice of prudential accommodation should promote assimilation into liberal political values raises the seemingly inescapable question: What about the Amish? Allowing Amish parents to pull their children out of high school does not promote assimilation into liberal values. On the other hand, the Amish were no threat to the larger society: they are "private persons standing in merely private relations to others," as Hegel said of the Quakers and Anabaptists.[43] This makes it much easier to recognize the law-abidingness and hard work that so impressed Justice Burger in his *Yoder* opinion.

We cannot be entirely happy about accommodating the Amish, however. And we certainly should not leap to the view that *Yoder* stands for a broad presumption in favor of religious accommodationism, or parental control over education. That the Amish are hardworking does not impugn the fact that, as Jeff Spinner argues, they are in other respects not good liberal citizens.[44] Amish society is patriarchal and insular—women are regarded as unequal helpers of men—and Amish children are not prepared for being critically reflective citizens. Although the state has no business promoting comprehensive philosophical ideals of individual autonomy, allowing Amish parents to withdraw their children from high school could thwart the children's ability to make informed decisions about their own futures. All children should have an education that provides them with the ability to make *informed* and *independent* decisions about how they want to lead their lives in our modern world. Liberal freedom to choose is the birthright of every child.

Spinner points out, however, that Amish communities are not quite as insular as idealized pictures might suggest. Amish teenagers sometimes go to Florida for spring break, and about 20 percent of them leave Amish communities altogether.[45] To the extent that there is a real "exit option" from the Amish community, that should soften our anxieties about the Amish high school exemption. Spinner suggests that our attitude toward the Amish should be one of "grudging tolerance": they are not good liberal citizens, but they do not wholly tyrannize their children, and they keep to themselves. We should not celebrate them, but we may tolerate them. This is far more appropriate than the common tendency to romanticize the Amish (and diversity in general) to the detriment of children's freedom. If we accommodate these Amish parents, we should do so on narrow grounds that do not necessarily apply to other religious groups.

There are, nevertheless, substantial reasons for wondering whether even Spinner's "grudging tolerance" (as applied to *Yoder*) goes too far. The fact that the Amish are relatively few in number and withdrawn from the society around them means they do not threaten us. But the strikingly insular, homogeneous, and intense nature of Amish community life—in which the "same people frequently work, play, and worship together"—increases the potential detriment of allowing the children to be withdrawn from high school. Moreover, the 20 percent attrition rate tells us only that whatever the degree of communal pressure and ignorance working to keep members in the community, a substantial portion of Amish children still leave. How high would the number be if Amish children had a fuller knowledge of the ways of life available to them in the modern world? The answer to this question is precisely what worried the Amish parents who sued the state of Wisconsin to have their children removed from high school.

In granting the Amish exemption, we are abetting the Amish parents and elders in preventing Amish children from making informed decisions about how they wish to lead their own lives. That the children are well prepared for life in the Amish community is not enough: it is for the children to say whether that is what they wish. To insist on this point does not require that I invoke anything as grand as "the Enlightenment project" or a comprehensive philosophy of autonomy, contrary to what William A. Galston has argued. We should as a civic matter insist on the overriding importance of suiting children to make informed decisions about their own future without being straitjacketed by their parents, their religious community, or anyone else.

I have come to believe that at the very least we should hope that *Yoder* remains a "dead end" in American constitutional law. Ideally, unless it can be shown that Amish children are not significantly impeded in making their own choices by ignorance and communal pressure, *Yoder* should at some point be overruled. Of course, the Amish should have the right to establish their own schools, subject to public regulation, like everyone else. But we should certainly refuse to join commentators like McConnell and Galston who would extend the principles of *Yoder* and regard them as modern beacons of the "Diversity State."[46]

All this makes clear that fundamentalist parents cannot claim the same grounds for exemption as the Amish. Fundamentalists are not sectarians living apart, but are a group that is increasingly politicized and hostile to many liberal values and practices.

I would defend a practice of accommodation—a second stage of exception making—that recognizes the supreme political importance of protecting the basic interests of children and constituting diversity for liberal civic ends. Let us note, in this regard, that Chief Justice Burger's opinion in the Amish high school case is not as bad in one respect as it may at first appear. Burger lauds the Amish for their law-abidingness and bourgeois virtue, and no doubt to many this seems a rather cramped and even illiberal basis for accommodating dissenters. Are only those communities that zealously promote "family values" to be accommodated? What about communities of Thoreauian individualists, or others? Surely not.

It is perfectly legitimate, however (assuming no basic interests are at stake), to ask whether accommodation promotes any of our public values, so long as they are not merely our values but also grounded in good public reasons. This point can be appreciated from both sides of the political spectrum. The case for accommodating pacifistic Quakers in cases of military service is similar in structure to Burger's argument. On the one hand, as a public matter we believe the Quaker position on military service to be deeply mistaken. On the other hand, as Rawls suggests (in a discussion that is a left-leaning version of Burger's *Yoder* opinion), the pacifism of the Quakers presents us with an intense version of some of our own values: they have been sterling examples of conscientious commitment to principle, even in the face of adversity, and they may remind us, as Rawls says, that governments are apt to commit serious wrongs in our name. And the Quakers have submitted to forms of alternative service—such as the ambulance corps—which are even more dangerous than military service. So even though we believe the Quakers to be wrong, we can see that accommodating them may well improve the moral quality of our society as a whole.[47]

There are various public bases for accommodating dissenters by making exceptions to general, publicly justified rules, but there is no general *right* of conscientious dissent. Liberal constitutionalism properly understood holds that laws must be based on reasonable public grounds. When faced with dissenters, who refuse to recognize the weight or authority of those grounds, we must not cast aside our public standards. We may sometimes accommodate or exempt dissenters but we cannot, at the stage of exception making, discover or construct some new or higher ground that promises necessarily to *reconcile* religious dissenters to the political order.

If religious minorities generate a large volume of requests for exceptions and exemptions, it may or may not be because of religious prejudice. On the one hand, political majorities may discount the interests of religious communities simply because they are religious minorities—that is, because of religious prejudice. Such a reason is unfair and a good ground for judicial intervention. On the other hand, some of the smaller religious communities may be unwilling to look at public policies from a public point of view and to acknowledge the authority of public reasons. Insofar as religious minorities suffer special burdens on account of their unwillingness to recognize the importance of basic public values—as with the *Mozert* families and, to some degree at least, nineteenth-century Catholics—we should be more skeptical of their claims. We want to make sure, in other words, that small religious communities are treated with equal concern and respect. We should also be prepared to allow, however, that the communities may be small precisely because of their resistance to basic civic values. We should not discount our political values simply because they are opposed on religious grounds, and we should try to avoid short-circuiting the transformative project. It would be perverse if we were to extend special political favor to groups whose "minority" status is a result precisely of its unwillingness to honor basic civic commitments.

Yet we must listen to dissenters and be willing to learn from them. Liberal public reasonableness would be betrayed by a pigheadedness that refuses to countenance the possibility that the political order has gone astray at some fundamental level. By insisting on at least an intermediate level of judicial scrutiny for religious pleas for accommodations and exemptions, we can help ensure that public officials and political majorities do not simply ignore complaining religious minorities.[48] We must also engage religious and other conscientious minorities in political conversation, practicing the virtues of democratic reciprocity that Gutmann and Thompson describe. Nevertheless we must, in the end, be prepared to acknowledge and defend our own liberal commitments. It is hard to see why we should do more.

It seems doubtful that we should leave the task of religiously based exception making to legislatures and executives: there is no reason to think that their virtues are alone adequate to this task. The worries advanced by Scalia, Berns, and others are weighty, but the legal process is not as inflexible or fragile as they assume. It will be hard to define with precision when exceptions will be made—but such is often the nature of exceptions and of equitable relief. General rules are only part of the material of law. Judgments about religiously based exceptions are likely to be highly complex and contextualized matters. That is an argument that judges should avoid broad pronouncements, not that they should altogether avoid getting involved. Given the complexity of the relevant judgments, the problematic status of this territory, and the not completely unreasonable fear of opening a Pandora's box of religiously based complaints, exemptions and exceptions should be carved out narrowly. But it can be done.

When complaints are advanced by small and politically weak religious groups, moreover, courts can help ensure that their concerns are taken seriously and that they are treated with equal concern and respect.[49] To leave accommodations and exceptions to the democratic branches is virtually to guarantee that complaints advanced by some minority religious communities will be slighted.

Berns and Scalia properly remind us that there is no general *right* of conscientious dissent, and that we cannot reach the mirage of "perfect fairness" for religious dissenters. Political liberalism holds that laws must be based on reasonable public grounds. When faced with dissenters who refuse to recognize the weight or authority of those grounds, we must not cast aside our public standards.[50]

The question of whether to make exceptions to public laws and if so, when, is vexing and complex but not really basic. The more basic point is that *we* must decide when we can afford to make exceptions in light of the full range of publicly accessible reasons as best we understand them. The grounds for exemptions and accommodation must be the principles and aims that *we* believe justified, and they should be consistent with—even supportive of—the preservation of a liberal civic order. We cannot allow that dissenters have a general right, on private, conscientious grounds, to opt out of generally applicable and publicly justifiable policies or rules.

CHAPTER 9

Divided Selves and Transformative Liberalism

In the preceding chapters of this part I have tried to flesh out a version of liberalism that owes a great deal to Rawls's political liberalism and to the distinctive and illuminating approach to public justification and diversity that he and others have developed. In this chapter, I want to consider whether the real lesson of this tale is that we were wrong to start with Rawls and liberal public reason in the first place. Let us weigh the charge that while this approach is coherent, it is neither necessary nor useful, but rather morally and politically debilitating.[1]

According to critics of Rawls's view, people should not be expected to invoke public reasons rather than their religious and other comprehensive moral views, even when justifying basic political principles. Joseph Raz argues that the "epistemic abstinence" on which political liberalism rests is impossible and, moreover, unnecessary. It is impossible because Rawls must assume some truths, such as that peace and freedom are good. It is unnecessary because even if people participate in politics with all of their moral and religious values engaged, worries about chaos and bloody conflict are unconvincing. The comprehensive conceptions widely held in our society prescribe persuasion rather than coercion as the proper approach to nonbelievers. Political stability, in any case, has more to do with affective ties than shared principles.[2]

Unrepentant comprehensive liberals reject the strategy of avoidance in favor of a strategy of engagement: they would invite our deepest disagreements onto the political stage to be grappled with directly. Allowing people to confront openly their deepest moral differences is more respectful (or at least respectful in a different way) than telling people to invoke reasons that they can share when considering the most important political matters, especially because doing so will be much harder for some people than for others. The strategy of avoidance robs our politics of its most profound sources of vigor, excitement, and importance, and it promotes forms of personality unencumbered by deep commitments to communities and ideals and a politics of mere proceduralism. Our deepest disagreements should be dealt with directly in politics, not moved off the political agenda wholesale. Dropping political liberalism's strategy of avoidance would, critics say, promote a wider and more profound diversity of political viewpoints, deeper forms of mutual respect, and a more robust political life.

Against these powerful criticisms, it must be allowed that the liberal ideal of public reason may not be the best ideal along every conceivable dimension. There are bound to be tradeoffs among competing values, and we must be satisfied if political liberalism and related versions of liberal public reason seem on balance best able to secure our most basic political aims. With this in mind, let me try to dispatch the critics.

Raz's charge that political liberalism rests on unacknowledged claims to truth appears itself to rest on a misunderstanding.[3] Political liberalism does not leave comprehensive questions aside altogether, but that is not the same as asserting a particular view of the whole truth. Any liberalism assumes a certain range of answers to many ultimate questions, and political liberals assert that the values supporting the liberal settlement—individual freedom, tolerance and respect for social diversity, and so forth—override competing sets of values. The important point is that asserting the public unacceptability (or even falsehood) of religious imperatives requiring the persecution of heretics—or other illiberal measures—does not depend on a particular account of religious truth. Citizens may adjust their religious convictions to shared political principles in their own way, and in any number of ways.[4] Liberalism cannot avoid making certain general assumptions about what does and does not have ultimate value; it need not rest on a particular comprehensive account of the truth or of good as a whole.

So claims about truth and human good as a whole *can* be largely excluded from the public justification of basic political principles and institutions, but why should they be if the major comprehensive views in our society generate from within many of the same limitations on the use of political power as political liberalism has? Insofar as the major comprehensive religious and philosophical views in a society do generate the same limits as political liberalism, it is hard to see what the disagreement is. Political liberalism is not essentially a claim about the inappropriateness of religious speech. The important thing for political liberalism is that we can share and publicly affirm the authority of public grounds that are adequate to justify the constitutional essentials. If religious people wish to bear witness to the justifiability of political liberalism from the point of view of their religious perspectives, this may be not only appropriate but helpful on certain occasions. Pointing out that publicly shared reasons gain further support from our extrapolitical conceptions of the truth as a whole might, for example, assuage the doubts of those who question the sincerity of our allegiance to political liberalism.[5]

But comprehensive moralities may *not* generate all of the same limits on the use of state power as does political liberalism. Political liberalism, as we have seen, provides good reasons for pulling up short at the comprehensive educational agenda of Deweyite liberalism, or any similar agenda.

Indeed, there are other ways that political liberalism seems better able than its competitors to promote trust. First, under political liberalism citizens share not only substantive principles but also a public form of reasoning and a common rationale for the basis of their political order. Leaving basic political arrangements dependent on radically different rationales invites division and distrust. Even if the major comprehensive religious and philosophical perspectives generate many or all of the same limits as political liberalism, it is not a bad thing to have a *shared account* of why those limits are so important: to have something like a "social contract" that we can hold in common, along with any additional reasons that we will not share with our fellow citizens. Where a political community shares not only substantive commitments but also a commitment to resolving fundamental disputes on the basis of publicly available reasons and evidence, this becomes part of its political culture and should have a broadly educative effect.

Second, political liberalism generates trust from its simplicity: it relies only on forms of reasoning and evidence that are available to citizens generally. Comprehensive liberals, on the other hand, are prepared to shape public power on the basis of principles subject to deep but reasonable disagreement, so it is hard to see why they would follow political liberalism's exclusion of complex and subtle forms of reasoning. Here again, comprehensive liberalisms appear to invite greater conflict and distrust.[6]

Political liberalism may have one other important advantage: it may be better able than comprehensive liberalisms to promote the transition of a modus vivendi (from a condition of mere peace—that is, a truce backed not by shared principles but only a balance of power) to a more principled public order. Suppose in a given society that people's religious views are deeply opposed and at odds with liberal principles, yet battle fatigue leads them to establish peace and to grudgingly accept the need for political cooperation. How could they move toward a more principled order?

Rawls suggests that political liberalism may be especially capable of taking advantage of "a certain looseness" in the comprehensive views of most people. Some people are bound to have religious or moral convictions that stand in some tension with liberal politics. They may not, however, have worked out all of the connections among their political and extrapolitical convictions and values. If so, it will be easier for them to live with and develop an allegiance to liberalism. Political liberalism will be especially able to take advantage of this intellectual loosejointedness: "there is lots of slippage, so to speak, many ways for liberal principles of justice to cohere loosely with those (partially) comprehensive views."[7] The thought here seems to be that by avoiding comprehensive claims to truth, political liberalism does not provoke the kinds of comprehensive reflection about the coherence and compatibility of one's values as a whole—one's religious and political values, for example—that might make it harder for some people to live with the liberal political order. So "many if not most citizens come to affirm the principles of justice . . . without seeing any particular connection, one way or the other, between those principles and their other views."[8] While such individuals may eventually reflect on the connections and possible incompatibilities among their political and extrapolitical values, political liberalism's strategy of avoidance makes it more likely that this will occur only after they have lived under liberal arrangements for a while. Then, when critical reflection does occur, Rawls suggests, prior experience of the great goods of the liberal order should help ensure that any incompatibilities are resolved by adjusting the comprehensive doctrines rather than by rejecting political liberalism.[9]

Political liberalism seems designed to ease the transition from a modus vivendi to a principled public order. But does political liberalism involve deception? Does it, in other words, succumb to the sort of esotericism that Straussian political theorists have explored, and according to some, practiced?[10] If comprehensive liberalisms make transitions to a liberal order more difficult by fostering broader and deeper reflection on the connections among our political lives and other spheres of value, they also in this way help ensure that these transitions are more informed and genuinely consensual. Political liberalism appears to exploit an implicit tradeoff between stable allegiances, on the one hand, and principled transparency and critical reflection, on the other.

The charges of deception are provocative but unsound. Every institution and practice is educative, after all, and no political order counts solely on self-conscious educative measures. Liberal constitutionalism is replete with institutions and structures of power justified in part by their ability to promote indirectly particular civic dispositions and traits. Such mechanisms are pervasive. Robert Post observes that American First Amendment law puts far less emphasis on group-based sources of offense than do the laws governing offensive speech in some other societies. The English law of blasphemy, for example, gives legal recognition to the offense that Christians would feel at having their God publicly vilified. Blasphemy laws might be justified on civil grounds as a way to promote mutually respectful interactions among groups, or among individuals whose religious convictions shape their identities. The law of blasphemy, Lord Scarman insisted not long ago, should protect religious beliefs from "scurrility, vilification, and contempt," and in a plural society like England or India, it should protect the religious sensibilities of *all* religious groups.[11]

American constitutional law, however, allows the state to protect individuals from personal libel and "fighting words" (face-to-face insults directed at an individual that provoke immediate violent conflict).[12] American First Amendment law is far more hostile to government attempts to protect group-based sensibilities, whether through blasphemy laws, group libel, or hate speech laws. Why? Is it that Americans *naturally* take less offense at having their religious beliefs publicly scorned? Or is it that American judges think in individualistic as opposed to group-based terms?

No doubt, Americans may tend to ignore or discount the harms that speech can do, especially to long-disenfranchised minority groups.[13] There are, however, legitimate grounds for worrying about the educative effects of group-libel laws. By recognizing and providing legal recourse for certain kinds of harms but not others, legal regimes represent us as certain kinds of persons with certain kinds of basic interests. If we give legal recognition to the offense of blasphemy or other forms of group libel, we may encourage group-based sensitivities. If there is no legal recourse for blasphemous speech, people may become less sensitive to vigorous religious disagreement. Whether or not we decide to legally recognize blasphemy or hate speech, the law will be educative. We need to consider what the aims of a transformative constitutional order should be. What sorts of identities do we want to encourage citizens to adopt? How will the recognition of certain interests affect identity formation?

In the British context, it is worth remembering that when some Muslims objected to the depiction of Allah in Salman Rushdie's *The Satanic Verses,* the British blasphemy law was their weapon. British Muslims argued that all they wanted were the same protections enjoyed by Christians. Rather than broadening the blasphemy law and allowing more prosecutions for insults to religion, the British would likely do better to move toward the American model. By not using criminal law to enforce acceptable modes of mutual interaction, we may help promote more fluid group memberships, and so social attitudes that are less sensitive and more tolerant.[14]

There are a host of ways in which our political institutions give preference to certain kinds of interests and seem to ignore others, in order to encourage the predominance of those interests that can serve as the basis for peaceful interaction in our diverse society. These practices are deeply, if indirectly, educative. Indirect civic education is, in fact, a pervasive if neglected feature of our political institutions and our public policies. If political liberalism has certain self-supporting educative dimensions, that is not a bad or surprising thing.

The fact is that by establishing liberal values and identities indirectly, we may establish them more effectively.[15] This points us in an important direction. While we must not flee from the deeply controversial imperatives of liberal civic education, public schools are far from being the only political levers we have with respect to citizens' attitudes, habits, and character traits. A wide range of political institutions and public policies appear to have neglected educational dimensions, and these are worth exploring (as I will do in a companion work).

There is nothing wrong with relying in part on indirectly educative mechanisms. What is most crucial is that political liberals are prepared fully and openly to justify the transformative institutions and practices they support. That is sufficient. While political liberalism may seem to make philosophy take a back seat to the practical imperatives of politics, we must remember that political liberalism views deep but reasonable disagreement about the good life as a permanent consequence of freedom in modern conditions. Political liberalism provides, indeed, a philosophical account of why it is that political justification need not and should not depend on a particular account of the whole truth.

Some comprehensive liberals will respond that all of this is unnecessary or worse because there is widespread agreement on many substantive political principles and procedures. They argue that we can afford to encourage comprehensive moral and religious opinions to grapple in the political realm in a way that Europeans of the sixteenth century could not and citizens of today's former Yugoslavia or Lebanon cannot. We are amply ballasted by agreement; we may indeed be overly ballasted by commercialism and political lethargy.

The question that these comprehensive liberals fail to address, however, is to what do we owe this political ballast, and what must we do to preserve it? The three great American religions are in many ways strikingly liberal, but where did our peculiar attitudes toward religion come from and what keeps them so?[16] If our political culture is dependent on our political institutions—including the work done by the political avoidance of religious controversy—then encouraging the politicization of the deepest and historically most destructive forms of disagreement could undermine the culture and unseat the ballast.

In any case, the critics of liberal public reason often miss an essential point: when determining the basic shape of the awful coercive powers of the modern state, should we not try to offer our fellow citizens reasons that they can accept without first accepting our convictions about the ultimate ends of human life? Civic liberalism offers the hope of politics as a shared moral order without depending on unrealistic expectations of agreement on life's most difficult questions.[17]

Further, the very fact that liberal public reason lays claim to only a part of the moral realm should help foster political moderation. Even if political liberalism tends to transform extrapolitical commitments in its own image, it also provides real space for religious communities and institutions to develop according to their own convictions and imperatives. The playing field may not be level when one compares the prospects of those religious communities in tune with and those averse to liberal democratic values, but it is hard to imagine how it could be otherwise or why we should strive to make it so. Liberal public reason bars governments and political actors from making comprehensive claims to value and meaning; it leaves our allegiances divided. According to civic liberalism, politics does not exhaust the entire realm of moral value. Focusing on the authority of public reasons that can be shared, and understanding these reasons as encompassing something short of the whole truth, discourages total investments of moral capital in the political realm, and that seems to me to be all to the good.

Diversity is often a great liberal resource, but not always. There are religious and other forms of diversity that we have no reason to embrace or even accommodate. The liberalism of public reason allows us to regard declarations of holy war as premature; but equally important, it should furnish liberals with sufficient spine to stand up for their own core values. It softens but does not eliminate the tension between a this-worldly politics and many religions. That must be good enough. To true believers we pledge ourselves to public justifications and the avoidance of both religious and philosophical ideals of life. We will sometimes accommodate dissenting groups, but we must remind fundamentalists and others that they must pay a price for living in a free pluralistic society.

Liberal Multiculturalism and Civil Society

Horace Kallen was not wrong to emphasize that ethnic groups may be "reservoirs of individuality" and "springs of difference." An important part of civic education involves acknowledging the contributions to our national project made by the many races, ethnic groups, religions, associations, and cultures that have composed the American experience. The liberal democratic state properly conceived does not belong to Anglo-Saxon Protestants, those of "European" descent, or particular racial, ethnic, or religious groups. We have no grounds, however, for surrendering our critical faculties or denying the basic importance of a shared civic identity defined by certain common virtues and publicly justified principles. The fact that we do not stand for a certain racial or religious identity does not mean that we stand for nothing. Many forms of cultural pluralism are to be celebrated, but we should make sure that the pluralism we embrace is compatible with a political program designed to foster peaceful diversity, mutual cooperation, and respect for the accomplishments of many cultures.

In addition, liberalism should include support for multiculturalism that, properly understood, is a vibrant part of civic life. A liberal civic education will insist that children learn that it is possible for fellow citizens who affirm the political supremacy of liberal values to disagree deeply about other matters: not only cultural tastes, but also deep religious convictions. A liberal pluralistic multiculturalism will insist on the good of political respect for many different religions and cultures, while acknowledging the political authority of a shared point of view. Multiculturalism properly understood is an important part of a liberal civic education.

Stephen Carter rightly emphasizes a point that I develop elsewhere: religious communities are vital components of the civil society institutions intermediate between the individual and the state. Much evidence suggests that Tocqueville was right to stress the importance of intermediate associations in promoting trust, cooperativeness, and civic activity in a mass democracy. Religious communities are among the most active and widespread types of intermediate association, especially in America.[18] Religions are particularly important components of civil society, for they often challenge the materialism, hedonism, and this-worldliness that is so dominant in our time. And religions provide sources of meaning outside of politics that should help keep alive the intellectual arguments by which truth is supposedly approached in a liberal polity.[19]

These are important and powerful public reasons for taking seriously the project of accommodation. They cohere nicely with the aims of liberalism and with the prudential accommodationism I recommended earlier. In Part Three I argue that the moral resources furnished by civil society institutions are crucial to liberal civic life. Carter supplies no warrant, however, for adopting an uncritical accommodationist stance toward religious communities that seek exemptions from generally applicable policies.

A policy of accommodation and support for particular groups and cultures has its place within a sensible liberalism. A liberal policy of accommodation and a pluralistic multiculturalism should not be confused with an uncritical embrace of diversity. Accommodation should not aim at the "equal" treatment of all religious beliefs and communities. We must not apologize for the fact that some communities will have a harder time than others retaining their members or convincing the young to join.

Liberal constitutionalism is not only about rights and freedom, after all: it is also about sustaining political and social structures that educate individuals and shape communities in ways that are congruent with the basic aspirations of liberal justice. This is not only legitimate but essential political work, which will nevertheless have very unequal consequences for different religious communities.

Some religious communities detract, in important ways, from the civic life of liberal democratic societies. As we saw in Chapter 5, the Roman Catholic hierarchy promoted political authoritarianism until the church embraced liberal freedoms at Vatican II. The Amish continue to stand at odds with a specifically liberal democratic civil society, and not only because of their attitudes toward high school education. A substantial body of evidence suggests that the civic virtues needed by modern democracies are nurtured where individuals are enmeshed in a variety of cross-cutting, only partially overlapping patterns of association. These complex patterns of membership nurture broad forms of trust and cooperation not only among those in one's particular group, but among citizens as a whole. The homogeneity and tribalistic insularity of the Amish community is at odds with the pluralistic patterns of membership that contribute to liberal freedom and democratic civil society.[20]

My plea is that while we endeavor to make adequate room for religious practices, and while we recognize the positive contributions to our shared political life of many religious and other forms of pluralism, let us not forget or neglect the supreme importance of protecting the basic rights of all and sustaining our shared political framework. Let us, moreover, have the honesty and toughmindedness to acknowledge that this framework—no matter how liberal—inevitably constrains diversity in direct and indirect ways. We should not, in particular, aim to create a level playing field for various faith communities, and we should remember that even on a level playing field, some will lose. We will need some fortitude in the face of those fundamentalists of all stripes who refuse ever to acknowledge the political authority of reasons, principles, and a point of view above our many narrower sectarianisms.

Civil Society versus Sectarian Sensitivity

Does liberal public reason require people to separate their religious and their public selves? Only if their religious or philosophical convictions move them to advance public policies that can only be justified on grounds that are unable to be publicly shared with others. Then, liberals will try and remind such people of the importance of being guided in politics by reasons we can share.

Those whose religious views stand in tension with liberal democratic political norms may be especially resistant to the division of our lives that is so crucial to liberalism. Those who cannot or will not distinguish their sectarian convictions about the truth as a whole from the public imperatives of citizenship—when these come into conflict—may feel especially vulnerable and sensitive to criticism.

This sensitivity is exhibited in Carter's stance toward religion. Many liberals will only be happy, Carter argues, if believers treat their religion as a hobby: discrete, unimportant, and confined to the weekend. Liberalism requires serious religious believers to "split their public and private selves," telling them that "it is fine to be religious in private, but there is something askew when those private beliefs become the basis for public action." And so Carter complains that the public square is "formally open" but "religious witness" is not welcomed there.[21]

It is not enough for Carter and others that the rights of religious people to speak and profess are respected. The fact that liberals disapprove of relying on religious reasons in politics is portrayed by Carter as liberal intolerance. In the same vein, Carter argues that *tolerance* of religion is not enough: "Tolerance without respect means little; if I tolerate you but do not respect you, the message of my tolerance, day after day, is that it is *my* forbearance, not *your* right, and certainly not *the nation's* commitment to equality, that frees you to practice your religion. You do it by my sufferance, but not with my approval."[22]

These observations appear strangely confused. Liberal citizens must *respect* each other's rights, but they need not approve of the choices that other people make within the limits of their rights. It is perfectly acceptable for a citizen to say, "I respect your right to talk bloody nonsense and will defend it to the death, but I certainly do not approve of the drivel you propose."[23] It would be self-defeating from a liberal standpoint to demand more than this, for the whole point of our freedom is to allow us to disagree vehemently but peacefully with other people about such matters as religious truth.

What Carter seems to want to protect is not the freedom to disagree vigorously, but the psychological fragility and sensitivity of religious believers, a sensitivity that is inconsistent with vigorous disagreement. This solicitude for sensitive psyches leads Carter to conflate intellectual disagreement and physical vulnerability. He goes so far as to portray proselytizing as a method of wiping people "off the face of the earth." "I have even heard it suggested," writes Carter, "that the idea that Christians should tolerate Jews developed hand-in-glove with the notion that Christians should try to persuade them to come to Christ. It is hard to be happy if one's religious choice is tolerated only in order to hasten its destruction. America should put no one to that choice. A vital security of life in a free society should be that, far from being tolerated, every religious person and every religious group can claim equal rights with every other."[24]

It makes all the difference in the world whether someone seeks to "destroy" a religion through voluntary conversion or force. Carter resists this basic distinction, however, and once again seems to want "equal concern and respect" not simply for person's rights as citizens, but for what every person professes.

This desire to protect people from offense is odd for someone such as Carter, who celebrates the "subversive independence" of religious communities and their ability to "mobilize passions" as opposed to reason, and who denies that we should try to "domesticate" religious enthusiasms.[25] In spite of this tough rhetoric, Carter seems to regard religious believers as a timid lot. They need not only liberty but approval, not simply the right to speak but a welcome mat at the public square.

Carter's version of multiculturalism exhibits a troubling combination of radicalism and sensitivity. On the one hand, Carter insists that religions are subversively and passionately independent.[26] On the other hand, religious people are "silenced" by disapproval and intimidated by attempts at persuasion and conversion. Cherishing our "epistemic diversity," for Carter, seems to mean not only ignoring the political authority of shared reasons, but also requiring everyone to avoid challenging and criticizing other people's religious convictions.[27]

This combination of solicitude for diversity and prickly sensitivity to offense is a prescription for illiberality. Ironically it is Carter who would "silence" vigorous disagreement in the name of his multiculturalism of mutual sensitivity. Contrary to Carter, it is important in a pluralistic society for people to become less sensitive to taking offense in response to views of which they disapprove.

Liberalism seeks to make possible a peaceful framework within which we acknowledge the political authority of mutually accessible reasons. We can concede this much to Carter: the rule of public reasons is not served when people gratuitously insult each other's religious beliefs or moral convictions. But people are free to disagree deeply and to try to convert one another. In a richly pluralistic society, we need to be careful not to encourage offense taking and feelings of vulnerability. From a public point of view, people's equal standing and the grounds of their self-respect are furnished by their status as equal citizens, with its attendant rights and opportunities. We need to be careful not to undermine the basis of a lively and peaceful civic life by encouraging citizens to take offense over religious and cultural matters about which they are free to disagree.

In Carter's overall stance there is a final irony, one that reinforces and makes more troubling the illiberal tendencies implicit in his position. While his book is laced with references to the Bible and his own religious beliefs, he also rather oddly seems to embrace a certain relativism or perhaps skepticism. He praises "epistemic diversity" and insists that "given its starting point and methodology, creationism is as rational an explanation as any other" (there is an awful lot built into that "given," but we will leave that aside).[28] The battle between creationism and those who defend evolutionary accounts of human origins is a "war . . . between competing systems of discerning truth." The victor in this battle, Carter seems to suggest, can be determined not by better reasons or superior insight but only by "power."[29]

This attitude toward truth—Hobbesian skepticism in service of cultural pluralism—may help explain both why Carter seems drawn toward a multiculturalism of mutual sensitivity and why such a position is so deeply at odds with liberalism. Liberals believe that public argument, debate, and reason giving help us distinguish better and worse answers to political questions.

For Carter, however, deep disagreements appear as clashes of rival epistemologies or worldviews without any way of judging among them. Carter seems to have come round to the position of Stanley Fish and others—namely, that confidence in public reason is really nothing more than one ultimate faith among others.[30] An ultimate skepticism of this sort helps explain why we might as well give in to those who resist critical thinking and public reason: we have no reason to regard these practices as having any special authority. Perhaps this is why Carter favors public sensitivity and equality of respect over robust argument. For the skeptic, robust argument has no point; it is only the dominant culture's way of asserting power.

It is hardly surprising, then, that Carter explicitly links his brand of cultural pluralism to calls for including creationism in the curriculum. If there are only disparate and conflicting worldviews with no means of adjudicating among them, why not treat them all as equally valid? Carter is simply being fair-minded in recognizing that creationists have as much claim to be accommodated as the favored constituencies of the political left.[31] But why stop there? If creationism has an equal claim to legitimacy with mainstream science, then so presumably do voodoo and witchcraft. And what of the long tradition of "Christian Identity," according to which Jews and homosexuals are agents of Satan? If the world is divided into merely *different* "worldviews" among which we cannot discern more or less justifiable positions, then any system of ideas, if maintained consistently—but, for that matter, why make a fetish of consistency?—or as part of a "way of life," merits respect.

This radically pluralist march away from public reason is a decisive step away from liberalism. If liberal claims to public authority rest on nothing more than superior power, then one cannot be said to have good reasons to favor liberal arrangements over the rivals: favoring individual rights and robust public argument is only a matter of taste and ultimately of political strength. Of course, if all we have in the end is a war of all against all with no privileged claims to authority and no shared public standards for adjudicating conflicting claims, then Hobbes may have been right to suppose that rule by a sovereign will is the safest course.

Carter does not defend anything like Hobbesian authoritarianism (indeed, he does not typically assert the radical implications of his own arguments). We can, however, see the germs of a soft form of intolerance in this intellectual stance. These germs are the overriding desire to protect fragile egos from the upsets of criticism and disagreement, and a skepticism about the possibility of distinguishing better and worse claims through vigorous and public debate. Sometimes these elements are combined with the notion that it is oppressed groups in particular whose group-based perspectives have been unfairly ignored or marginalized by "mainstream" political, scientific, and cultural centers of power. Such a stance may attract powerful constituencies to the cause of deep pluralism.

The fact is, however, that the causes of equality and justice for long-disenfranchised groups will not be advanced by embracing an epistemological pluralism, or by skepticism about the possibility of shared moral standards. If the oppressed share no common standards of right or justice with their oppressors, then they lose the ability to appeal to standards that ought to control their oppressors. Oppressed and marginalized groups have the most to lose by dividing the world into segmented epistemological and moral units.

Carter is right to suppose that some religious people will have a hard time recognizing the political authority of reasons that can be shared with fellow citizens of different faiths. Carter's mistake is in supposing that this means something is wrong with liberalism. As I have argued in preceding chapters, a good citizen in a pluralistic modern society acknowledges the fact of reasonable pluralism and recognizes the importance of finding shared grounds for basic political principles. Carter's political sectarian cannot be a good citizen in this respect. We should beware an overweening desire to protect such sensitivities at the expense of the norms that make a shared civic life possible.

It is important to remember that most Americans do not experience a profound tension or split between their religious and political convictions because they are not inclined to impose their religious beliefs on others through politics. Indeed, Alan Wolfe's research on the religious convictions of ordinary Americans reinforces the contention that Will Herberg advanced nearly forty years ago: the major religions of America accept and support the core liberal political conviction that religious beliefs should not be imposed on others through politics.[32]

Conclusion

The civic liberalism we have begun to explore offers a way of holding out our hand to religious believers and others who reject the comprehensive ideals sometimes associated with liberalism. It seeks reasons widely acceptable to reasonable people, and it rejects all forms of moral totalism, whether the ecumenical Protestantism of a Horace Mann, the secular humanism of a John Dewey, or the fundamentalist biblical totalism of a Vicki Frost. Liberal public reason seeks to respect not one party's conception of the whole truth, but the reasonableness that we all might share. It also permits us, as I have argued, to go beyond the anxious conservatism of Berns and Scalia to consider possible exceptions and exemptions partly on the basis of our own shared values and aims.

As Amy Gutmann has noted, it would be wrong to claim that any version of liberalism is uncontroversial, and it would be mistaken to minimize the consequences and ramifications of life within liberal institutions.[33] Even though political authority stakes out a philosophically limited realm, the educative realm thus covered in practice is rather broad, extremely important, and is bound to exercise a pervasive influence on people's lives as a whole. We should acknowledge all this, lest it appear that political liberalism is a Trojan horse for a more comprehensive conception. If we believe in the authority of public reasons, then we must candidly admit and defend the full breadth of our partisanships.

In his book *Liberal Purposes*, William Galston chides the present author, among others, for picking too many fights with religious "true believers." "Civic tolerance of deep differences," he claims, "is perfectly compatible with unswerving belief in the correctness of one's own way of life . . . Civic deliberation is also compatible with unshakable personal commitments."[34] As we have seen, however, not all religions are equally amenable to the political authority of public reasons.

Galston gets closer to the truth when he writes that "[i]f, to be wholly effective, a religious doctrine requires control over the totality of individual life, including the formative social and political environment, then the classic liberal demand that religion be practiced privately amounts to a substantive restriction on the free exercise of that religion."[35] This assertion is certainly right: the readiness to put religion aside in politics constitutes an important concession for many religious people.

Many traditional religious concerns can be translated into public terms and can thereby make an important contribution to public policy debates. Instead of invoking "Judeo-Christian" values on behalf of profamily policies, for example, one could argue in appropriately secular terms that stable two-parent families are important social institutions. And yet many believers, fundamentalists included, pay a substantial price for life in a liberal society. It cannot be the case that all religions prosper equally in a liberal regime, and Galston certainly admits this. A moment of silence in public schools, which Galston offers as the happy meeting ground of liberals and religious types, will not make everyone equally happy.[36]

A political or civic liberalism, honoring as it does the important but limited authority of public reasons, allows us to soften some sources of tension between a secular, permissive, this-worldly politics and some religions. It seems hard to imagine that we could do better than that. To true believers we must pledge ourselves to public justifications and the avoidance of both religious and philosophical ideals of life. Perhaps we can sometimes accommodate dissenting groups when significant disparate burdens are imposed on them. We must also remind fundamentalists and other dissenters that they must pay a certain price for living in a pluralistic society. In the end, true believers say nothing that should shake our faith in the legitimacy of a regime dedicated to peaceful pluralism and individual freedom.

Fastening our bayonets should be a last resort. There is plenty to discuss before we get to that point. The only way to satisfy our own moral convictions is to keep explaining and answering objections as best we can, even if there is no guarantee that we can convince everyone. In any case, we cannot say in advance what might or might not convince religious people to go along with the liberal settlement, or even to affirm the principled case for political liberalism. Our politics might well come down to holy war with some people, but we don't know in advance with how many or exactly whom.

PART III

School Reform and Civic Education

Public schooling has been and remains a source of some of the deepest moral conflicts that our polity has witnessed. One increasingly attractive response has been to avoid the conflicts by overturning the model of common schooling that has dominated America since the time of Horace Mann—that is, by getting the government out of the business of promoting civic values through formal educational institutions, by providing much greater scope for parental choice and school competition, and by narrowing the focus of public educational policies to the pursuit of widely acceptable aims such as improving test scores, lowering dropout rates, and efficiency.

We return, then, to the strategy of avoidance discussed in the Introduction, which would dissociate public policy toward education from our deepest civic purposes. This strategy appeals to widely felt libertarian convictions: to the desire to respect parental control over children and the integrity of families, to cultural and religious pluralism, and to the faith in competition and free markets. The turn away from common schooling certainly appeals to latter-day heirs to the position of Bishop Hughes, according to which a public stance of "perfect neutrality" toward religious diversity can only be achieved by a system of parental choice among schools, including religious schools.

A principal thrust of this book has been that proponents of diversity and choice often underestimate the extent of our legitimate civic purposes with respect to education. Arguments for school reform need to be examined in a context that takes seriously the full measure of our civic ambitions. To insist that we need to place public school reform in a civic context is not to argue against reform. On balance there may well be good reasons to support some of the reforms now being proposed, at least in some places. We will, however, think about reform differently and more effectively if we keep civic aims in view.

The one thing we should not do is to ignore the civic purposes that have so powerfully shaped the institution of public schooling. While the extent and nature of common *schooling* is always subject to reasonable debate, the imperatives of common civic *education* must be pursued somehow.[1] We have no reason to expect citizenship to take care of itself.

In Chapter 10 I focus on a variety of moral arguments designed to establish the priority of parental and private purposes with respect to education. Just how powerful are arguments for parental rights, and for the priority of educational diversity over civic purposes? In Chapter 11, I turn to the question of school reform more broadly. Reform proposals most often focus on urban school systems, and more especially on the scale and anonymity of big urban high schools. The "shopping mall" high school is intended to contain the diversity and reflect the emphasis on choice that characterize the Great Society beyond the walls of the school. It is not difficult to imagine that this model needs rethinking, but it should be recast from a perspective that pursues, as effectively as possible, the full range of our civic purposes. Without attempting anything like a comprehensive analysis of the many school reform proposals that compete for our attention—magnet schools, charter schools, vouchers, and school choice—I want to raise the question: How do such reforms measure up to our civic ideals?

CHAPTER 10

Civic Purposes and Public Schools

The themes of diversity and distrust are never far from the foreground in debates over public school reform. On the one side, school autonomy, competition, and parental choice are often touted as panaceas, or at least as keys to vast improvement. Get the government out of the way; allow schools to diversify, define distinctive missions, and to compete. Trust parents to decide what is best for their children. Indeed, reform often seems to mean trusting choice-based diversity to do better than an inefficient, one-size-fits-all government monopoly.

On the other side, among those who fear reform, distrust is often the key. Amy Gutmann expresses this perspective well:

> History suggests that without state provision or regulation of education, children will be taught neither mutual respect among persons nor rational deliberation among ways of life. To save their children from future pain, especially the pain of eternal damnation, parents have historically shielded their children from diverse associations, convinced them that all other ways of life are sinful, and implicitly fostered (if not explicitly taught them) disrespect for people who are different.[1]

This may be slightly overstated, but it contains an important element of truth. To cast school reform as a matter of trusting competition and consumer choice to "outperform" a government-run, single-provider system is to miss the whole point of common schooling. Public schools are supposed to contribute to the creation of a common civic identity.

That the schools bring children from many backgrounds together in a common institution is the whole point: it does not make sense to say that school choice and competition will "outperform" the common school system if one central desired "output" of the public system is simply left off the balance sheet. A profound choice among educational *ends*, not only *means*, may well be at stake here.

Defenders of the current system are not all wrong to worry that radical school reforms could lead to schools in thrall to various forms of localism and particularism: to schools run by Scientologists, black nationalists, or white supremacists. And yet it is doubtful that many such schools would come into being under even the most radical of reforms.

Let us consider the moral and civic elements of the case for retaining something like the traditional common school system, and then for placing much greater emphasis on parental rights, freedom of choice in education, and diversity.

The reigning system of publicly run common schools is not simply outmoded or empty from the standpoint of political morality. The common school ideal stands for educational institutions that contain society's diversity in a tolerant, respectful cooperative context. Common schools remain especially appropriate vehicles for inculcating the civic virtue of mutual respect for those who differ with us in their religious convictions or beliefs about the good life. As Eamonn Callan puts it, common schools are a "setting that really includes students and teachers whose diverse ethical voices represent the pluralism of the larger society." It is not simply, or perhaps even principally, the substantive curriculum of these schools that is crucial. Common schools have a "hidden curriculum" suggesting "that at least in this environment one can and perhaps should study literature, discuss moral problems and so on, in a way that sets aside commitments to separate educational values which, for their adherents [at least in the extreme instances], can never be justifiably set aside."[2] Such institutions embody the fundamental liberal civic commitment to mutual understanding, respect, and cooperation among reasonable fellow citizens who may disagree about their ultimate religious and philosophical commitments.

In addition, as Meira Levinson has argued, common schools are importantly "detached" from the beliefs of parents and the particular normative communities with which families identify. Publicly run common schools represent, therefore, the basic fact that children are independent persons-in-the-making with their own basic interests and their own lives to lead. Those families whose beliefs have no place for liberal civic ideals, such as the fundamentalist families in *Mozert* or others who are intent on binding children to the convictions of their parents, may well view the common schools with hostility.[3]

Common Schooling and Mutual Respect

The current system of public schooling aims to promote directly certain core liberal civic values. Big schools and big school districts are designed to foster a broad social mixing and, it is hoped, more tolerant and inclusive attitudes. And so Abigail Thernstrom properly suggests that something of value could be lost if we embrace reform proposals and retreat from the ideal of the big, diverse city schools.[4] We could lose an educative institution that embodies the diversity and openness of the cosmopolitan liberal society and that, as a consequence, should help inculcate liberal virtues of toleration, openness, self-criticism, and mutual respect.

Public school advocates tell a story about civic education that is reminiscent of the traditional argument for common schooling. For much of our history, distrust focused on religious and ethnic outsiders such as Irish Catholics. Today's public school proponents focus their distrust on fundamentalists, creationists, racists, Nazis, black separatists, Afrocentrists, multiculturalists, and others who, in one way or another, espouse particular religious, ethnic, or racial identities at the expense of civic norms of toleration, mutual respect, and the authority of public reason. Now, as before, parents are often portrayed as sources of bigotry and religions are frequently depicted as sources of prejudice and disrespect, all of which need to be counteracted by public education. Without public schools, Gutmann argues, Protestant parents would have continued to teach disrespect for Catholicism, and "the religious prejudices of Protestant parents would have been visited on their children." Catholics who now support privatization and parental control have the luxury of building on the "moral capital created by public schooling" over many decades, but in doing so they would prevent the building of such capital for blacks and Hispanics.[5]

When we turn from theory to practice, it does indeed appear that public schools are often animated by an ethos of tolerant pluralism and mutual respect. Arthur G. Powell, Eleanor Farrar, and David K. Cohen found that even teachers critical of the laxity of big city public high schools praised their ethos of tolerance: "The one theme that schools can rally around is *tolerating* differences. This is what they are least neutral about . . . Indeed, the only objective officially listed by the school which bore on moral character was the intention that students become 'more understanding of the problems of others, and more appreciative of the strengths of others.' The 'others' included those of different race, religion, cultural background, economic status, talent, sex, and mental or physical capacities."[6]

Big, inclusive public schools teach toleration because "the whole society is there"—they are microcosms of the diversity of society as a whole—and when "racial or ethnic slurs occurred within classrooms, teachers virtually never ignored them. They pounced on them as educational opportunities."[7] Admittedly some observers, such as Gerald Grant, characterize the achievement more modestly as mere peaceful coexistence with little positive affirmation of the virtues of diversity.[8]

The "shopping mall" high school is not morally neutral: it stands for mutual respect for students of different religious, racial, and cultural backgrounds, and it stands for choice and individuality, as we will see. The structure and ethos of common schooling, as well as the power conferred by a public system with a monopoly on government support—and, in many instances, a certain degree of remoteness from parental demands—help public schools to advance values that overarch more particular communities.

The actual effectiveness of public schools at teaching toleration is hard to gauge. It is difficult to detect important differences among public and private school students with respect to attitudes about tolerance and respect for liberal rights. One study finds that Catholic school students (especially blacks) are more feminist than their public school counterparts: another shows that Catholic schooling seems to make Catholic students more religiously tolerant and supportive of civil liberties than does public schooling.[9] Andrew Greeley finds that while Catholic schools have fewer minority students, they are better integrated than in public schools. Socioeconomic classes are much better mixed in Catholic schools.[10] The comparative success of different types of schools at teaching civic virtues is not much studied, but today's Catholic schools do not appear detrimental to the achievement of our civic aims.

In addition, racist attitudes have declined markedly over the last thirty years, but how much credit do the public schools deserve for this happy development?[11] Between 1968 and 1972, thanks to court orders and new federal requirements, school segregation declined significantly: the percentage of blacks in predominantly minority schools declined from 77 to 64 percent, and the percentage of blacks in schools with a minority composition of more than 90 percent declined from 64 to 39 percent. Political control over schooling allowed significant strides to be made toward racial integration and, later, the "mainstreaming" of students with disabilities. In many places, public school integration was thwarted by "white flight" and the unwillingness of courts and other political actors to override popular opposition to large-scale busing across district lines. Since the early seventies, racial integration has not improved much, and some argue it has worsened in recent years.[12] Even critics of the size and impersonality of today's urban high schools allow that racial harmony within the schools has improved markedly since the early days of integration.[13]

Should we conclude that public schools do nothing to promote liberal civic attitudes and virtues? Not necessarily. One unstated assumption in many skeptical critiques of public schools is that the reformed system of the future will resemble the civically happy Catholic schools of today. But will they? Private schools have not, for a long time, been more than a very small part of the overall educational establishment; their performance, like everything else in our society, may be indebted to the wider social influence of the dominant common school regime. It is impossible to say for sure what schools would look like were we really to take privatization and parental choice seriously. And it must be remembered that Catholic schools represent a declining portion of nonpublic schooling.

Given the centrality of civic purposes to public schools it is ironic that studies of "effective schools" pay so little attention to civic ends.[14] Reform could change the moral nature of all schools. Of course, even if we were to eliminate common schooling as we have known it, that does not mean we will forgo regulating all schools receiving public moneys. There are, in addition, many ways to pursue our civic educational aims outside of formal educational institutions. A serious shift of authority toward parents and particular communities must be attended by a certain risk.

Despite these empirical questions, the common school has an enduring appropriateness as an apt instrument for the pursuit of weighty moral and political concerns. It would be foolish to cast aside on light and narrow grounds an instrument fit for such an important purpose. The public schools' actual civic effectiveness is open to dispute, and some public school systems may be "failing" in various ways. But in the end, the case for reform is circumstantial and local, not based on sweeping matters of first principle.

Public Education, Civic Autonomy, and Neutrality

Public schools have also been defended as appropriate means for guarding the basic moral interests of children as independent persons with their own lives to lead. In common schools, as opposed to schools affiliated with particular moral or religious communities, children are exposed to a variety of alternatives and allowed to choose for themselves. One vexing question is just how far it is proper for public institutions to go in promoting not only children's basic interests in education and independence but their individuality and autonomy.

Big public schools that embody the diversity of a liberal society and introduce children to a variety of options seem well designed to promote a child's right to live his or her own life. Like the liberal social order itself, public schools contain children from many backgrounds. Big public schools are the kinds of places that Justice Douglas celebrated in his dissent in the Amish education case, *Wisconsin v. Yoder.* An Amish child

> may want to be a pianist or an astronaut or an oceanographer. To do so he will have to break from the Amish tradition . . . If a parent keeps his child out of school beyond the grade school, then the child will be forever barred from entry into the new and amazing world of diversity that we have today . . . If he is harnessed to the Amish way of life by those in authority over him and if his education is truncated, his entire life may be stunted and deformed.[15]

Public schools seem well designed to make effective the child's right to separate from the moral ideals and religious convictions of his or her parents. The public schools are an antidote to all forms of sectarian indoctrination.

James S. Coleman and Thomas Hoffer describe the mission of today's public high schools as that of freeing children from the inevitable limitations of the particular families and communities into which they are born. Public high schools aim to liberate children by introducing them to the broader culture and stripping away ethnic and other particular attachments.[16] Public schooling is thus a way of guaranteeing what Joel Feinberg has called a child's right to "an open future."[17]

Bruce Ackerman presses this line of argument even further by arguing that, like the political system as a whole (as he understands it), schools should try to be "neutral" with respect to the choices that children might make. The "mission" of the "liberal" school is "to provide the child with access to the wide range of cultural materials that he may find useful in developing his own moral ideals and patterns of life."[18] Children need training for self-control, and guidance as to the feasibility and costs of various alternatives, but to otherwise push them in a particular direction—whether parents or public authorities are doing the pushing—is to tyrannize them.[19]

As I have argued throughout this book, "neutrality" is not a basic demand of liberal justice, and it is hard to see why either parents or schools should be straitjacketed in the manner Ackerman suggests. Neither parents nor the democratic community should be allowed to confine children's options within narrow limits, or deny any child the right to pursue his or her own path in life. The right to freedom is not, however, the right to a level playing field: the child can rightfully be subjected to parental or public efforts to inculcate their visions of good character so long as these efforts are not repressive, and so long as the child is also presented with information about alternative ways of life. Neither political societies nor parents may rightly seek to indoctrinate children, but much of what actually happens in schools today falls between repression and Ackerman's neutrality.[20] As Gutmann observes, "To focus exclusively on the value of freedom, or even on the value of moral freedom, neglects the value that parents and citizens may legitimately place on partially prejudicing the choices of children by their familial and political heritages." Both parents and the political community have a right to promote reasonable visions of good character.[21]

Similarly, the goals of "liberation" or of providing a child with a perfectly "open" future goes too far. Schools should not aim to strip away all of the beliefs and allegiances that parents might seek to inculcate in their children. Nor should we be troubled if, especially in the early years of schooling, public educational authorities seek to foster in children a feeling of attachment to community and country, and an aversion to bigotry and prejudice. As Gutmann observes, it is altogether appropriate to first teach young children to be repelled by bigotry, and later to teach them why.[22]

Liberal education should not stand for a neutral educational environment, one that is "nonjudgmental" with respect to the choices people make or to the forms of good and valuable lives: to the contrary, we want children to learn that there are better and worse ways of using their freedom. What is crucial from a liberal standpoint is that no one educational authority should totally dominate: that children acquire a measure of distance on all claims to truth in order to be able to think critically about our inclusive political ideals and detect conflicts between those inclusive ideals and their more particular moral and religious convictions. The point is not to promote a comprehensive philosophical doctrine of autonomy or individuality, but to make sure that no authority imposes an intellectual tyranny on children, which would thwart their right to freedom.

Public schools have several advantages with respect to these aims. Because they are democratically controlled and generally locally controlled, they are unlikely to be at radical loggerheads with the views of most parents. In addition, they are public, common institutions, and so are suited to representing our broadest and most inclusive educative ambitions. Gutmann adds that the role of educational professionals may also be important: professionalism among teachers may help the schools stand for a measure of critical independence from both civic and parental convictions.[23]

Civic liberalism will insist that children learn that the freedom to choose is the birthright of every citizen of a liberal political community: that they are rights holders, and that as adults they may leave oppressive associations and relationships without losing their status as equal citizens. Children must at the very least be provided with the intellectual tools necessary to understand the world around them, formulate their own convictions, and make their own way in life. Within those limits, both parents and the state should take care to promote broader and higher notions of excellence in children.

Is there not a danger of our broadly civic ideals becoming a form of comprehensive liberalism? That is, does not the emphasis on equal liberty, critical independence, an awareness of the world and its options, and the ability to reflect on one's particular convictions and aims for the sake of doing justice come very close to a comprehensive philosophical ideal of individuality or autonomy?

The fact is that a broad (not comprehensive) commitment to critical thinking is inseparable from the core civic capacities of good liberal citizens. Liberal citizens should be committed to honoring the public demands of liberal justice in all departments of their lives. They should be alert to the possibility that religious imperatives, or even inherited notions of what it means to be a good parent, spouse, or lover, might in fact run afoul of guarantees of equal freedom. A basic aim of civic education should be to impart to all children the ability to reflect critically on their personal and public commitments for the sake of honoring our shared principles of liberal justice and equal rights for all. Only in this way can citizens reassure themselves and their fellow citizens that they are alert to possible conflicts among their nonpublic imperatives and commitments and the demands of liberal public reasonableness.

Public educational institutions should not promote comprehensive ideals of life as a whole, but that does not mean that public schools are limited to a narrowly political agenda. Our civic ideals are not narrowly political. The promotion of these ideals (as opposed to the basic educational prerequisites of personal independence) are not imperatives of basic justice, but they are surely within the range of legitimate discretion of democratically constituted educational institutions, which may—and should—promote the ideal of a broadly educated and civically engaged citizenry.

No doubt some of the distinctions that separate a civic liberalism from a comprehensive liberalism are fairly subtle, but they are as important now as they were in 1840. Public schoolteachers and authors of materials for public schools should avoid advancing the notion that children need to think about their religious beliefs critically for the sake of better understanding religious truth. Yet, good liberal citizens will be alert to possible conflicts between their religious convictions and civic demands. All citizens should be capable of thinking critically about their private beliefs for the sake of honoring the demands of liberal justice. All children should be made aware of the ethnic, racial, and religious diversity that constitutes our society so that they can think as citizens and so that they will not live in a mental straitjacket at odds with freedom. As a practical matter, this aspect of education needs to be approached with great sensitivity.

The crucial point is to celebrate critical thinking and autonomy for broadly civic purposes, not to advance particular religious or comprehensive philosophical convictions. It is of course true, and inevitable, that our broad civic ideals (and even our narrowest and most basic political aims) are more compatible with some religions than with others. But we should not exaggerate the extent of direct conflict: nothing I have said denies the truth of biblical literalism as a religious matter.[24]

The proponents of the current educational regime do not make the mistake of leaving the civic dimensions of education aside. The case for preserving common schooling relies on some of the most basic liberal political values: toleration, mutual respect, and the ability to reflect critically on political matters and develop a measure of personal independence. Distrust plays an important role in these arguments: the worry is that particular communities, especially those that are highly insular, may so envelop a child's commitments and beliefs that the child is effectively denied the capacity to exercise his or her basic freedoms. Such arguments, if sometimes overstated, are far from wrong: the state helps make real freedom possible by providing children with vantage points outside of particular groups.[25]

School Reform, Parental Rights, and Family Life

Let us turn now to a very different set of arguments: those proposing that school reform take its bearings not from civic purposes but from the private right that many Americans hold dearest: the right of parents to control the education of their children. On what grounds do many academics and ordinary Americans believe that the parental and familial interests at stake in education "trump" public purposes?

As we have already seen, some moral arguments against the common school regime are rooted in claims of fundamental justice. Echoing certain aspects of the Supreme Court's decision in *Pierce v. Society of Sisters,* some critics argue that public schools are an assault on parents' rights to control the education of their children. More moderate, and as it turns out, more plausible, critics of today's dominant public school model argue that the public system, while it does not violate fundamental rights, does neglect the importance of the moral resources furnished by small communities. We can begin with the more radical critics and move toward the more plausible ones.

Now as in the 1920s, there are those who argue that public schools usurp parental rights and undermine the good of the family as a distinctive and especially important form of moral community. But this line of argument is quite weak. Consider first the claim that we should regard parents as having a right to choose among educational options because shaping a child's education is so central to the flourishing of parents, and the good of family as a community.

Certain basic and important human goods arise from the deep and extensive bonds of caring and love, knowledge and intimacy, that constitute families. Here as in few if any other human relationships, a willingness to sacrifice all for another is not unusual. The intensity of family relations stems from such things as the uniqueness of the biological tie, the great dependence of children on their parents and the sustained nurturing and sacrifice that childrearing requires, and long shared experiences and common projects. As Loren Lomasky puts it,

> having children is often an integral component of persons' projects . . . And having children in whom one invests one's devotion is to undertake a commitment that spans generations and creates personal value for the parent that transcends his or her own span of life . . . Few people can expect to produce a literary or artistic monument, redirect the life of a nation, garner honor and glory that lives after them. But it is open to almost everyone to stake a claim to long-term significance through having and raising a child.[26]

We all care about the well-being of children, but parents (as a rule) care intensely about their own children. In general, we do well to trust parents to make decisions for their children within a wide but not unlimited range of discretion. As Stephen G. Gilles argues, one reason is that parents can generally be trusted better than anyone else to pursue the child's best interests.[27] This is good not only for children, but also for parents, whose own flourishing is bound up with the freedom to shape their children's education.

Choice in education would bolster parental control by encouraging schools to extend and complement the authority of parents and the moral communities with which parents identify. When governments run schools in the name of shaping what children will learn, however, the polity effectively denies the educational autonomy of families and claims joint responsibility with parents for childrearing. It is as though every child gains a third adoptive parent with lengthy and long-term visitation rights. Early opponents of public schooling, such as Boston Irish Catholics, argued that when the state "adopts" the child it weakens "the ties which bind it to the parent." By taking away responsibility from parents, public institutions can dilute but not replicate parental love.[28] And so, Gilles argues, parents should be required to provide children with a "basic education that equips the child to speak, read, write, calculate, and reason" and thus to be enabled for "normal human flourishing in our society."[29]

This line of argument, flowing from worries about the dilution of parental affection, is reminiscent of Aristotle's criticisms of Plato's utopian scheme for holding women and children in common: "there will be less affection where children and women are common." What Aristotle says of property applies to children as well: "it makes an immense difference with respect to pleasure to consider a thing one's own." Where children are held in common, familial affection is not universalized; instead,

> affection necessarily becomes diluted through this sort of partnership, and the fact that a father least of all says "mine" of his son, or the son of his father. Just as adding much water to a small amount of wine makes the mixture imperceptible, so too does this result with respect to the kinship with one another based on these terms, it being least of all necessary in a regime of this sort for a father to take thought for his sons as sons, or a son for his father as a father, or brothers for one another [as brothers]. For there are two things above all which make human beings cherish and feel affection, what is one's own and what is dear; and neither of these can be available to those who govern themselves in this way.[30]

It seems right to say that it is immensely important for every child to have parents of his or her own. It would be foolish to think that state agencies or other societywide institutions could substitute for the intensely personal and particularized bonds of family life. Without parental attention and affection, children are liable to find themselves adrift in a sea of mild and distant affections.

But what reason do we have to think that public schools undermine parents' affection for, and attention to the well-being of, their children? It seems unlikely that mandatory schooling, and a public educational agenda wider than that recommended by Gilles, lessens parental attachment to children. After all, there really is no dispute that parental authority over children is limited: there are things that parents must do for their children, and there are things that they may not do. The authority of parents over their children is qualified by the collective insistence that children have certain basic interests that even parents may not deny or ignore. The only issue here is the range of public authority.

The justification for some measure of public authority lies in the fact that children are not simply creatures of their parents, but are independent persons with their own lives to lead. Children have basic interests in food, shelter, affection, and other aspects of basic well-being, including education. In part, our collective insistence on qualifying parental authority flows from these basic interests. It is not so much that the public insists on acting as a third adoptive parent, but rather that governments and the democratic community recognize the moral independence of each individual and insist on due regard for that independence, even from parents.

Parental authority is properly qualified on other grounds as well, for children are also future citizens—members not only of families, but also of local and national political communities. In addition to the basic aspects of human well-being, it also seems right to say that additional grounds for a range of public authority with respect to public education are furnished by our desire to shape future citizens.

Another approach to this question is suggested by the remarks of Lomasky and Gilles, quoted earlier. It might be thought that public schools undermine important goods intrinsic to family life because they impede a family's ability to pursue the good life, or a particular conception of religious truth, as a family. The pursuit of happiness is every individual's right, but it requires other people with whom to share the pursuit. For many people, the most important such others are family members. Family members typically share an especially rich, deep, and long-term history constituted by shared commitments to basic goods. The most natural thing in the world, according to Gilles, is for committed and loving parents to "wish their vision of education to be given full effect."[31] If we deprive parents of the opportunity to nurture their own orientations toward religion and meaning in their children, we will deny parents the ability to express many of their most basic values in the context of their most important associations.

Once again, the problem is that children are not just family members pursuing common family goals: they are independent individuals with their own lives to lead, and they are future citizens. The family is an especially important form of community—and I have conceded that parents have a right and indeed a responsibility to teach their children about the excellences of human character, as best they understand them—but the family's prerogatives should not be allowed to override the basic interests of children as individuals and future citizens. The extensive and intense ties of affection and concern that distinguish families from other associations help explain why public interventions in matters of education are so fraught with controversy. Whatever some parents might wish, it has been a very long time since we viewed it as a matter of fundamental right for parents to give "full effect" to their vision of education for their children: to do so gives *no effect* to the moral and political independence of children.[32]

It is hard for me to see how the arguments put forward by Lomasky and Gilles provide convincing grounds for shifting our educational aims away from civic purposes and toward greater control for parents. The traditional American system of educational funding does not run afoul of either fundamental rights or the basic interests of families and parents properly conceived. The common school ideal still accords most educational authority to parents: children spend their earliest years under the guidance of their parents, and parents maintain ongoing control outside of school hours. In addition, while public funds support public schools, parents remain free to send their children to nonpublic schools at their own (or some other private party's) expense. Further, we provide churches and non-profit schools with tax-exempt status. Of course, the institution of common schooling is not *compelled* by basic principle either: it would not necessarily be a gross violation of children's rights were we publicly to decide to move *closer* to the system Gilles and Lomasky advocate (at least, perhaps, if we augment somewhat Gilles's account of the child's interest in civic competence). Gilles himself allows that children's education "must both be consistent with, and prepare them for, their future autonomy as adults," and that "excessive intolerance" is undesirable, because it will often spill over into public life.[33] Any sensible view will qualify parental control: it is hard to see why we should not press those qualifications further than Gilles.

Amy Gutmann has emphasized, there is room for democratic discretion here. While we might publicly decide to cede more authority to parents in order better to realize our civic ends broadly conceived, it is hard to see why we should recognize any fundamental parental right that precludes the longstanding public practices of selective school funding. Indeed, as I argued earlier, we have good reason to value a division of educational authority. Parents will always have considerable control, due to their extensive nurturing responsibilities. And local and national political communities properly ensure that children's basic interests and a variety of civic interests are advanced.[34] The last thing we want is any one source of authority dominating education.

It is also worth remembering that in spite of what Gilles and Lomasky argue, there is no great tension between the aims of common schooling and the moral aspirations of the vast majority of parents. Few parents reject either our basic civic values or the notion that their children should lead independent lives. We have no reason, either in morality or prudence, to design public policy around those few parents who reject these reasonable propositions.

Our conclusions here are largely negative, but they are important. If there are good reasons for significant school reform, we need to be careful to be clear about them, for such reasons will help determine the nature of reform and the standards by which we judge its success. There are no parental interests decisive enough to displace shared civic considerations. The good reasons for reform have to do with the well-being of children, families, and the wider political community.

School Reform and the Good of Social Diversity

It may be, however, that certain broader social goods are sacrificed in an educational environment that inculcates too singlemindedly the virtues of toleration, openness to diversity, appreciation for pluralism, and so on. That is, a moral education in which too much emphasis is placed on tolerance for other faiths and philosophies may be an education with too little room for deeply developing particular ways of life that make social diversity rich and give individuals distinctive sources of meaning and direction.

Liberal values are distinctive and substantive values. Moral and religious communities that embrace Socratic virtues (reflective self-criticism) and Millian values (social diversity and choice) will regard the public school regime as a complement to communal life. Most communities are not Amish, in part because of the long pressure of public schools and other agencies of social mixing and assimilation. Why not stand unflinchingly behind public schools in the hope that these will transform all communities and integrate them ever more fully into this pluralistic tolerant society?

The question is whether liberal democratic virtues can be pressed so far or so relentlessly—in a combination of formal and informal educational settings—as to rob particular communities of the chance to develop rich moral and cultural traditions. Are we creating a tolerant and "open" society that is also a bland and homogeneous mass? This worry encourages us to focus not on the prerogatives of parents and families, but on the distinctiveness and depth of the cultural and moral alternatives that our society contains, and that our educational institutions either foster or fail to foster.

It would be not simply boring, but unimaginable for one's moral compass to be set entirely by liberal democratic convictions. (Taking such a stand would be almost as pointless as being committed to "communitarianism" without feeling an attachment to the special worth of any particular community.) Liberal democratic values and virtues should be important in the lives of liberal citizens, but those citizens should also have their own interests, convictions, and commitments beyond public concerns that make their lives distinctive. Liberal democratic principles and aspirations are substantive moral commitments, but being a good liberal democrat is not meant to be the whole of one's moral personality. The good society is not simply marked by toleration and cooperation, but also real (if not violent or destructive) conflict and contestation among communities.

It is conceivable that in some places the educational status quo could be criticized for pressing so hard on values such as tolerance, self-criticism, friendliness to diversity, and openness to change that the survival of all significant forms of diversity is threatened. Recall, after all, the description by Powell, Farrar, and Cohen of today's high schools as shopping malls, where a "do-your-own-thing attitude prevails," and which "take few stands on what is educationally or morally important" beyond tolerating diversity.[35] Consider also Tocqueville's worries: "The state receives, and often takes, the child from its mother's arms to hand it over to its functionaries; it takes the responsibility for forming the feelings and shaping the ideas of each generation. Uniformity prevails in schoolwork as in everything else; diversity, as well as freedom, is daily vanishing."[36] By educating too intently for some liberal virtues, we could flatten the landscape of choice and undermine freedom's value. An education wholly dominated by the virtues of toleration and mutual respect could render pale and shallow the forms of diversity available to children.

John Stuart Mill opposed government control over schools because he feared uniformity:

> That the whole or any large part of the education of the people should be in State hands, I go as far as any one in deprecating. All that has been said of the importance of individuality of character, and diversity in opinions and modes of conduct, involves, as of the same unspeakable importance, diversity of education. A general State education is a mere contrivance for moulding people to be exactly like one another . . . it establishes a despotism over the mind.[37]

Mill's point is misstated, however, for state-imposed uniformity is not the only path to mental despotism: nonpublic groups—including families and churches—can be oppressive as well. Nevertheless, the point remains that the value of freedom may depend upon preserving a measure of real social diversity.

Depriving particular groups and associations of the space and collective freedom to develop their distinctive ways may undermine social diversity: as commitments to particular ways of life become less deep, choice may range more widely and freely but only across a landscape now gray and featureless. If the value of choice is partly a function of the depth and richness of the available options, then we must beware of uniformity: the freedom to choose among options that are only superficially distinct is not very valuable. We may overlook an important tradeoff between the Socratic virtues (critical reflection, insistence on evidence, and public reasons) and Millian values (the range and depth of choices available in society). Are we giving too much weight to common educational values and not enough space and authority to the development of distinctive ways of life?

One way of casting this problem is by worrying that an education that emphasizes rational criticism of alternatives is itself an education in a particular way of life, and that certain deep alternatives to the life of rational criticism may become impossible to imagine or consider. Eamonn Callan reminds us that trust in God is central to many forms of religious life: faith in the face of evidence to the contrary. With respect to religious practice so understood, "strict fidelity to the rational critical principle" makes "the option of religious practice virtually ineligible; and where that option does more or less disappear, it is not clear that one enjoys an ampler range of choice than the indoctrinated zealot who cannot seriously consider alternatives to his faith."[38] Advocates of critical reflection might assert that the important thing is that *tenable* options persist, and those may not include many forms of religious faith that rest on blind faith. It is, however, hard to rest altogether easy with this assurance: "The problem seems to be that in order *seriously* to reject, much less accept, the life of faith one needs to examine it from a perspective other than the disengaged outsiders'. One needs to enter, at least imaginatively, into a way of seeing the world where some central beliefs are sustained more by heroic (or foolhardy?) hope than by anything that could properly be described as evidence and argument."[39]

Callan alerts us to the danger of a Socratic dogmatism: the inability to entertain seriously alternatives to the life of critical reason, because such alternatives have been driven out of existence by the very pervasiveness of the Socratic virtues. Unless deep and unwavering faith is kept alive in some communities, we may lose the ability to consider the possible limits of the basic commitment to critical questioning. This is one argument for protecting communities such as the Amish that are no great threat to the mainstream of liberal democratic politics but that remind us of the distinctiveness and limits of our own deep commitments (although respecting the Amish is not without its cost, especially with respect to the opportunities of Amish children, as mentioned earlier).

We want to be very careful, however, not to press a provocative line of thought too far. For one thing, Socratic dogmatism is a bit of a ruse, for it is open to those who think critically to reflect upon the limits of the examined life, as indeed some philosophers have done.[40] The question of the limits of rational self-examination is itself grist for the Socratic mill.

In addition, and most important, it is difficult to imagine by what standard one would judge that Americans are "too rational" or too wedded to the Socratic virtues of critical reflection. Just the opposite would appear to be true: too many Americans hold all sorts of irrational beliefs. Furthermore, whether rational or not, America is outstanding as a country in which religious faith is very much alive. Indeed, there has been a striking shift in recent decades away from "mainline" Protestant denominations toward more evangelical churches. As a nation we simply are not overly committed to critical reflection or rational self-examination, and to the extent that we are wedded to these "Socratic values," they most assuredly have not undermined the religious faith of Americans. The real problem, as we saw at the end of Chapter 4, is that adults are not exercising enough authority in the schools on behalf of *any* values except tolerance and mutual respect.[41]

There is a more generalized version of this worry that pulls away from the alleged tension between critical reflection and deep religious faith. The more general concern focuses on the observation that there may be costs to displacing educational institutions that reinforce and deepen children's commitments to particular communities: the liberal social goods of self-critical reflection and choice themselves depend upon a clash of significantly different conceptions of the good life. Significant alternatives are nurtured by particular moral communities, and educational institutions are the ways that communities develop and transmit their distinctive values. The more control those communities have over educational institutions, the more children will be educated in the ways of the group, and the more deeply varied the social landscape will become. The homogenizing effects of a public school system may, however, promote not the preconditions of a lively and deeply reflective public life, but a flattened social order without much at stake. Some might say that the shallowness of discourse and the blandness of public life in American testify to the overweening success of a common educational regime.

It might be suggested that the popularity of extreme philosophies, cults, and oddball communities of one sort or another results from the frailty of more mainstream moral and religious communities, whose blandness and superficiality make them incapable of rousing the deepest moral enthusiasms. Consequently, those who are searching for deeper and more encompassing forms of meaning will be left to search outside the cultural mainstream and may resort to gangs, cults, sects, or extreme political movements.

The problem with this line of criticism is that it is so large and abstract. How much social diversity is enough? Which forms of difference are deep, and which are shallow? And from a more practical standpoint, how do we go about fostering forms of significant diversity that are nevertheless congruent with our basic civic values?

These questions do not have simple or easy answers. Even if we credit concerns about the depth and distinctiveness of social diversity, moreover, it is far from clear that the answer is to overturn the system of common schooling in favor of a system of publicly supported educational diversity.

In some parts of the country—certain suburbs, perhaps—some forms of diversity may be lacking. But school choice is unlikely to provide it. With respect to some public educational institutions—big city urban high schools, for example—it might well be an improvement for the school itself to be more of a community: a smaller and more personalized institution with a greater sense of shared ethos and purpose. As I suggest in the next chapter, however, that issue can be addressed without overturning the system of common schooling. In other respects as well, public schools should have more substantial moral ambitions than they now have. Our moral expectations with respect to schooling should increase, but that can be done without shifting to a choice-based system.

At its most abstract, the argument from social diversity is difficult to assess. It is, at best, a rather amorphous and indirect argument for educational choice. In the world in which we actually live, it is hard to say that there is a shortage of cultural and religious diversity, and as I have emphasized throughout, many forms of diversity are simply not worth promoting. Indeed, those forms of diversity most in tension with the core civic aims of common schooling are least worth promoting, but parents who subscribe to these forms may be the most eager to resort to highly "distinctive" educational institutions.

We should prize and preserve the tension between the shared civic values represented by public schools and the particular moral and religious values of families, churches, and other moral communities. No one source of authority should dominate the educational landscape. Further, this division of educational authority is part of the larger mix of political institutions in an "extended republic" that fosters cross-cutting memberships and complex identities. The fragmentation and multiplicity of our social lives means that our identities will also be fragmented, and our associations with others always partial and provisional. There will be no simple answer to the question, "Who am I?"

The multiplicity of our memberships and affiliations is itself an important element of civic education, for that multiplicity deters the tribalistic and unified identities that may go along with the deepest forms of communal affiliation but at the expense of breeding hostility to outsiders. It will be hard in a social structure like America's—pluralistic rather than tribalistic, characterized by cross-cutting rather than consistently reinforcing memberships—to settle comfortably and permanently on final answers to many of life's questions. A measure of alienation from any and all associations and commitments goes with modern freedom, and some will find this unnerving.[42]

No doubt those who reject the pattern of pluralistic affiliations and the fragmented identities have reason to oppose common schooling. School differentiation and parental choice should make it possible for more parents to select schools that reinforce the convictions of the particular communities with which they identify, thereby avoiding the conflicts that may go with their children's attendance at schools representing larger civic purposes. It would truly be unfortunate if many people had psychological needs that could only be satisfied in all-encompassing associations. Then we would have to radically rethink the value of the liberal civic order explored here. As things stand, however, cults and all-encompassing forms of identity raise troubling problems for a liberal democratic society, but only at the margins. There are people in society, as Nancy Rosenblum argues, whose peculiar psychological makeup means that they need deeper forms of membership than those that tend to be fostered by liberal civic life. Most people are not like that, but within limits we should allow havens outside the mainstream for those with peculiar needs. Rosenblum's study shows that there are now many such havens outside the mainstream, and that is how it should be in a free society.[43]

It is very hard to see, however, why public educational policy should be guided by the peculiarities of a small number of people whose needs for psychological closure place them in opposition to liberal democratic civic practices and virtues, including mutual respect amidst diversity and cooperation across group lines. As I have emphasized previously, we sometimes have good reason to accommodate groups who bear special burdens on account of holding views in tension with those in the mainstream. Yet we should not overturn a cosmopolitan social order that satisfies the needs of most people while fostering freedom and peace based on the needs of a few.

Conclusion

Arguments for school reform based on parental rights or the goods of family life are not very powerful. Public educational institutions appear to run afoul of parental rights or the goods of family life only when these private imperatives are exaggerated at the expense of basic interests of children as independent persons and as future citizens.

Somewhat more compelling are arguments for school reform based on the importance of significant social diversity to a liberal democratic society. It is possible that the common school system is partly to blame for the prevalence, even among religious people, of the rather anemic nonjudgmentalism that observers such as Alan Wolfe identify. Ordinary Americans increasingly seem to be embarrassed not simply about imposing their religious beliefs on other people—which is good—but of advancing any interpersonal moral claims at all. Wolfe describes a middle class strikingly averse to moral conflict and to imposing "personal judgments" on others. The result is not unlike what Allan Bloom described a decade ago: a dogmatic moral subjectivism in which nobody has the right to judge anyone else.[44]

Similarly, J. Budziszewski worries that a false tolerance—one of indifference and skepticism—is coming to dominate all other virtues in our society. "True tolerance," according to Budziszewski, "is not forbearance from judgment, but the fruit of judgment"; it is a matter of putting up with things that you regard as wrong or mistaken. We need a tolerance, Budziszewski argues, rooted in confidence in our ability to make judgments about how people ought to live their lives. What we need is a truer vision of tolerance, and a more judgmental form of pluralism.[45] Invigorating local, particularistic communities might well be a way of making people more judgmental. Hopefully, it would not make people markedly less tolerant. I doubt, however, that it is as easy to reconcile tolerance and strong sectarian convictions as Budiszewski thinks.

Shifting authority over schooling away from common institutions toward more particular moral and religious communities could be one way of increasing the cultural weight of these communities, which are liable to be less concerned about reinforcing our overarching civic ideals, and more concerned about educating children in their particular ideals. Making people more judgmental would be a way of stirring the cultural pot. But would it also make people less tolerant and cooperative?

These large cultural concerns are provocative, but they are also too far removed from the problems of the most troubled public school districts to yield much leverage over the problem of school reform. The case for publicly funded vouchers that could be used to subsidize a private school education is strongest when applied to poor children left behind in the most troubled urban school systems. There, however, the case for reform has little to do with arguments for deeper social diversity. The attraction of Catholic schools in the most troubled urban areas has more to do with higher expectations, greater discipline, and the sense of shared purpose that those schools seem to generate. The argument from deeper social diversity seems misplaced and superfluous in those places that are actually experimenting with vouchers, as we will see. The diversity argument might carry more weight in suburban districts, but there parents are happier with their public schools.

The primary conclusion of this chapter is that the current publicly controlled system does not run afoul of basic principles. This negative conclusion is nevertheless important because it means that we have no reason to put aside our basic civic imperatives with respect to education when taking up the question of reform. We should, rather, take up this question from the point of view of our shared civic values, asking whether those values would be better served by a reformed system.

CHAPTER 11

The Case for Civically Minded School Reform

Common educational institutions are, as I argued in Chapter 10, apt instruments for pursuing basic civic aims and for securing the basic interests of children as independent persons with their own lives to lead. We have no reasons of basic principle to put aside these civic aims when considering school reform; to the contrary, the most convincing cases for reform will take account of our widest civic purposes.

There are arguments for school reform more promising than those considered in the previous chapter. Those who shaped the development of the public school system in this century may not always have given adequate weight to the contributions that small communities can make to the moral economy of a modern liberal democracy. During the twentieth century, the scale and ethos of public schools were transformed, as epitomized by the rise of the big urban high school. Nowadays, important arguments for school reform are grounded in a reappreciation of the virtues of small communities.

I will not attempt a comprehensive survey of policy arguments surrounding school reform. Many of those arguments are, indeed, driven by imperatives quite different from those that I will discuss. In addition, the civic factors on which I focus are difficult to assess, incapable of precise measurement, and hard to compare across different schools and different segments of the population. It is worth emphasizing at the outset, however, that the standard policy debates over effective schools—typically involving either comparisons between public and private schools or school choice experiments—are also extremely difficult to assess. Even when focusing only on narrow indices of school performance—student test scores, dropout rates, and the like—predictions made by advocates of a choice-based educational system are neither particularly reliable nor dramatic.[1]

Critics of public schools charge that bloated and rigid public school bureaucracies stifle change and thwart accountability for educational outcomes. The costs of public schooling, say critics, have increased considerably since the early 1960s, while scholastic achievement has either declined or remained stagnant. Teachers' salaries have increased, but teachers do not measure up to the standards of old. Public schools are just not working.

Defenders of public schools rightly point out that, in important respects, society has increased the demands that it has placed on public schools. We have used public schools to pursue the great social purpose of racial integration, for example. Our success at integration has been mixed, but there is no question that the costs to public schools have been considerable not only in terms of increased costs for transportation, but also in terms of the disruption of the workings of many schools. In addition to racial integration, "special needs" students once excluded from public school classrooms are now being "mainstreamed." This is a great step forward in terms of equal opportunity for all, but services for special needs students are costly.

The issue of rising public school teachers' salaries and declining teacher competence is also far from clear-cut. In the old days, there were few professions open to women; as a consequence, the pool of schoolteachers was artificially overqualified and underpaid. The opening to women of a broader array of career opportunities means that those days are gone. The prestige of teaching careers may have consequently declined as well.[2]

Another factor that makes it so difficult to compare today's public schools with those of a generation or two ago is that families are no longer what they were. The proportion of stable two-parent families has declined considerably. Where two parents are still present, it is now much more common than it once was for both parents to work outside of the home. Schoolchildren watch much more TV, and their parents probably spend less time making sure that they do their homework. Many high-school-aged children also appear to be working a great deal more than they used to, and, as Patricia Albjerg Graham notes, the reason is not to support their families but to provide themselves with major consumer items such as cars and motorcycles. A New Hampshire survey suggested that 84 percent of children in the tenth, eleventh, and twelfth grades are working, and 45 percent are working over twenty hours a week. These statistics almost certainly reflect a cultural shift with respect to our expectations for children: away from academic achievement and toward consumerism.[3]

Scores on the Scholastic Aptitude Test (SAT) and other indices of educational achievement may have declined during the 1960s and 1970s but the causes are bound to be complex. Most of the decline in the 1960s seems to have been the consequence of a much larger base of students taking the SAT. Many more children from deprived backgrounds are taking the SAT, and their scores increased between 1972 and 1992. The scores of white students declined somewhat, but the proportion of white seventeen-year-olds taking the SAT rose from 19 percent in 1976 to 25 percent in 1992. The pool of test takers has become a less elite group, which is good, but this fact also creates an apparent but false "decline" in overall student performance. From 1976 to 1992, the percentage of seventeen-year-olds taking the SAT and doing well on it increased considerably. Even if longer stretches of recent history are considered, it seems that broad levels of achievement are not declining. One thing we know for sure is that since World War II our expectations for schools have increased and broadened—"more learning for more people"—as Graham puts it.[4] The higher branches of education are no longer an elite enterprise, so of course there will be perceptions that quality and achievement are declining.

Even defenders of public schools allow that bureaucratic rules, detailed curricular requirements, and the unwillingness of some teachers' unions to allow merit to be assessed and rewarded may stifle improvement and inhibit teacher creativity. But decentralization of control and greater discretion for school principals and teachers creates dangers of corruption and incompetence.[5]

We need to be cautious with respect to bold pronouncements about the superiority of older public schools, private schools, or choice-oriented schools. The fact is that in order to compare the performance of schools, we would need to control for all of the other differences between them, including disparities in parent involvement and other differences among students' families and culture. School choice experiments often bring infusions of cash, talent, and enthusiasm that will not easily be recreated on a larger scale.

Although I will not suggest that all is well, the fact is that our educational system seems to be producing the bulk of skills needed by today's employers. Indeed, in certain respects, our schools supply a more educated workforce than our economic system can utilize. True enough, there are rising economic returns to education. In 1979 college graduates earned 38 percent more than high school graduates, but by the early 1990s, they earned 57 percent more. And yet many college graduates take jobs that do not require college degrees. In 1990, 20 percent of college graduates either could not find work or had jobs that did not require higher education. Richard Rothstein points out that there are 644,000 college graduates working as retail salespersons, and 166,000 driving trucks or buses. Moreover, the main concern of employers is not the academic skills of job applicants but attributes like work ethic and deportment. According to the Commission on the Skills of the American Workforce, the primary concern of more than 80 percent of employers is with qualities like reliability, work ethic, "a good attitude," "pleasant appearance," and "a good personality." The absence of these qualities reflects at least as poorly on families and the wider community as it does on the school system.[6]

The Shopping Mall High School Revisited

Today's urban high schools draw the most intense complaints about public education. These schools embody the variety and choice of the liberal community as a whole: they aim not to reinforce particularistic communal norms but to provide access to a world beyond the family and its closest affiliations. But mirroring the diversity and openness of the larger society does not create an effective educational environment for many children. A wide variety of arguments for school reform hone in on the importance of a sense of community to effective schools.[7]

In his study of the quintessential American high school, Gerald Grant argues that today's schools contain "more justice, more equality, fairer treatment for the disabled, and more protection of faculty rights" than was the case in the 1950s. On the other hand, "Tardiness and absenteeism are too common; high expectations and high ideals are too rare. Cheating is widespread. It is an individualistic, bureaucratic world, where altruism makes only an occasional visit. Like many schools in America, it is plagued by a sense of unease about the role of moral education . . . [S]tudents wonder whether faculty really care, and if so, about what."[8] What Grant and many other observers of today's urban public high schools describe is an impersonal, demoralized, and anomic environment that stands in sharp contrast to the shared ethos and sense of common purpose that seem to characterize Catholic schools.

In their permissiveness and their extreme individualism, public schools in big cities mirror some of the deep tendencies of the liberal society as a whole, rather than counteracting, balancing, or tempering those tendencies. A powerful case has been made in the literature on school reform that urban schools should take more seriously the moral resources generated by smaller size and greater choice.

Our thinking about political and moral education should take account of changes in social institutions. Stable two-parent families, neighborhoods, and other forms of local community life provided vital social capital that supported the educational mission of the school.[9] Given the breakdown or at least attenuation of these social institutions, schools cannot be expected to function as they once did.[10] Arguably, schools themselves must be reformed to try to replace some of the moral resources that could once be taken for granted.

The Mismatch of School Reform and Civic Purposes

In the Introduction, I discussed the narrowness of prominent policy-oriented cases for school reform. That narrowness is surprising not only because the case for reform based on achievement standards alone is far from overwhelming, but also because a more adequate civic case *can* be made for at least some forms of school reform. Reformers often urge that we should reappreciate the virtues of small communities, but we want to make sure that we take account of these virtues within an adequate civic framework. Reformers often seem prepared to revolutionize the main institution by which our polity has directly educated children for citizenship without considering the moral and political consequences or devising alternative accounts of how civic aims can be achieved.

Exactly this neglect besets an otherwise interesting defense of reform by Clifford Cobb.[11] The key to renewed schooling, Cobb argues, is a voucher system that would allow schools to be agents of particular communities rather than the proponents of the values of society as a whole. In part, Cobb's argument recalls those by commentators surveyed in Chapter 1 who embrace diversity and choice uncritically. Cobb likens the moral conflicts surrounding public schools to the religious conflicts that would surround an established church: "rather than expecting the state to resolve our disagreements with each other on moral issues, we should learn to rely on participatory communities to guide the behavior of individuals."[12] In the main, however, Cobb favors parental choice not simply to avoid conflict, but primarily because he believes that a reformed school system would help us address the cause of many of our social problems, namely, the decline of local communal institutions.

According to Cobb, today's public schools are part of a wider cultural problem because they are excessively bureaucratic, remote, and skewed too far toward the values of individuality, freedom, and choice. Cobb echoes Gerald Grant's observation that the typical post-1960s American high school has lost its sense of ethos and adult moral leadership.[13] Parental choice would allow the formation of schools with clear values and goals and a greater ability to maintain discipline and order.

Cobb's desire to link school reform to the moral resources of smaller communities is far from eccentric. It is, however, troubling in that he ignores the possibility of tradeoffs between the moralities of particular communities and the inclusive commitments of the liberal social order as a whole. In this, Cobb recalls Horace Kallen's uncritical embrace of cultural pluralism. It is as though Cobb would resolve the conflict between assimilation and ethnic separateness by letting people choose whether to go to ethnically unified or mixed schools. That is not a resolution but rather an evasion of our basic civic problem. Urban education may benefit from renewed communities, as Cobb suggests, but not all communities are equally worthy or capable of helping to revive urban civic life.

Cobb, like many other reformers, seems to assume that choice-based schools of the future will resemble today's inner-city Catholic schools, but it is far from clear that this hopeful expectation is to be counted upon. Like some other reform advocates, Cobb also fails to acknowledge that public schools stand for any public values at all: they are, he says, "a neutral, value-free zone."[14] But this is not true, for even now public schools stand for toleration, respect for diversity, and other civic values that are not neutral. Cobb is unwilling to face the hard questions and difficult tradeoffs that must attend a substantial shift of authority away from common educational institutions and toward those representing particular communities within the polity. His rhetorical question, "Community or Communities?" is all too reminiscent of Horace Kallen's stark choice of "Kulture Klux Klan or Cultural Pluralism."[15] It also represents a false choice. Reinvigorated communities may be an important part of educational reform, but only insofar as they contribute to the full range of our public purposes, which includes the well-being of children, the health of local communities, and the larger civic ideals of the nation.

The Return of Catholic Schooling?

Cobb's endorsement of smaller, more community-oriented schools is worth taking seriously, but we need to place this suggestion in a more civic context. James Coleman and his associates argue that the organization of schools matter, and that Catholic schools appear to have an advantage over public schools and private secular academies alike. Catholic schools and other religiously affiliated schools seem to do an especially good job of generating social capital on behalf of education: effective schools (those with lower dropout rates and higher academic achievement) are agents of families who actually know and interact with each other, as people once did more routinely in small towns or traditional neighborhoods.[16] The right sorts of interactive, functional communities have a degree of what Coleman calls "closure": repeated interactions among adults and children make it possible to monitor behavior, exchange information, and enforce norms. To put it simply, in the right sorts of face-to-face communities, people get to know each other and each other's children, reputations develop and circulate, and individuals acquire an incentive to look after their reputations. Community members are liable to learn about and care about the good behavior or misbehavior of adults and children: they hold each other accountable.[17]

Andrew M. Greeley also finds that Catholic schools do an especially good job of educating disadvantaged students, who seem to benefit most from the moral resources that religious schools generate. Coleman plausibly suggests that the reason for this is that children from disadvantaged backgrounds (especially when they suffer from broken homes) will tend to reap particular advantages from the communal structures and the shared sense of purpose provided by Catholic schools.[18]

The Coleman-Greeley thesis has been usefully expanded by Anthony S. Bryk, Valerie E. Lee, and Peter B. Holland. These authors allow that, as Christopher Jencks and others have pointed out, on average students in Catholic schools do not appear to enjoy a great advantage in academic achievement. Bryk and his colleagues argue, nevertheless, that Catholic schools have another advantage that is most relevant from a civic standpoint: Catholic schools are powerful equalizers, helping children from disadvantaged backgrounds overcome the accidents of fate. Even if the overall academic superiority of Catholic schools is not large, therefore, they do appear to help boost the achievement of less well-off students.[19]

It is not difficult to imagine that today's 5,000-student "shopping mall" high schools are far from ideal environments for adolescents and young adults, especially those from difficult family circumstances. But are we to conclude from this that separating church and school is, as some have argued, bad for education, especially for the education of the urban poor?[20]

While insisting that civic aims must be attended to, we should not romanticize public schools or any of the institutions that we have relied upon in the past. Fresh thinking about public policy is to be welcomed, and in any case is to be expected in a nation dedicated to newness. But if the idolization of familiar institutions is one danger, another of at least equal significance is a kind of amnesia with respect to the basic civic requirements of a liberal democracy such as ours.

We need to look more critically at the advantages and disadvantages of those reform proposals that increase our reliance on particular communities.

Reformed Schools and Communities outside the School

One way in which school reform can tap into the social resources associated with communities is to shift public support toward schools that are affiliated with particular communities *outside* the school. Many Catholic schools seem to have an educational advantage over public schools because they tap into communities of families who interact with each other across many different situations, not just at school. According to researchers, the social capital generated by religious communities is especially beneficial to children without stable families, children whose stock of social capital is low.[21]

Voucher proposals that would give parents a per-pupil cash grant to be "spent" at a school of the parents' choice would make it easier for parents who wish to do so to avail themselves of religious schooling. But it is important to stress that market mechanisms like school competition and consumer choice do not necessarily tap into communities outside the school, for parents may not choose to send their children to a school affiliated with their church or some other community to which they belong. Independent private schools are, in fact, highly individualistic in that parents who send their children to private academies often have no other interaction with each other. Indeed, James Coleman has claimed that nonreligious private schools have dropout rates that are even higher than those in the public system. Independent private schools seem to lack even the thin forms of community available to public schools, which at least contain students from the same (albeit sometimes extensive) geographical area.[22]

Vouchers providing parents with choice among public or private schools represent a turning away from the common school ideal. Something like a voucher system was in place before the common school system took hold, and some cities and states are experimenting with the idea once again.

Many clearly believe it would be wise to put greater trust in the educational benefits of schools affiliated with particular religious or moral communities. The Catholic Church has undergone a transformation and embraced American civic values. Bryk and his coauthors acknowledge the importance of this transformation to the case for school choice. Indeed, the greater discipline of Catholic schools might address employers' worries about the work ethic and demeanor of today's graduates. With respect to Catholic schools as currently constituted, there may not be a tradeoff between public and particular purposes; indeed, the Catholic schools may advance many of our civic aims more effectively than do public schools.

Catholic school enrollments, however, have declined precipitously over the past three decades: from a high of 5.5 million students (or 12 percent of the school-age population) in 1965, to 2.5 million (or 5.4 percent) in 1990. Yet enrollment in evangelical and Orthodox Jewish academies has skyrocketed.[23] School choice would shift public support to a variety of private schools, not only the dwindling number of Catholic schools.

At the very least, we must allow for the tradeoffs that are likely to accompany educational reform. Allowing schools to generate "social capital" might be good for student discipline and academic performance, but as I have emphasized, schools close to particular moral or religious communities reinforce *that* community's morality.[24] That is why Catholics have always insisted on autonomous schools. The moralities of particular communities—religious, ethnic, even racial—will not necessarily track our common political morality, which overarches our particularisms and unites diverse communities.

It is hardly surprising that schools serving more cohesive communities may have an easier time generating trust among students, teachers, and indeed parents. After all, in common schools—schools containing students from diverse religious, racial, ethnic, and class backgrounds—a certain amount of energy will have to be expended to build the trust and mutual understanding that more homogeneous schools can (to a greater degree) take for granted. Schools that contain students and teachers from different communities may need to expend time and energy helping students and teachers to negotiate transitions across the boundaries that divide particular communities. More homogeneous schools may transfer some of these resources more directly into teaching and learning.

From the point of view of achievement narrowly conceived, putting scarce resources into the negotiation of cultural, economic, and racial boundaries looks like a waste. Here as elsewhere, however, the narrow view of public educational aims is simply mistaken. The health of our political society requires that we learn how to negotiate cultural boundaries and promote wider sympathies among citizens. Far from being a waste, this is crucial political work. Where will this work be done if not in the common schools? This is not an easy question to answer, and to pose it is not to reject reform. It does no good to neglect the potential tradeoff between the social capital generated by cohesive communities on behalf of academic achievement, and the more specifically political imperatives of liberal civic education, which might "cost" us something in terms of achievement.[25] Let us, at least, think about educational reform as citizens of a liberal democratic polity, not just as consumers of educational services, or as competitors (and the parents of future competitors) in the marketplace.

Privately controlled educational institutions are not only more or less effective and efficient than public educational institutions, they are different in nature. We cannot substitute a system of publicly subsidized but privately controlled institutions for our current system on the basis of the simple claim that doing so will make education work better. This is not to say that it is always and everywhere wrong for public authorities to make it easier for parents to send their children to religious or other private schools. There are school districts that are in such a horrible state, and where the reform of public schools is so difficult, that voucher proposals are on balance advantageous.[26]

Schools as Moral Communities

The second way of invoking "community" in educational reform is less troubling than the first. The sensible suggestion of some reformers is that the sorts of advantages displayed by Catholic schools could be available to other schools—including public schools—if those institutions were granted a greater degree of autonomy to define their mission, select their own students and teachers, and enforce their own standards. The very act of choosing a school might help get more parents involved in their children's education. The "Catholic school advantage" may be available to smaller, choice-based public schools.

The public high school could be more like the Catholic school by being organized on a scale capable of sustaining a sense of community among students and teachers. The schools must also have enough autonomy so that they can be self-governing and develop a shared ethos. An element of parental choice is important so that children want to be there. Individual schools should have the ability to hire and fire teachers to ensure that a shared sense of mission and purpose can be sustained—that is, to ensure that the teachers want to be there as much as the students do.

One way of pursuing this notion of community within the school is through a "charter school." Many states now allow groups of teachers and administrators to start such schools, which have an unusual degree of autonomy from district and school board regulation. Typical charter schools are smaller than public schools (they are often formed within existing public school buildings), and they depend on their ability to attract students who wish to attend.

Paul T. Hill, Laurence C. Pierce, and James W. Guthrie have argued that the public school system as a whole should move in the direction of the charter school model. They propose what they call a "contracting" model, according to which school districts would no longer operate schools, but rather set standards and try to ensure an adequate array of alternatives. Schools would be far more autonomous and run under contracts with school districts, subject to the schools' ability to attract a sufficient number of students. Discrimination on grounds of race, religion, and ethnicity would be strictly forbidden, and it would be possible to allocate seats in oversubscribed schools on the basis of a lottery or some other mechanism, which could include preferences for children from deprived backgrounds (a good way of avoiding segregation by class and race). The schools would set their own mission, govern themselves to a much higher degree, and hire and fire their own teachers. This proposal combines public control with a much greater degree of school autonomy and parental choice. To a greater degree than is now the case, schools within the public system would be voluntary communities.[27] Hill, Pierce, and Guthrie, along with other advocates of contract or charter schools, argue that parental choice, a measure of competition, and the virtues of a small community can be introduced within the public system without surrendering public oversight and ultimate public control.

Building on the charter school or contract school model is a promising avenue of reform in those districts where there is the most dissatisfaction with public schools. Such proposals recognize that "choice" is to be thought of as a means of pursuing public ends, not as a rights-based alternative in which public ends are marginal or irrelevant. Peter W. Cookson Jr. points out that systems of "controlled choice" have helped school districts in Massachusetts and elsewhere pursue racial integration more effectively. He sensibly rejects the most radical arguments for school choice, and drawing on the work of Charles Willie and others, insists that reform should be guided by our basic commitments to justice and equal opportunity. He argues that parental involvement in choosing schools has increased parents' sense of ownership and involvement in education. Cookson argues, not unlike Hill, Pierce, and Guthrie, that all public schools should be "magnet" schools and choice schools. He goes so far as to suggest that at least where children from deprived urban environments are concerned, choice in education should extend to state-provided vouchers that could be used in private schools, including parochial schools.[28]

But on what basis will parents choose among schools? Can we trust families to exercise their ability to choose on the proper grounds, or will schools be chosen based on nonacademic factors such as athletic programs and the like? Of course, as I have argued, parental choice is not without its risks, but recent findings from voucher programs in Milwaukee and Cleveland are quite hopeful: according to Paul E. Peterson and his coauthors, the most important factors to the poor inner-city parents participating in these choice programs is academic quality and school safety: of parents questioned, 85 percent and 79 percent cited these reasons, respectively, for choosing a school, while only 37 percent mentioned religious reasons, and even fewer (20 percent) the fact that their children's friends went to the school. Peterson's studies of the choice experiments in Milwaukee and Cleveland also indicate significant increases in parental satisfaction and student achievement.[29]

These studies seem to indicate, first, that parents in voucher experiments are choosing schools based on respectable, sensible, and nonthreatening, grounds, such as academic quality and safety. Second, and unsurprisingly, they show that what parents want out of their children's schools is narrower than what we as a polity want from these institutions.

An impressive number of educational researchers support the notion that the properties that make some schools more "effective" than others are linked with the qualities of schools as communities of shared purpose. As James Q. Wilson argues, "public schools that combine academic demands and high disciplinary standards produce greater educational achievement than public schools that do not."[30] By the same token, James S. Coleman, Thomas Hoffer, and Sally Kilgore argue that the main reason for the superiority of private schools is that "achievement and discipline are intimately intertwined," and private and parochial schools are, on the whole, better able to define and enforce demanding standards of behavior.[31]

Paul T. Hill, Gail E. Foster, and Tamar Gendler argue that when public schools are not required to serve all the disparate interests of a large school zone, but are allowed to develop a particular educational "focus," they can generate many of the advantages of Catholic schools: a sense of shared purpose, a strong sense of authority within the school, better discipline, and improved academic achievement.[32] The problems of public schooling would seem to have less to do with democratic control per se (as John E. Chubb and Terry M. Moe contend) than with excessively centralized control, bureaucratization, and a lack of positive ethos. Coleman and his associates—Chubb and Moe, and Hill, Foster, and Gendler—argue that it is very important for schools to acquire a distinctive sense of purpose and a shared ethos.[33] Individual choice and market competition are not educational cure-alls.[34] But a wide range of educational researchers converge on a similar set of qualities having to do with schools as communities. Too many public schools have become "formal agencies of government, not intimate and personalized community resources for nurturing children." Direct control by relatively remote political agencies has encouraged an excessive concern with "standardization" and "avoidance of controversy."[35]

Choice is not panacea; indeed, a greater reliance on parental choice would make it harder to pursue some public purposes. Similarly, the more autonomous schools are, the less accountable they will be to public authorities. And, as Amy Gutmann emphasizes, state-sponsored "controlled choice" plans mean that there will be less local democratic deliberation about school curricula and policies: less of an opportunity for citizens to engage in what she calls "conscious social reproduction" by defining the mission of local public educational institutions.[36]

Nevertheless, it seems plausible that a greater measure of school autonomy would provide a greater opportunity for adults within schools to nurture a measure of shared purpose and generate a positive ethos. Choice may well be an effective public tool for promoting moral community as well as school accountability for performance. A greater measure of parental choice of schools, and a greater degree of freedom on the part of school principals to hire and fire teachers, would help make the school more of a voluntary community, albeit one still subject to public norms of nondiscrimination and openness. Bryk, Lee, and Holland emphasize that the voluntary nature of the Catholic school helps give students, parents, and teachers a sense of ownership; foster the development of a sense of mission; and generate and informally enforce norms of good behavior.[37]

There are no guarantees. More autonomous schools and parental choice will not improve educational quality or the achievement of other civic ideals unless parents and their children choose wisely. School autonomy will only improve schools if school principals and teachers care enough to do their jobs well. From many angles, however, aspects of the public school sector stand accused of a similar set of charges: even those sympathetic to the urban public high school regard it as a demoralized environment. The least well-off children may suffer the most, and the least well-off families also have the least choice: suburban schools already compete with each other to attract new residents to their communities, and better-off parents can already afford to move to affluent suburbs or send their children to private schools. Where public schools are characterized by anonymity, demoralization, and bureaucratic, uncaring attitudes, and where the communities that surround them are likewise attenuated, then reforms that emphasize a smaller and more personal scale, and a greater sense of shared purpose, seem all to the good. This, surely, is one way that public schools may need to change in order to "fit" the changing nature of families and communities. Certainly we are increasingly asking schools to perform many of the tasks formerly expected of families. Preschooling, breakfast and lunch programs, extended monitoring of various sorts, sex education, help with single parenting, and counseling of all kinds are among the ways that schools have changed to fit the needs of families, and they must continue to do so. As schools develop these broader responsibilities, it may be important for them to become more caring communities, and (in spite of reservations stated earlier) for schools to develop links with caring communities outside their walls.[38]

Reconsidering Civically Minded School Reform

On either version of the small community argument, the "shopping mall" high school appears wanting: it lacks the support of any cohesive community outside the school, and so too it fails to create a community within its walls. We should keep in mind the two different strains of argument. Creating community within schools may be a way of better promoting not only academic achievement but also the civic purposes of schools. Yet to shift control of schools to private communities and build success based on the linkages between schools and particular normative communities represents a more fundamental turning away from the common school idea.

Of the two alternatives, the less radical is that public schools should themselves exist on a scale that allows them to be real communities in which teachers and administrators know students personally, and the students know each other. The best and brightest high school students will thrive anywhere, and indeed they may benefit from the labs and computers and other specialized resources that only a very large school can provide. But average students, and especially students from socially and economically deprived backgrounds, seem to benefit from schools that offer personalized attention, familiarity, caring, and accountability, rather than only choices.[39]

Smaller size, greater school autonomy, and choice within the public system seem to me to be reforms worth pursuing where citizens and parents are dissatisfied with their public schools. It seems to me very likely indeed that our public school system of the post–World War II era—along with many of our other major public institutions—neglected the value of small-scale organization and interpersonal familiarity. If mass anonymous institutions are bad for adults, how can they be good for adolescents?[40]

The more radical tack for reform is the idea that academically effective schools depend upon gathering students from particular communities outside the school. This is one important rationale for moving toward a voucher system. Such proposals are a very significant break with the tradition of common schools. They shift educational authority away from public institutions to private groups and, given the institutional history surveyed in Part One, they represent a historic reversal.

Nevertheless, throughout much of our history common schools have been primarily neighborhood schools. And because America was far more homogeneous throughout the early decades of common schooling, most families and local communities tended to unite in support of these institutions. Diane Ravitch emphasizes, indeed, that throughout much of the twentieth century, many progressive reformers aimed to curb neighborhood control by centralizing and professionalizing the schools, but they did not seek to abolish neighborhood schooling: the schools continued to draw their students from geographical neighborhoods that were often strikingly homogeneous. European immigrants in New York City in the 1930s and 1940s still lived clustered in slums and attended neighborhood schools. "Integration," as Ravitch emphasizes, was not an issue with respect to European immigrants; it emerged as a rallying cry only in the 1950s and with respect to race.[41] We should not exaggerate the amount of cross-class and cross-race mixing that has taken place in public schools.

And yet, neighborhood schools, or other public schools that are fairly homogeneous, are still *public* institutions serving public purposes. They may serve narrower geographical areas, but they were at least formally open to all. The principle on which the school was based was, formally speaking, a public principle, not an ethnic and exclusive one. In addition, the schools themselves represented the common language of public life, and the civic ideals of a self-governing republic. Schools whose primary constituency is not the public as a whole but a more particular community will tend to stand, internally, for the values of that community.

Of course, we could and should temper the civic costs of any choice programs via public regulation. We could require that schools receiving public vouchers must open their doors to all. Catholic schools already educate children from an impressive variety of religious, racial, and class backgrounds.

Would a voucher plan, whether advantageous or not from a public policy standpoint, be unconstitutional if it were to include religious schools? Not necessarily, though allowing such a program to stand would alter the contours of our constitutional arrangements. It would be crucial that vouchers be given to parents, and that they could be spent on a wide variety of schools, public as well as private, secular as well as religious. The Supreme Court has already accepted the notion that state income tax deductions for educational expenses may be extended broadly to include expenses incurred by parents with children in secular and religious schools, and at public as well as private schools.[42]

Vouchers go a step beyond tax exemptions, however, and provide parents with a portion of public moneys. Typically, the voucher does not cover the full cost of education in a private school, and that could be important, for it allows one to justify the voucher as a way of paying for children to be educated in those portions of private school education that are of shared civil interest. The partial nature of a voucher also means that the funding system will still be tilted in favor of common schooling, which is good.

Public vouchers should be accompanied by public conditions and regulations: both for the sake of constitutional concerns, and to ensure that civic purposes are served. The Milwaukee Parental Choice Program is instructive. It will provide vouchers worth an average of nearly $5,000 to as many as 15,000 students. Families can choose public or private schools, including religious schools. But the Milwaukee school vouchers come with important strings attached. First, schools can decide how many voucher children to admit, but if the school is oversubscribed, students are chosen by lottery (with preference given to siblings of students already enrolled). There is, in addition, an opt-out requirement: schools receiving vouchers may not require students to participate in any religious activity that they or their parents find objectionable.[43]

These conditions seem to me to be vital. The first helps ensure that public funds will not be used to support narrowly sectarian institutions. The second helps guarantee that children will not have religious exercises imposed upon them. The conditions raise obvious problems of definition (what counts as a "religious exercise"?) and enforcement. Catholic and many other church-affiliated schools have accepted the conditions. But it is notable that the most conservative Protestant schools—the ones in which "[e]verything is taught with regard to God's word and how it applies in our lives"—have refused to accept voucher students. They worry that the restrictions will undermine their ability to preserve a religious atmosphere and student discipline. It seems to me altogether appropriate, however, that publicly funded vouchers should contain conditions that have the effect of excluding pervasively sectarian institutions.[44]

"Controlled choice" could well allow us to pursue our public purposes more effectively than the current system of common schooling. The resources now available to different public school districts are grossly unequal, as Jonathan Kozol has eloquently explained. The flight of middle-class families to suburbs has deprived urban school districts of resources, and more importantly, it has drawn off many of the most educated and active parents and many of the most capable students. Mayor John O. Norquist of Milwaukee defends school choice as a way of attracting middle-class families back to the city, and one hopes that he is right. Ideally, state-designed voucher schemes should allow a choice of schools across entire metropolitan areas, and they should (as many do) concentrate extra resources on the poorest children from the worst performing schools. School choice can and should be designed in such a way as to help us overcome the grossly disparate opportunities provided to inner-city and suburban children.[45]

The choice to transfer some authority to a private agency does not stop us from setting the terms on which public funds can be spent. Even if these terms are not fully enforced, they may still curb pressures on children to conform with religious exercises in publicly funded schools. It may be that, in practice, problems will develop that make the provision of vouchers to religious schools an unconstitutional option, but the experiment should not be closed off on constitutional grounds.

On more practical, political grounds, it is worth keeping in mind that while the embrace of vouchers would represent a principled shift in educational policy of historic proportions, vouchers have been debated for decades, and there is no evidence of a massive trend in their direction. Schooling remains the province of state and local governments, and what we have to look forward to are experiments with vouchers here and there, such as those taking place in Milwaukee and Cleveland. Let us see how these local reforms work out before passing judgment.

Most parents are reasonably happy with their public schools. Disaffection focuses on urban areas, and here, as we have seen, the social capital that might be generated by religious schooling might do the most good. In cities where public education seems to be failing the most needy students, it is hard to condemn a state-supported voucher program, such as Cleveland's, which gives vouchers only to families whose income is below 200 percent of the poverty level.

Some of our civic worries about voucher programs can be assuaged by setting limits to the kinds of schools that would be eligible. But of course, hard questions will remain. What of all-male academies, for example? The budding sexual impulses of adolescents give same-sex schools a plausible rationale. The Detroit public school system tried to begin several all-male, Afrocentric academies, but these were blocked by a federal judge, who ruled that such programs deny young women the right to an equal education. These academies were a special governmental initiative that left women out, which is a prima facie violation of equal protection. If there had been a comparable parallel initiative for young women, the same-sex schooling would have been constitutionally permissible.[46] Whether same-sex education has any real educational or developmental advantages is another question, which I will not try to address. Some studies show that girls benefit more than boys from single-sex education, but these findings have been disputed.[47]

There is a plausible rationale for same-sex education, but I see no comparable rationale for racially exclusive institutions. Schools founded on a racially or ethnically exclusive basis should not be publicly funded, even when they are desired by minority groups. Minority student groups within schools may well serve important functions, and there is ample public reason to foster racial mixes in publicly supported schools. Racial exclusion and race pride have too long and horrible a history in America to make racially exclusive public institutions acceptable.[48]

Many of the questions raised by a voucher system do not have particularly satisfying answers. Even where the answers seem clear, public aims will be open to interpretation and implementation by organizations that do not at base represent public purposes. That is the worrisome crux of the voucher idea, and no set of public conditions will altogether address those concerns. We should proceed with caution, and that is exactly what is happening, for in spite of all the talk about vouchers, there has been no rush to embrace them. The enormous investments that have gone into public schools—economic, political, and psychological—will not be quickly swept away.

This civic perspective on reform is circumstantial and complex. We should take reform seriously, so long as a reasonable case can be made for it in terms of our civic values broadly conceived.

Conclusion

As we saw in Chapter 10, public school preservationists speak to the need to foster tolerant attitudes and to the worry that parental choice and public purposes may be at odds. Reformers respond to the concern that schools are not educating children as well as they should, that students lack an adequate moral anchoring, that our problem is not one of overly deep commitments but of thin and faltering ones.[49] Each of these perspectives carries some weight in the current circumstances.

Partiality and extremism characterize both sides of the school reform debate. Each side grasps part of a complex truth, but misses the whole. On the one hand, those who would preserve the current system are not wrong to express some distrust of parents and local communities, and they are right to insist on the enduring and basic importance of civic aims. The primary goal of public education policy should be to secure a system of liberal self-government in which citizens are mutually respectful and cooperative. The proponents of reform, on the other hand, often praise diversity, parental authority, and community uncritically, and sometimes seem to see nothing of value in the common school regime. A disturbing civic forgetfulness characterizes many arguments for school reform.

How should we strike the balance between the virtues and values of the liberal society as a whole, and those of the more local communities that often exist in some tension with our most inclusive ideals? No one account of these tradeoffs applies to society as a whole. In many school districts, parents and children are happy with their schools. In many others, families no doubt have reason to be dissatisfied. The strongest case for shifting some educational authority toward smaller communities is in urban areas, where there may be the greatest need to tap into the moral resources of small communities, and where frustration with the bureaucratic rigidity of public schools is felt most keenly. If the case for school reform is not only hard to assess but also circumstantial, it should be some consolation that radical and sweeping educational reform is unlikely anytime soon.

The institution of public schooling has played a central role in the project of creating American citizens. But common schools are means to civic ends, not ends in themselves. It makes a great deal of sense at this juncture to experiment with educational reforms such as choice and competition. It may turn out to make sense to increase our public reliance on private educational institutions. We should not, however, increase our *dependence* on the vagaries of markets and consumer choice. We should rather formulate a plan to help ensure that the new educational regime serves public purposes more effectively than the one we currently have.

Conclusion: Public Reasons, Private Transformations

For much of this book, I have argued that the *ends* of civic education in a liberal democratic state are deeper and more controversial than is usually allowed. While I have also argued for the value of casting liberalism as something less than a fully comprehensive philosophical system, there is no question that the civic liberalism I have defended has broad implications for the shape of people's lives as a whole.

My main purpose has been to urge the importance of facing up to liberalism's civic ambitions: to argue that we should not allow liberalism's most alluring features—broad freedoms, limited government, and the great pageant of diversity—to obscure other dimensions of a healthy, free, self-governing society. Our central aims are the protection of individual freedom and preservation of stable, limited, and orderly government, but to plan for these great political goods we need to think very broadly about how liberal citizens become capable of their great office.

There will be some who will see this book, I suspect, as anything but liberal. To some, my account will seem too concerned with collective outcomes, insufficiently attentive to family and communal freedom, inadequately respectful of people's deepest moral and religious commitments, too friendly to the tutelary state, and far too distrustful of social diversity.

I believe that those who would level such criticisms simply take too much for granted. The success of individual freedom, the rule of law, and constitutionally limited government depend upon profound transformations in systems of belief and culture. This crucial political work must be done somehow, if not by government policy then by constitutional structures, background social practices, and institutional arrangements. I may seem to put too much emphasis on political constructivism while giving short shrift to the "spontaneous," unplanned mechanisms that help coordinate individual activities in conditions of freedom. It may be that once certain large political and economic structures are in place, the system is largely self-governing.

Markets and other examples of what Friederich Hayek called "spontaneous" social order may be largely self-regulating, but they are not entirely so. They are supported by legal and political frameworks that must be understood and consciously maintained. Citizens themselves must accept many forms of self-restraint for free markets to work, they must be prepared to engage in cooperative relations with strangers, and they must understand and support the benefits of individual freedom.[1]

It may also be that I have put too much weight on the *problem* of cultural and religious diversity. It could be said, I suppose, that the core features of modern liberty—broad individual freedoms, the rule of law, constitutionally limited government, representative democracy, and capitalism—are a successful, stable, self-supporting, and deeply attractive package. Our political concern should be to protect and perfect these core institutions. We can count on people being reasonable enough to recognize the intrinsic attractions of the modern commercial republic, and, given those intrinsic attractions, the project of civic education is simply not very important.

I do not want to disparage the reasonableness of most citizens of advanced and stable democratic societies. Much of this book has been a discussion of the reasonableness that prevails in a successful modern democracy. Nevertheless, it would be foolish to regard the dangers of religious enthusiasm, or of various forms of tribalism, as problems that are superseded once and for all as a polity matures. An economic, military, or environmental crisis could greatly exacerbate latent hostilities. In addition, there are new fault lines emerging that could threaten social stability and fidelity to our shared political project. It is possible to be an avid proponent of commercial enterprise and the wonders of a free market economy while worrying about the social fissures that may result from the growing economic and social inequalities that divide many inner cities from the rest of America. It is possible to insist on respect for a wide range of personal freedoms while worrying about the difficulty of finding substitutes for the more stable family structures of the past. It is simply not obvious that the difficulties of sustaining responsible self-government have been solved.

Of course, ill-considered government interventions can make even a bad situation worse. Nevertheless, it has been too easy for libertarians and free market advocates (with whom I sympathize across a great range of issues) to make the case for public school failure. Typically, those who argue in this vein ignore or heavily discount the civic purposes and wider aims of public education policy. It may well be that many public schools are failing, but let us make the case on the basis of an adequate account of "success" and "failure," one that does not ignore such legitimate civic goods as racial integration, the mainstreaming of handicapped children, and social mixing across lines of class.

With respect to public school policy, I believe that we should do two different things. First, we should welcome educational experimentation, especially choice within the public system and experiments with vouchers for poorer children in those places where frustration with public schools is greatest. At the same time, we should think about the means of civic education—the project of shaping citizens—in much broader terms than we usually do. Far too much weight has been placed on formal schooling as the means of promoting civic ends. The quickened pace of school reform provides an appropriate occasion for considering a wider variety of ways of gaining political leverage over the civic habits and attitudes of citizens.

We should, I will argue in another volume, promote our civic goals using all of the instruments of public policy. One way to proceed is to think about how public policy can intervene gently in the sphere of free association to encourage people to use their freedoms in ways that support civic values. Patterns of social life are themselves educative, not just for children, but for adults as well.

The fact is that our freedom to associate operates in an environment that is shaped pervasively and inevitably by institutional structures, laws, and public policies. These in turn create incentives and shape social norms and meanings that mold individual choices and character.

We already intervene gently in the sphere of private freedom—in the *most* private spheres of freedom—to influence the ways that people use their freedom and to promote certain virtues. We accord certain benefits to marriage in order to encourage people to settle down in stable relationships and discipline their sexual lives. We regard this intervention in the most private and personal relations as beneficial for society and good for the character of the parties involved.[2] Intervening in this way does not mean that we are on a slippery slope to Plato's elaborate state-administered birth formulas.

Some of the most important instruments of civic education lie beyond the schools. To the extent that public policies influence patterns of free association, we acquire crucial, indirect means to shape the character of citizens. We should be open and self-critical in our pursuit of civic ends. We should also, however, realize that major institutions and public policies have a wide variety of social consequences.

Recent versions of liberalism have tended to put so much emphasis on the definition and defense of the most basic rights and principles of justice that they have neglected the wider set of somewhat less basic principles and institutions that are nevertheless crucial to the health of a liberal democratic society. It is possible to be so riveted by interesting questions concerning the boundaries and limits of individual rights and the content of fundamental justice that we forget the larger project of sustaining healthy patterns of liberal democratic social life. I have tried to shift the discussion to civic questions without, I hope, disparaging problems of liberal justice and rights. It is not that we need to think less about what is legally permitted in our society, but we do need to think more about what is encouraged.

We should adopt a more judgmental liberalism, one that is prepared to make and defend moral judgments about the way that people use their rights. Whether we like it or not, whether we attend to it or not, our collective and individual lives are shaped by a richer set of social forces than can be captured in such ideas as law, rights, and justice. We should adopt an adequately subtle account of the virtues on which a healthy liberal democracy depends, and a correspondingly complex account of the institutional means of political education.

Throughout this book, I have tried to argue that we should not dismiss out of hand suspicions and anxieties about diversity, and about tensions between particular moral and religious communities and our larger civic ambitions. We should not take for granted a shared civic life robust enough to master the many centrifugal forces to which modern life gives rise. A shared liberal democratic civic identity has taken centuries to achieve and solidify in those few places on the globe where it seems secure for now.

It seems to me unrealistic at the moment (but perhaps not crazy in the longer run) to worry about the possibility of liberal values crowding out all competitors and thereby eliminating all deep debate about liberalism itself. That worry can, however, be stated and addressed within a liberal civic context: liberalism properly understood stands for a self-critical embrace of liberal values. Liberal self-criticism depends upon social contestation. For the time being, we have certainly not fully realized liberal justice, and we have a number of serious social and political problems about which there is considerable and heated debate. It is part of the health of this political order, moreover, that there should exist sufficient social space for various conceptions of the good life to flourish. We need real disagreement to keep us alert to the meaning of our own principles, to keep liberalism a "fighting faith." About this Mill was surely right.[3]

In this regard it should be noted that public schools have an important moral advantage with respect to civic education: they pursue our deepest civic purposes *openly* and allow people to argue about these purposes in local as well as national democratic venues. The vice of a too-heavy reliance on indirect modes of civic education is that we might be led to exploit false consciousness. If we were to opt for handling our most basic conflicts via the silent operation of institutional biases that are never explicated and defended, we would forgo the project of public justification.

Let us, here as elsewhere, address concerns about disagreement and diversity with our critical faculties engaged, and with the realization that disagreement and diversity are qualified values. Democratic deliberation and debate depend upon shared support for norms of civility, and on a common aspiration to deal with disputes reasonably. Our good fortune in having developed institutions that foster these shared civic values must neither lull us into complacency nor encourage reforms that rashly overlook the advantages of the system we have.

Notes

Introduction

1. Richard E. Flathman's criticisms of traditional liberals for seeking to impose "unicity" or "singularity" on the polity are in this vein. In his view, the proponents of unicity include Stalinists, Titoists, imperialists, and liberals who advocate reasonableness and civic virtue. See his *Reflections of a Would-be Anarchist: Ideals and Institutions of Liberalism* (St. Paul: University of Minnesota Press, 1998). See also J. Donald Moon, *Constructing Community* (Princeton: Princeton University Press, 1993), an excellent critique of various attempts to suggest that liberalism is exclusionary and silencing with respect to difference.

2. *Regents of the University of California v. Bakke,* 438 U.S. 265 (1978). The phrase "equal concern and respect" is taken from Ronald Dworkin's defense of liberalism; see Dworkin, *Taking Rights Seriously* (Cambridge: Harvard University Press, 1977), 180–183, 272–278.

3. Rogers M. Smith, *Civic Ideals: Conflicting Visions of Citizenship in U.S. History* (New Haven: Yale University Press, 1997), 503, Amy Gutmann and Anthony Appiah, *Color Conscious* (Princeton: Princeton University Press, 1996).

4. Many political scientists have pointed out the extent to which respect for basic civil liberties has become much more widely and consistently held in twentieth-century America. See, for example, Herbert McCloskey and John Zaller, *The American Ethos: Public Attitudes toward Capitalism and Democracy* (Cambridge: Harvard University Press, 1984). With respect to the decline of racist attitudes among whites, see Stephen Thernstrom and Abigail Thernstrom, *America in Black and White: One Nation, Indivisible* (New York: Simon and Schuster, 1997).

5. Alan Wolfe, *One Nation, After All: What Middle-Class Americans Really Think about God, Country, Family, Racism, Welfare, Immigration, Homosexuality, Work, the Right, the Left, and Each Other* (New York: Viking, 1998).

6. See Adam Smith, *An Inquiry into the Nature and Causes of the Wealth of Nations,* ed. R. H. Campbell, A. S. Skinner, and W. B. Todd (Oxford: Clarendon Press, 1976), vol. 2, esp. 781–796.

7. Consider the recurring "nativist" reactions to immigration, discussed in Chapter 2, from the "Know-Nothings" of the 1850s to the "100 percent Americanizers" of the early decades of this century. An excellent overview can be found in Philip Gleason, "American Identity and Americanization," in William Petersen, Michael Novak, and Philip Gleason, *Concepts of Ethnicity,* (Cambridge: Harvard University Press, 1982). See also David H. Bennett's masterful *The Party of Fear: From Nativist Movements to the New Right in American History* (Chapel Hill: University of North Carolina Press, 1988).

8. See the rather startling findings in James L. Gibson, "The Political Consequences of Intolerance: Cultural Conformity and Political Freedom," *American Political Science Review* 86 (June 1992).

9. This point has been amply and importantly documented. See, e.g., Smith, *Civic Ideals,* and Bennett, *Party of Fear.*

10. See Stephen Macedo, "Community, Diversity, and Civic Education: Toward a Liberal Political Science of Group Life," *Social Philosophy and Policy* 13 (Winter 1996), which is part of a longer work in progress on liberal civil society.

11. Jonathan Rieder, *Canarsie: The Jews and Italians of Brooklyn against Liberalism* (Cambridge: Harvard University Press, 1985), 6.

12. See Sandel's development of these claims in *Liberalism and the Limits of Justice* (Cambridge: Cambridge University Press, 1982), 175–183, and *Democracy's Discontent: America in Search of a Public Philosophy* (Cambridge: Harvard University Press, 1996).

13. Some versions of liberalism emphasize the importance of government neutrality toward conceptions of the good life. See, for example, Ronald Dworkin's "Liberalism," in Dworkin, *A Matter of Principle* (Cambridge: Harvard University Press, 1985), and Bruce Ackerman, *Social Justice in the Liberal State* (New Haven: Yale University Press, 1980). See also Charles Larmore's impressive, but I believe unsuccessful, argument for neutrality in *Patterns of Moral Complexity* (Cambridge: Cambridge University Press, 1988). The reliance on neutrality has been rejected by a number of liberals, including the present author: see Stephen Macedo, *Liberal Virtues: Citizenship, Virtue, and Community in Liberal Constitutionalism* (Oxford: Clarendon Press, 1992); William A. Galston, *Liberal Purposes* (Chicago: University of Chicago Press, 1991), and John Rawls, *Political Liberalism* (New York: Columbia University Press, 1993).

14. Benjamin Constant, "The Liberty of the Ancients Compared with That of the Moderns," speech at the Athénée Royale in Paris, 1819, in Biancamaria Fontana, ed., *Constant: Political Writings* (Cambridge: Cambridge University Press, 1988), 309–328, 310–311.

15. Isaiah Berlin, "Two Concepts of Liberty," in Berlin, *Four Essays on Liberty* (Oxford: Oxford University Press, 1979).

16. Berlin, "Introduction," *Four Essays,* lviii.

17. Constant, "Liberty of the Ancients," 311, 328.

18. Such is the entire point of Alexis de Tocqueville's *Democracy in America,* ed. J. P. Mayer (New York: Random House, 1969). His claims are amply confirmed by subsequent political science, especially the "civic culture" literature, which includes Gabriel A. Almond and Sidney Verba, *The Civic Culture: Political Attitudes and Democracy in Five Nations* (Princeton: Princeton University Press, 1963); Peter L. Berger and Richard John Neuhaus, *To Empower People: The Role of Mediating Structures in Public Policy* (Washington, D.C.: American Enterprise Institute, 1977); Alan Wolfe, *Whose Keeper? Social Science and Moral Obligation* (Berkeley: University of California Press, 1989); Robert D. Putnam, *Making Democracy Work: Civic Traditions in Modern Italy* (Princeton: Princeton University Press, 1993); the useful summary overview in E. J. Dionne, "Why Civil Society? Why Now?" *The Brookings Review* 15, no. 1 (Fall 1997): 4–7; and Richard Rose, "Postcommunism and the Problem of Trust," *Journal of Democracy* 5, no. 3 (July 1994): 18–50.

19. I provide an account of this perspective in *Liberal Virtues.* See also the sources in ibid.

20. I should emphasize at the outset that I am referring to liberal constitutionalism in the contemporary sense as it would apply to the basic elements of the American political system. I do not mean to exclude democratic values, even if I regard them as secondary to the protection of individual liberty. In some instances here, "political" might do as well as "constitutional," but I favor the latter word because it seems to me that the transformative ambitions of a liberal democratic polity such as ours are especially liable to be missed by legalistic understandings of liberalism.

21. Walter F. Murphy, "Civil Law, Common Law, and Constitutional Democracy," *Louisiana Law Review* 52, no. 1 (1991): 129. For another important presentation of the argument that the American constitutional tradition tends to define the aims of politics negatively, as merely "an enterprise for drawing a protective circle around the individual's sphere of self-interested action," see George F. Will, *Statecraft as Soulcraft: What Government Does* (New York: Simon and Schuster, 1983), 45.

22. I defend all of this in *Liberal Virtues.* For my particular formulation here, and elsewhere in this book, I am indebted not only to John Rawls, *Political Liberalism,* but also to the complementary account of deliberative democratic principles in Amy Gutmann and Dennis Thompson, *Democracy and*

Disagreement (Cambridge: Harvard University Press, 1996). See my discussion in Chapter 6.

1. Diversity Ascendant

1. I explored the views of Fuller, Hayek, and Oakeshott and this conception of law with far more sympathy in "The Public Morality of the Rule of Law: A Critique of Ronald Dworkin," *Harvard Journal of Law and Public Policy* 8, no. 1 (1985).
2. John Locke, *Two Treatises of Government: Second Treatise,* ed. Peter Laslett (New York: Mentor, 1963), 348, para. 57. See also Thomas Hobbes, *Leviathan,* ed. C. B. Macpherson (Harmondsworth, Eng.: Penguin, 1981), ch. 30, 388.
3. John E. Coons, "School Choice as Simple Justice," *First Things* (April 1992): 15–22, and Coons and Stephen D. Sugarman, *Education by Choice: The Case for Family Control* (Berkeley: University of California Press, 1978).
4. Stephen Arons, *Compelling Belief: The Culture of American Schooling* (New York: McGraw Hill, 1983).
5. Ibid., 3.
6. Ibid., 5–6. "Values clarification" is discussed in Chapter 1.
7. Dorothy Nelkin, *Science Textbook Controversies and the Politics of Equal Time* (Cambridge: MIT Press, 1977), quoted in Arons, *Compelling Belief,* 37.
8. Arons, *Compelling Belief,* 37.
9. Rockne McCarthy, Donald Oppewal, Walfred Peterson, and Gordon Spykman, *Society, State, and Schools: A Case for Structural and Confessional Pluralism* (Grand Rapids, Mich.: Eerdmans, 1981), 148–149.
10. Arons, *Compelling Belief,* 205.
11. Ibid., 207; see also 214–221. For a provocative attempt (from an economic perspective) to explain public school organization as guided by an imperative of indoctrination, see John R. Lott, "An Explanation for Public Provision of Schooling: The Importance of Indoctrination," *Journal of Law and Economics,* 33 (April 1990); and Lott, "Why Is Education Publicly Provided? A Critical Survey," *Cato Journal* 7 (Fall 1987). Lott's imaginative arguments ignore the possibility that even a free society counts on shaping the ideas of citizens.
12. Michael McConnell, "Multiculturalism, Majoritarianism, and Educational Choice: What Does Our Constitutional Tradition Have to Say?" *University of Chicago Legal Forum* (1991): 123–151, 133, 145.
13. Arons, *Compelling Belief,* 207. Arons is an egalitarian libertarian: he wants some equalization of educational resources to make equal opportunity possible, but otherwise he wants political institutions to remain neutral about educational ideals and purposes.

14. Ibid., 153.
15. Harry A. Eckstein, "A Theory of Stable Democracy," research monograph 10, Woodrow Wilson School of Public and International Affairs, Center of International Studies, Princeton University, Princeton, N.J., 1961, 47.
16. John E. Chubb and Terry M. Moe, *Politics, Markets, and America's Schools* (Washington, D.C.: Brookings, 1990).
17. Chubb and Moe argue that more effectively organized schools may increase student achievement by more than one full year during the normal four-year high school experience. Quotation from ibid., 226; see also 1–25, 140, 180–182, and 215–229 generally.
18. Quotation from ibid., p. 217. Myron Lieberman provides an accurate account of the failures of an over-bureaucratized public system, but he resolutely ignores the civic purposes of education. See his *Public Education: An Autopsy* (Cambridge: Harvard University Press, 1993).
19. See, for example, the argument of Arthur Schlesinger Jr., *The Disuniting of America: Reflections on a Multicultural Society* (New York: Norton, 1992).
20. See the following judicious surveys of the relevant evidence: K. L. Alexander and A. M. Pallas, "School Sector and Cognitive Performance: When Is a Little a Little?" *Sociology of Education* 58 (1985): 115–128; Christopher Jencks, "How Much Do High School Students Learn?" *Sociology of Education* 58 (1985): 128–135; and John F. Witte, "Public Subsidies for Private Schools: What We Know and How to Proceed," *Educational Policy* 6, no. 2 (1992): 206–227. Jencks argues that there is reasonably strong evidence that students learn "slightly more" in Catholic high schools, and that there is "suggestive" evidence that the effect is greatest for students from disadvantaged backgrounds. The jury is still out on these matters. Important recent arguments for the advantages of school choice programs and vouchers can be found in Jay P. Greene, Paul E. Peterson, and Jiangtao Du, "Effectiveness of School Choice: The Milwaukee Experiment," occasional Paper 97–1, Program on Education Policy and Governance, Center for American Political Studies, Harvard University, Cambridge, Mass., March 1997. See also Jay P. Greene, William G. Howell, and Paul E. Peterson, "An Evaluation of the Cleveland Scholarship Program," also published by Harvard's Program on Education Policy and Governance (September 1997).
21. John E. Chubb and Terry M. Moe, "America's Public Schools: Choice Is a Panacea," *Brookings Review*, no. 3 (Summer 1990): 4–12.
22. See Foucault's *The Order of Things: An Archeology of the Human Sciences* (New York: Vintage, 1970), and *Discipline and Punish: The Birth of the Prison* (New York: Vintage, 1979); also William E. Connolly, *Identity/Difference: Democratic Negotiations of Political Paradox* (Ithaca, N.Y.: Cornell University Press, 1991), ch. 3: "Liberalism and Difference."
23. Iris Marion Young, *Justice and the Politics of Difference* (Princeton: Princeton University Press, 1990), 7, 95, 174, 88, 118, 181; see also 100–107, 112–115.

24. Ibid., 37.
25. Ibid., 227, and see ch. 8 generally.
26. Richard E. Flathman, "'It All Depends on How One Understands Liberalism': A Brief Response to Stephen Macedo," *Political Theory* 26, no. 1 (February 1998): 82.
27. Richard E. Flathman, *Willful Liberalism: Voluntarism and Individuality in Political Theory and Practice* (Ithaca, N.Y.: Cornell University Press, 1992), quotations from 211, see also 222–223.
28. Rogers M. Smith, *Civic Ideals: Conflicting Visions of Citizenship in U.S. History* (New Haven: Yale University Press, 1997).
29. Stanley Fish, "Mission Impossible: Settling the Just Bounds between Church and State," *Columbia Law Review* 97, no. 8 (December 1997).
30. John Locke, *A Letter Concerning Toleration,* ed. James H. Tully (Indianapolis: Hackett, 1983), 26.
31. Ibid., 38, emphasis in original. See James Madison's "Memorial and Remonstrance against Religious Assessments," in *The Papers of James Madison,* vol. 8, ed. Robert A. Rutland et al. (Chicago: University of Chicago Press, 1973); and Thomas Jefferson, *Notes on the State of Virginia* in *The Life and Selected Writings of Thomas Jefferson,* ed. Adrienne Koch and William Peden (New York: Random House, 1944), query 17, pp. 272–277.
32. Locke, *Letter,* 47; Jefferson, *Notes,* query 17, p. 275.
33. Locke, *Letter,* 46; see also 33.
34. See John Stuart Mill, *On Liberty,* ed. David Spitz (New York: Norton, 1975), esp. ch. 3.
35. Locke, *Letter,* 51–56.
36. Ibid., 33.
37. See James H. Tully, Introduction to Locke's *Letter.*
38. Locke, *Letter,* 23.
39. Ibid., 46. See the excellent discussion in John Marshall, *John Locke: Resistance, Religion, and Responsibility* (Cambridge: Cambridge University Press, 1994), 376–383.
40. U.S. law exempts from combatant military service those persons conscientiously opposed to participation in "war in any form" by reason of their "religious training and belief." The question for the courts has been how broadly to define "religious" in this context; that is, whether it should include a deeply held ethical creed. See, for example, *United States v. Seeger,* 380 U.S. 163 (1965); *Welsh v. United States,* 398 U.S. 333 (1970); and *Gillette v. United States,* 401 U.S. 437 (1971). The peyote case is *Employment Division of Oregon v. Smith,* 494 U.S. 872 (1990); see the discussion later, Chapters 6–7. The Christian Science case, from Massachusetts, is *Commonwealth v. David R. Twitchell,* 416 Mass. 114 (1993). The highway case is *Lyng v. Northwest Indian Cemetery Protective Association,* 485 U.S. 439 (1988). I have benefited from the [richly detailed] survey of religion clause issues in John H. Mansfield, "The Religion Clauses of the First

Amendment and the Philosophy of the Constitution," *California Law Review* 72 (1984). See also the account of the relationship between religious enclaves and democratic civil society in Judith Lynn Failer, "The Draw and Drawbacks of Religious Enclaves in a Constitutional Democracy: Hasidic Public Schools in Kiryas Joel," unpublished essay on file with the author.

41. Locke, *Letter,* 48, 49.
42. Ibid., 33–34.
43. Ibid., 51. For a powerful exploration of the ways in which private religious communities generate their own law, see Robert M. Cover's "Foreword: Nomos and Narrative," *Harvard Law Review* 97, no. 4 (1983).
44. Locke also argues, famously but not convincingly, that atheists should not be tolerated because they cannot be trusted to abide by "promises, covenants, and oaths, which are the bonds of human society." Nearly everyone in Locke's day, and many thereafter, believed that divine punishment was a crucial motive for good conduct; see Locke, *Letter,* 51, and Tully, "Introduction."
45. Locke, *Letter,* 49.
46. Ibid., 47, see also Jefferson, *Notes,* Query 17, p. 263.
47. See the insightful discussion in Don Herzog, *Happy Slaves: A Critique of Consent Theory* (Princeton: Princeton University Press, 1989), 162–171.
48. Locke, *Letter,* 46. See the discussion in Marshall, *John Locke,* ch. 8.
49. Jonathan Kaufman, "Many Poles Dismayed by Pope's Criticisms," *Boston Globe,* June 10, 1991, 1, 8.
50. Promise Keepers' founder Bill McCartney, on NBC's *Meet the Press,* October 5, 1997.
51. Jeremy Waldron, "Toleration and the Rationality of Persecution," in *John Locke: A Letter Concerning Toleration, in Focus,* ed. John Horton and Susan Mendus (London: Routledge, 1991), 98–124, 99.
52. Sidney Verba, Kay Lehman Schlozman, and Henry E. Brady, *Voice and Equality: Civic Voluntarism in American Politics* (Cambridge: Harvard University Press, 1995).

Part I. Public Schooling and American Citizenship

1. Stephen V. Monsma, *When Sacred and Secular Mix: Religious Nonprofit Organizations and Public Money* (Lanham, Md.: Rowman and Littlefield, 1996), 139–140; John E. Coons, "School Choice as Simple Justice," *First Things* (April 1992): 15–22, 19.
2. Myron Lieberman, *Public Education: An Autopsy* (Cambridge: Harvard University Press, 1993), 15.
3. See David Nasaw, *Schooled to Order: A Social History of Public Schooling in the United States* (New York: Oxford University Press, 1979), 27–28, 35–37, 40–41; and Stanley K. Schultz, *The Culture Factory: Boston Public Schools, 1789–1860* (New York: Oxford University Press, 1973), 130–131.

4. Paul E. Peterson, *The Politics of School Reform, 1870–1940* (Chicago: University of Chicago Press, 1985), 9–10. Peterson emphasizes that political power, not economic imperatives, drove school reform.

5. Rogers M. Smith, *Civic Ideals: Conflicting Visions of Citizenship in U.S. History* (New Haven: Yale University Press, 1997).

2. Civic Anxieties

1. I draw here on the provocative discussion in Bernard Bailyn, *Education in the Forming of American Society* (New York: Norton, 1960), quotation from 27. William E. Nelson traces the "gradual breakdown of ethical unity" in Massachusetts, beginning in the 1780s, as manifested in the common law. See his fascinating study, *The Americanization of the Common Law: The Impact of Legal Change on Massachusetts Society, 1760–1830* (Cambridge: Harvard University Press, 1975). He attributes this breakdown primarily to religious fragmentation as well as economic growth and competition; see pp. 4–7. See also Lawrence A. Cremin, *American Education: The Colonial Experience, 1607–1738* (New York: Harper, 1970), 22–23.

2. Alexis de Tocqueville, *Democracy in America*, ed. J. P. Mayer (New York: Random House, 1969), 44–45, and app. 1. Massachusetts was ahead of other colonies with respect to education.

3. For examples in Massachusetts and Virginia, see David J. Rothman, *The Discovery of the Asylum: Social Order and Disorder in the New Republic* (Boston: Little, Brown, 1971), 14, and ch. 1 generally; and Bailyn, *Education*, 22–24. See also Steven Mintz and Susan Kellog, *Domestic Revolutions: A Social History of American Family Life* (New York: Free Press, 1988), ch. 3. I have benefited as well from Laura J. Scalia, "Constitutions as Constituting People: The Interaction of Good Laws and Good Men; Massachusetts as a Case Study, 1641–1853," an excellent unpublished paper presented at the 1997 Annual Meeting of the American Political Science Association, Washington, D.C.

4. See Rothman, *Discovery of the Asylum*, 13, 18–20.

5. "His virtues, his vices, his wisdom and his folly, excite here much the same attention, and are examined in much the same manner, as in a country village," Timothy Dwight, *Travels in New-England and New York*, 4 vols. (New Haven, 1821–1822), 4:449–452, 466–469, quoted in Stanley K. Schultz, *The Culture Factory: Boston Public Schools, 1789–1860* (New York: Oxford University Press, 1973), 114. Population statistics from ibid. and Alfred D. Chandler Jr., *The Visible Hand: The Managerial Revolution in American Business* (Cambridge: Harvard University Press, 1977), 15–17; and Adna Ferrin Weber, *The Growth of Cities in the Nineteenth Century: A Study in Statistics* (New York: Macmillan, 1899), 1, 20.

6. Rothman, *Discovery of the Asylum*, 16, 19.

7. Barry Alan Shain, *The Myth of American Individualism: The Protestant*

Origins of American Political Thought (Princeton: Princeton University Press, 1994), 65.

8. Adam Smith, *An Inquiry into the Nature and Causes of the Wealth of Nations*, vol. 2, ed. R. H. Campbell, A. S. Skinner, and W. B. Todd (Oxford: Clarendon Press, 1976), 788. On the democratizing currents that fed and fed off the American Revolution, see Gordon S. Wood's marvelous study, *The Radicalism of the American Revolution* (New York: Random House, 1991). The new American constitutional system was not expected to operate without the support of civic virtue, as is sometimes suggested. See the discussion in Stephen Macedo, *Liberal Virtues: Citizenship, Virtue, and Community in Liberal Constitutionalism* (Oxford: Clarendon Press, 1990), ch 4; and the extensive discussion in Lorraine Smith Pangle and Thomas L. Pangle, *The Learning of Liberty: The Educational Ideals of the American Founders* (Lawrence: University Press of Kansas, 1993).

9. Benjamin Rush, *Letters of Benjamin Rush,* edited by L. H. Butterfield, 2 vols. (Princeton: Princeton University Press, 1951), 1:lxvii, quoted in Lawrence A. Cremin, *American Education: The National Experience, 1783–1876* (New York: Harper and Row, 1980), 116. See also Noah Webster, "On the Education of Youth in America" (1790), in Frederick Rudolph, ed., *Essays on Education in the Early Republic* (Cambridge: Harvard University Press, 1965), 64, 66.

10. See the writings collected in Rudolph, *Essays on Education,* especially Rush's "Plan for the Establishment of Public Schools and the Diffusion of Knowledge in Pennsylvania; To Which Are Added, Thoughts upon the Mode of Education Proper in a Republic" (1786); Webster's "On the Education of Youth"; and Robert Coram's "Political Inquiries: To Which is Added, a Plan for the General Establishment of Schools throughout the United States" (1791). See also the discussion in Cremin, *American Education,* 103–114.

11. Figures are from Diane Ravitch, *The Great School Wars* (New York: Basic Books, 1974), 27. The situation was similar in Boston, though immigrants arrived somewhat later. See Oscar Handlin, *Boston's Immigrants: 1790–1865* (Cambridge: Harvard University Press, 1941); and David B. Tyack, *The One Best System: A History of American Urban Education* (Cambridge: Harvard University Press, 1974), 74–77.

12. Ravitch, *School Wars,* 30–33.

13. Tyack, *One Best System,* 33–35. Early school reformers such as William Ellery Channing, James Carter, and Horace Mann were deeply impressed by continental European state intervention on behalf of national uniformity. See Charles Leslie Glenn Jr., *The Myth of the Common School* (Amherst: University of Massachusetts Press, 1988), esp. chs. 1 and 3, and Jonathan Messerli, *Horace Mann: A Biography* (New York: Knopf, 1972), 405–407.

14. Stanley K. Schultz, *The Culture Factory: Boston Public Schools, 1789–1860* (New York: Oxford University Press, 1973), 58–59; David Nasaw, *Schooled*

to Order: A Social History of Public Schooling in the United States (New York: Oxford University Press, 1979), ch. 1; and Mintz and Kellog, *Domestic Revolutions*, 50–55.

15. Robert H. Wiebe, *Self-Rule: A Cultural History of American Democracy* (Chicago: University of Chicago Press, 1995), 31; Horace Mann, "Prospectus of the Common School Journal," *Life and Works of Horace Mann*, vol. 7 (Boston: Lee and Shepard, 1891), 7, 14; Ravitch, *School Wars*, 17–24; and Ellwood P. Cubberley, *Changing Conceptions of Education* (Boston: Houghton Mifflin, 1909) 30–36. For statistics on rising participation in presidential elections, see Rogers M. Smith, *Civic Ideals: Conflicting Visions of Citizenship in U.S. History* (New Haven: Yale University Press, 1997), 201; and Carl Kaestle, *Pillars of the Republic: Common Schools and American Society, 1780–1860* (New York: Hill and Wang, 1983), 72–73, 81–83, 169. On the importance of property ownership to citizenship in the eighteenth century, see Shain, *Myth*, 180–186. On the support of the Workingman's Party for universal education, see Ravitch, *School Wars*, 23–24; the important discussion in Ira Katznelson and Margaret Weir, *Schooling for All: Class, Race, and the Decline of the Democratic Ideal* (New York: Basic Books, 1985), esp. ch. 2; and Judith N. Shklar, *American Citizenship: The Quest for Inclusion* (Cambridge: Harvard University Press, 1991), 77.

16. "We see, and feel, the havoc and the ravages of their tiger-passions, now, when they are full-grown," Mann continued with characteristic color, "but it was years ago that they were whelped and suckled." See his "Lectures on Education," lecture 1: "Means and Objects of a Common School Education," in *Life and Works*, 7:41. Jay Fleigelman's excellent *Prodigals and Pilgrims: The American Revolution against Patriarchal Authority, 1750–1800* (Cambridge: Cambridge University Press, 1982) argues that literature was a crucial mechanism for popularizing Locke's emphasis on parents' responsibility to prepare their children for rational independence and moral autonomy; see 1–6, 60–66, 111–112.

17. Rothman, *Discovery of the Asylum*, 65, and ch. 3. Michel Foucault has made much of the ways that various reform institutions should be seen as manifestations of a new determination by society to extend the disciplines of normality to groups who had in the past been let alone. See, for example, Foucault, *Discipline and Punish: The Birth of the Prison*, trans. Alan Sheridan (New York: Vintage, 1979). See also Gideon F. Thayer, "On Courtesy: A Lecture Delivered in Boston, before an Audience of Female Teachers Engaged in Elementary Instruction, on Wednesday, January 23, 1839," *Common School Journal* 2 (December 15, 1840): 378, quoted in Schultz, *Culture Factory*, 54, 48–55. These changes no doubt began much earlier, see Mintz and Kellog, *Domestic Revolutions*, 20–21.

18. Messerli, *Mann*, 109. And in Rothman's, *Discovery of the Asylum*, the author emphasizes the Jacksonian conviction that "the child offender, no less than the adult one, was a casualty of his upbringing," 76 and ch. 3

generally. American religious thought increasingly emphasized the importance of educational and other reforms as means of hastening the "consummation of that ultimate amelioration of society proposed in the Christian scriptures," as the religious leader Alexander Campbell put it in his publication, "The Millenial Harbinger," January 4, 1830, and as quoted and discussed in Ernest Lee Tuveson, *Redeemer Nation: The Idea of America's Millennial Role* (Chicago: University of Chicago Press, 1968), 81 (see generally Tuveson's useful discussion, pp. 52–90).

19. Messerli, *Mann*, 122–137, 134; and Cremin, *American Education*, 137–142.

20. Timothy L. Smith, "Protestant Schooling and American Nationality, 1800–1850," *Journal of American History* 53 (March 1967): 681–683.

21. On the prehistory of common schooling, see Cremin, *American Education*, 47–48; and Kaestle, *Pillars*, x, 33. Class-based thinking was not absent from America, however; see the discussion in Messerli, *Mann*, 271–272. On the plight of early teachers, see the accounts in Messerli, *Mann*, 254–255, 284–288.

22. Kaestle, *Pillars*, 30–33, 37, 51.

23. On New York, see Smith, "Protestant Schooling," 682–685, and Ravitch, *School Wars*, 19. On Massachusetts, see Messerli, *Mann*, 304–305.

24. Messerli, *Mann*, 306–307; Kaestle, *Pillars*, 55–56.

25. The American pattern of institutional development in education was unusual. In England between 1818 and 1858, the proportion of children ages three to fifteen in school increased from approximately one-fifth to one-half. Given that the average length of time in school was 5.7 years, many more than half of these British children were receiving significant formal schooling by midcentury, even without substantial public support (which arrived only in 1870). See John R. Lott Jr., "Why Is Education Publicly Provided?" *Cato Journal* 7 (Fall 1987): 475–501, 480. In some places, such as France, public educational initiatives were designed to supplant private schooling and actually led to substantial declines in formal education. See the valuable study by Glenn, *Myth*, 16, 22–23; Glenn also has some interesting observations on the Netherlands and Prussia.

26. William Oland Bourne, *History of the Public School Society of the City of New York* (New York: William Wood, 1870), 109; Kaestle, *Pillars*, 55–57; and Smith, "Protestant Schooling," 681–684.

27. DeWitt Clinton, Address of December 11, 1809, reprinted in Bourne, *History of the Public School Society*, 14–24, quote from 15; James G. Carter, "Speech of Mr. Carter, of Lancaster, Delivered in the House of Representatives of Massachusetts, February 1837" (Boston, 1837), quoted in Messerli, *Mann*, 224.

28. Selwyn K. Troen, *The Public and the Schools: Shaping the St. Louis System, 1838–1920* (Columbia: University of Missouri Press, 1975), 12–13; "1828 Appeal from Trustees of the Public School Society," reprinted in Bourne,

History of the Public School Society, 110–118, quotations from 115, 114; and Ravitch, *School Wars,* 17–24. It is interesting to see the language of positive rights used so early here.

29. Troen, *Public and the Schools,* 52–53.

30. W. S. Dutton, "The Proposed Substitution of Sectarian for Public Schools," *Common School Journal* 10, no. 11 (June 1, 1848): 166–168, quoted and discussed in Glenn, *Myth,* 223–224.

31. See David B. Tyack and Elizabeth Hansot, *Managers of Virtue: Public School Leadership in America, 1820–1980* (New York: Basic Books, 1982), 19–31.

32. Tuveson, *Redeemer Nation,* 52–53, 58, 61, 63–64, 74, 81–82, and ch. 3 generally; see also Tyack and Hansot, *Managers of Virtue,* 72–74.

33. Nathan O. Hatch, *The Democratization of American Christianity* (New Haven: Yale University Press, 1989), 9–11. Richard Hofstadter says similar things about the Great Awakening of the mid-eighteenth century: "[B]y achieving a religious style congenial to the common man and giving him an alternative to the establishments run by and largely for the comfortable classes, the Awakening quickened the democratic spirit in America . . . the revivalists broke the hold of the establishments and heightened that assertiveness and self-sufficiency which visitor after visitor from abroad was later to find characteristic of the American people." The Great Awakening, Hofstadter notes, also gave a spur to such humanitarian causes as antislavery and the conversion of the slaves and Indians, for there "was no soul to whose welfare the good awakener was indifferent." See Hofstadter, *Anti-Intellectualism in American Life* (New York: Vintage, 1963), 74. It should be noted, however, that Hofstadter's primary concern throughout his wonderful study is the fate of high culture and the life of the mind, and this leads him to consider only the coarser aspects of religious enthusiasm.

34. Hofstadter, *Anti-Intellectualism,* 56, 57, 81–85; Hatch, *Democratization,* 11.

35. Michel Chevalier, *Society, Manners, and Politics in the United States: Being a Series of Letters from North America* (Boston, 1839), 317, quoted in Hatch, *Democratization,* 58. American Christianity has retained this populist impulse to a remarkable degree; see Hatch, *Democratization,* ch. 8.

36. Tyack and Hansot, *Managers of Virtue,* 28, 35. On the extent to which school reformers employed the model of the camp meeting and religious revival, and indeed used religious networks for publicity and to generate support, see 47–49, 54–55.

37. Smith, "Protestant Schooling," 680. See also Kaestle, *Pillars,* 57–58. On the relationship between Protestantism and the American creed, see Samuel P. Huntington, *American Politics: The Promise of Disharmony* (Cambridge: Harvard University Press, 1981), 14–15, 154–159. Huntington suggests that the lack of an established church contributed to the development of a national creed and attendant practices with religious functions, and so he quotes Chesterton's well-known remark that America is "a nation with the

soul of a church" (159). See also Robert N. Bellah, "Civil Religion in America," in his *Beyond Belief: Essays on Religion in a Post-Traditional World* (Berkeley: University of California Press, 1991), 168–191, which emphasizes the inclusive aspects of our civil religion.

38. Lawrence A. Cremin, *Traditions of American Education* (New York: Basic Books, 1976), 49, 50; see also Kaestle, *Pillars*, x.

39. Horace Mann, "Prospectus of the Common School Journal" (1838), *Life and Works of Horace Mann*, vol. 7 (Boston: Lee and Shepard, 1891), 29, 3. See also Tuveson, *Redeemer Nation*, ch. 4.

40. Kaestle, *Pillars*, 101, 144–146. See also the later discussion of the Senate debates on the Blaine Amendment.

41. A resident of Atchison, Kansas, writing in *Freedom's Champion*, a local newspaper, put it this way: "This age is purely American . . . Americanism is Protestantism . . . Protestantism is Life, is Light, is Civilization, is the spirit of the age. Education with all its adjuncts, is Protestantism. In fact, Protestantism is education itself." Quoted in James Carper, "A Common Faith for the Common School? Religion and Education in Kansas, 1861–1900," *Mid-America: An Historical Review* 60, no. 3 (1978): 149 (see also 147–161); and discussion in Tyack and Hansot, *Managers of Virtue*, 76.

42. Kaestle, *Pillars*, 98–103; Tyack and Hansot, *Managers of Virtue*, 30–31, 34–38, 43–44, 74–75.

43. Illinois Department of Public Instruction, Seventh Biennial Report of the Superintendent . . . 1867–1868 (Springfield, 1868), 229, quoted in Smith, "Protestant Schooling," 694.

44. Daniel Webster, *Works*, 6 vols (Boston: Little, Brown, 1854), 6:161, quoted in Josiah Strong, *Our Country: Its Possible Future and Its Present Crisis* (Garden City, N.Y.: Doubleday, 1912), 109.

45. "Remonstrance of the Executive Committee of the Public School Society," reprinted in William Oland Bourne, *History of the Public School Society*, 181–182; and from Cincinnati, Argument of W. M. Ramsey in *Minor v. Board of Education of Cincinnati* (1870), reprinted in Robert G. McCloskey, ed., *The Bible in the Public Schools: Arguments before the Superior Court of Cincinnati in the Case of Minor v. Board of Education of Cincinnati (1870)* (New York: Da Capo Press, 1967), 25–58, esp. 52.

46. Smith, "Protestant Schooling," 684–685.

47. The naturalization period remained five years until 1906. My account here is drawn from Philip Gleason's excellent "American Identity and Americanization," in William Petersen, Michael Novak, and Philip Gleason, *Concepts of Ethnicity* (Cambridge: Harvard University Press, 1982), 65–67.

48. *Notes on The State of Virginia*, Query 8: "Population," 124–125.

49. Gleason, "American Identity," 65–67. See also the useful tables in Gerald Shaughnessy, *Has the Immigrant Kept the Faith? A Study of Immigration and Catholic Growth in the United States, 1790–1920* (New York: Macmillan, 1925), 100–101, 189, 209.

50. Tyler Anbinder, *Nativism and Slavery: The Northern Know Nothings and*

the Politics of the 1850s (New York: Oxford University Press, 1992), 3, 9; and John Tracy Ellis, *American Catholicism* (Chicago: University of Chicago Press, 1956), 64, 70. On America and Catholicism in this period in general, see also Vincent P. Lannie, "Alienation in America: The Immigrant Catholic and Public Education in Pre–Civil War America," *The Review of Politics* 32 (1970): 503–521; and George Weigel, "Catholicism and Democracy: The Other 20th-Century Revolution," in Brad Roberts, ed., *The New Democracies: Global Change and U.S. Policy* (Cambridge: MIT Press, 1990), 17–37.

51. Josiah Strong, *The New Era; or, The Coming Kingdom* (New York: Baker and Taylor, 1893), 354; Tuveson, *Redeemer Nation*, ch. 5; and Milton M. Gordon, *Assimilation in American Life: The Role of Race, Religion, and National Origins* (New York: Oxford University Press, 1964), ch. 4.

52. Strong, *Our Country*, 220–221. This vastly popular work, originally published in 1886, was an expansion and rewriting of material first published by the Home Missionary Society in 1842, according to Tuveson, *Redeemer Nation*, 165.

53. John L. Motley, "Historical Introduction to *The Rise of the Dutch Republic*," in *The Complete Works of John L. Motley* (New York: Society of English and French Literature, 1900), quoted in Tuveson, *Redeemer Nation*, 146, 148 (see also 126–128, 132–133).

54. Reginald Horsman, *Race and Manifest Destiny: The Origins of American Racial Anglo-Saxonism* (Cambridge: Harvard University Press, 1981), 250, 4–6, 42–61, 172–173. See also Smith's comprehensive survey of the influence of these racialist ideas, in *Civic Ideals*.

55. In "Quanta Cura," of Dec. 8, 1864. See *The Papal Encyclicals, 1740–1878*, ed. Claudia Carlen, Immaculate Heart of Mary (Raleigh: McGrath Publishing Co., 1981), 381–386, 382. See also Pope Gregory XVI's encyclicals "Mirari Vos," August 13, 1832, 235–241, and "Singulari Nos," June 25, 1834, 249–251. Pope Pius IX's infamous "Syllabus of Errors" was quoted at length by U.S. Senators in support of the Blaine Amendment. See *Congressional Record*, vol. 4, pt. 6, 44th Cong., 1st sess., (August 14, 1876), 5587–5588, 5591, and the discussion later in the present work. Recent studies support the notion that until quite recently, until after Vatican II in fact, Catholic countries tended to be politically authoritarian. See the discussion later.

56. Gregory XVI, "Singulari Nos," 251.

57. Archbishop John McCloskey of New York to Archbishop Martin J. Spaulding of Baltimore, in Thomas W. Spaulding, *Martin John Spaulding: American Churchman* (Washington: Catholic University of America Press, 1973), 241.

58. Address before Congress, January 8, 1826, in *The Works of the Right Reverend John England, First Bishop of Charleston*, ed. Sebastian G. Messmer, 7 vols. (Cleveland, Ohio: Arthur H. Clarke, 1908), 7:9–43. I draw here on

Gleason, "American Catholics and Liberalism, 1798–1960," in R. Bruce Douglass and David Hollenbach, ed., *Catholicism and Liberalism: Contributions to American Public Philosophy* (Cambridge: Cambridge University Press, 1994), 47–50.

59. Ellis, *American Catholicism,* 45–46; Gleason, "American Identity," 69–74; and Anbinder, *Nativism,* 26–29. Senator Bogy, a Catholic, speaking in the Senate debate over the Blaine Amendment, attempted to portray Pope Pius IX's Syllabus of Errors as merely a religious rather than a political teaching, and a religious teaching (no less!) in support of religious liberty and the separation of church and state (*Congressional Record,* vol. 4, pt. 6, 44th Cong., 1st sess., [August 14, 1876], 5589). When challenged to explain the grounds for this liberal interpretation of the pope's "clear and explicit" teaching to the contrary, Bogy admitted, "It is very hard to explain, very hard to vindicate these things . . . It is hard to explain; I do not rise to do it myself" (5591).

60. From Anbinder, *Nativism,* 120, quoting the *Visitor* (Rising Sun, Indiana), October 20, 1855, and the New York *Express,* September 10, 1855.

61. Albany *State Register,* September 12, 1855, quoted in Anbinder, *Nativism,* 113.

62. Vincent P. Lannie, *Public Money and Parochial Education: Bishop Hughes, Governor Seward, and the New York School Controversy* (Cleveland: Case Western Reserve University Press, 1968), 34; Tyack, *One Best System,* 65–70, 79–83.

63. See Kaestle, *Pillars,* 40–42, 52–58, 104–117, 144–152; and Smith, "Protestant Schooling," 687.

64. See Messerli, *Mann,* 332–334, 410–412; Tyack and Hansot, *Managers of Virtue,* 30–31, 34–38, 61–62; and James S. Coleman and Thomas Hoffer, *Public and Private High Schools: The Impact of Communities* (New York: Basic Books, 1987), 6–7.

65. See Mann's Twelfth Annual Report, *Annual Reports of the Secretary of the Board of Education* (Boston: Lee and Shepard, 1891); and the discussion in Tyack and Hansot, *Managers of Virtue,* 61. See also the excellent discussion in Mustafa Emirbayer, "Moral Education in America, 1830–1990: A Contribution to the Sociology of Moral Culture (Ph.D. diss., Harvard University, 1989), ch. 3.

66. Argument of W. M. Ramsey in *Minor et al. v. Board of Education of Cincinnati* (1870), reprinted in McCloskey, *Bible in the Public Schools,* 49.

67. As described by Senator Edmunds in the Congressional debate over the Blaine Amendment, *Congressional Record,* vol. 4, pt. 6, 44th Cong., 1st sess. (August 14, 1876), 5588. When Mann had difficulty gaining acceptance for nonsectarianism in the schools, he concentrated his efforts on the normal schools that were to train teachers. Charles Leslie Glenn emphasizes the Unitarian influence over normal school governance by stressing that the claim of the public system to being truly "common" was a myth; see Glenn,

Myth, 134–145. It is too simple to say that the common schools were instruments for establishing Mann's Unitarianism. According to Messerli, the overwhelming number of orthodox ministers (at least in the Northeast) seem to have supported Mann, see Messerli, *Mann,* 309–315, 410–412, 432–435. It is important, moreover, that the common schools did *not* take a stand for Unitarianism as against Trinitarianism, but rather avoided this theological controversy. Avoidance of controversy—at least among Protestants—was, and was understood to be, the whole point, and the common schools would otherwise have failed. Glenn discounts the relevant civic purposes.

68. See Ravitch, *School Wars,* 35.
69. Argument of J. B. Stallo in *Minor et al. v. Board of Education of Cincinnati* (1870), reprinted in McCloskey, *Bible in the Public Schools,* 59–105, esp. 65.
70. Ravitch, *School Wars,* 35.
71. *Common School Journal,* August 15, 1843, quoted in Glenn, *Myth,* 143–144. See also the account in Lannie, "Alienation in America," 507–515.
72. This view was suggested in Glenn, *Myth,* 143–144. There is an important distinction, which I will take up in Part Two, between religious and civil doctrines of toleration: a religious doctrine of toleration, such as the one advanced by Mann here, would say that all religions are the same in the eyes of God, whereas a civil doctrine would say *only* that they are all the same in the eyes of the state. Liberal states should confine themselves to civil doctrines.
73. Kaestle, *Pillars,* 158–164.
74. Bourne, *History of the Public School Society,* 160–163.
75. Ravitch, *School Wars,* 34–35; and Anbinder, *Nativism,* 10–11.
76. Quotes are from Lannie, *Public Money,* 32–34. These documents were apparently not reprinted in Bourne, *History of the Public School Society,* but for related documents, see his 196–201.
77. Kaestle, *Pillars,* 168–171; and Anbinder, *Nativism,* 11–12. In 1889, Bishop Gibbons accepted the place of Protestantism in public schools on the condition that some public aid be extended to denominational schools for the support of secular portions of education. See Ellis, *American Catholicism,* 11–12.
78. Quoted in Charles Leslie Glenn, "Religion, Textbooks, and the Common Schools," *The Public Interest* (Summer 1987): 33. Similarly, the National Teachers Association (the forerunner of the NEA) resolved in 1869 that "the Bible should not only be studied, venerated, and honored as a classic for all ages, people, and languages . . . but devotionally read and its precepts inculcated in all the common schools of the land." Immediately thereafter, as Tyack and Hansot report, the association resolved "that the teaching of partisan or sectarian principles in our public schools, or the appropriation of

public funds for the support of sectarian schools, is a violation of the fundamental principles of our American system of education" See *Addresses and Proceedings of the NEA* (1869), quoted in Tyack and Hansot, *Managers of Virtue*, 24–25.

79. *New York Freeman's Journal*, July 11, 1840, quoted in Lannie, *Public Money*, 30.

80. For example, Catholic Democratic Senator Kernan, of New York, argued in the debates on the Blaine Amendment, "Where free public schools are taught for all, there they must be free from any religious teaching at all. They must be . . . just like a school to teach mechanics . . . to which every child in the State can go and get secular learning without there being anything offensive to the creed of anyone." Only by avoiding any creed, even a very generalized Protestant, biblical religiosity, could offense to religious sensibilities be avoided; see *Congressional Record*, vol. 4, pt. 6, 44th Cong., 1st sess. (August 14, 1876), 5586. The problem with this view is that most Americans—of many denominational stripes—believed biblical religion to be the foundation of public morality.

81. Speech of Bishop Hughes in the Debate on the Claim of Catholics to a Portion of the Common School Fund, in Bourne, *History of the Public School Society*, 220. See also the excellent discussion in Ravitch, *School Wars*, 52–55, from which I have benefited greatly. Catholics in the Netherlands raised objections to common schools much like those in New York; see Glenn, *Myth*, 50–55.

82. It was also called this in debates over the Blaine Amendment; see later. These complaints against the public schools are interestingly similar to those which were to be leveled in the next century by Protestant fundamentalists (see Part Two): neutrality through inclusion brackets the truth question, neutrality through exclusion treats religion as a hobby. Catholicism (at least in the nineteenth century), like twentieth-century fundamentalism, makes pervasive demands on people's lives, and so the liberal attempt to carve out a shared politically authoritative space will appear to some as an assault on religion.

83. Some Protestant fundamentalists voice these same objections today (see Part Two).

84. Argument of J. B. Stallo in *Minor et al. v. Board of Education of Cincinnati*, reprinted in McCloskey, *Bible in the Public Schools*, 64.

85. Lannie, *Public Money*, 59.

86. Speech of Bishop Hughes in Bourne, *History of the Public School Society*, 286; Lawrence Kehoe, ed., *Complete Works of the Most Rev. John Hughes, D.D.*, 2 vols. 2d ed (New York: American News Company, 1865), 1:63, quoted in Lannie, *Public Money*, 59.

87. Bourne, *History of the Public School Society*, 235, 237.

88. Speech of Theodore Sedgwick in ibid., 229–230.

89. Ibid., 235. For the offer to join with Catholics in expurgating offensive materials and compiling a set of mutually acceptable materials, see 237, 263, 317, 321, 386, 409; and Lannie, *Public Money*, 80–81, 110–115.

90. Speech of Theodore Sedgwick in Bourne, *History of the Public School Society*, 236–237.

91. Speech of Bishop Hughes in ibid., 219.

92. Ravitch, *School Wars*, 47–51; quotation from p. 47.

93. Tyack and Hansot, *Managers of Virtue*, 75–79; Tyack, *One Best System*, 108; Paul E. Peterson, *The Politics of School Reform, 1870–1940* (Chicago: University of Chicago Press, 1985), 55–57; and Troen, *Public and the Schools*, ch. 3. Many supported German language instruction because German was seen as representing an advanced culture; the attitudes of many shifted decisively when the proposed languages of study were Italian, Hungarian, and Polish. See Tyack and Hansot, *Managers of Virtue*.

94. In Kaestle, *Pillars*, 158, 170. See also Smith, "Protestant Schooling," 684–687. Smith makes clear that while there was some opposition to the religious thinness of nondenominational common schooling, the notion gained much wider and readier acceptance in the United States than in England.

95. Philip Gleason, "American Catholics," 45–75, 52.

96. Bible reading was rejected elsewhere as well. See McCloskey, *Bible in the Public Schools*, x–xi; and Morton Keller, *Affairs of State: Public Life in Late Nineteenth-Century America* (Cambridge: Harvard University Press, Belknap Press, 1977), 136–142.

97. Strong, *Our Country*, 103, 102; and 101–108 generally.

98. Messerli, *Mann*, 309–315, 410–412, 432–435. I speak of perceptions because schooling's actual effectiveness at shaping values and attitudes is hard to measure; see my later discussion.

99. Anbinder, *Nativism*, 24. By 1890, the Catholic schools had enrolled over 625,000 students and formed the largest "alternative system" to the public schools. See Tyack and Hansot, *Managers of Virtue*, 75–78. For the shift in the Catholic position, see Lannie, "Alienation in America," 515–519.

100. In 1855, the Know-Nothings controlled six states and elected seventy-five representatives to Congress. See Gleason, "American Identity," 70–71; and Anbinder, *Nativism*, ch. 5.

101. See *Commonwealth v. Cooke*, 7 Am.L.Reg. 417, 425–426 (Mass. Police Ct. 1859); *Donahoe v. Richards*, 38 Me. 379, 399–401 (1854), cited in Marvin E. Frankel, "Religion in Public Life: Reasons for Minimal Access," *George Washington Law Review* 60 (1992): 633–644. Only Massachusetts required Bible reading in the nineteenth century (most school superintendents permitted it), but between 1913 and 1930, eleven states and the District of Columbia passed similar laws. See David Tyack, Thomas James, and Aaron Benavot, *Law and the Shaping of Public Education, 1785–1954* (Madison: University of Wisconsin Press, 1987), 164–165.

102. *Report of the Annual Examination of the Public Schools of the City of*

Boston, 1850 (Boston, 1850), 29–30, quoted in Schultz, *Culture Factory,* 291. In similar language, St. Augustine spoke of the need to persecute heretics: we must "compel them to come in," as he wrote in his letter "To Boniface [On the Treatment of the Donatists]," letter 185, ch. 24, reprinted in *The Fathers of the Church,* vol. 30: *Saint Augustine, Letters, vol. 4,* trans. Sister Wilfrid Parsons, Sisters of Notre Dame (New York: Fathers of the Church, 1955), quotation from 165.

103. John Higham, *Strangers in the Land: Patterns of American Nativism, 1860–1925* (New York: Atheneum, 1970), ch. 2.

104. "General Grant's Des Moines Speech: The Circumstances of a Remarkable Utterance" [an article containing the text of Grant's speech], *Century Magazine* 55 (March 1898): 785–788.

105. *Congressional Record,* vol. 4, 44th Cong., 1st sess. (December 14, 1875), 205.

106. The amendment introduced by Blaine can be found at ibid.; a revised Senate version can be found at ibid., 5453. I am greatly indebted to Gary D. Glenn's excellent discussion, "The Blaine Amendment's Application of the Religion Clauses to the States: Differences between a Congressional and a Judicial Understanding of Church/State Separation," unpublished manuscript on file with the author.

107. Sen. Frelinghuysen in the Senate Debate on the Blaine Amendment, *Congressional Record,* vol. 4 pt. 6, 44th Cong., 1st sess. (August 14, 1876), 5562. The aptly named Sen. Christiancy articulated well the principle behind the amendment: "In a country situated like ours, where the conscience is left free, where religious toleration is universal, where the people are divided into a great number of churches and sects, with a very large proportion, if not a majority, of the population belonging to no church or sect, and where our public schools could never be maintained unless placed upon a footing of substantial equality among all people who may choose to send them, it would be wrong to raise money by taxation or to appropriate property belonging to the whole people for the support of any one of those denominations" (5583).

108. Sen. Frelinghuysen, ibid., 5562, or as Senator Edmunds put it, the religion that can be taught in public institutions "without violating" anyone's creed consists of "the duty of man to man, the obligation to truth and personal purity, charity, virtue, intelligence, cleanliness, honor, all those can go into the orphan asylum [or the school]. The great and golden rule that is in his creed and mine, that you shall do unto others as, under similar circumstances, you would wish them to do to you" (5588). What cannot be taught, Edmunds insisted, is either "a trinity or unitarian doctrine, or whether in the holy sacrament the elements show the real presence or only the symbolic and memorial one" (5588).

109. See, in ibid.: Sen. Randolph, 5455; Sen. Frelinghuysen, 5561, 5562; Sen. Christiancy, 5583; Sen. Morton, 5585; Sen. Kernan, 5586.

110. Sen. Kernan, ibid., 5586.
111. Ibid., 5587.
112. *Congressional Record,* vol. 4 (August 11, 1876), 5455.
113. Quoted in ibid. Catholics such as Senator Bogy could agree that "the great principles of liberty are founded on . . . the 'divine law'" without supporting either the Blaine Amendment or the common school regime.
114. Based on Gary D. Glenn's analysis of Michael Angelo Musmanno, *Proposed Amendments to the Constitution,* 70th Cong., 2d sess. 1929, H. Doc. 551, see Glenn, "Blaine Amendment." See also Tyack and Hansot, *Managers of Virtue,* 77; Keller, *Affairs of State,* 141–142; James Hennessey, S. J. *American Catholics: A History of the Roman Catholic Community in the United States* (New York: Oxford University Press, 1981), 184–186.
115. Strong, *Our Country,* 101. See the excellent discussion of Strong's relation to American postmillennialism in Jean B. Quandt, "Religion and Social Thought: The Secularization of Postmillenialism," *American Quarterly* 25 (1973): 390–409.
116. Strong, *Our Country,* 98–99.
117. Ibid., 108–110.
118. On this shift, see Lannie, "Alienation in America," 515–519.
119. Isaac T. Hecker, *Catholics and Protestants Agreeing on the School Question* (New York: Catholic Publication Society, 1881), 6–7. The monograph was originally published in *The Catholic World* (February 1881).
120. Ibid., 7, 13, 14, 16.
121. See *Engel v. Vitale,* 370 U.S. 421 (1962), striking down a school "non-denominational" prayer; and *Abington School District v. Schempp,* 374 U.S. 203 (1963), overturning bible reading in public schools. See also *Everson v. Ewing Township,* 330 U.S. 1 (1947), permitting the public provision of free buses for children attending religious as well as public schools; and *McCollum v. Board of Education,* 333 U.S. 203 (1948), striking down a school board's practice of permitting students to attend sectarian classes held in public schools during school hours and taught by parochial school instructors. But cf. *Zorach v. Clausen,* 343 U.S. 306 (1952), and the discussion later in this book.
122. See, for example, Glenn, *Myth.*
123. Kehoe, *Works of Hughes,* 1:46–47, 51–52, 151; Lannie, *Public Money,* 109–110.
124. Speech of Bishop Hughes in Bourne, *Public School Society,* 282.
125. Locke, *Letter,* 33–34.

3. Civic Excess and Reaction

1. Michael McConnell, "Multiculturalism, Majoritarianism, and Educational Choice: What Does Our Constitutional Tradition Have to Say?" *University of Chicago Legal Forum* 1991 (1991): 123–151, 141; Kenneth B. O'Brien

Jr., "Education, Americanization, and the Supreme Court: The 1920s," *American Quarterly* 13, no. 2 (1961): 171.

2. Selwyn K. Troen, *The Public and the Schools: Shaping the St. Louis System, 1838–1920* (Columbia: University of Missouri Press, 1975), 62–63. In San Francisco, residents born in Germany and France made up 11.5% of the population by 1870, and the city enacted an accommodating policy for foreign-language instruction. So did Chicago; see Paul E. Peterson, *The Politics of School Reform: 1870–1940* (Chicago: University of Chicago Press, 1985), 53–60. On blacks and Asians, see Peterson, *Politics of School Reform*, ch. 5.

3. Diane Ravitch, *The Great School Wars* (New York: Basic Books, 1974), 174; and John Higham, *Strangers in the Land: Patterns of American Nativism, 1860–1925* (New York: Atheneum, 1970), 46, 54–55, 59–63.

4. Theodore Roosevelt, "American Ideals," *The Forum* (Feb. 1895), reprinted in *The Works of Theodore Roosevelt,* ed. Hermann Hagedom, vol. 15: *Citizenship, Politics and the Elemental Virtues* (New York: Scribners, 1925), 3–14, esp. 5.

5. From *The Forum* (April 1894), reprinted in *Works,* 15:15–31, 27. See also Philip Gleason, "American Identity and Americanization," in William Peterson, Michael Novak, and Philip Gleason, *Concepts of Ethnicity* (Cambridge: Harvard University Press, 1982), 80–83.

6. Josiah Strong, *Our Country: Its Possible Future and Its Present Crisis* (Garden City, N.Y.: Doubleday, Page & Co., 1912), 219–220, 222, 227.

7. Milton M. Gordon, *Assimilation in American Life: The Role of Race, Religion, and National Origins* (New York: Oxford University Press, 1964), 97–98.

8. John R. Commons, *Races and Immigrants in America* (Chautauqua, N.Y.: Chautauqua Press, 1908), 1, 7.

9. Ellwood P. Cubberley, *Changing Conceptions of Education* (Boston: Houghton Mifflin, 1909), 15–16. Cubberley headed and drastically reformed the Education Department at Stanford, was a widely influential editor and author of education textbooks, and was one of the nation's leading proponents of educational professionalization and reform. See the account of Cubberley's career in David Tyack and Elizabeth Hansot, *Managers of Virtue: Public School Leadership in America, 1820–1980* (New York: Basic Books, 1982), 121–128.

10. Cubberley, *Changing Conceptions,* 15–16. John R. Commons wrote in 1907 of a line drawn across Europe that separated the north and west of the continent from the south and east: "It separates Protestant Europe from Catholic Europe; it separates countries of representative institutions and popular government from absolute monarchies; it separates lands where education is universal from lands where illiteracy predominates . . . it separates an educated, thrifty peasantry from a peasantry scarcely a single generation removed from serfdom; it separates Teutonic races from Latin, Slav,

Semitic and Mongolian races." Commons warned that the shift of immigration from one side of the line to the other "should challenge the attention of every citizen." Commons, *Races and Immigrants,* 69–70.

11. The proportion of Americans living in cities of 8,000 or more rose from 8.5% in 1840 to nearly 30% in 1890, and in 1900, immigrants and their children constituted 75% of Boston's population. See Adna Ferrin Weber, *The Growth of Cities in the Nineteenth Century: A Study in Statistics* (New York: Macmillan, 1899), 22; and Mustafa Emirbayer, "Moral Education in America, 1830–1990: A Contribution to the Sociology of Moral Culture" (Ph.D. diss., Harvard University, 1989), 144, and ch. 4 generally. See also Higham, *Strangers in the Land,* 59–63.

12. Cubberley, *Changing Conceptions,* 16–21. This analysis has some similarities to that advanced more recently and elaborately by James S. Coleman; see Coleman's *Foundations of Social Theory* (Cambridge: Harvard University Press, 1990), ch. 22. In Coleman's language, Cubberley is bemoaning the loss of "social capital."

13. Cubberley, *Changing Conceptions,* 62–67.

14. Tyack and Hansot, *Managers of Virtue,* 114–128. On Addams's views, see Jane Addams, *Twenty Years at Hull House* (New York: Macmillan, 1937).

15. Roosevelt, "Religion and the Public Schools," *Works,* 15:32–39.

16. Ibid.; see also *Works,* 15:18, 24, 25, 36–37. See also "The Bible and the Life of the People," ibid., 606–616.

17. Ibid., 34, 25, 28, 29; see also Gordon, *Assimilation,* 82–84, 98–102.

18. Roosevelt, *Works,* 15:30–31, quoting the Honorable Richard Guenther of Wisconsin, "at the time of the Samoan trouble."

19. See the excellent account of the ghetto life of eastern European immigrants, and the fear of subversion that surrounded the anarchist trial of *Abrams v. U.S.,* 250 U.S. 616 (1919) in Richard Pollenberg, *Fighting Faiths: The Abrams Case, the Supreme Court, and Free Speech* (New York: Viking, 1987), 72.

20. *Meyer v. Nebraska,* 262 U.S. 390 (1923).

21. *Pierce v. Society of Sisters,* 268 U.S. 510 (1925).

22. Sanford Levinson, "Some Reflections on Multiculturalism, 'Equal Concern and Respect,' and the Establishment Clause of the First Amendment," *University of Richmond Law Review* 27 (1993): 989–1021, 999, 1002.

23. See Ronald Dworkin's insightful account in his *Taking Rights Seriously* (Cambridge: Harvard University Press, 1979), chs. 2–3.

24. For an important warning of the dangers of allowing conflicting political principles to be displaced, see Bonnie Honig, *Political Theory and the Displacement of Politics* (Ithaca, N.Y.: Cornell University Press, 1993).

25. In *Lochner v. New York,* 198 U.S. 45 (1905), the Supreme Court struck down a New York law setting maximum working hours for the employees of bakeries. In more recent times, *Meyer* and *Pierce* are seen as providing support for privacy rights and other personal liberties.

26. See *Report of the Commissioner of Education for 1893–1894,* vol. 2 (Wash-

ington, D.C.: Government Printing Office, 1896), cited in Barbara Woodhouse, "Who Owns the Child? *Meyer, Pierce* and the Child as Property," *William and Mary Law Review* 33 (Summer 1992): 995–1123, 1004, 1006. In 1852, fiscal support for Spanish-language schools was abruptly terminated in California, and in 1855 the California State Bureau of Public Instruction required that instruction in all schools be conducted in English. See Fred G. Burke, "Bilingualism/Biculturalism in American Education: An Adventure in Wonderland," *Annals of the American Academy* 454 (March 1981): 164–177.

27. Woodhouse, "Who Owns the Child?" 1004–1005.

28. Ibid., describing a series of articles that ran in the *Literary Digest* and elsewhere.

29. Troen, *Public and the Schools,* 66–67.

30. A study of Nebraska schools by a professor of Slavic languages at the University of Nebraska found that in 1918, fifty-nine counties reported having schools with instruction in languages other than English, and seven counties with schools whose instruction was altogether in German. See Robert N. Manley, "Language, Loyalty, and Liberty: The Nebraska Council of Defense and the Lutheran Church, 1917–18," *Concordia Historical Institute Quarterly* 37, no. 1 (1964): 1–16, esp. 9.

31. See Lloyd P. Jorgenson, "The Oregon School Law of 1922: Passage and Sequel," *Catholic History Review* 54 (1968–1969): 455–466.

32. Justice McReynolds, Opinion of the Court, Meyer v. Nebraska, 402. Manley, "Language, Loyalty, and Liberty," 14–15.

33. Argument (Affirmative) submitted by H. Baldwin and others, in behalf of the Compulsory Education Bill, *Official Pamphlet Distributed Among Voters Prior to Election of Nov. 7, 1922,* State of Oregon. Printed in Brief for Appellee, app. 1, 19–43, *Pierce v. Society of Sisters,* 24. See the excellent account by Clement E. Vose, "The Catholic School Issue," in *Constitutional Change: Amendment Politics and Supreme Court Litigation since 1900* (Lexington, Mass.: D.C. Heath, 1972), 139–160, 143. See also the helpful account in David Tyack, Thomas James, and Aaron Benavot, *Law and the Shaping of Public Education, 1785–1954* (Madison: University of Wisconsin Press, 1987), ch. 7.

34. Vose, "Catholic School Issue," 143.

35. Argument (Negative) Submitted by the Catholic Civil Rights Association of Oregon, by J. P. Kavanaugh and others, opposing the Compulsory Education Bill, *Official Pamphlet. . .Election of Nov. 7, 1922,* quoted in ibid., 144.

36. Brief for Appellant Governor of Oregon, *Pierce v. Society,* at 46, quoted in Vose, "Catholic School Issue," 155.

37. Justice McReynolds, Opinion of the Court, *Pierce v. Society of Sisters,* 535.

38. My revisionist account of these two cases is deeply indebted to Barbara Woodhouse's excellent account in "Who Owns the Child?"; on *Meyer,* see 1002–1016.

39. See ibid., 1016–1019.

40. Appendix to Brief on Behalf of Appellee at 24–25, *Pierce v. Society of Sisters* (no. 583), Official Ballot Argument (Affirmative), quoted in Woodhouse, "Who Owns the Child?" 1018.

41. See Woodhouse, "Who Owns the Child?" 1032–1035. On labor union support for public education and opposition to child labor, see Peterson, *Politics of School Reform,* 35–40.

42. Woodhouse, "Who Owns the Child?" 1059–1068.

43. *Hammer v. Dagenhart,* 247 U.S. 251 (1918).

44. Woodhouse, "Who Owns the Child?" 1076–1078.

45. Bryan to Austin Peay, June 27, quoted in O'Brien, "Education, Americanization," 168.

46. See Stephen Macedo, *New Right v. The Constitution* (Washington, D.C.: Cato Institute, 1987).

47. Woodhouse, "Who Owns the Child?" 1000–1001.

48. Ibid., 1007; see also Troen, *Public and the Schools,* 53–78. Peterson, discusses similar episodes in San Francisco and Chicago in his *Politics of School Reform,* 52–71.

49. Troen, *Public and the Schools,* 62.

50. Gordon, *Assimilation,* 102–103; and Gleason, "American Identity," 89–93, Smith, *Civic Ideals,* 442–443.

51. Horace M. Kallen, *Culture and Democracy in the United States: Studies in the Group Psychology of the American People* (New York: Boni and Liveright, 1924), 117, 122. Compare Kallen's emphasis on the inevitability and the good of cultural group ties beyond the scope of individual choice with Michael J. Sandel's notion of "constitutive commitments" in Sandel, *Liberalism and the Limits of Justice* (Cambridge: Cambridge University Press, 1982), 84–86, 92–95.

52. Kallen, *Culture and Democracy,* 140–141, 124, 122.

53. Ibid., 50.

54. Ibid., 52–56.

55. Ibid., 59–60.

56. Ibid., 57.

57. Ibid., 59–60, 61, 92, 114–115, 176. Against claims on behalf of environment and nurture, Kallen was adamant: "the blood remains . . . heredity remains" (175).

58. Ibid., 121, emphasis in original, 61.

59. Ibid., 115, 35, 119–120.

60. Ibid., 43. See also the excellent discussions and criticisms of Kallen's position in Gleason, "American Identity," 97–107; and Gordon, *Assimilation,* 140–150.

61. See Gleason, "American Identity," 99–105.

62. Amy Gutmann observed this in her review article, "Communitarian Critics of Liberalism," *Philosophy and Public Affairs* 14, no. 3 (Summer 1985): 308–322.

63. Kallen, *Culture and Democracy,* 230, 112–114.
64. See also the later collection: Horace M. Kallen, *Cultural Pluralism and the American Ideal: An Essay in Social Theory* (Philadelphia: University of Pennsylvania Press, 1956).
65. See the discussion in Gordon, *Assimilation,* 150–154. Kallen's racialism still has its proponents.
66. Kallen, *Culture and Democracy,* 65.
67. Ibid., 64.
68. Ibid., 229.
69. Ibid., 63, 200–201.

4. The Decline of the Common School Idea

1. See the account in Herbert J. Storing, *What the Antifederalists Were For* (Chicago: University of Chicago Press, 1981).
2. David B. Tyack, *The One Best System: A History of American Urban Education* (Cambridge: Harvard University Press, 1974), 89, 24–25.
3. Diane Ravitch, *The Great School Wars* (New York: Basic Books, 1974), 176–177.
4. Tyack, *One Best System,* 94–95.
5. John Snyder, "Snyder Says, 'For Shame,'" *St. Louis Republic,* Nov. 7, 1881, quoted in Selwyn K. Troen, *The Public and the Schools: Shaping the St. Louis System, 1838–1920* (Columbia: University of Missouri Press, 1975), 210–211.
6. Adele Shaw, "The Public Schools of a Boss-Ridden City," *World's Work* 7 (February 1904): 4460–4466; Edward C. Eliot, "School Administration: The St. Louis Method," *Educational Review* 26 (December 1903): 464–475, esp. 466–467; and Eliot, "A Non-Partisan School Law," *NEA Addresses and Proceedings, 44th Annual Meeting* (Asbury Park, Ocean Grove, N.J., 1905), 223–231, esp. 226; all quoted in Tyack, *One Best System,* 154–155, 158. Tyack makes clear that similar calls for reform were voiced in New York, Philadelphia, San Francisco, St. Louis, and elsewhere (156–167). See also Ravitch, *School Wars,* ch. 13.
7. Stephen Olin, "Public School Reform in New York," *Educational Review* (June 1894): 1–6, quoted in Ravitch, *School Wars,* 138.
8. Ellwood P. Cubberley, *Rural Life and Education: A Study of the Rural-School Problem as a Phase of the Rural-Life Problem* (Boston: Houghton Mifflin, 1914), 70–71: and see discussion in Tyack, *One Best System,* 22.
9. Ravitch, *School Wars,* 158.
10. Nearly 40% were Republicans, more than half were merchants, and many others were lawyers, doctors, and other professionals. See Ravitch, *School Wars,* 152.
11. William Taggert, as quoted in Tyack, *One Best System,* 155, and Ravitch, *School Wars,* ch. 14.

12. The warning about aristocracy is from a circular prepared for a mass protest meeting for teachers, "Public Schools in Danger!" New York Municipal Archives, Mayoral Papers, undated [1896], Board of Education. President Robert Maclay's remarks were published in the weekly newspaper *School,* Feb. 27, 1896. The third quotation is from the same issue. See Ravitch, *School Wars,* 154–155.

13. Paul E. Peterson, *The Politics of School Reform, 1870–1940* (Chicago: University of Chicago Press, 1985), 9–10, 13–15, 35–42, 69–71, 152–153, and Troen, *Public and the Schools,* 218–225.

14. See Peterson, *Politics of School Reform,* ch. 4, esp. 86–94.

15. Troen, *Public and the Schools,* 225.

16. Tyack, *One Best System,* 24–26.

17. The reforms seem to have been successful in this endeavor, according to Tyack, *One Best System,* 89, 94–95, 127–129, 156–157. See also Ravitch, *School Wars,* 134–139, 181–186, and Mustafa Emirbayer, "Moral Education in America, 1830–1990: A Contribution to the Sociology of Moral Culture" (Ph.D. diss., Harvard University, 1989), ch. 4, material accompanying nn. 71–75.

18. See David Boaz, "The Public School Monopoly: America's Berlin Wall," in David Boaz, ed., *Liberating Schools: Education in the Inner City* (Washington, D.C.: Cato Institute, 1991), figures from material accompanying fn. 38. By 1980, according to Sam Peltzman, local school boards raised only about 40% of their own funds. See Boaz, "Declining Student Performance," *American Enterprise* (July/Aug. 1993): 45–49, esp. 47.

19. See table 2.2 in Paul E. Peterson, "Monopoly and Competition in American Education," in William H. Clune and John Witte, eds., *Choice and Control in American Education* (London: Falmer, 1990).

20. The proportion of high schoolers taking Latin dropped from nearly half to under 10% between 1910 and 1950, and a proliferation of new, nonacademic courses sprang forth: courses in driver education, home economics, personality problems, auto repair, etc. See Richard Hofstadter, *Anti-Intellectualism in American Life* (New York: Vintage Books, 1962), 341–343.

21. Ibid., 345.

22. See Robert C. Post's discussion of the individualistic basis of the rise of First Amendment protections for expression: "Cultural Heterogeneity and the Law," ch. 3 of Post, *Constitutional Domains: Democracy, Community, Management* (Cambridge: Harvard University Press, 1995).

23. *Minersville School District v. Gobitis,* 310 U.S. 586 (1940). See also the interesting background account and materials presented in Walter F. Murphy, James E. Fleming, and Sotirios A. Barber, *American Constitutional Interpretation,* 2d ed. (Westbury, N.Y.: Foundation Press, 1995), 1165–1174.

24. *West Virginia v. Barnette,* 319 U.S. 624 (1943), 640–642.

25. *Tinker v. Des Moines School District,* 393 U.S. 503 (1969), 505.

26. *Board of Education v. Pico,* 457 U.S. 853 (1982), 869.
27. Justice Brennan's plurality opinion, ibid.
28. *Pierce v. Society of Sisters,* 268 U.S. 510 (1925), 534.
29. *Bethel School District v. Fraser,* 755 F.2d 1363 (1985). I am indebted to the account in Michael A. Rebell, "Values Inculcation and the Schools: The Need for a New *Pierce* Compromise," in Neal E. Devins, ed., *Public Values, Private Schools* (New York: Falmer Press, 1989), 44–46.
30. Bethel *School District v. Fraser,* 106 S.Ct. 3159 (1986), 3164–3165.
31. *Hazelwood School District v. Kuhlmeier,* 484 U.S. 260 (1988), 271–272.
32. *Everson v. Ewing Township* 330 U.S. 1 (1947), Justice Black writing for the Court, 16.
33. Ibid, 17–18.
34. *Board of Education v. Allen,* 392 U.S. 236 (1968); *Mueller v. Allen,* 463 US 388 (1983).
35. *Lemon v. Kurtzman,* 403 U.S. 602 (1971).
36. *Meek v. Pittinger,* 421 U.S. 349 (1975).
37. See *Engel v. Vitale,* 370 U.S. 421 (1962); *School District of Abington Township v. Schempp,* 374 U.S. 203 (1963); *Lee v. Weisman,* 505 U.S. 577 (1992); and *Stone v. Graham,* 449 U.S. 39 (1980).
38. Michael McConnell, "Multiculturalism, Majoritarianism, and Educational Choice: What Does Our Constitutional Tradition Have to Say?" *University of Chicago Legal Forum* 1991 (1991): 123–151, esp. 140–141, 127.
39. Justice Stewart dissenting in *Abington,* 313.
40. The prayer read, "Almighty God, we acknowledge our dependence upon Thee, and we beg Thy blessings upon us, our parents, our teachers and our Country," quoted in *Engel,* 422.
41. *Walz v. Tax Commission,* 397 U.S. 664 (1970); *Rosenberger v. University of Virginia,* 515 U.S. 819 (1995).
42. See Neal Devins, "State Regulation of Christian Schools," *Journal of Legislation* 10 (1983): 351–381, esp. 351, n. 3.
43. Sonia L. Nazario, "Schoolteachers Say It's Wrongheaded to Try to Teach What's Right," *Wall Street Journal,* April 6, 1990, B1, B8.
44. Frances FitzGerald's observations on changes from the 1950s to the 1970s in American history textbooks is instructive, see his *America Revised: History Schoolbooks in the Twentieth Century* (New York: Vintage, 1979), 7–13, 16, 209. See also Gerald Grant, *The World We Created at Hamilton High* (Cambridge: Harvard University Press, 1988).
45. See Arthur G. Powell, Eleanor Farrar, and David K. Cohen, *The Shopping Mall High School: Winners and Losers in the Educational Marketplace* (Boston: Houghton Mifflin, 1985), 57–65.
46. See the account in Grant, *Hamilton High,* 185–189, and the poll he cites: Kevin Ryan and Michael G. Thompson, "Moral Education's Muddled Mandate: Comments on a Survey of Phi Delta Kappan's," *Phi Delta Kappan* 56 (June 1975): 663–666.

47. It was a set of values clarification textbooks that were burned in Warsaw, Indiana, in the incident related by Stephen Arons and discussed in the introduction.

48. My source is Sidney B. Simon, Leland W. Howe, and Howard Kirschenbaum, *Values Clarification: A Handbook of Practical Strategies for Teachers and Students*, rev. ed. (New York: Hart, 1978), 11–22.

49. See Strategies 31, 35, and 36, in ibid. The authors also provide a kind of values clarification hymn, called "I Am Proud," with lyrics that are rather easy to remember: "I am proud, I am Proud, I am Proud of what I do. I am proud and I'll tell you." Composed by Marianne Simon, of the Center for Humanistic Education; see ibid., 327–328.

50. Ibid.

51. Grant, *Hamilton High*, xx; and Amy Gutmann, *Democratic Education* (Princeton: Princeton University Press, 1987), 55–56.

52. Michael J. Sandel advances these charges in his typically provocative treatment "Political Liberalism (Review of Rawls's Political Liberalism)" *Harvard Law Review* 107 (1994): 1765–1794. It must be allowed that some versions of liberalism, especially perhaps those that place neutrality at their center, may be vulnerable to Sandel's critique. There are, however, other versions of liberalism. In choosing to criticize neutralist liberalism, it seems to me that Sandel, like so many other critics of liberalism, chooses a particularly vulnerable rather than a particularly powerful target. I do not believe that the version of liberalism defended here is vulnerable to Sandel's charges (it may be vulnerable to others, but we shall see).

53. *Keyishian v. Board of Regents of the University of the State of New York*, 385 U.S. 589 (1967), 603, and see Stanley Fish, "Children and the First Amendment," *Connecticut Law Review* 29 (Winter 1997): 884.

54. See, for example, Michael J. Sandel, *Democracy's Discontent: America in Search of a Public Philosophy* (Cambridge: Harvard University Press, 1996), and Sandel, "Political Liberalism."

55. This point was forcefully made to me by Jane J. Mansbridge. I explore these virtues, and their connection with liberal politics, in *Liberal Virtues: Citizenship, Virtue, and Community in Liberal Constitutionalism* (Oxford: Oxford University Press, 1990). It has to be admitted that what evidence there is, and there is not much, does not suggest that public schools actually do a better job at civic education. See Andrew M. Greeley and Peter H. Rossi, *The Education of Catholic Americans* (Chicago: Aldine, 1966); and Andrew M. Greeley, *Catholic High Schools and Minority Students* (New Brunswick, N.J.: Transaction, 1982). Greeley advances the powerful claim that Catholic schooling has the greatest advantage over public schooling with respect to the education of children from economically and socially deprived backgrounds, so that Catholic schools rather than public schools are the true promoters of the democratic ideal of equal opportunity. These arguments are developed in Antony Bryk, Valerie E. Lee, and Peter B. Holland, *Catho-*

lic Schools and the Common Good (Cambridge: Harvard University Press, 1993). It should be noted that for Bryk and his colleagues in particular, the ability to make a civic case for Catholic schooling depends on the transformation of Catholicism symbolized by Vatican II. This seems to me crucial as well, for reasons to be considered in Chapter 5. On the ideal of the "detached school," see Meira Levinson's *The Demands of Liberal Education* (Oxford: Oxford University Press, 1999).

56. See, for example, the account in Peterson, *Politics of School Reform*, ch. 5.

57. See, for example, Richard Kluger, *Simple Justice* (New York: Vintage, 1975); and Taylor Branch, *Parting the Waters: America in the King Years* (New York: Simon and Schuster, 1988).

58. The quotation from President Lyndon Johnson is from his "Remarks on Project Head Start, May 18, 1965," *Public Papers of the Presidents of the United States: Lyndon B. Johnson, 1965,* 2 vols. (vol. 1: Washington, D.C.: Government Printing Office, 1966), 1:556. On the history of education in this era generally, see Lawrence A. Cremin, *American Education: The Metropolitan Experience, 1876–1980* (New York: Harper & Row, 1988), 314–320.

59. Peterson, "Monopoly and Competition," 63–66. Ira Katznelson and Margaret Weir emphasize the decisive role that courts played in forcing desegregation on city school districts. See their *Schooling for All: Class, Race, and the Decline of the Democratic Ideal* (New York: Basic Books, 1985), ch. 7.

60. See Powell et al., *Shopping Mall,* 57–65.

61. Ravitch, *School Wars,* 261; Paul E. Peterson, "Are Big City Schools Holding Their Own?" occasional paper 91–4, Center for American Political Studies, Harvard University, Cambridge, Mass., January 1991.

62. See James S. Coleman and Thomas Hoffer, *Public and Private High Schools: The Impact of Communities* (New York: Basic Books, 1987), 6–8.

63. Powell et al., *Shopping Mall,* 3.

64. Coleman and Hoffer, *Public and Private,* xvi–xvii, 3–4.

65. Powell et al., *Shopping Mall,* 40; see also 62–65 and chs. 2 and 5 generally.

66. Grant, *Hamilton High,* 4–5.

67. Ibid., 51.

5. Civic Ends

1. I provide an account of this dependence in "Community, Diversity, and Civic Education: Toward a Liberal Political Science of Group Life," *Social Philosophy and Policy* 13, no. 1 (Winter 1996).

2. See John Tracy Ellis, *American Catholicism* (Chicago: University of Chicago Press, 1956), 105. I am indebted in this paragraph generally to Ellis's insights.

3. Ibid., 107–108.

4. Robert D. Putnam, *Making Democracy Work: Civic Traditions in Mod-*

ern Italy (Princeton: Princeton University Press, 1993), 100, 107, 126, 172, 175–176.

5. Kenneth A. Bollen, "Political Democracy and the Timing of Development," *American Sociological Review* 44, no. 4 (1979): 572–587, 583; and Samuel Huntington, *The Third Wave: Democratization in the Late Twentieth Century* (Norman: University of Oklahoma Press, 1991), 75.

6. Huntington, *Third Wave*, 77.

7. George Weigel, "Catholicism and Democracy: The Other Twentieth-Century Revolution," in Brad Roberts, ed., *The New Democrats: Global Change and U.S. Policy* (Cambridge: MIT Press, 1990), 17–37, 24–25. See also *The Documents of Vatican II*, ed. Walter M. Abbott, S.J. (New York: Herder and Herder, 1966), esp. 672–688; and *American Participation in the Second Vatican Council*, ed. Vincent A. Yzermans. (New York: Sheed and Ward, 1967). See also the discussions in Huntington, *Third Wave*, 77–78, and John Cogley, *Catholic America* (New York: Dial Press, 1973), in which Cogley emphasizes the extent to which the Catholic Church made concessions to liberalism and "modernity" in Vatican II: "[T]he long Catholic cold war against liberalism was unobtrusively brought to an end during the Second Vatican Council. If a winner were to be named, it would probably have to be liberalism" (190; see also 185–193 generally). American Catholics were not alone in pushing for liberalization within the Catholic Church. On the role of European, especially French, Catholics, and the relationship between changes in the Catholic Church and political and social liberalization, see Gene Burns, "The Politics of Ideology: The Papal Struggle with Liberalism," *American Journal of Sociology* 95, no. 5 (1990): 1123–1152. See also the illuminating philosophical perspective on this story in Lief Wenar's excellent article, "Political Liberalism: An Internal Critique," *Ethics* 105 (October 1995). I have also benefited from conversations on these topics with Mark Brewer, Margaret Susan Thompson, and Paul Sigmund.

8. Weigel traces the origins of the Catholic post–Vatican II position to a letter by Pope Gelasius I to the Byzantine Emperor Anastasius in 494. See his "Catholicism and Democracy," 25–26.

9. See Philip Gleason, "American Identity and Americanization," in William Petersen, Michael Novak, and Philip Gleason, *Concepts of Ethnicity* (Cambridge: Harvard University Press, 1982).

10. See Will Herberg, *Protestant, Catholic, and Jew: An Essay in American Religious Sociology* (Garden City, N.Y.: Anchor, 1960), esp. ch. 5. It may go too far to say that people must regard their religious views as politically irrelevant. What is required is that they have secular grounds for their political views, but these may be colored by their wider views.

11. *New York Times*, December 23, 1952, quoted in ibid., 84. In 1948, Eisenhower said, "I am the most intensely religious man I know. Nobody goes through six years of war without faith. That doesn't mean I adhere to any sect. A democracy cannot exist without a religious base. I believe in democ-

racy." *New York Times,* May 4, 1948, quoted in Ellis, *American Catholicism,* 155.

12. Barnett, "God and the American People," *Ladies Home Journal* (November 1948): 235–236, quoted in Herberg, *Protestant, Catholic, and Jew,* 76.
13. Herberg, *Protestant, Catholic, and Jew,* 76.
14. Ibid.
15. See also the discussions of religion in America in Daniel J. Boorstin, *The Genius of American Politics* (Chicago: University of Chicago Press, 1953), discussed later.
16. Sanford Levinson, "The Confrontation of Religious Faith and Civil Religion: Catholics Becoming Justices," *DePaul Law Review* 39 (1990): 1047–1081, 1049.
17. I should emphasize that just because transformative mechanisms are subtle and indirect does not mean that they cannot be publicly defended. See Part Two.
18. *The Bible in the Public Schools: Arguments before the Superior Court of Cincinnati in the case of* Minor v. Board of Education of Cincinnati *(1870),* ed. Robert G. McCloskey (New York: Da Capo, 1967), 437.
19. Among the important recent treatments of Dewey are Robert B. Westbrook, *John Dewey and American Democracy* (Ithaca, N.Y.: Cornell University Press, 1991); Alan Ryan, *John Dewey and the High Tide of American Liberalism* (New York: W. W. Norton, 1995); David M. Steiner, *Rethinking Democratic Education: The Politics of Reform* (Baltimore: Johns Hopkins University Press, 1994), and David Fott, *John Dewey: America's Philosopher of Democracy* (Lanham, Md.: Rowman and Littlefield, 1998).
20. John Dewey, "The School as a Means of Developing Social Consciousness and Social Ideas in Children," *Journal of Social Forces* 1 (Sept. 1923): 515.
21. John Dewey, *A Common Faith* (New Haven: Yale University Press, 1934), quotations from 30, 14, 16, 33. See also "Reconstruction," *The Early Works,* ed. Jo Ann Boydston, 5 vols. (Carbondale: Southern Illinois University Press, 1969–1975), 4:101.
22. Dewey, *Common Faith,* 33.
23. Ibid., 32, emphasis added. Westbrook rightly describes Dewey's conception of science as "latitudinarian but imperial," in his *Dewey,* 142.
24. Dewey, *Common Faith,* 39.
25. Ibid., 28, 86; see also Westbrook's account, *Dewey,* 423–428. The question for Dewey was not this or that belief, but the underlying method: "The theological philosophers of the Middle Ages had no greater difficulty in giving rational form to all the doctrines of the Roman church than has the liberal theologian of today" (ibid., 33–34; see generally 30–35).
26. Dewey, *Common Faith,* 46, 80–81, 85. Elsewhere Dewey writes that "full victory will not be won until every subject and lesson is taught in connection with . . . the kind of power of observation, inquiry, reflection and testing that are the heart of scientific intelligence." See "The Relation of Science and

Philosophy as a Basis of Education," in *School and Society* 47 (April 9, 1938): 470–473, reprinted in *John Dewey on Education: Selected Writings,* ed. Reginald D. Archimbault (Chicago: University of Chicago Press, 1974), quotation from 19.

27. Dewey, "Christianity and Democracy" (1892), *Early Works,* 4:10.
28. Ibid., 4:9.
29. John Dewey, "The Relation of Philosophy to Theology" (1893), *Early Works,* 4:368, 367; see also the excellent discussion in Westbrook, *Dewey,* 78–79. Elsewhere Dewey notes that true revelation is science, see "Christianity and Democracy," 6.
30. Dewey, "Religion and Our Schools" (1908), *The Middle Works: 1899–1924,* ed. Jo Ann Boydston, 15 vols. (Carbondale: Southern Illinois University Press, 1976–1983), 4:167–168; and Westbrook's discussion in *Dewey,* 418–428.
31. Dewey, "Religion and Our Schools," 168.
32. Ibid., 175.
33. Ibid., 169. For an excellent discussion of Dewey's relationship with American religious traditions, including the postmillennial reformism of Josiah Strong and others, see Jean B. Quandt, "Religion and Social Thought: The Secularization of Postmillennialism," *American Quarterly* 25 (1973): 390–409.
34. Westbrook, *John Dewey,* 418–419, n. 40.
35. Dewey, "Religion and Our Schools," 175.
36. Dewey, *The Public and Its Problems* (New York: Holt, 1927), 148–149.
37. Ibid., 178–181.
38. Steven C. Rockefeller, *John Dewey: Religious Faith and Democratic Humanism* (New York: Columbia University Press, 1991), 562.
39. Ronald F. Thiemann, *Religion in Public Life: A Dilemma for Democracy* (Washington, D.C.: Georgetown University Press, 1996), 169.
40. Weigel, "Catholicism and Democracy," 28–29, quoting in part John Paul II's "Instruction on Certain Aspects of the 'Theology of Liberation.'"
41. Again, see Weigel, "Catholicism and Democracy," 30–31; and John Finnis, "Is Natural Law Compatible with Limited Government?" in Robert George, ed., *Natural Law, Liberalism, and Morality* (Oxford: Oxford University Press, 1996).
42. Amy Gutmann, *Democratic Education* (Princeton: Princeton University Press, 1987), 45.
43. Gleason, "American Identity," 140–143.

Part II. Liberal Civic Education and Religious Fundamentalism

1. Interesting work on the complementarity of the two religion clauses has been done by Abner S. Greene; see his "The Political Balance of the Religion Clauses," *Yale Law Journal* 102 (1993): 1611–1644. See also the important

work of Christopher L. Eisgruber, which overlaps in important ways with the perspective advanced in this book: "Madison's Wager: Religious Liberty in the Constitutional Order," *Northwestern University Law Review* 89 (1995): 347–410.

2. As Neal Devins reports in his excellent account, "Fundamentalist Christian Educators v. State: An Inevitable Compromise," *George Washington Law Review* 60 (1992): 818–840, esp. 819.

3. See Douglas Laycock, "Summary and Synthesis: The Crisis in Religious Liberty," *George Washington Law Review* 60 (1992): 841–856, esp. 842; Mary Ann Glendon and Raul F. Yanes, "Structural Free Exercise," *Michigan Law Review* 90 (1991): 477–550; Nomi Maya Stolzenberg, "'He Drew a Circle That Shut Me Out': Assimilation, Indoctrination, and the Paradox of a Liberal Education," *Harvard Law Review* 106 (1993): 581–667; and Stephen Carter, "Evolutionism, Creationism, and Treating Religion as a Hobby," *Duke Law Journal* 1987 (1987): 977–996. In her provocative and searching article, Stolzenberg is mainly concerned with highlighting the seriousness of fundamentalist complaints, though she also evinces a good deal of sympathy for those complaints. Like Stolzenberg, Sanford Levinson emphasizes the moral costs to people with totalistic faiths of the liberal "privatization" of religion, giving too much weight to religious objections. See Levinson, "The Confrontation of Religious Faith and Civil Religion: Catholics Becoming Justices," *DePaul Law Review* 39 (1990): 1047–1081, and "Religious Language and the Public Square (Review of Michael Perry, *Love and Power: The Role of Religion and Morality in American Politics*)," *Harvard Law Review* 105 (1992): 2061–2079.

4. Douglas Laycock, "Crisis," p. 841.

5. Michael W. McConnell, "Multiculturalism, Majoritarianism, and Educational Choice: What Does Our Constitutional Tradition Have to Say?" *University of Chicago Legal Forum* 1991 (1991): 123–151.

6. Multiculturalism and the Religious Right

1. *Wisconsin v. Yoder*, 406 U.S. 205 (1971), 218.

2. Ibid., 211.

3. Ibid., 235, 225–226, 233.

4. *Employment Division, Dept. of Human Resources of Oregon v. Smith*, 110 S. Ct. 1595 (1990), 1597–1598.

5. Ibid., 1600.

6. Ibid., 1604–1606, and see *Gobitis*, 310 U.S. 586.

7. Statement of the Hon. Stephen J. Solarz, *Hearing before the Subcommittee on Civil and Constitutional Rights of the Committee on the Judiciary, House of Representatives*, 101st Cong., 2d sess., on H.R. 5377, Religious Freedom Restoration Act of 1990, ser. 150 (Washington, D.C.: U.S. Government Printing Office, 1991), 13.

8. *Dred Scott v. Sanford,* 60 U.S. (19 How.) 393 (1857), see Statement of Nadine Strossen, *Hearing before the Committee on the Judiciary, United States Senate, 102nd Congress, 2nd Sess., on S.2969, A Bill to Protect the Free Exercise of Religion,* Senate Hearing 102–1076, Sept. 18, 1992, ser. J-102–82, (Washington D.C.: U.S. Government Printing Office, 1993), 171.

9. *Report of Mr. Brooks, from the Committee on the Judiciary, Together with Additional Views, to Accompany HR 1308, Religious Freedom Restoration Act of 1993,* Report 103–88, House of Representatives, 103d Cong., 1st sess., 6.

10. "Remarks by the President at Signing Ceremony for the Religious Freedom Restoration Act," White House Press Release, Office of the Press Secretary, The White House, November 16, 1993. Emphasis in the original. RFRA was struck down by the Supreme Court in *City of Boerne v. Flores,* 521 U.S. 507 (1997).

11. *Mozert et al. v. Hawkins County Public Schools* 579 F.Supp. 1051 (1984) (hereafter *Mozert* 1), 1052. The five sets of published opinions that form the core of the *Mozert* litigation are, in addition to the case just cited, *Mozert v. Hawkins County Public Schools (Mozert 2),* 582 F. Supp. 201 (E.D. Tenn. 1984); *Mozert v. Hawkins County Public Schools (Mozert 3),* 765 F.2d 75 (6th Cir. 1985); *Mozert v. Hawkins County Public Schools (Mozert 4),* 647 F. Supp. 1194 (E.D. Tenn. 1986); and *Mozert v. Hawkins County Public Schools (Mozert 5),* 827 F.2d. 1058 (6th Cir. 1987), *cert. denied,* 484 U.S. 1066 (1988). Fundamentalist parents Bob Mozert and Vicki Frost testified that plaintiffs in this case objected to passages in public school reading texts that "expose their children to other forms of religion and to the feelings, attitudes and values of other students that contradict the plaintiffs' religious views without a statement that the other views are incorrect and that the plaintiffs' views are the correct ones." See Chief Judge Lively's opinion for the Court in *Mozert 5,* 1062.

12. It was noted, for example, "that of 47 stories referring to, or growing out of, Religions (including Islam, Buddhism, American Indian religion and nature worship), only 3 were Christian, and none Protestant." See Danny J. Boggs, Circuit Judge, concurring opinion in *Mozert 5,* pp. 1080–1081, fn. 13.

13. Opinion of Judge Lively, *Mozert 5,* 1061, quoting the testimony of Vicki Frost.

14. Stolzenberg, "Circle," 594. See also Stephen Bates's valuable account of the litigation and the larger political struggle in *Battleground: One Mother's Crusade, the Religious Right, and the Struggle for Control of Our Classrooms* (New York: Poseidon, 1993).

15. See *Mozert 5,* 1059–1060; *Mozert 4,* 1196–1198.

16. *Mozert 4,* 1199; Stolzenberg, "Circle," 596–597. My account here is indebted to the excellent discussion in Stephen Bates's *Battleground.*

17. *4*, see Bates, *Battleground*, chs. 4 and 5.
18. *Mozert 1*, 1052–1053. See also *Mozert 2*, 202.
19. *Mozert 3*, 765 F.2d 75 (1985), 78.
20. *Mozert 4*, 1200.
21. Ibid., 1202–1203.
22. For good measure, Chief Judge Hull of the Federal District Court, who wrote the opinions in *Mozert 1*, *Mozert 2*, and *Mozert 4*, also awarded the families $50,000 in damages against the school board. See *Mozert 5*, 1059, 1063.
23. *Mozert 5*.
24. See the helpful discussion in George W. Dent Jr., "Religious Children, Secular Schools," *Southern California Law Review* 61 (1988): 863–941. Dent points out that states often excuse religious children by statute from particular parts of the curriculum: New York, for example, excuses Christian Science children from health classes, and some localities allow children to be excused from sex education classes on religious grounds (924, fn. 337).
25. There is no "establishment" worry in *Mozert;* in other words, there was no attempt by the *Mozert* parents to change the curriculum for all, or to impose their beliefs on others. See *Mozert 4*, 1195. See also *Grove v. Mead School District No. 354*, 753 F.2d 1528 (9th Cir. 1985); cert. denied, 106 S.Ct. 85 (1985). A student objected to reading *The Learning Tree* on religious grounds. The student was allowed to do alternative reading, but then also sued to have the book removed from the school, alleging violation of free exercise and of the establishment clause.
26. Jeff Spinner calls them "partial citizens" in his important book, *The Boundaries of Citizenship: Race, Ethnicity, and Nationality in the Liberal State* (Baltimore: Johns Hopkins University Press, 1994).
27. *Mozert 5*, 1064. On these grounds, Judge Lively distinguished other cases where interference with religious freedom was found; see 1065–1066. See also *West Virginia State Board of Education v. Barnette*, 319 U.S. 624 (1943).
28. *Mozert 5*, 1063. Some school officials denied that any values at all were being taught. County Superintendent Snodgrass, for example, said that the schools do not teach "any particular values" and that they "teach and promote reading, not values." Quoted in *Mozert 5*, opinion of Judge Boggs, 1077.
29. *Mozert 5*, Judge Boggs concurring, 1075–1076.
30. These points are forcefully developed in Stolzenberg, "Circle," 599–611. On the notion of unconstitutional conditions in the education context, see Michael W. McConnell, "The Selective Funding Problem: Abortions and Religious Schools," *Harvard Law Review* 104 (1991): 989–1050.
31. *Mozert 5*, 1080.

32. Ibid.
33. There are most certainly more adequate and suitably critical versions of multiculturalism, which I consider later.
34. Stolzenberg, "Circle," 583, 582. Stolzenberg is mainly concerned with highlighting the seriousness of fundamentalist complaints, though she also evinces a good deal of sympathy for those complaints. Like Stolzenberg, Sanford Levinson highlights the moral costs to people with totalistic faiths of the liberal "privatization" of religion, and he also gives too much weight to religious objections. See Levinson, "The Confrontation of Religious Faith and Civil Religion: Catholics Becoming Justices," *DePaul Law Review* 39 (1990): 1047–1081, and "Religious Language and the Public Square (Review of Michael Perry, *Love and Power: The Role of Religion and Morality in American Politics*)," *Harvard Law Review* 105 (1992): 2061–2079.
35. This is Ronald Dworkin's felicitous phrase, found in his *Taking Rights Seriously* (Cambridge: Harvard University Press, 1977), 180–183, 272–278.
36. Will Kymlicka argues eloquently that this multicultural concern will be especially important for minority cultures that find themselves at odds with more mainstream cultural attitudes and that are liable to be disadvantaged by the public policies that flow from those attitudes. See Kymlicka, *Liberalism, Community, and Culture* (Oxford: Oxford University Press, 1989), and *Multicultural Citizenship* (Oxford: Oxford University Press, 1995). Kymlicka is not an uncritical multiculturalist. His argument, indeed, seems not to apply to cultural minorities generally but to "distinct peoples" who never became full members of the shared political order: the Quebecois, who reserved rights to cultural distinctness in the Canadian Constitution, and to native peoples who reserved the right to remain distinct peoples. Kymlicka's model does not seem to me to apply within an immigrant society that is, or properly aspires to be, one political community. For an important critical discussion of these matters, see John Tomasi, "Kymlicka, Liberalism, and Respect for Cultural Minorities," *Ethics* 105 (April 1995). I am also indebted to discussions with Tomasi.
37. Bates, *Battleground*, 314, quoting Philip H. Walking and Chris Brannigan, "Anti-Sexist/Anti-Racist Education: A Possible Dilemma," *Journal of Moral Education* 15 (January 1986): 21–22.
38. Bates, *Battleground*, 314.
39. Ibid., 317.

7. Diversity and the Problem of Justification

1. I draw heavily on John Rawls's account in *Political Liberalism* (New York: Columbia University Press, 1993).
2. Almost 40 percent of the American public believes that the Bible is literally true, according to George A. Gallup Jr. and Jim Castelli, *The People's Faith: American Faith in the 90's* (New York: Macmillan, 1989), 61. This does *not*

show that the belief is reasonable. What political liberalism would resist—properly, I think—is the blanket judgment that belief in the literal truth of the Bible is a false *religious* belief.

3. See Rawls, *Political Liberalism*, xxi–xxiv.

4. Underlying Hobbes's political view is the conviction that moral notions such as good and evil are "ever used with relation to the person that useth them: there being nothing simply or absolutely so," not any common meaning "to be taken from the nature of the objects themselves." Thomas Hobbes, *Leviathan*, ed. C. B. Macpherson (Harmondsworth, Eng.: Penguin, 1968), pt. 1, 120.

5. John Locke emphasized that people who differ over religion nevertheless share certain "civil interests," the protection of which furnished a shared ground for political unity. These civil interests were "things of the body not the soul," and included the preservation of every person's life, liberty, and property; an effective rule of law; and enforcement agencies to provide security and peace. In the *Second Treatise,* Locke insists that these basic "civil interests" are backed by certain ideas of natural law and natural rights: people have inalienable rights to life, liberty, and property, and a natural law—known to all people of ordinary understanding—prescribes that everyone should respect these rights. To illustrate that an understanding of natural law is innate, Locke speaks of Adam: created as "in full possession" of "strength and reason," and so "capable from the first instant of his being to . . . govern his actions according to the dictates of the law of reason which God had implanted in him." *Two Treatises of Government,* ed. Peter Laslett (New York: Mentor, 1965), *Second Treatise,* 347, par. 56. The Lockean approach is promising, but the notion that all normal, mature people have easy access to an objective moral law now seems unconvincing. A vast amount has been written on the relationships among Locke's philosophical, religious, and political ideas. For an excellent recent contribution, see John Marshall, *John Locke: Resistance, Religion and Responsibility* (Cambridge, Cambridge University Press, 1994).

6. *Mozert v. Hawkins County Board of Education,* 827 F.2nd 1058 (6th Cir. 1987), (hereafter *Mozert 5*), 1069, and 1068, quoting *Bethel School District no. 403 v. Fraser,* 106 S.Ct. 3159, 3164 (1986).

7. *Mozert 5,* quoting the testimony of parent Vicki Frost.

8. Ibid., 1069. In fact, Judge Kennedy seemed basically to take this route as well, emphasizing that the legitimate state interest includes inculcation of "the habits and manners of civility as values in themselves conducive to happiness and as indispensable to the practice of self-government." Ibid., 1071–1072.

9. Ibid., 1069.

10. See Amy Gutmann and Dennis Thompson, *Democracy and Disagreement* (Cambridge: Harvard University Press, 1996), discussed later.

11. Rawls, *Political Liberalism*, Lecture III.

12. Ibid., 77–81, 154.
13. One who believes this might say, for example: "Your Catholicism absurdly defers to the authority of the Bishop of Rome, but I welcome you as a fellow citizen whose reasonableness is shown by the fact that you do not seek to impose your religious beliefs on me by political means, but instead join with me in acknowledging the political authority of reasons we can share."
14. See Rawls's discussion of the "burdens of judgment" in *Political Liberalism*, 54–58.
15. John Rawls, *A Theory of Justice* (Oxford: Oxford University Press, 1971), 214, 132.
16. See Joshua Cohen's helpful discussion, "Moral Pluralism and Political Consensus," in David Copp, Jean Hampton, and John Roemer, eds., *The Idea of Democracy* (Cambridge: Cambridge University Press, 1993). See also T. M. Scanlon, "Contractualism and Utilitarianism," in Amartya Sen and Bernard Williams, eds., *Utilitarianism and Beyond* (Cambridge: Cambridge University Press, 1982), 103–128.
17. Ronald Dworkin, *Taking Rights Seriously* (Cambridge: Harvard University Press, 1977), 166.
18. Gutmann and Thompson, *Democracy and Disagreement*, 2; see also 255.
19. Rawls, *Political Liberalism*, 49; Gutmann and Thompson, *Democracy and Disagreement*, 55. See my discussion of moral motivation in Stephen Macedo, *Liberal Virtues: Citizenship, Virtue, and Community in Liberal Constitutionalism* (Oxford: Oxford University Press, 1990), 133–142.
20. Rawls, *Political Liberalism*, pp. 54–57.
21. Gutmann and Thompson, *Democracy and Disagreement*, 56–57.
22. Ibid.
23. A popular version of this charge—directed at American liberalism in general rather than political liberalism in particular—can be found in Stephen L. Carter's *Culture of Disbelief: How Law and Politics Trivialize Religious Devotion* (New York: Basic Books, 1993). Rawls clarifies his position in "The Idea of Public Reason Revisited," *University of Chicago Law Review* 64, no. 3 (1997).
24. Rawls, *Political Liberalism*, p. 222.
25. *Mozert 5*, 1069.
26. *Scopes v. State* 289 S.W. 363 (1927), 368–369.
27. According to this view, students might be allowed to describe and defend their religious views in certain ways, and so as Kent Greenawalt properly suggests to me religion need not be kept altogether out of the public schools. For another view of the *Mozert* case, see Joe Coleman, "Civic Pedagogies and Liberal Democratic Curricula," *Ethics* 108 (July 1998).
28. John Dewey, *A Common Faith* (New Haven: Yale University Press, 1934), 32.
29. *Mozert v. Hawkins*, 582 F.Supp. 201 (1984) (hereafter *Mozert 2*), 202.
30. Ibid.

31. Distinguishing exposure and indoctrination, as George Dent explains, is liable to depend on context and other complex matters. See Dent, "Religious Children," 891–892.

32. Amy Gutmann emphasizes the former point in "Civic Education and Social Diversity." The commitment to public reason sometimes influences the resolution of substantive decisions; see Macedo, "In Defense of Public Reason: Are Slavery and Abortion Hard Cases?" *American Journal of Jurisprudence* 42 (1997).

33. See Hobbes, *Leviathan,* pt. 3.

34. Jean-Jacques Rousseau, *On the Social Contract* in *On the Social Contract, Discourse on the Origins of Inequality, Discourse on Political Economy,* ed. Donald A. Cress (Indianapolis: Hackett, 1983), bk. 4, 102–103.

35. Rawls, *Political Liberalism,* 195–200.

36. See Rawls, *Political Liberalism,* 191–194.

37. See the discussion in Chapter 2, and that in Vincent P. Lannie, *Public Money and Parochial Education: Bishop Hughes, Governor Seward, and the New York School Controversy* (Cleveland: Case Western Reserve University Press, 1968), 59.

38. See Michael J. Sandel's account in *Liberalism and the Limits of Justice* (Cambridge: Cambridge University Press, 1982).

39. See Rina Verma, "Secularism and Communal Violence in Indian Politics," thesis prospectus, Department of Government, Harvard University, May 20, 1992, on file at the department. Note Verma's observation that "equidistance produces communalism by producing insecurity and disequilibrium among religious communities. Instead of remaining at an equal distance from the different religions, the state progressively becomes entangled in trying to please 'all of the communities all of the time.' If it grants one concession to one group, it must grant one to another group, and so on. The process, instead of making all groups feel secure about their position, actually never reaches an equilibrium, increases the burden on the state, and ends up antagonizing all groups involved" 10).

40. Niklas Luhmann writes, "[I]n highly complex societies none of the central functions of the societal system can be assumed by a unified organization"; see Luhmann, *The Differentiation of Society,* trans. Stephen Holmes and Charles Larmore (New York: Columbia University Press, 1982), 80. See also ch. 4 and the useful introduction by Holmes and Larmore, (ix–xxxvi).

41. "Organizational plans and directives are evaded, distorted, redefined, or intentionally derailed at the level of interaction. The slack relation between official Church dogma and ordinary confessional practice . . . offers a good example of this process of routine deviation." Ibid., 79.

42. See Nomi Maya Stolzenberg, "'He Drew a Circle That Shut Me Out': Assimilation, Indoctrination, and the Paradox of a Liberal Education," *Harvard Law Review* 106 (1993): 581–667, esp. 616–634.

43. The phrase "liberal Protestantism" was widely used and often equated with

"modernist" impulses, to be discussed later. See the important conservative Protestant critique of Christian liberalism and modernism in J. Gresham Machen, *Christianity and Liberalism* ([1923]; Grand Rapids, Mich.: Eerdmans, 1981).

44. See William R. Hutchinson, *The Modernist Impulse in American Protestantism* (Durham, N.C.: Duke University Press, 1992), 2–5. According to Hutchinson, "Protestant modernism" dominated perhaps one-third of Protestant churches by 1920.

45. Ibid., 44–47.

46. David Swing advanced such views and was charged with promoting a religion of "mere morality" and with heresy; see ibid., 52–56. Charles Briggs embraced this historicist attitude and argued that it allowed one to think of theology itself as a science; ibid., 91.

47. Hutchinson, *Modernist Impulse*, 255. It would be wrong, however, to characterize this debate as one within Protestantism. There was and is, rather, a larger conflict between religious traditionalists, who want to hold on to time-honored truths and immunize them from not only science but critical inquiry, and religious modernists and "liberals," who want to revise their religious beliefs in order to bring them into harmony with the claims of science and critical inquiry more broadly (which for many will include what they understand as "liberal" attitudes toward social and religious pluralism and progressive attitudes toward political and social reform). For a Catholic volley against Modernism, see the "Encyclical of Pope Pius X on the Doctrines of the Modernists, *Pascendi Dominici Gregis,*" September 8, 1907, reprinted in *The Papal Encyclicals,* vol. 3: 1903–1939, ed. Claudia Carlen, Immaculate Heart of Mary (Raleigh, N.C.: McGrath, 1981). Pius X denies that it is possible to place religious truth into a different realm than science and philosophy, for "man does not suffer a dualism to exist in him, and the believer therefore feels within him an impelling need so to harmonise faith with science." He thus insists, quoting Pius IX, "In matters of religion it is the duty of philosophy not to command but to serve, . . . not to scrutinise the depths of the mysteries of God but to venerate them devoutly and humbly . . . The Modernists," he concluded, "completely invert the parts." Ibid., 78.

48. Ibid., 260–264. See also Norman F. Furniss, *The Fundamentalist Controversy, 1918–1931* (Hampden, Conn.: Archon Books, 1963), esp. 22–34.

49. Nathan O. Hatch, *The Democratization of American Christianity* (New Haven: Yale University Press, 1989), 213–215. For readable fundamentalist polemics, see William B. Riley, *The Finality of the Higher Criticism; or, The Theory of Evolution and False Theology* ([1909]; New York: Garland, 1988); and William Jennings Bryan, *Orthodox Christianity versus Modernism* (New York: Fleming H. Revell, 1923).

50. Stolzenberg, "Circle," 614. Vincent P. Branick lucidly presents the fundamentalist viewpoint: Historical criticism "lacks a certain seriousness. At times it smacks of the playfulness of a game. A game may, of course, involve

exhausting activity and energy and within its own context elicit intense seriousness. Yet a game can be put aside at will. A game is bounded off from the whole of life without direct claim on outside areas. It may suggest or represent the whole in microcosm. That is what makes it absorbing. But a game does not engage the whole. That is what makes it fun. To the degree that the historical-critical method requires that I distance myself and my life decisions from the matter at hand, to the degree the method renders me a detached observer of the Bible 'out there,' it becomes a game. Such playfulness fails to do justice to the subject matter of Scripture . . . To speak of the 'myth of Resurrection' effectively brackets the question of the reality or truth of the Resurrection. It is neither affirmed nor denied. It is only analyzed as to its meaning. As simply having a particular meaning, it makes no claim on my existence. It summons me to no response, positive or negative." See Vincent P. Branick, "The Attractiveness of Fundamentalism," in Marla J. Selvidge, ed., *Fundamentalism Today: What Makes It So Attractive?* (Elgin, Ill.: Brethren Press, 1984), quotation from 22–23, discussed in Stolzenberg, "Circle" 626. Fundamentalists are, in the terminology of Michael J. Sandel, unwilling to be disencumbered of their religious commitments; see his *Liberalism and the Limits of Justice* (Cambridge: Cambridge University Press, 1982).

51. It is not true, then, that liberalism is based on religious uncertainty or value subjectivism, as Stolzenberg suggests in "Circle," 587, 647–665.

52. This is an important concession in the context of the *Mozert* controversy, because some of the most influential shapers of American public schooling have advocated comprehensive liberalisms diametrically opposed to fundamentalism. See Dewey, *Common Faith*.

53. As Thomas Nagel argues: "The true liberal . . . is committed to refusing to use the power of the state to impose paternalistically on its citizens a good life individualistically conceived," *Equality and Partiality* (Oxford: Oxford University Press, 1991), 165.

54. Stephen L. Carter, "Evolutionism, Creationism, and Treating Religion as a Hobby," *Duke Law Journal* 1987 (December 1987): 977–996, esp. 978. I am indebted to Glyn Morgan for discussions on this topic.

55. Stanley Fish, "Liberalism Doesn't Exist," *Duke Law Journal* 1987 (December 1987): 997–1001, esp. 1001.

56. Rawls, *Political Liberalism*, 127–129.

57. Clinton, "Remarks by the President at Signing Ceremony for the Religious Freedom Restoration Act," White House Press Release, The White House, Office of the Press Secretary, November 16, 1993.

8. The Mirage of Perfect Fairness

1. William A. Galston, *Liberal Purposes: Goods, Virtues, and Diversity in the Liberal State* (Cambridge: Cambridge University Press, 1991), 298. See also 117, where Galston cites an unpublished paper by Jon Gunneman.

2. See William A. Galston, "Two Concepts of Liberalism," *Ethics* 105 (April 1995).

3. Douglas Laycock distinguishes formal and substantive notions of neutrality or liberty in "Summary and Synthesis: The Crisis in Religious Liberty," *George Washington Law Review* 60 (1992): 848–849. Formal neutrality requires only that religious associations not be singled out for especially harsh treatment, but it is satisfied if religious groups receive the same treatment as other groups in society, or if general rules and restrictions are applied evenhandedly to religious associations along with all others. On Laycock's view, formal neutrality is not enough to satisfy the "free exercise" clause of the Constitution; I agree. See also the instructive paper by Abner S. Greene, "The Political Balance of the Religion Clauses," *Yale Law Journal* 102 (1993): 1611–1644.

4. Greene, "Political Balance."

5. John Rawls, *Political Liberalism* (New York: Columbia University Press, 1993), 197–200.

6. Consider the mail fraud charges brought against the wife and son of Guy W. Ballard, "alias Saint Germain, Jesus, George Washington, and Godfrey Ray King" and founder of the "I am" movement, who claimed that Jesus stood behind him and dictated the tracts that he distributed through the mail: *U.S. v. Ballard,* 322 U.S. 78 (1944), and *Ballard v. U.S.,* 329 U.S. 187 (1946). How, as Walter Berns asks, is a court to decide whether people got what they paid for? See Walter Berns, "Religion and the Supreme Court," in *The First Amendment and the Future of American Democracy* (New York: Basic Books, 1970), 39–40.

7. Berns, "Religion," 38.

8. Ibid., 49–50.

9. Ibid., 50, 44, 48.

10. See the helpful discussion of *Goldman* by Michael J. Sandel, "Moral Argument and Liberal Toleration: Abortion and Homosexuality," *California Law Review* 77, no. 3 (1989).

11. *Employment Division, Department of Human Resources of Oregon, et al. v. Smith,* 110 Sup. Ct. 1595 (1990).

12. Ibid., 1605.

13. See Scalia's "The Rule of Law as a Law of Rules," *University of Chicago Law Review* 56 (1989), 1175–1188.

14. *Minersville School District v. Gobitis,* 310 U.S. 586 (1940). The Court reversed itself three years later in *West Virginia State Board of Education v. Barnette* 319 U.S. 624 (1943).

15. Thomas Hobbes, *Leviathan,* ed. C. B. Macpherson (Harmondsworth, Eng.: Penguin, 1968), pt. 1, ch. 15.

16. Getting the fundamentalists out of their hair seems to be what the school board had in mind. See Stephen Bates, *Battleground: One Mother's Crusade, the Religious Right, and the Struggle for Control of Our Classrooms* (New York: Poseidon, 1993), 87–88.

17. Liberals should not, I think, allow that there is such a thing as "sovereign legislative discretion."

18. *Wisconsin v. Yoder,* 406 U.S. 205 (1972). In 1948 Congress granted conscientious objector status to those whose objections stemmed from religious beliefs, which Congress specified to mean "belief in a relation to a Supreme Being" rather than "essentially political, sociological, or philosophical views." The Court extended coverage first to someone with "a religious faith in a purely ethical creed," and then to someone with deeply held pacifist views grounded in the study of "history and sociology"; see *U.S. v. Seeger,* 380 U.S. 163 (1965), and *Welsh v. U.S.,* 398 U.S. 333, 341 (1970). For an important argument by a liberal who takes a very different view of the *Yoder* case, see Shelley Burtt, "In Defense of *Yoder:* Parental Autonomy and the Public Schools," in Ian Shapiro and Russell Hardin, eds., *NOMOS XXXVIII: Political Order* (New York: New York University Press, 1996).

19. The Court has not always adhered to its occasional expansive pronouncements on behalf of free exercise challenges to laws with disparate effects. The courts can manipulate the idea of a "burden" on religion to sidestep the problem of free exercise protection; see the discussion in Ira C. Lupu, "Where Rights Begin: The Problem of Burdens on the Free Exercise of Religion," *Harvard Law Review* 102 (1989): 933.

20. I sympathize with the flexible standards discussed in Mary Ann Glendon and Raul F. Yanes, "Structural Free Exercise," *Michigan Law Review* 90 (1991): 477–550, esp. 523, at least with respect to free exercise complaints.

21. Rina Verma suggests this potential outcome in her "Secularism and Communal Violence in Indian Politics," thesis prospectus, Department of Government, Harvard University, May 20, 1992, on file at the department.

22. Rawls suggests as much in his *Political Liberalism.* See also Joshua Cohen's helpful discussion, "Moral Pluralism and Political Consensus," in David Copp, Jean Hampton, and John Roemer, eds., *The Idea of Democracy* (Cambridge: Cambridge University Press, 1993).

23. William A. Galston, "Two Concepts of Liberalism," *Ethics* 105, no. 3 (1995): 524.

24. See James Q. Wilson's foreword to George L. Kelling and Catherine M. Coles, *Fixing Broken Windows: Restoring Order and Reducing Crime in Our Communities* (New York: Free Press, 1996), xvi.

25. For Justice Marshall's complaints about the rigid categorical approach, see *San Antonio Independent School Board v. Rodriguez,* 411 U.S. 1 (1973). For Justice Stevens's views, see, for example, *R.A.V. v. City of Saint Paul,* 505 U.S. 377 (1992).

26. Glendon and Yanes, "Structural Free Exercise."

27. See the very skeptical account of political socialization through schooling in Tyll van Geel, "The Search for Constitutional Limits on Governmental Authority to Inculcate Youth," *Texas Law Review* 62 (1983): 197–297, esp.

262–266. See also van Geel's "The Prisoners' Dilemma and Education Policy," *Notre Dame Journal of Law, Ethics, and Public Policy* 3 (1988): 301–374.

28. There is little evidence for the proposition that public schools (on the whole, and as currently constituted) do a better job than religious schools of teaching civic virtues, or even toleration, but these issues are little studied. The fact is that the overwhelming preoccupation of comparative school studies is academic achievement. Andrew M. Greeley finds that Catholic school students (especially blacks) are more feminist than their public school counterparts, and that Catholic schools have only a marginal impact on religious devotion and make virtually no difference on where students place themselves on a liberal/conservative scale. He finds, too, that whether a student attends Catholic school has no effect on his or her access to birth control information. See Greeley, *Catholic High Schools and Minority Students* (New Brunswick, N.J.: Transaction Books, 1982), 54–55. See also Andrew M. Greeley and Peter Rossi, *The Education of Catholic Americans* (Chicago: Aldine, 1966), 153–155, which confirms that Catholic schooling seems to make Catholic students more religiously tolerant and supportive of civil liberties than does public schooling. Note as well the civic case for Catholic schooling advanced in Antony Bryk et al., *Catholic Schools and the Common Good* (Cambridge: Harvard University Press, 1993), which is discussed in Part Three. A number of commentators regard such findings as highly significant; see, for example, van Geel, "Search for Constitutional Limits"; and George W. Dent Jr., "Religious Children, Secular Schools," *Southern California Law Review* 61 (1988): 907–910, 932. While such evidence is important, it is scanty and rather soft: the general topic is not much studied, and there are inherent difficulties in such studies (especially that of "selection bias": it is difficult to measure the effectiveness of different kinds of schools when certain favorable selection mechanisms tend to explain why particular children are in private schools in the first place).

29. This claim can be made without invoking a comprehensive commitment to individual autonomy.

30. In *Pierce v. Society of Sisters*, 268 U.S. 510 (1925), the Supreme Court sustained a challenge by the operators of parochial and private schools to a law requiring attendance at public schools. I owe this objection to Jon Fullerton and Sanford Levinson.

31. Discussed in Chapter 3.

32. See Neal E. Devins, "State Regulation of Christian Schools," *Journal of Legislation* 10 (1983), esp. 359–363, and Dent, "Religious Children," 909–912.

33. I advance this principle as a corollary to *Pierce*.

34. It will not always be easy to say what is central and what is not, but the ability to read is certainly a basic skill, and, likewise, knowledge of the

diversity that constitutes our history and the importance of tolerance are clearly among the core civic aims.

35. See the account by Paul C. Vitz, *Censorship: Evidence of Bias in Our Children's Textbooks* (Ann Arbor, Mich.: Servant Books, 1986). A second stage of exception making would help give independent meaning to the Constitution's free exercise clause, which it would seem to lack if all that is required is the assurance that laws have public grounds.

36. Rawls also allows comprehensively based arguments in extraordinary moments; see his *Political Liberalism,* 247–254.

37. See Walter Berns, "Religion and the Supreme Court," in *The First Amendment and the Future of American Democracy* (New York: Basic Books, 1970); and Justice Scalia's opinion in *Employment Division, Department of Human Resources of Oregon, et al. v. Smith,* 110 Sup. Ct. 1595 (1990), esp. 1605. Both writers overemphasize the fragility of the rule of law.

38. I elaborate on these themes in Stephen Macedo, "The Rule of Law, Justice, and the Politics of Moderation," In Ian Shapiro, *NOMOS XXVI: The Rule of Law* (New York: New York University Press, 1994).

39. Kymlicka emphasizes this point in his *Multicultural Citizenship* (Oxford: Oxford University Press, 1995), 177.

40. Neal E. Devins reported in 1983 that between 8,000 and 10,000 Christian schools had been established since the mid-1960s, enrolling approximately 1 million students. See Devins, "State Regulation of Christian Schools," 351–381. See also Devins, "Fundamentalist Christian Educators v. the State: An Inevitable Compromise," *George Washington Law Review* 60 (1992): 818–840.

41. See Bates, *Battleground,* 81–92.

42. A valid point made by Stephen L. Carter, *Culture of Disbelief: How American Law and Politics Trivialize Religious Devotion* (New York: Basic Books, 1993), 56.

43. G. W. F. Hegel, *The Philosophy of Right,* trans. T. M. Knox (Oxford: Oxford University Press, 1952), 168, fn. to par. 270.

44. Jeff Spinner, *The Boundaries of Citizenship: Race, Ethnicity, and Nationality in the Liberal State* (Baltimore: Johns Hopkins University Press, 1994), 87–108.

45. Ibid. Most of those who leave the Amish community become Mennonites, not ballet dancers and astronauts as Justice Douglas seemed to hope.

46. For an account of the Amish community see the essays in *The Amish and the State,* ed. Donald B. Kraybill (Baltimore: Johns Hopkins University Press, 1993); The quoted description is from Kraybill's essay "Negotiating with Caesar," 8. My thinking about *Yoder* was influenced by the opportunity to review Brian Barry's provocative and important manuscript, *Culture & Equality: An Egalitarian Critique of Multiculturalism,* on file with the author. See also Galston's contrary views, "Two Concepts of Liberalism," 524–525.

47. See Rawls, *Theory of Justice,* sec. 56. See also Ronald Dworkin, *Taking Rights Seriously* (Cambridge: Harvard University Press, 1977), ch. 8, for a related discussion.

48. I am grateful to Annabelle Lever for stressing this point to me, though what I write here will probably not adequately reassure her.

49. Christian Scientists, for example, are not especially numerous, but the church is well funded and organized. Members of the Church of the Lukumi Babaya Aye, on the other hand, are quite poor, and so perhaps especially liable to not being adequately represented in elected branches. See Linda Greenhouse, "Court, Citing Religious Freedom, Voids a Ban on Animal Sacrifice," *New York Times,* June 12, 1993, 1, 9.

50. See Hegel's useful discussion of Quakers and Anabaptists, who "fulfill their direct duties to the state in a passive way," and who may be tolerated but cannot claim "the rights of citizenship," in the long fn. to par. 270 in *Philosophy of Right,* 168–169.

9. Divided Selves and Transformative Liberalism

1. See Sanford Levinson's concluding remarks in his "Religious Language and the Public Square (Review of Michael Perry, *Love and Power: The Role of Religion and Morality in American Politics),*" *Harvard Law Review* 105 (1992): 2061–2079; and Kent Greenawalt's important work, *Religious Convictions and Political Choice* (New York: Oxford University Press, 1988), esp. 12, 35. I have learned a lot from Greenawalt, though I believe that he may construe the demands of public reasonableness very stringently, perhaps too stringently; see ibid., 153–156. See also Rawls's discussion in his *Political Liberalism* (New York: Columbia University Press, 1993), lect. 6, sec. 7; and Amy Gutmann and Dennis Thompson, "Moral Conflict and Political Consensus," *Ethics* 101 (October 1990). An excellent discussion of liberal public justification and its relationship to liberal institutions and practices can be found in Gerald F. Gaus, *Justificatory Liberalism: An Essay on Epistemology and Political Theory* (New York: Oxford University Press, 1996). This section is indebted to discussions with Lief Wenar and Michael Sandel.

2. Joseph Raz, "Facing Diversity: The Case of Epistemic Abstinence," *Philosophy and Public Affairs* 19 (1990): 3–46.

3. The fact that it rests on a misconception is perfectly understandable given that Raz's judgment was rendered well before the appearance of Rawls's *Political Liberalism.*

4. See Rawls's discussion in ibid., 209–211. The constraints generated by the political conception "do not refer to, although they limit, the substantive content of comprehensive conceptions of the good."

5. Again, I draw here freely on Rawls's "The Idea of Public Reason Revisited," *University of Chicago Law Review* 64 (Summer 1997): 765–807.

6. All of this is based on Rawls's discussion in his *Political Liberalism,* 162.

7. Ibid., 159, 160.

8. Ibid.

9. Ibid., last paragraph of 160, and 208.

10. See Leo Strauss, "Persecution and the Art of Writing," in *Persecution and the Art of Writing and Other Essays* ([1952]; Chicago: University of Chicago Press, 1988).

11. Scarman was defending the application of the law of blasphemy to a gay publication that contained a poem describing promiscuous homosexual practices of Jesus Christ in *Regina v. Lemon,* 1979 App. Cas. 617, 658; described in Robert C. Post, *Constitutional Domains: Democracy, Community, Management* (Cambridge: Harvard University Press, 1995), ch. 3: "Cultural Heterogeneity and the Law: Pornography, Blasphemy, and the First Amendment." See also *Gay News Ltd. v. United Kingdom,* 5 Eur. Comm. H.R. 123 (1982), denying any inconsistency between the conviction and the European Convention on Human Rights.

12. *Chaplinsky v. New Hampshire,* 315 U.S. 568 (1942).

13. Mari J. Matsuda, Charles R. Lawrence III, Richard Delgado, and Kimberle William Crenshaw argue this point in their *Words That Wound: Critical Race Theory, Assaultive Speech, and the First Amendment* (Boulder, Colo.: Westview, 1993).

14. See Robert C. Post, *Constitutional Domains,* ch. 3

15. This discussion of government by indirection is indebted to Harvey C. Mansfield's "Hobbes and the Science of Indirect Government," *American Political Science Review* 65 (1971): 97–110.

16. See Will Herberg, *Protestant, Catholic, and Jew: An Essay in American Religious Sociology* (Garden City, N.Y.: Anchor Books, 1960), esp. ch. 5.

17. Michael J. Sandel tries to suggest that there is just as much reasonable disagreement about issues of basic justice as there is about religious truth and other ultimate questions. See his "Political Liberalism (Review of Rawls's *Political Liberalism*)," *Harvard Law Review* 107, no. 7 (1994). This seems to me wrong. There does not seem to be any reasonable disagreement about the core meaning of the constitutional basics: the good of basic democratic procedures and a range of long established civil liberties. Of course, there are myriad disputes outside the core. Likewise, questions of distributive justice (aside from the existence of a basic safety net) are more difficult and should for that reason not be regarded as among the constitutional essentials (as indeed they are not at present).

18. For some recent evidence, see Robert Putnam's *Making Democracy Work: Civic Traditions in Modern Italy* (Princeton: Princeton University Press, 1993).

19. Stephen L. Carter, *Culture of Disbelief: How American Law and Politics Trivialize Religious Devotion* (New York: Basic Books, 1993), 134, 179.

20. For empirical support for my view of civil society, see Putnam, *Making*

Democracy Work. Also see Stephen Macedo, "Community, Diversity, and Civic Education: Toward a Liberal Political Science of Group Life," *Social Philosophy and Policy* 13, no. 1 (Winter 1996).

21. Ibid., 26–33, 8, 54; see also 56, 63, 230.

22. Ibid., 93.

23. See the interesting discussion of related notions in John Tomasi, "Individual Rights and Community Virtues," *Ethics* 101 (1991): 521–536.

24. Carter, *Culture of Disbelief*, 94. Note also that Carter dedicates the book to his children with the wish that they "should be able to live in a world that respects your choices instead of tolerating them." Elsewhere he argues that "it is possible to maintain that crucial separation [of church and state] while treating religious beliefs with respect" (16), and "religious pluralism and equality—never mere 'toleration'—should be essential parts of what makes American democracy special" (21).

25. Ibid., 42–43.

26. Ibid., 213. The phrase is reminiscent of some feminists' insistence on a "women's way of knowing."

27. See also Iris Young, *Justice and the Politics of Difference* (Princeton: Princeton University Press, 1990).

28. Carter, *Culture of Disbelief*, 175, 230.

29. Ibid., 175–176.

30. See Stanley Fish, "Liberalism Doesn't Exist," *Duke Law Journal* 1987 (December 1987): 997–1001, which is a reply to "Evolutionism, Creationism, and Treating Religion as a Hobby," *Duke Law Journal* 1987 (December 1987): 977–996, an early version of a portion of Carter's book.

31. Carter, *Culture of Disbelief*, 180–182.

32. Alan Wolfe, *One Nation, After All: What Middle-Class Americans Really Think about God, Country, Family, Racism, Welfare, Immigration, Homosexuality, Work, the Right, the Left, and Each Other* (New York: Viking, 1998).

33. Amy Gutmann, "Civic Education and Social Diversity," *Ethics* 105 (April 1995): 557–579.

34. William A. Galston, *Liberal Purposes: Goods, Virtues, and Diversity in the Liberal State* (Cambridge: Cambridge University Press, 1991), 291–293, 253. I might add that I believe Galston inflates my commitment to autonomy, which I describe in *Liberal Virtues: Citizenship, Virtue, and Community in Liberal Constitutionalism* (Oxford: Clarendon Press, 1990), though my discussion is not nearly as clear as it should have been. If I were writing the book today, I would stress that autonomy is an important civic virtue in that thinking critically about received political ideas is a civic virtue. I also emphasized that political autonomy is liable to spill over into other spheres of life and foster critical attitudes toward religious beliefs and other forms of authority. I did not mean, however, to grant the state the authority to pro-

mote autonomous attitudes with respect to all questions. On all of this see Rawls, *Political Liberalism,* 77–81, "Full Autonomy: Political Not Ethical." See also the valuable debate over these matters in Eamonn Callan, "Political Liberalism and Political Education"; Kenneth A. Strike, "Must Liberal Citizens Be Reasonable?" and Callan, "Last Word," all in *Review of Politics* 58, no. 1 (1996).

35. Galston, *Liberal Purposes,* 277.
36. Ibid., 281–289, 117. See also George A. Gallup Jr. and Jim Castelli, *The People's Faith: American Faith in the 90's* (New York: Macmillan, 1989), 61, reporting that the percentage of Americans believing in the literal truth of the Bible has declined by half in a recent quarter-century span. Of course, one needs to think about the extent to which religious arguments can be translated into acceptable secular terms. As Robert George put it to me, if the translation is perfect, isn't the only point of such an exercise to force a certain deception onto believers? If translation is incomplete, isn't that unfair to believers? The answer to both questions is "no."

Part III. School Reform and Civic Education

1. I owe this formulation to Eamonn Callan, "Common Schools for Common Education"—see my "Liberal Civic Education and Its Limits: A Comment on Eamonn Callan"; both documents are in *Canadian Journal of Education* 20, no. 3 (1995). See also the useful discussion in Terrence H. McLaughlin, "Liberalism, Education, and the Common School," *Journal of the Philosophy of Education* 29, no. 2 (1995).

10. Civic Purposes and Public Schools

1. Amy Gutmann, *Democratic Education* (Princeton: Princeton University Press, 1987), 30–31.
2. Eamonn Callan, "Common Schools for Common Education," *Canadian Journal of Education* 20, no. 3 (1995): 1.
3. Meira Levinson, *The Demands of Liberal Education* (Oxford: Oxford University Press, 1999).
4. Abigail Thernstrom, "Is Choice a Necessity?" *The Public Interest,* no. 101 (Fall 1990).
5. Gutmann, *Democratic Education,* 32.
6. Arthur G. Powell, Eleanor Farrar, and David K. Cohen, *The Shopping Mall High School: Winners and Losers in the Educational Marketplace* (Boston: Houghton Mifflin, 1985), 57.
7. Ibid., 57–58; see also 199.
8. Gerald Grant, *The World We Created at Hamilton High* (Cambridge: Harvard University Press, 1988), 112–113.

9. See Greeley, *Catholic High Schools and Minority Students* (New Brunswick, N.J.: Transaction Books, 1982), 54–55; and Andrew M. Greeley and Peter H. Rossi, *The Education of Catholic Americans* (Chicago: Aldine, 1966), 153–155. This evidence is surveyed and expanded in Anthony Bryk, Valerie E. Lee, and Peter B. Holland, *Catholic Schooling and the Common Good* (Cambridge: Harvard University Press, 1993).

10. Greeley, *Catholic High Schools*, 9–10.

11. See William Julius Wilson, *The Declining Significance of Race: Blacks and Changing American Institutions*, 2d ed. (Chicago: University of Chicago Press, 1980), esp. 150–154, and the studies discussed on 168. If school reform holds out the hope of improving big city schools and helping minority children out of poverty, then school choice will advance the cause of racial equality.

12. Paul E. Peterson, "Are Big City Schools Holding Their Own?" occasional paper 91–4, Center for American Political Studies, Harvard University, Cambridge, Mass., January 1991, 28, and table 12. See also the important argument in Jennifer L. Hochschild, *The New American Dilemma: Liberal Democracy and School Desegregation* (New Haven: Yale University Press, 1984); and the helpful discussion by Robert K. Fullinwider in his article, "The State's Interest in Racially Non-Discriminatory Education," in Neal Devins, ed., *Public Values, Private Schools* (London: Falmer, 1989).

13. Grant, *Hamilton High*, ch. 4.

14. It is well documented that greater education leads to increases in tolerance, but only Greeley asks whether different types of schools (public, private, secular, or Catholic) contribute equally to increased tolerance. See Greeley, *Catholic High Schools*, 9–10, ch. 5.

15. 406 U.S. 205 (1972), 244–246.

16. James S. Coleman and T. Hoffer, *Public and Private High Schools: The Impact of Communities* (New York: Basic Books, 1987), xvi–xvii, 3–4. The current public system may promote the sort of democratic individuality that George Kateb lauds, a "positive individuality" that requires "a break with habit, convention, and custom, all of which work to condition us to accept the oppression of others . . . and to respond in an impoverished manner to difference." See Kateb, "Democratic Individuality and the Meaning of Rights," in Nancy L. Rosenblum, ed., *Liberalism and the Moral Life* (Cambridge: Harvard University Press, 1989), 183–206, esp. 192.

17. Joel Feinberg, "A Child's Right to an Open Future," in William Aiken and Hugh LaFollette, eds., *Whose Child?* (Totowa, N.J.: Littlefield, Adams, 1980).

18. Bruce A. Ackerman, *Social Justice and the Liberal State* (New Haven: Yale University Press, 1980), 155–156.

19. Ibid., ch. 5.

20. Gutmann, *Democratic Education*, 43–47, quotations from 43, 44.

21. Ibid., 43.
22. Ibid.
23. Ibid., 75–79.
24. Recall here the remarks of Theodore Sedgwick, Chapter 2, text accompanying notes 94–95.
25. I discuss this in a forthcoming book on liberal civil society.
26. Loren E. Lomasky, *Persons, Rights, and the Moral Community* (New York: Oxford University Press, 1987), 167. I have learned much from Lomasky's discussion.
27. Stephen G. Gilles, "On Educating Children: A Parentalist Manifesto," *University of Chicago Law Review* 63 (Summer 1996): 952–953.
28. Quotation from the *Boston Pilot*, April 24, 1852, quoted in Stanley K. Schultz, *The Culture Factory: Boston Public Schools, 1789–1860* (New York: Oxford University Press, 1973), 306; see also 34–36.
29. Gilles, "Educating Children," 952; see also 985.
30. Aristotle, *The Politics*, trans. Carnes Lord (Chicago: University of Chicago Press, 1985), bk. 2, 59; see also 59–63. My argument here is indebted to conversations with Peter Berkowitz.
31. Gilles, "Educating Children," 966.
32. See here Amy Gutmann's discussion and rejection of "The State of Families" in her *Democratic Education,* ch. 1.
33. Gilles, "Educating Children," 951, 981.
34. Gutmann, *Democratic Education,* chs. 2 and 3.
35. Powell, Farrar, and Cohen, *Shopping Mall,* 3.
36. Alexis de Tocqueville, *Democracy in America,* ed. J. P. Mayer (New York: Random House, 1969), 680–681.
37. John Stuart Mill, *On Liberty,* ed. David Spitz (New York: Norton, 1975), 98.
38. Eamonn Callan, "Faith, Worship, and Reason in Religious Upbringing," *Journal of Philosophy of Education* 22, no. 2 (1988): 192. Callan's discussion is, as always, very provocative.
39. Ibid.
40. See, for example, Bernard Williams, *Ethics and the Limits of Philosophy* (Cambridge: Harvard University Press, 1985).
41. Alan Wolfe's evidence suggests that many Americans may tend toward a bland nonjudgmentalism in many areas of religious and moral controversy. But according to Wolfe, Americans remain deeply religious, and their nonjudgmentalism reflects, at least in part, a disposition to think well of one's fellow citizens. See *One Nation, After All: What Middle-Class Americans Really Think about God, Country, Family, Racism, Welfare, Immigration, Homosexuality, Work, the Right, the Left, and Each Other* (New York: Viking, 1998). Nothing in Wolfe's book suggests that Americans have become excessively committed to critical self-examination.
42. I explore these themes at greater length in *Liberal Civil Society.*

43. Nancy L. Rosenblum, *Membership and Morals: The Personal Uses of Pluralism in America* (Princeton: Princeton University Press, 1998).
44. Wolfe, *One Nation,* 281–286; Allan Bloom, *The Closing of the American Mind* (New York: Basic Books, 1987).
45. J. Budziszewski, *True Tolerance: Liberalism and the Necessity of Judgment* (New Brunswick, N.J.: Transaction Books, 1992), 7, 5. The phrase "judgmental pluralism" was suggested to me by Michael J. Sandel.

11. The Case for Civically Minded School Reform

1. In spite of several decades of intensive study by scholars—including Andrew M. Greeley, James S. Coleman, Anthony S. Bryk, and more recently, Paul E. Peterson—and the numerous colleagues of these scholars, there is no scholarly consensus that school choice yields substantial educational benefits. See for example, K. L. Alexander and A. M. Pallas, "School Sector and Cognitive Performance: When Is a Little a Little?" *Sociology of Education* 58 (1985): 115–128; Christopher Jencks, "How Much Do High School Students Learn?" *Sociology of Education* 58 (1985): 128–135; Jay P. Greene, Paul E. Peterson, and Jiangtao Du, "Effectiveness of School Choice: The Milwaukee Experiment," occasional paper 97–1, Program on Education Policy and Governance, Center for American Political Studies, Harvard University, Cambridge, Mass.; and Antony Bryk, Valerie E. Lee, and Peter B. Holland, *Catholic Schools and the Common Good* (Cambridge: Harvard University Press, 1993). Nevertheless, I write in some sympathy with the arguments for choice, as will become clear.
2. See the useful overview in Richard Rothstein, "The Myth of Public School Failure," *The American Prospect,* no. 13 (Spring 1993). A lengthier overview is Edith Rasell and Richard Rothstein, eds., *School Choice: Examining the Evidence* (Washington, D.C.: Economic Policy Institute, 1993).
3. Patricia Albjerg Graham, *S.O.S.: Sustain Our Schools* (New York: Hill and Wang, 1992), 66–67, which cites for the survey figures Bruce D. Butterfield, "Children at Work: Long Hours, Late Nights, Low Grades," *Boston Globe,* April 24, 1990, 12. See also Graham's "What America Has Expected of Its Schools over the Past Century," *American Journal of Education* 101 (February 1993).
4. Graham, *S.O.S.,* 31–32. For the changes in SAT scores among seventeen-year-olds, see Rothstein, "Myth of Public School Failure," 26–27.
5. Rothstein, "Myth of Public School Failure," 28–29.
6. Ibid., 22, 34.
7. James S. Coleman and T. Hoffer, *Public and Private High Schools: The Impact of Communities* (New York: Basic Books, 1987), xvi–xvii, 3–4.
8. Gerald Grant, *The World We Created at Hamilton High* (Cambridge: Harvard University Press, 1988), 6.
9. Sobering evidence on the importance of stable two-parent families is dis-

cussed in Barbara Dafoe Whitehouse, "Dan Quayle Was Right," *Atlantic Monthly* (April 1993).

10. For a concentrated version of this argument, see James S. Coleman, "Families and Schools," *Educational Researcher* 16 (August–September 1987): 32–38.

11. Clifford Cobb, *Responsive Schools, Renewed Communities* (San Francisco: Institute for Contemporary Studies, 1992).

12. Ibid., 202. Cobb is not alone in drawing an analogy between public control over schooling and religious establishments: Arons makes the connection, as noted in the introduction, as do Rockne McCarthy, Donald Oppewal, Walfred Peterson, and Gordon Spykman in their *Society, State, and Schools: A Case for Structural and Confessional Pluralism* (Grand Rapids, Mich.: Eerdmans, 1981).

13. Grant, *Hamilton High.*

14. Cobb, *Responsive Schools,* 102, 112, 205, 2.

15. This is the title of ch. 13 of ibid.

16. Coleman and Hoffer, *Public and Private,* esp. 3–27, 211–243. For a useful summary of the findings of Coleman et al., see Coleman, "Families and Schools."

17. Coleman and Hoffer, *Public and Private,* 225–227. See also James S. Coleman, *Foundations of Social Theory* (Cambridge: Harvard University Press, 1990), ch. 22.

18. Andrew M. Greeley, *Catholic High Schools and Minority Students* (New Brunswick, N.J.: Transaction Books, 1982), ch. 7; Coleman and Hoffer, *Public and Private,* 213.

19. See Anthony Bryk, Valerie E. Lee, and Peter B. Holland, *Catholic Schooling and the Common Good* (Cambridge: Harvard University Press, 1993), 53–56, for a useful overview of the research comparing Catholic and public schools.

20. Coleman and Hoffer, *Public and Private,* xxvi, 6–11; and Greeley, *Catholic High Schools,* ch. 7.

21. Coleman, "Families and Schools," 36–37.

22. Coleman and Hoffer, *Public and Private,* 217.

23. Figures on Catholic schools are from Bryk et al., *Catholic Schooling,* 33; those on evangelical and Orthodox Jewish schools are from Peter W. Cookson Jr., *School Choice: The Struggle for the Soul of American Education* (New Haven: Yale University Press, 1994), 32, quoting Donald A. Erickson, "Choice and Private Schools: Dynamics of Supply and Demand," in Daniel C. Levy, ed., *Private Education: Studies in Choice and Public Policy* (New York: Oxford University Press, 1986), 82–109.

24. Student attitudes across types of schools (public/private and secular/religious) have not been much studied, but see Greeley, *Catholic High Schools,* 54–55; and Andrew M. Greeley and Peter H. Rossi, *The Education of Catholic Americans* (Chicago: Aldine, 1966), 153–155.

25. The preceding paragraphs are greatly indebted to conversations with Elizabeth Hansot, and to a set of highly provocative discussions sponsored by the Spencer Foundation and the U.S. Department of Education's Office of Educational Research and Improvement, June 24–25 at Stanford University. I am especially indebted to materials supplied on that occasion by Chandra Muller and Vanessa Siddle Walker.

26. The church-school connection appears to be extremely important; for example, choice plans would allow schools to grow up around black inner-city churches. See Susan Chira, "Black Churches Turn to Teaching the Young," *New York Times,* August 7, 1991, 1, 19. See also the excellent account of the advantages of smaller schools in Deborah Meier, *The Power of Their Ideas: Lessons for America from a Small School in Harlem* (Boston: Beacon, 1995).

27. See Paul T. Hill, Lawrence C. Pierce, and James W. Guthrie, *Reinventing Public Education: How Contracting Can Transform America's Schools* (Chicago: University of Chicago Press, 1997).

28. Cookson, *School Choice.* "Controlled choice" plans have been instituted to overcome residential segregation without resort to forced busing. In practice, *control* has been emphasized for the sake of racial mixing. See Abigail Thernstrom's study, "School Choice in Massachusetts," Pioneer Paper no. 5 Pioneer Institute for Public Policy Research, Boston, 1991. For a more hopeful view of controlled choice, see Charles L. Glenn, "Controlled Choice in Massachusetts Public Schools," *Public Interest,* no. 103 (Spring 1991): 88–105.

29. See Jay P. Greene, Paul E. Peterson, and Jiangtao Du, "Effectiveness of School Choice: The Milwaukee Experiment," occasional paper 97–1, Program on Education Policy and Governance, Center for American Political Studies, Harvard University, Cambridge, Mass., March 1997; see also Jay P. Greene, William G. Howell, and Paul E. Peterson, "An Evaluation of the Cleveland Scholarship Program," also published by Harvard's Program on Education Policy and Governance (September 1997).

30. James Q. Wilson, *On Character: Essays by James Q. Wilson* (Washington, D.C.: American Enterprise Institute, 1991), 14–15.

31. James S. Coleman, Thomas Hoffer, and Sally Kilgore, *High School Achievement: Public, Catholic, and Private Schools Compared* (New York: Basic Books, 1982), 187; see also 97–115.

32. See Paul T. Hill, Gail E. Foster, and Tamar Gendler, *High Schools with Character* (Santa Monica, Calif.: Rand, 1990), 15–20, 54–56. Reform could allow public schools to develop the norms of small societies and the kinds of mechanisms that we associate with Catholic schools: uniforms, strict rules about lateness and attendance, and a distinctive sense of mission that is shared by administrators, teachers, and students. Of course, the power of teachers' unions is one major obstacle to reform: principals must be freer to

select and dismiss staff. Hill et al., suggest that low teacher pay is also a feature of focus schools: it helps ensure that teachers share the mission of the school and are not doing the job simply for the money (20). All of this parallels the findings of some important studies of bureaucratic effectiveness; see James Q. Wilson, *Bureaucracy: What Government Agencies Do and Why They Do It* (New York: Basic Books, 1989), esp. 109–110, 366–368.

33. Coleman, Hoffer, and Kilgore, *High School Achievement*, 236; and John E. Chubb and Terry M. Moe, *Politics, Markets, and America's Schools* (Washington, D.C.: Brookings Institution Press, 1990). See also Hill, Foster, and Gendler, *High Schools with Character*.

34. Chubb and Moe, *Politics, Markets, and America's Schools*.

35. Hill, Pierce, and Guthrie, *Reinventing Public Education*, 31–32.

36. Amy Gutmann, *Democratic Education* (Princeton: Princeton University Press, 1987), 45–47.

37. Bryk et al., *Catholic Schooling*, 312–316.

38. See Coleman's suggestions in "Families and Schools." On schools changing to fit changing families, see Graham, *S.O.S.*, ch. 2.

39. See Coleman, Hoffer, and Kilgore, *High School Achievement*, 143–146, 177–178; and Bryk et al., *Catholic Schooling*, 56–58, 269–271.

40. See Stephen Macedo, "Community, Diversity, and Civic Education: Toward a Liberal Political Science of Group Life," *Social Philosophy and Policy* 13, no. 1 (1996).

41. Diane Ravitch, *The Great School Wars* (New York: Basic Books, 1974), 244–245.

42. In *Mueller v. Allen*, 463 U.S. 388 (1983), the Court found constitutional state income tax deductions of up to $700 for educational expenses incurred by parents of children in secondary schools ($500 for children in primary schools), including public or private, religious or secular schools.

43. See Joe Loconte, "Paying the Piper: Will Vouchers Undermine the Mission of Religious Schools?" *Policy Review* (January–February 1999): 33–34.

44. Quotation from Nona Zellmer, a teacher at Garden Homes Lutheran School in Milwaukee, from ibid., 34.

45. Jonathan Kozol, *Savage Inequalities: Children in America's Schools* (New York: HarperCollins, 1991): John O. Norquist, *The Wealth of Cities: Revitalizing the Centers of American Life* (Reading, Mass.: Addison-Wesley, 1998), ch. 5.

46. See Isabel Wilkerson, "To Save Its Men, Detroit Plans Boys-Only Schools," *New York Times*, August 14, 1991, A1, A17; and "U.S. Judge Blocks Plan for All-Male Public Schools in Detroit," (AP) *New York Times*, August 15, 1991, C7. See also the successful challenge to single-sex education at Virginia Military Academy, *U.S. v. Virginia*, 135 L.Ed. 735 (1996).

47. Bryk et al. argue that Catholic girls' schools are "empowering environments

for young women"; see their *Catholic Schooling*, 235. But see also Wendy Kaminer, "The Trouble with Single-Sex Schools," *Atlantic Monthly* (April 1998): 22, 24–26, 34–35.

48. For an important critique of minority race pride, see Randall Kennedy's "Reflections on Black Power," in Stephen Macedo, ed., *Reassessing the Sixties: Debating the Political and Cultural Legacy* (New York: W. W. Norton, 1997). A contrary view is advanced by many advocates of African-American schools; see Wil Haygood, "On Schools, Many Blacks Return to Roots," *Boston Globe*, November 16, 1997, A1.

49. See William A. Galston's discussion, "Civic Education in the Liberal State," in Nancy L. Rosenblum, ed., *Liberalism and the Moral Life* (Cambridge: Harvard University Press, 1989). I have only canvassed some of the reasons why liberals might favor institutions of separate as opposed to common schooling. For some additional considerations, see T. H. McLaughlin, "The Ethics of Separate Schools," in Mal Leicester and Monica Taylor, eds., *Ethics, Ethnicity and Education* (London: Kogan Page, 1992); and Shelley Burtt, "Religious Parents, Secular Schools: A Liberal Defense of Illiberal Education," *Review of Politics* 56 (1994).

Conclusion

1. See F. A. Hayek, *The Constitution of Liberty* (London: Routledge, 1960).

2. See Stephen Macedo, "Sexuality and Liberty: Making Room for Nature and Tradition," in David M. Estlund and Martha C. Nussbaum, eds., *Sex, Preference, and Family: Essays on Laws and Nature* (New York: Oxford University Press, 1997).

3. John Stuart Mill, *On Liberty,* ed. David Spitz (New York: W. W. Norton, 1975).

Index